IRISH DRAMA AND THE OTHER REVOLUTIONS

Edinburgh Critical Studies in Modernism, Drama and Performance

Published
The Speech-Gesture Complex: Modernism, Theatre, Cinema
Anthony Paraskeva

Irish Drama and the Other Revolutions: Playwrights, Sexual Politics and the International Left, 1892–1964
Susan Cannon Harris

Forthcoming
Beckett's Breath: Anti-theatricality and the Visual Arts
Sozita Goudouna

Modernism and the Theatre of the Baroque
Kate Armond

Russian Futurist Theatre: Theory and Practice
Robert Leach

Greek Tragedy and Modernist Performance
Olga Taxidou

IRISH DRAMA AND THE OTHER REVOLUTIONS

Playwrights, Sexual Politics and the International Left, 1892–1964

Susan Cannon Harris

EDINBURGH
University Press

for Liza and Zoe
with hope for the future

Edinburgh University Press is one of the leading university presses in the UK. We publish academic books and journals in our selected subject areas across the humanities and social sciences, combining cutting-edge scholarship with high editorial and production values to produce academic works of lasting importance. For more information visit our website: edinburghuniversitypress.com

© Susan Cannon Harris, 2017, 2019

Edinburgh University Press Ltd
The Tun – Holyrood Road
12(2f) Jackson's Entry
Edinburgh EH8 8PJ

First published in hardback by Edinburgh University Press 2017

Typeset in Sabon and Gill Sans by
Servis Filmsetting Ltd, Stockport, Cheshire,
and printed and bound in Great Britain by
CPI Group (UK) Ltd, Croydon CR0 4YY

A CIP record for this book is available from the British Library

ISBN 978 1 4744 2446 2 (hardback)
ISBN 978 1 4744 5197 0 (paperback)
ISBN 978 1 4744 2447 9 (webready PDF)
ISBN 978 1 4744 2448 6 (epub)

The right of Susan Cannon Harris to be identified as the author of this work has been asserted in accordance with the Copyright, Designs and Patents Act 1988, and the Copyright and Related Rights Regulations 2003 (SI No. 2498).

CONTENTS

Acknowledgements	vi
Introduction	1
1 Desiring Women: Irish Playwrights, New Women and Queer Socialism, 1892–1894	16
2 Arrested Development: Utopian Desires, Designs and Deferrals in *Man and Superman* and *John Bull's Other Island*	57
3 We'll Keep the Red Flag Flying Here: Syndicalism, Jim Larkin and Irish Masculinity at the Abbey Theatre, 1911–1919	96
4 Mobilising Maurya: J. M. Synge, Bertolt Brecht and the Revolutionary Mother	135
5 The Flaming Sunflower: The Soviet Union and Sean O'Casey's Post-Realism	169
Epilogue: What The Irish Left – Sean O'Casey, Samuel Beckett and Lorraine Hansberry's *The Sign in Sidney Brustein's Window*	213
Works Cited	241
Index	258

ACKNOWLEDGEMENTS

It will be impossible to thank all the people who helped make this book a reality, but it is my privilege to try. I owe a special debt to those who read and commented on earlier versions of these chapters, especially Margot Backus, Helen Burke, Elizabeth Cullingford, Sarah McKibben, Paige Reynolds and Mary Trotter. I am grateful to everyone who helped me in the search for a publisher, especially Elizabeth Cullingford, Valerie Sayers, Jesse Lander, Maud Ellmann and David Kornhaber, as well as my series editor, Olga Taxidou, and my editors at Edinburgh University Press, Jackie Jones and Adela Rauchova. Thanks go to the Keough-Naughton Institute for Irish Studies and the Institute for Scholarship in the Liberal Arts at the University of Notre Dame for their financial support for this project. I appreciate all the support I have received from my colleagues at the University of Notre Dame.

I thank the *Illustrated London News* for permission to reproduce the images from *The Sketch* that appear in Chapter 1. I am grateful to Josephine Johnson and Colin Smythe Limited for permission to reproduce the images of Florence Farr that appear in the same chapter. I cite Sean O'Casey's unpublished typescripts, letters and notebooks with the kind permission of the Estate of Sean O'Casey. I thank the Society of Authors, on behalf of the Bernard Shaw Estate, for their permission to quote from Shaw's unpublished typescripts. I thank the New York Public Library Archives & Manuscripts department for permission to cite material from the Henry W. and Albert A. Berg Collection of English and American Literature, New York Public Library, Astor, Lennox and Tilden Foundations. John Todhunter's unpublished typescripts are cited here by permission of the University of Reading Special Collections. I would also thank all the staff who helped me access archival material at these libraries, as well as the staff of the British Library, the Victoria and Albert Museum, the National Library of Ireland and the Special Collections Research Center at the Morris Library of Southern Illinois University.

An early version of Chapter 4 was originally published in *Modern Drama* as 'Mobilizing Maurya: J. M. Synge, Bertolt Brecht and the Revolutionary Mother' (*Modern Drama*, 56(1) (2013), 38–59), and portions of Chapter 5 originally appeared in the *Princeton University Library Chronicle* as part of

'Red Star Versus Green Goddess: Sean O'Casey's *The Star Turns Red* and the Politics of Form' (*Princeton University Library Quarterly*, 68 (2006–7), 357–98). I thank the University of Toronto Press and the Princeton University Library, respectively, for permission to include that work in this manuscript. I thank Suhrkamp Verlag for their permission to use the poetry of Bertolt Brecht, including the English translation of 'Der Requisiten Der Weigel' published in Wolfgang Pintzka's *Helene Weigel: Actress. A Book of Photographs* (Leipzig: VEB Edition, 1961). John Willett's English translation of Bertolt Brecht's 'Weigel's Props' (1961) and David Constantine and Tom Kuhn's English translation of Bertolt Brecht's 'The Actress in Exile' are used by permission of Liveright Publishing Corporation.

This book owes a special debt to Barbara Harlow (1948–2017). Barbara's scholarship, her uncompromising rigour and her profound commitment to human rights and social justice have been an inspiration to me for more than twenty years. For her dedication to her students, for her courage in the face of injustice, and for her indomitable spirit, I am forever grateful.

I also want to thank those whose contributions are less easy to document but no less important. This category includes my graduate students, who continue to instruct and inspire me: Stephanie Pocock Boeninger, Brooke Cameron, Heather Edwards, Lindsay Haney, Eric Lewis, Angel Matos, Ana Jimenez-Moreno, Robinson Murphy, Katie Osborne, Julieann Ulin and Nicole Winsor. Thanks also to all my colleagues in the Hyde Park Community Players, who have been keeping my love for theatre alive since 2009. I thank my parents, John and Elin Harris; my sister Lynn and her family; my brother John and his family; my wife's parents, Bill and Pauline Reynolds; and my sister-in-law Jane and her family, for supporting me on this quixotic endeavour. Last and most important, I thank my wife Liza and our daughter Zoe. Without their constant love and support, and their faith in me and my writing, this book would not exist. I can never thank them enough.

Edinburgh Critical Studies in Modernism, Drama and Performance
Series Editor: Olga Taxidou

Editorial Board:

Penny Farfan (University of Calgary); Robert Leach (formerly of Edinburgh and Birmingham Universities); Ben Levitas (Goldsmiths, University of London); John London (Goldsmiths, University of London); Laura Marcus (University of Oxford); Marjorie Perloff (University of Stanford); Kirsten Shepherd-Barr (University of Oxford); Alexandra Smith (University of Edinburgh)

Edinburgh Critical Studies in Modernism, Drama and Performance addresses the somewhat neglected areas of drama and performance within Modernist Studies, and is in many ways conceived of in response to a number of intellectual and institutional shifts that have taken place over the past 10 to 15 years. On the one hand, modernist studies has moved considerably from the strictly literary approaches, to encompass engagements with the everyday, the body, the political, while also extending its geopolitical reach. On the other hand, performance studies itself could be seen as acquiring a distinct epistemology and methodology within modernism. Indeed, the autonomy of performance as a distinct aesthetic trope is sometimes located at the exciting intersections between genres and media; intersections that this series sets out to explore within the more general modernist concerns about the relationships between textuality, visuality and embodiment. This series locates the theoretical, methodological and pedagogical contours of performance studies within the formal, aesthetic and political concerns of modernism. It claims that the 'linguistic turn' within modernism is always shadowed and accompanied by an equally formative 'performance/performative turn'. It aims to highlight the significance of performance for the general study of modernism by bringing together two fields of scholarly research which have traditionally remained quite distinct – performance/theatre studies and modernism. In turn this emphasis will inflect and help to re-conceptualise our understanding of both performance studies and modernist studies. And in doing so, the series will initiate new conversations between scholars, theatre and performance artists and students.

INTRODUCTION

THE OTHER REVOLUTIONS

Irish Drama and the Other Revolutions re-examines the Irish dramatic revival in the context of two international revolutions that unfolded alongside the Irish struggle for national independence. These 'other' revolutions are: (1) a socialist movement which increased in scope, strength, and militancy from the 1880s into the 1950s, and (2) a campaign for gender and sexual liberation whose harbingers were the New Woman and the queer man, and whose emergence was closely linked to the late nineteenth-century European 'free theatre' movement and the twentieth-century avant-garde drama that arose from it. These revolutions came together in London at a time when the first generation of modern Irish writers – including W. B. Yeats, George Bernard Shaw and Oscar Wilde – were trying to establish literary careers there. Being, by virtue of their Irishness, excluded from what constituted normativity there, these self-displaced Irish playwrights were drawn into the web of influence and inspiration created by the interconnected struggles for sexual and social liberation. From the Ibsen revolution of turn-of-the-century London to the height of the Cold War on Broadway, Irish playwrights were enmeshed in both of these liberation struggles and impelled by their desires. Strategies that Irish playwrights developed for negotiating the interchange between socialist and sexual politics were then taken up, changed or contested by playwrights outside of Ireland. By examining the work of these Irish playwrights in the context of two other revolutions that defined the twentieth century, then, we will reach a richer understanding of the contributions of Irish playwrights to modern European drama, and of the interactions between embodiment and ideology that continue to define the possibilities and limitations of left politics in the twenty-first century.

By 'left politics' I mean the network of anticapitalist ideologies that proliferated rapidly around the globe during the nineteenth and twentieth centuries. These include Marxism, anarchism, syndicalism, anarcho-syndicalism, Communism (and its national variations in England, Spain, Germany, the USA, and the Soviet Union), and quite a few flavours of socialism. To attempt to maintain impermeable definitional boundaries around each one of these ideologies at all times would be as maddening and futile as trying to establish a bright-line rule for separating naturalism from realism. When the analysis requires more technical terminology – as it often does – I will use it. One of the things that makes the special case of Irish revival playwrights so illuminating, however, is the Irish left's history of doctrinal impurity. Marx's atheism, for instance, was never embraced by the Irish left – from Oscar Wilde, who devotes a considerable chunk of 'The Soul of Man Under Socialism' to discussing Jesus, to Sean O'Casey, whose enthusiasm for all things Soviet never put a dent in his love of biblical cadences and Christian symbolism. Percy Shelley's romantic idealism, with its fusion of political and sexual liberation, continued to influence Irish left playwrights after it had been snuffed out in left culture elsewhere. Of all the playwrights we will examine, Shaw was most attracted to doctrine and dialectics; but once we understand how his politics relate to his embodiment as an Irish man, they become murkier than he would have us believe. To understand the contributions these playwrights have made to left culture, and the impact that left politics had on modern Irish drama, therefore, we have to employ a broad and flexible conception of the 'left' as well as a detailed knowledge of more specific formations.

I use the term 'sexual revolution' to refer to the struggle for gender equality and sexual freedom which dominated progressive culture and anticapitalist theater in *fin-de-siècle* London. Yeats, Shaw and Wilde were producing their first plays during the era of the New Woman – the educated feminist who could earn her own income, live independently, and reject marriage and motherhood if she chose. *Fin-de-siècle* London was also the time and place in which 'homosexuality *came out* as a major cultural influence' (Woods, *Homintern*, 29). Even before the Oscar Wilde scandal of 1895 made an Irish playwright the most notorious queer man in modern Europe, the interpenetration of socialism, feminism and queer activism in London's progressive community exerted a formative influence on Yeats and Shaw. While Wilde does figure in my discussion of this cultural moment in Chapter 1, I have chosen to focus on the period just *before* his trials in order to reveal the aspects of this history that have been obscured by what Eibhear Walshe has called 'Oscar's shadow'. It is in the same spirit that Chapter 1 focuses instead on a queer New Woman, Florence Farr, whose impact on Yeats's and Shaw's formation as playwrights has attracted less critical attention than her impact on their personal lives.

London was, during the same decade, somewhat belatedly joining an international theatrical revolution. As playwrights and performers became frustrated with the commercial theatre and its stifling conventions, they established 'free theatres' – independent venues and companies which would allow them to produce innovative material using innovative techniques. The groundbreaking realism of Henrik Ibsen and Émile Zola helped inspire André Antoine to found the Théâtre Libre in Paris in 1887. It was soon followed by Berlin's Freie Bühne (1889), the Scandinavian Experimental Theatre (1889) and London's Independent Theatre (1891). Of the six original plays in English that the Independent Theatre produced before it folded, three were by Irish playwrights. When Yeats, Edward Martyn and Lady Gregory had that fateful meeting at Coole Park in 1897, their decision to found a literary theatre was not made spontaneously or in isolation. Though not named in the title, this theatrical revolution is part of the context for our investigation; and for that reason, Wilde, who between 1892 and 1895 enjoyed the warm embrace of the commercial theatre, is less central to this project than his Irish contemporaries.

Many of the plays we will investigate as we excavate the intersections of the Irish, socialist, sexual and theatrical revolutions were rejected decades ago as bad investments. While Yeats, Shaw, Synge and O'Casey are central to this book, we will also encounter playwrights with much shorter afterlives: the forgotten John Todhunter, the mysterious A. Patrick Wilson, the contrarian St. John Ervine, and others. Precisely because they were central to the history of the political and cultural left, many of these plays don't fit easily into dominant narratives about literary modernism, avant-garde drama or the Irish revival. All of this is partly a function of the fact that the relevance of the twentieth-century left is widely held to have died with the Soviet Union. Marxist theory, of course, will be with us as long as we have capitalism; but the material applications and cultural expressions of Marxism that shaped the first half of the twentieth century have long been marked as failures from which we have little to learn apart from the impracticability of utopian ideologies.

Before asking you to invest in the following chapters, then, it behooves me to answer some of the questions that naturally arise, such as: why, nearly a quarter of the way into the twenty-first century, is it useful or necessary to reopen this particular chapter of twentieth-century history? If we are going to rake over the cultural bones of a failed and destructive Communist revolution, why make gender and sexuality central to that project? In the age of digital humanities and the 'global turn', why invest so much time and money in chasing down a scattered archive of obscure documents in pursuit of such rich contextualisation for such a small sample of plays and performances? What is the purpose of trying to ignite critical interest in plays which are no longer viable on the contemporary stage?

The short answer to these questions is the one I gave in 2005 while attempting to inspire graduate students at my alma mater with a sense of the continued relevance of scholarship in a post-9/11 world: 'We are searching through the past looking for ways to spring the traps that have closed on the present' (Harris, 'What Still Matters'). The feminist and queer liberation movements that emerged in London in the late nineteenth century critiqued the interdependence of property ownership, landlordism, class privilege and marriage, holding that freedom from the heterosexual family unit was inseparable from freedom from economic oppression and political tyranny. The formations of left politics that were so important to the Irish playwrights we are about to examine, and to which they contributed so much, thus offer us the opportunity to re-vision possibilities foreclosed by our current conditions. At the same time, as we approach the Cold War, we will witness a fatal divergence between the two revolutions, as feminist and queer utopian dreams give way to a militant labour movement, and finally to a totalitarian state engaged in the aggressive imposition of a global left orthodoxy. In describing the arc that extends from Yeats's and Shaw's immersion in London's progressive community to Sean O'Casey's romance with Stalin and the Soviet Union, we get an edifying view of the utopian possibilities created by the cooperation of socialist and sexual radicals – and of some of the consequences of the reassertion of hegemonic masculinity within the international left.

There is, of course, a longer answer. I will provide it by situating this study in the context of the 'global turn', arguing against the utility of the kind of totalising theory of 'world literature' set forward in Pascale Casanova's *The World Republic of Letters*. I will then explain why Irish drama's special relationship to fantasies about utopia, and to nightmares about reproduction and productivity, demands that we approach the history of Irish drama's engagement with the left through the lens of contemporary queer theory. Finally, I will justify this project's focus on socialism as a set of material and cultural practices, rather than as an abstract ideology or political programme.

Other Places

The new millennium has seen a shift away from both nationalism and specialisation in favour of comparative and transnational projects able to claim global significance. Within Irish studies, this has renewed interest in figures like George Bernard Shaw and Samuel Beckett, whose work was never overtly or obviously 'Irish'. This study benefits from much of this recent work, including Michael McAteer's *Yeats and European Drama*, Ben Levitas's work on the history of Irish working-class urban drama, and Anthony Roche's investigation of Synge's German connections. The Celtic Tiger boom, and its apocalyptic bust, piqued scholarly interest in the socialist dimension of Irish revolutionary politics, especially after Joe Cleary's 2007 *Outrageous Fortune: Culture and Capital in Modern Ireland* put forward a new grand narrative about twentieth-century Irish literature's relationship to global capitalism. Similarly, while my own *Gender and Modern Irish Drama* was pioneering, in 2002, in its sustained focus on gender and sexual politics as part of the context for the Irish dramatic revival, there is now a substantial body of work investigating modern Irish drama from a gender studies perspective.

This book combines all of these approaches. At the core of this project is my interest in the relationship between sexual and social politics, and how that relationship carried plays and playwrights across national and cultural boundaries. My practice throughout is to investigate the most illuminating points of intersection, even where the Irish playwright might be peripheral. To understand Irish drama and the left, we must treat Ireland as one node in a system of influences and exchanges which incorporates multiple cities, languages and nations, and treat the 'other' plays and locations as worthy of analysis in their own right.

This book seeks, therefore, not to establish a linear chain of influence, but to describe the operations of an international network of left organisations, people, parties and states within which these Irish playwrights moved and through which their work circulated. In so doing, I argue for the importance of an internationalism which informed and inspired modernist performance, and which has, in part because of its association with Marxism, receded from view as we pursue a dematerialised and deterritorialised 'global' methodology. For this reason, I have put aside, along with the word 'global', a range of 'world literature' paradigms which are not designed to explain or even identify the patterns of connection that this study illuminates.

I prefer 'international' to 'global' for another, simpler reason, which is that my analysis inevitably will be constrained by the conceptual and geopolitical space which I personally have the power to illuminate. The world of literary modernism as most Anglophone critics apprehend it is typically restricted to 'Europe and the shores of the Mediterranean, plus the two-way traffic across the Atlantic' (Woods, *Homintern*, xii). 'Looked at from a global perspective', Gregory Woods observes, 'this cosmopolitanism is really quite local – as readers in the the southern hemisphere will be quick to observe' (ibid.).

Moreover, 'world systems' paradigms based on evolutionary theory or market theory are so wedded to the developmental logic of capitalism that they render left theatre's internationalism invisible. This is especially true for the model elaborated in Pascale Casanova's *The World Republic of Letters*, which had a major influence on Irish studies after its English translation was published in 2004. Casanova devotes special attention to the Irish literary revival as a case study which validates her theory of world literary space, and demonstrates in microcosm 'virtually the entire range of literary solutions to the problem of domination' (Casanova, *The World Republic of Letters*, 320).

The problem with Casanova's argument, for my purposes, is that it uses the logic of capitalism to objectify a concept of literary value that would otherwise be recognisable as subjective. Her conception of 'literary value' may not *be* economic value, but it *works* in exactly the same way. Literary value is conflated with literary influence, which must be achieved using the processes that define success in a capitalist economy. Riches breed more riches; a successful investment is one whose value increases with time; more shall be given always and only to those who have. Time is value; the older a literature is, the richer it becomes. Since 'literary power' emerged in continental Europe first (ibid., 11), belated literatures cannot achieve the autonomy that produces innovation; they can only borrow it from the nearest major European centre (ibid., 109). Casanova's world literary space thus does not allow for contrarian systems driven by an anticapitalist definition of 'value'. But it was precisely that kind of counter-system that enabled the encounters, exchanges and mutual transformations that this book investigates. These Irish plays traveled the world via pathways cobbled together from labour unions, political parties, national liberation movements and Soviet influence. This Internationale-ism, if you will, constituted an intentionally anticapitalist system of exchange whose operations cannot be accounted for by market theory.

For a more appropriate comparative paradigm, I turn to Natalie Melas's *All the Difference in the World: Postcoloniality and the Ends of Comparison*, which argues that the global turn has, ironically, effaced the anti-imperialist internationalisms of postcolonial studies. Melas calls into question the 're-emergence of systematic approaches' to world literature 'based on sociological and scientific models' which often simply represent the contemporary rebranding of Eurocentric comparativism (Melas, *All the Difference in the World*, 33). In rejecting a unified system of world literature, Melas rejects not merely a centre-periphery model which unfailingly locates the West at the hub and the Rest at the margins, but a teleological understanding of temporality and modernity which takes the 'here and now' as the natural state towards which everything has always been moving. In her 'refusal of the "normalization of the present"' (ibid., 40), Melas puts forward a comparative model that incorporates Bertolt Brecht's conception of history as contingent rather than providential: things happened this way, but they *could* have, *should* have, happened another way. We should not, therefore, reject a text, or a time, or a place, as irrelevant simply because it has been excluded from the causal narratives that are held to have produced the present moment. 'Postcolonial literature', Melas suggests, is drawn precisely to that which an evolutionary or teleological paradigm would read as failure, seeking to '[give] expression to all that is left over, forgotten, or unaccomplished in history's rapid march' (ibid.).

INTRODUCTION

Left over, forgotten, or unaccomplished: all of these terms are as applicable to the utopian projects of the nineteenth- and twentieth-century left as they are to postcolonial literature. Every chapter in this book investigates something that remained left over, forgotten or unaccomplished after the establishment of the Irish dramatic canon: John Todhunter's reviled and unpublished *Comedy of Sighs*; the utopian land-nationalisation scheme that was ripped out of *John Bull's Other Island*; Daniel Corkery's uneven but fascinating dramatisation of Ireland's already-vanishing Bolshevist moment in *The Labour Leader*; Bertolt Brecht's transformation of *Riders to the Sea* into a Spanish civil war propaganda play whose value in Casanova's 'world literary space' is asymptotically approaching zero; Sean O'Casey's attempt to fuse Shakespearean richness and Communist content in *The Star Turns Red*; Lorraine Hansberry's vastly under-appreciated exploration of the postwar American left's existentialist crisis in *The Sign in Sidney Brustein's Window*. Melas's approach suggests that in examining the broken lines and snapped threads that failed to terminate in a utopian present, we might discover materials out of which to build an unexpected future.

OTHER TIMES

Judith Halberstam, in *The Queer Art of Failure*, argues that failures like these plays can model ways to 'escape the punishing norms that discipline behavior and manage human development' (Halberstam, *Queer Art of Failure*, 3) and pursue possibilities excluded from the realm of 'success'. In observing that '[f]ailing is something that queers do and have always done exceptionally well' (ibid.), Halberstam reprises Samuel Beckett's injunction in *Worstward Ho* to 'Fail again. Fail better.' Failing is something that the Irish, too, have always done exceptionally well – in some of the same ways and for some of the same reasons. The Irish themselves perennially have been accused of failing at productivity; the Irish modern dramatic tradition is marked by the failure of re-productivity. This failure is especially acute in the work of J. M. Synge, whose plays often seem to deny even the possibility of a next generation. But Yeats's fascination with degeneration testifies to a similar scepticism; and Shaw was obsessed with the inadequacy of sexual reproduction as a means of ensuring a better future. It is in this realm of failed re/production that Irishness and queerness meet; and it is for this reason that queer theory will be central to this study. To the realm of the generative failure we must also assign the utopian desires of Marxism, which reject the future continually being reproduced by capitalism in favour of another future whose production is never assured.

Apart from the historical conditions that bring sexual and social politics together at the beginning of this history, it is the reproductive nexus that makes it imperative to look at socialist and sexual politics together in the context of modern Irish drama. Lee Edelman has argued in *No Future: Queer Theory and the Death Drive* that the 'queer' is precisely that which is outside of and antagonistic to what he calls 'reproductive futurism' (Edelman, *No Future*, 2). For Edelman, the price of entering the political sphere in thought, word or deed – the price of entering the social order at all – is to bind oneself to work for the production and/or the protection of future generations. Edelman embodies this irresistible demand in the terrifying allegorical figure of the Child whose 'coercive universalization . . . serves to regulate political discourse – to prescribe what will *count* as political discourse' (ibid., 11). It is this refusal of the reproductive mandate, Edelman argues, that excludes queer people from a social order which

> exists to preserve for this universalized subject, this fantasmatic Child, a notional freedom more highly valued than the actuality of freedom itself, which might, after all, put at risk the Child to whom such a freedom falls due. Hence, whatever refuses this mandate by which our political institutions compel the collective reproduction of the Child must appear as a threat not only to the organization of a given social order but also, and far more ominously, to social order as such, insofar as it threatens the logic of futurism on which meaning always depends. (Ibid.)

I argue that it was precisely because queer culture had to disrupt the 'logic of futurism' that it became so intimately associated with utopian socialism. In this I draw on José Muñoz's concept of 'queer futurity', which opposes the power of reproductive futurism with the power of a future which is queer precisely because it can never become the present moment. In that sense, the queer socialism that exerted such a formative influence on modern Irish drama provides – for a time – a crucial corrective to the authoritarian socialism so vigorously anathematised by Matthew Yde in *Bernard Shaw and Totalitarianism*.

Other Marxisms

Queer theory, rooted as it is in the problem of embodiment, calls us down from the vertiginous heights of Marxist theory to witness the messy, ugly and often tragic material history of socialist practice. It is partly to resist Marxism's tendency towards abstract universalism that I insist on reading the sexual and socialist revolutions together. Feminist and queer theorists have long acknowledged and incorporated the insights of Marxist theory; Marxists haven't always returned the favour. As Halberstam notes, 'many Marxist scholars have characterized and dismissed queer politics as "body politics" or as simply superficial', rejecting queer theory's claim that 'alternative forms of embodiment and desire are central to the struggle' (Halberstam, *Queer Art of Failure*, 29). The view from the field of praxis is different. For better and for worse, for instance, the Bolsheviks recognised the 'ideological importance of sex as a topic of public discussion' and the 'ideological uses' that could be 'made of the body at a concrete historical moment when theory is put into practice' (Naiman, *Sex in Public*, 4–5). It is partly because this study takes such a keen interest in that transition from theory to practice that I use queer theory to keep the body and sexuality central to this project.

Halberstam suggests that for the thinkers who defined postmodern Marxism – Fredric Jameson, Raymond Williams, Edward Soja, David Harvey, etc. – hegemonic masculinity is fused with both working-class identity and intellectual/ideological rigour. This assumption manifests in part as a preference for the 'hard' disciplines of political science and economics over the fuzziness of cultural studies. Cleary's *Outrageous Fortune*, for instance, begins by dismissing feminist and queer studies as novelty acts in an 'intellectual circus' whose razzle-dazzle fools bourgeois academics into believing that they are accomplishing something when in fact their work leaves untouched the 'complex "sociological" questions' that might advance the revolution (Cleary, *Outrageous Fortune*, 3–5). This attitude is not confined to Irish studies; Helen Bruder and Tristanne Connolly, for instance, lament the efforts of Marxist romanticists to transform the fascinatingly perverse William Blake into a 'healthy, macho, rough and ready, "typical" English working class' subject (Bruder and Connolly, *Queer Blake*, 5). They sum up the 'politico-sexual subtext' of this move with beautiful pithiness: 'Queer is for poofy toffs; transgender softness for bleeding-heart liberals' (ibid.).

For all these reasons, this book necessarily rejects the idea of gender and sexual politics as distractions away from which we must tear ourselves before we can buckle down to a 'more materialist' (Cleary, *Outrageous Fortune*, 9) analysis. As Muñoz argues, to accept that argument is to forget or deny Marxism's 'interest in the transformative force of *eros* and its implicit relationship to political desire' (Muñoz, *Cruising Utopia*, 31). To write off the power of *eros* and thereby impoverish our understanding of embodiment is to undermine the effectiveness of Marxism as a mode of analysis. Perversely, indeed, this denial of the body produces an idealised conception of capitalism itself which impairs our ability to imagine a future without it.

Halberstam argues that it was precisely by excluding sexuality from analysis that Jameson et al. produced a conception of capitalism as eternally dominant and all-encompassing. An omnipotent and invulnerable capitalism ensures the perpetual dominance of Marxist theory; if nothing ever can be outside capitalism, then a sufficiently penetrating analysis of capitalism will in theory explain all of human experience. This level of abstraction must be maintained by dismissing 'the concrete, the specific, the narrow, the empirical, and even the bodily' (Halberstam, *In a Queer Time*, 11) in order to misrepresent the normal as the universal. '[N]ormativity, as it has been defined and theorized within queer studies', Halberstam observes, 'is the big word missing from almost all the discussions of postmodern geography within a Marxist tradition' (ibid., 7).

According to this totalising logic, because capitalism can never be subverted *everywhere*, it can never be meaningfully challenged *anywhere* (ibid., 12).

Both of the centuries this book excavates testify to the flexibility, resilience and adaptability of a global capitalism which periodically immolates itself only to rise, with hideously augmented strength, from its own ashes. To understand modern Irish drama's involvement in the social and sexual revolutions of the long twentieth century, however, we must relinquish the fantasy of capitalism as a complete and perfect system. This fantasy was, as we will see, extremely attractive to George Bernard Shaw, who succeeded in building it into the foundations of English naturalism. And yet, as David Lloyd, Seamus Deane, Joe Cleary and others have argued, Ireland's subjection to Britain created a distinctively Irish modernity remarkable for its anomalies – including some major deviations from Marxist narratives about economic development.

The birth of modern Anglophone drama occurs in the political and cultural ferment following one of these deviations: the Irish Land War of 1879–82. The history of the left in twentieth-century Ireland, meanwhile, cannot be profitably approached via any comparative paradigm which partakes of the imperialist conception of 'the world as an empirical totality' (Melas, *All the Difference in the World*, xii). The history of colonial oppression that led to the entanglement of sectarian animosity with Irish national politics made it difficult to establish a robust political left anywhere on the island. The history of the left in Ireland is instead dominated by syndicalism, a worldwide radical labour movement with an intentionally 'non-theoretical character' (Darlington 18) which made its impact not 'in terms of *ideological* doctrine, but as a mode of action, a *practical* social movement engaged in working class struggle' (Darlington, *Syndicalism*, 7). The social revolution thus came to Ireland as a lived experience of which ideology was only one dimension. Ireland's contribution to left culture must be understood *through* embodiment.

This book therefore treats the material realisations of left politics as inseparable from their theoretical or ideological articulations. In doing so I am, in one sense, simply following the time-honoured tradition of beginning any Marxist analysis of modern drama with the ritual invocation of Raymond Williams. His foundational essay 'Base and Superstructure' gave us this important elaboration of Gramsci's concept of hegemony:

> [W]hat I have in mind is the central, effective, and dominant system of meanings and values, which are not merely abstract but which are organized and lived ... It is a whole body of practices and expectations; our assignments of energy, our ordinary understanding of the nature of man and his world. It is a set of meanings and values which as they are experienced as practices appear as reciprocally confirming. It thus constitutes a sense of reality for most people in the society, a sense of absolute because

experienced reality beyond which it is very difficult for most members of the society to move, in most areas of their lives. (Williams, *Culture and Materialism*, 38)

Williams describes a hegemony generated by the drives of capitalism, revealing to us how our complex emotional responses to literary texts are conditioned by the 'body of practices and expectations' in which a capitalist economy imbricates us. But anticapitalist politics also constitute 'a set of meanings and values' which are 'experienced as practices', and not simply as a belief system or an economic theory. Certainly this was true for people who made left theatre – theatre being, in itself, material and therefore its own 'experienced reality'. It was also true for socialism, syndicalism, Communism and anarchism. For the adherents of these ideologies, the attempt to realise a utopian vision of a different world transformed the practice of daily life in both dramatic and subtle ways.

In keeping with this conviction of the value of the concrete, the material and the local, I have chosen depth over breadth. Much of the value of the scholarly monograph surely lies in the time and space it allows for the synthesis of different methodologies and disparate types of archival evidence. Each of the book's chapters focuses on two or three plays by major authors whose performance histories open out into a more expansive discussion of left culture, modern drama and sexual politics. In devoting so much attention to specific cases, I seek to provide a sustained, continuous and revelatory account of a tradition of modern performance which has remained illegible partly because of the labour and time involved in reconstituting its archive. The world electronic space has been shaped by many of the same forces crystallised in Casanova's conception of literary value. This particular revolution has not been digitised.

THE CHAPTERS

In the first chapter, 'Desiring Women: Irish Playwrights, New Women and Queer Socialism, 1892–1894)', I show how the interrelationship between sexual and social revolutions in late nineteenth-century London helped determine the contours of both the Irish dramatic revival and twentieth-century English drama. W. B. Yeats and George Bernard Shaw, while living and working in London, gravitated towards a specific version of socialism rooted in the radical *eros* that animated the work of their role model Percy Bysshe Shelley. This Shelleyan socialism was developed in the Victorian era by Yeats's and Shaw's mutual friend William Morris, by their fellow-expatriate Oscar Wilde, and by the pioneering queer socialist Edward Carpenter. Drawing on the theory of José Muñoz, Lee Edelman and J. J. Halberstam, as well as Patrick Mullen's work on queer Irish modernism, I identify this utopianism as a 'queer socialism' defined by an insistence on pleasure as both the practice and the objective of social progress. Through a reading of Shaw's collaborations with the English actress, activist and New Woman Florence Farr, focusing on his participation in the season of avant-garde drama that Farr produced at the Avenue Theatre in 1894, I show that Shaw was attracted to queer socialism while fearful of the consequences of identifying himself with homosexuality. His public repudiation of queer socialism was, I argue, catalysed by the audience's hostile response to the Avenue Theatre season's opening night programme, which featured Yeats's *The Land of Heart's Desire* and their Irish colleague John Todhunter's *A Comedy of Sighs*. The audience's rejection of the Yeats/Todhunter double bill was largely a response to both plays' depictions of desire between women, which drew on their authors' shared occult fascinations to mythologise the New Woman's transgressive sexuality. To save himself from similar punishment, Shaw revised *Arms and the Man* and replaced Farr with a more gender-conforming actress. The success of *Arms and the Man* created a split between Yeats – who took his supernatural women and their unholy desires with him to Dublin and the Irish Literary Theatre – and Shaw, who remained in London to found a more straightforwardly socialist English dramatic revival.

The second chapter draws on queer theories of futurity and the history of British socialism to explore Shaw's radical ambivalence about Irishness and about utopian desire – which were, I argue, intimately linked for him. Drawing on José Muñoz's analysis of the relationship between queer identity and utopian desire, I show how Shaw's repudiation of socialist praxis in favour of reproductive futurism in *Man and Superman* masks his shame about the anti-productivity associated with Irishness. Shaw's treatment of Ireland and Irishness in *Man and Superman*, nevertheless, becomes an outlet for his deep discomfort with the developmental logic undergirding both evolutionary theory and capitalism. Shaw recognised the Ireland depicted by the Irish Players during their London visits in 1903 and 1904 as a place outside of developmental logic, in which Shaw might re-present the utopian desires he had rejected after the Avenue Theatre catastrophe. By excavating the role that Ebenezer Howard's Garden City project once played in *John Bull*'s construction, I show how deeply bound up Shaw's first Irish play was with the socialist dream of land nationalisation and with William Morris's faith in design. Through my reading of Father Keegan, I show that the play's failure to develop a coherent plot helps preserve the hope that Ireland might yet become the site of radical change.

In Chapter 3, 'We'll Keep The Red Flag Flying Here: Syndicalism, Jim Larkin and Irish Masculinity at the Abbey Theatre, 1911–1919', I examine the drama of syndicalist labour during Ireland's revolutionary period, focusing on the shift in left culture and masculinity sparked by the rise of militant labour. I trace the influence of syndicalism on representations of working-class masculinity in three strike plays staged at the Abbey Theatre during Ireland's revolutionary period: St. John Ervine's 1911 *Mixed Marriage*, Andrew Patrick Wilson's 1914 *The Slough* and Daniel Corkery's 1919 play *The Labour Leader*. All three plays were inspired by syndicalist labour actions carried out in Irish cities and led by the Liverpool-born organiser James Larkin, whose agitational style incorporated some aspects of queer socialism into a more normative masculinity founded on the capacity for violence. Larkin's ability to inspire working-class men to share his own emotions was, as I show, a source of anxiety for Ervine, whose *Mixed Marriage* focuses on the heterosexual 'mixing' named in the play's title in order to suppress the disruptive potential of the homosocial 'mixing' of Catholic and Protestant men enabled by Larkin's organising. The counter-revolutionary family plot that Ervine constructs for *Mixed Marriage* promotes the dramatic conventions of the irresponsible working-class father and the strong but apolitical working-class mother, which are replicated in A. Patrick Wilson's Lockout play *The Slough* and then amplified in O'Casey's *Juno and the Paycock*. Daniel Corkery, however, was fascinated by Larkin's sensibilities. His 1919 play *The Labour Leader* uses Larkin's debt to queer socialism to explore the emotional landscape of working-class masculinity while demonstrating the potential of a revolutionary theatre capable of harnessing syndicalism's passions.

The fourth chapter examines the impact on modern drama of the establishment of the Soviet Union through in-depth investigation of a special case: Bertolt Brecht's transformation of J. M. Synge's 1904 *Riders to the Sea* into a 1937 Spanish Civil War play called *Señora Carrar's Rifles*. I argue that Synge and Ireland were not, for their own sakes, important to Brecht; he was drawn to *Riders* as a model which might help him solve the problem of how to radicalise the working-class mother. As I show, after the disastrous 1935 production of Brecht's *The Mother* by the New York City-based Theatre Union, Brecht concluded that the technical demands of epic theatre were beyond the capacity of these amateur ensembles. Synge's unusual treatment of maternal grief at the end of *Riders* helped Brecht envision a means of producing the effects of epic theatre while using the techniques of realism. Re-presenting Maurya's refusal to grieve for Bartley in both *Señora Carrar's Rifles* and *Mother Courage* helped Brecht refine his understanding of alienation in ways which made epic theatre more pleasurable for spectators without requiring Brecht to acknowledge that pleasure as a desired effect.

In the fifth chapter, I take up Sean O'Casey's late career, during which he settled in England and abandoned tenement realism. Many of the plays O'Casey wrote after his move to England in 1928 become legible only in the context of the history charted during the first four chapters, the Stalinised British left organisations with which O'Casey worked, and the genre of socialist realism. O'Casey's realistic Dublin trilogy represents a temporary disruption in his overall artistic trajectory. O'Casey saw the Soviet Union as a market for the kind of ideologically-committed and antirealist drama that neither the Abbey Theatre's directors nor London's commercial producers wanted. Through my investigation of the genesis and performance history of O'Casey's 1940 Communist play *The Star Turns Red*, I show how O'Casey's post-realist aesthetic derives from the literary tradition of queer socialism, which reached him through the work of Shelley and Larkin. O'Casey's ambivalence about British left culture masks an unbounded admiration of the kind of proletarian literature which O'Casey believed – thanks to his limited and misleading contact with it – was represented by socialist realism. He was also strongly drawn to Soviet conceptions of gender and sexuality, a fact which explains some unusual things about his reception.

In an epilogue, I consider the impact of Irish playwrights on an American left that had been decimated by anti-Communist persecution. A few months prior to the New York premiere of Samuel Beckett's *Waiting for Godot*, O'Casey made his comeback on Broadway in 1956 with his last Dublin Lockout play, *Red Roses For Me*. I show how the queer African-American playwright Lorraine Hansberry, whose interest in O'Casey is typically supposed to be limited to *Juno and the Paycock*, suspends the antirealist effects of these two different Irish premieres within her 1964 play *The Sign in Sidney Brustein's Window*, which chronicles the existential crises faced by a group of New York progressives after the destruction of the American cultural left. I argue that Hansberry deftly separates O'Casey's and Beckett's most promising techniques from the masculinist foundations on which they were originally reared, redeploying them in order to help Sidney Brustein – and, by extension, the white left – resolve the impasse in which they have been trapped, by abandoning a definition of struggle based on a self-defeating attachment to a heroic masculinity which was never attainable.

I conclude by considering some of the possible implications of this study for a world in which the persistence of globalisation as most of the twenty-first century has known it can no longer be taken for granted. I argue that it is imperative for us to relearn the value of internationalisms which are unbounded by, and antagonistic to, the 'globe' of late capitalism, and which therefore might help combat a reactionary politics of toxic protectionism that seeks to 'restore' an imaginary past by expelling immigrants and others perceived to be threatening the economic security of the white working class. By demonstrating the necessity of reading socialist and sexual politics together, this investigation into the participation of Irish playwrights in the international political and cultural left hopes to contribute to the project of reimagining a left politics in which anticapitalist politics and identity politics are no longer perceived to be in competition with each other. *Irish Drama and the Other Revolutions* thus hopes to contribute to the larger conversation about the internationalism of Irish modernism, and of modernist performance more generally, by calling attention to the ways in which Irish playwrights have dramatised the simultaneous embodiment of socialist and sexual politics.

1

DESIRING WOMEN:
IRISH PLAYWRIGHTS, NEW WOMEN
AND QUEER SOCIALISM, 1892–1894

INTRODUCTION

On 28 March 1894, the day before W. B. Yeats saw a play of his produced for the first time, Yeats wrote to John O'Leary of his dreams for the future. Florence Farr, an English feminist turned actress, had persuaded the Manchester tea magnate Annie Horniman to subsidise a season of original plays in English that she would produce at the Avenue Theatre in London. Yeats's fellow-expatriate George Bernard Shaw was working on a comedy called *Arms and the Man*; but the first night would feature Yeats's one-act *The Land of Heart's Desire*, followed by John Todhunter's *A Comedy of Sighs*. If all went well, Yeats thought he might stay in London, and he hoped Farr would produce and star in a play he was writing. Yeats described this play – eventually titled *The Shadowy Waters* – as

> a wild mystical thing carefully arranged to be an insult to the regular theatre goer who is hated by both of us. All the plays [Florence Farr] is arranging for are studied insults. Next year she might go to Dublin as all her playwrights by a curious chance are Irish. (Yeats, *Collected Letters*, I, 384)

This letter captures a moment when the future of literary drama in English is in flux. The Irish Literary Theatre is three years in the future. Although invested in the idea of an Irish literary revival, Yeats has been concentrating his efforts in London. He doesn't have an explanation for the 'curious chance' that brought three aspiring Irish playwrights together in London, or for what it means that Farr has attracted so much Irish talent to a venture with no national ambitions. For Yeats, insulting the 'regular theatre goer' is the project that holds the Avenue Theatre season together. The Irishness of the participants matters less than Farr's challenge to commercial theatre.

The future Yeats imagines here did not materialise. On opening night, Todhunter's *A Comedy of Sighs* met with a catastrophically hostile reception. When equally hostile reviews appeared the following morning, Shaw's *Arms and the Man* was rushed into production. *Arms* replaced *Comedy* on April 21.[1] Yeats's *Land of Heart's Desire* was soon replaced with *The Man in the Street*, a one-act comedy by a seasoned London hack named Louis N. Parker.[2] A humiliated Todhunter said goodbye to the theatre and hello to obscurity. Yeats, having failed to create an audience for his work in London, dedicated himself to launching an Irish dramatic revival in Dublin. Shaw, on the other hand, was encouraged by the brilliant success of *Arms and the Man*. He remained both immersed in the London theatre scene and stridently critical of it; and when, in 1895, Oscar Wilde's rising star went supernova, Shaw had a clear field on which to build an *English* dramatic revival.

The importance of the Avenue Theatre season in determining the character of both of these national dramatic revivals has never been fully appreciated. This is largely because the play that caused most of the trouble – *A Comedy of Sighs* – was never published. The surviving typescript has yet to be digitised, and Todhunter – a physician turned poet and member of the Order of the Golden Dawn who was at the time a more experienced and successful playwright than either Yeats or Shaw – has been largely forgotten. My primary purpose in beginning this book by re-examining the Avenue Theatre incident, however, is not to simply to excavate a crucial piece of theatre history; less still is it to make room in the Irish dramatic revival for John Todhunter, who (apart from being dead, white and male) fails most of the tests for canonical literary status. I begin with the story of what went wrong at the Avenue Theatre because it shows us how and why, at the origin point of modern drama in English, Irish revival drama and the British left became mutually exclusive.

That was not a foregone conclusion. During the late Victorian era, there was significant cooperation between Irish nationalists and British socialists. Radicals on both islands considered private ownership of land to be the root of all evil. Irish land agitation during the 1880s sought to end landlordism, as Michael Davitt rallied Irish nationalists behind the slogan 'the land of Ireland for the people of Ireland' (Moody, *Davitt and Irish Revolution*, 271). London's Social Democratic Federation was committed to land nationalisation partly due to the influence of expatriate Irishman James Bronterre O'Brien (Bevir, *Making of British Socialism*, 107–11). Liberal tolerance for policies used to quell land agitation in Ireland contributed to the spread of socialism in London by radicalising English progressives (ibid., 39–40). Land use and rent were core concerns of the Fabian Society when it formed in 1884 (ibid., 133). When the Irish Land Leaguer William O'Brien was imprisoned, the Irish National League and the Social Democratic Federation organised a protest in London to demand his release (ibid., 40). On 13 November 1887, this protest was joined by about 10,000 'unemployed workers, Radicals, Anarchists and Socialists', who processed towards Trafalgar Square (McCarthy, *William Morris*, 537). On the way, they were ambushed by police and treated to 'the most ruthless display of establishment power that London has ever seen' (ibid.). Police attacked in several locations, injuring hundreds and preventing the protest from occupying the square (ibid., 569). The confrontation between this crowd of protestors and the London police was christened 'Bloody Sunday'. There would be others.

The English poet, artist, and socialist William Morris marched that day; so did his friend and collaborator George Bernard Shaw (Peters, *Bernard Shaw*, 94). Though Shaw wrote far less about Bloody Sunday than Morris did, I will suggest here that this 'ruthless' exercise of state power had far-reaching consequences for the constitution of the Irish and English dramatic revivals. I argue that Shaw's encounter with state violence on Bloody Sunday greatly reduced his appetite for direct action, and taught him a fear of punishment which prompted him to respond to the failure of *Comedy of Sighs* with a decisive repudiation of the version of Irish drama modelled by Yeats and Todhunter that night. Shaw's handling of the Avenue Theatre incident was, I will show, an early and revealing expression of his ambivalence about the version of utopian socialism articulated and practiced by Morris and his circle. For a time, this conception of socialism was big enough for both Yeats and Shaw. The Avenue Theatre incident is the best clue we have as to why by the time Yeats helped found the Irish Literary Theatre in Dublin in 1897, that was no longer true.

Shaw and Yeats were part of the community of artists and activists that Morris presided over at his home in Hammersmith, during which time Yeats identified as a socialist and was inspired by the anarchist principles of Morris's friend Prince Kropotkin to write *Where There is Nothing* (McAteer, *Yeats and European Drama*, 22–4). During the decade leading up to the Avenue Theatre experiment, Morris's conception of socialism was transformed, with the help of Oscar Wilde and the queer English socialist Edward Carpenter, into a discursive formation that I will refer to as 'queer socialism', which foregrounded the interrelationship between socialism and sexual liberation. Both *Land of Heart's Desire* and *Comedy of Sighs* engaged current debates about feminism by mythologising the New Woman's transgressive erotic potential. This was partly due to Florence Farr herself, who was an outspoken feminist, an occult adept, a vocal critic of the institution of marriage, and a woman already identified – at least by Yeats, Todhunter and Shaw – as queer. Both plays were haunted by the spectre of desire between women, and the audience's violent rejection of the Yeats/Todhunter double bill showed Shaw just how much punishment the representation of queer desire could incur. Scrambling to avoid humiliation, Shaw alienated himself from the Irish revival *by* attempting to purge his dramatic universe of this transgressive *eros*. Shaw's obliteration of *Comedy of Sighs* with *Arms and the Man* thus publicly distanced him from an emerging Irish aesthetic already being marked as queer; it also constituted a rejection of the romantic socialism so closely associated with New Women and queer men. Yeats took his desiring women back to Dublin, leaving Shaw to cultivate a more straightforwardly socialist drama in London.

Idealism, Shelley and Radical *Eros*

To understand the relationship between Shaw's socialist formation and the Avenue Theatre incident we must turn back towards the desperate 1880s, when revolution seemed 'self-evidently imminent' (Livesey, 'Morris, Carpenter, Wilde', 601) to the collection of visionaries, poets, feminists, Marxists, anarchists, radicals and cranks that made up London's progressive community. Shaw's political formation took place at a time when the lecture circuit on which he would so indefatigably distinguish himself was dominated by Morris and Carpenter, who 'shared a vision of the subject under socialism' which was idealist in its origins and utopian in its faith that socialism would allow 'the self' to achieve its 'fullest expression, clearest realization' and 'true manhood' (ibid., 603). Oscar Wilde articulated a variation on this individualist theme in 'The Soul of Man Under Socialism', in which he attacked Morris's and Carpenter's ideas about the dignity of labour (Livesey, 'Morris, Carpenter, Wilde', 607–8) while theorising a socialism which was, like theirs, founded on the idealist recognition of beauty as a transcendent good.

The dominant narrative of Shaw's ideological formation has long been that Shaw's relationship to this strain of idealist, aesthetic and utopian socialism was purely oppositional. Though, as Matthew Yde and others have noted, Shaw's politics changed considerably over the course of an extraordinarily long career, he is forever identified with the Fabian Society, which formed in 1884 to promote a more 'scientific' socialism (Bevir, *Making of British Socialism*, 133–4). These 'gradualist socialists' (Livesey, 'Morris, Carpenter, Wilde', 603) were more preoccupied with economics than aesthetics, and focused on practical objectives rather than utopian alternatives (Bevir, *Making of British Socialism*, 133–4). Livesey, while arguing that the Fabian Society was more supportive of aesthetic socialism than it pretended to be ('Morris, Carpenter, Wilde', 606), nevertheless concurs with generations of Shavians in interpreting Shaw's politics as an outright 'dismissal of Carpenter's idealism' (ibid., 604) and identifying Shaw as 'pre-eminently responsible for separating out this association of socialist politics and the aestheticization of manly labor' (ibid., 614). Shaw, in this narrative, is the one who redefined socialism as the opposite of romantic – as a grueling and joyless struggle to 'reshape the material basis of society' one municipal regulation at a time (ibid.).

Certainly this was the impression Shaw intended to convey by staking out anti-utopian positions in innumerable lectures and essays. But one of my objectives is to liberate Shaw from the tyranny of his own voluminously expressed intentions, which have too long exerted a constraining influence on Shaw scholarship and a deadening effect on Shaw's drama. Shaw's compulsive generation of prefaces, afterwords and epilogues, in which he prescribes the authoritative reading of a play that is all but smothered beneath them, is partly responsible for the depreciation of his stock since the theory revolution. Protecting his own authority by striving to eliminate lack, subtext or ambiguity, Shaw foreclosed the kinds of reading that the past half-century has shown to be most generative. We cannot fully understand Shaw's drama *or* his politics, and we cannot understand his Irishness at all, if we accept this authority and assume that he alone somehow made language do exactly what he wished it to do. We must instead investigate the subvocal preoccupations that Shaw was reluctant to avow – many of which centred on the human body (Yde, *Bernard Shaw and Totalitarianism*, 3). We will begin by examining the ways in which the aesthetic socialism expounded by Morris and Carpenter linked socialism, theoretically and practically, with contemporary gender and sexual liberation movements.

Much of the Marxist scholarship done on modern Irish literature – Cleary's *Outrageous Fortune*, for instance, and Levitas's *The Theatre of Nation* – has focused on Ireland's distinctive formations of naturalism. The story of Irish drama's relationship with the British left, however, begins with the persistence of idealism. In *Henrik Ibsen and the Birth of Modernism*, Toril Moi argues that modernism and naturalism emerged, not in opposition to each other, but in opposition to the idealism that had become the dominant aesthetic paradigm of nineteenth-century Europe. At the beginning of the nineteenth century, she argues, idealist philosophy – derived from Plato, and popularised throughout Europe by Kant, Hölderlin, Hegel, Schiller and other German romantics – produced 'one of the most powerful and inspiring accounts of the nature and purpose of art and literature the world has ever seen' (Moi, *Henrik Ibsen and the Birth of Modernism*, 70). This idealist conception of art as a link between the material world and the transcendent ideal of which that world is the shadow was fervently embraced by the British romantic poets; but it survived the vogue of romantic literature. According to Moi, '*some* version of this account, however debased, diluted, vulgarised, and simplified, shows up practically everywhere in nineteenth-century aesthetic discussions' right to the end of the century (ibid.).

What survives into the Victorian period is the cult of beauty, 'the key term of aesthetic idealism' (ibid., 72). Beauty is 'both sensuous and spiritual' and therefore 'offers us an image of our own lost wholeness' (ibid.). Linking the beautiful with the true and the good, idealism fused art 'with ethics and religion' to create an 'optimistic, utopian vision of human perfection' (ibid., 73). As developments in science and technology increased the cultural power of materialism, however, idealist aesthetics degenerated into a system of restrictive literary conventions. Victorian idealism presents itself to the *fin-de-siècle* avant-garde as a willful denial of modern realities, and becomes 'identical with hypocritical, anti-artistic, moralistic conservatism' (ibid., 93). Modernism, like naturalism and realism, is then 'built on the negation of idealism' (ibid., 67).

In Ireland, this history played out differently. The Irish revival identified itself with the idealism that modernism and naturalism were challenging in England and on the Continent. The mission statement circulated in 1897 by Yeats, Gregory and Edward Martyn to raise funds for the Irish Literary Theatre promised 'to show that Ireland is not the home of buffoonery and of easy sentiment . . . but the home of an ancient idealism' (Gregory, *Our Irish Theatre*, 20). Yeats's own idealism was romantic; Yeats always wrote out of a desire to create beauty and out of a belief in an immaterial, occult realm which is the true 'reality' and which controls the comparatively minor portion of the universe which is perceptible to the senses. As Joseph Valente has demonstrated, however, it was *Victorian* idealism which was incorporated into Irish myth and legend by revival translators, who 'undertook, for strategic reasons, to retrofit the bardic heritage to the canons of late Victorian respectability' and Irish heroes to Victorian notions of masculine virtue (Valente, *The Myth of Manliness*, 141). Idealism attained specific political dimensions in Irish nationalist discourse, as Irish idealism was continually opposed to English materialism and Irishmen and -women were exhorted to choose Ireland and idealism over, as Maud Gonne once put it, 'England, flesh, and the devil' (quoted in Harris, *Gender and Modern Irish Drama*, 30–41, 61–8).

None of this would matter, for our purposes, were it not for the fact that another 'home' romantic idealism found when it was driven into exile was the radical left. The 'utopian vision of human perfectibility' that powered Schiller's aesthetics 'had a strong afterlife in the Marxist tradition' (Moi, *Henrik Ibsen and the Birth of Modernism*, 74). This was certainly true in nineteenth-century England, where poet-radicals were very much a part of left theory and practice. The paradigmatic example is Percy Bysshe Shelley. Shelley's 1813 poem *Queen Mab* became 'the "Bible" of the Chartist movement in the 1840s, and continued to influence British Socialist thinkers into the twentieth century' (Nichols, 'Liberationist Sexuality', 25). *The Mask of Anarchy*, Shelley's excoriation of the authorities who ordered and carried out the Peterloo Massacre in 1819, articulated what was 'perhaps the first modern statement of the principle of nonviolent protest' (ibid., 23).

All the Irish playwrights involved in the Avenue Theatre venture had two things in common: they were devoted to Florence Farr, and they were devoted to Shelley. For Yeats, Shelley was a personal role model as well as a poetic influence (Bornstein, *Yeats and Shelley*, xi); and when Shaw turned up at the inaugural meeting of the Shelley Society in March 1886, he declared that he was, 'like Shelley', a 'socialist, an atheist, and a vegetarian' (Shaw, *Bernard Shaw: The Diaries*, 152). Todhunter was a founding member of the Shelley Society and a lifelong Shelley scholar. The London production of Shelley's tragedy *The Cenci* by the Shelley Society in 1886, in which Todhunter and Shaw were involved, was one of the first shots fired in the modern revolt against London's commercial theare.

The Licensing Act of 1737 subjected England's patent theatres to state censorship. All original plays slated for performance at a licensed playhouse had to be submitted to the Lord Chamberlain's office for approval ahead of time. The topic of incest was categorically forbidden, which meant that *The Cenci* – in which the sadistic Count Cenci rapes his daughter Beatrice, who then organises his assassination – would never be licensed for public performance. The Shelley Society needed a way to produce *The Cenci* without the Lord Chamberlain's approval. Michael Orme credits the Shelley Society with the 'discovery' of the strategy that her husband, J. T. Grein, would adopt when he founded the Independent Theatre in 1890: they made the performance a private event by collecting subscriptions in advance (Orme, *J. T. Grein*, 74). Because '[t]he general public was not admitted' to the invitation-only affair, the Lord Chamberlain's office had no jurisdiction (ibid.). The 'private club' ruse would be exploited by 'amateur' groups producing theatre with challenging political content until the end of the censorship in 1968. Subscriptions became a business model for 'independent' or 'literary' theatres which could not support themselves through conventional ticket sales (Archer, *Royal Court Theatre*, 3). The Shelley Society thus invented, for the purpose of staging Shelley's attack on patriarchal tyranny, some of the strategies that made the English dramatic revival possible.

As the plot of *The Cenci* hints, Shelley's radicalism was multidimensional. The fact that Shelley was an idealist who sought to apprehend the immaterial, *and* a passionate opponent of tyranny, *and* the sworn enemy of patriarchy and its institutions (including the monarchy, marriage and organised religion), *and* a literary celebrity who conducted his sex life with flagrant contempt for his culture's rules of engagement, had a profound impact on the history we are about to investigate. The visionary idealism that attracted Yeats to Shelley's poetry fuelled the same polemical outrage that attracted Shaw; and neither Shelley's aesthetics nor his politics were separable from his avid pursuit of sexual liberty. 'Shelley adopted a poetics of love', according to William Ulmer, 'in part because it could accommodate his political commitments' (Ulmer, *Shelleyan Eros*, 18). Samuel Lyndon Gladden argues that Shelley 'masks political rhetoric by way of erotic narratives ... in which pleasure and love are posed as symbols for liberation from oppressive regimes' (Gladden, *Shelley's Textual* Seduction, 7–9). In Shelley's poetry, '[t]he body ... represents a repository of revolutionary potential, and sensuality a political weapon' (Ulmer, *Shelleyan Eros*, 55). In this respect, Shelley's work challenged not only conventional morality but the anti-corporeal bias that Moi identifies as foundational to idealism.

Shelley's radical *eros* is thus one of the origin points for an embodied, desire-driven, pleasure-seeking socialism which challenges the contempt for sexuality that still recurs in some strains of Marxism. José Muñoz argues that those 'theorists of postmodernity' who have 'narrated sex radicalism as a turning away from a politics of the collectivity toward the individualistic and the petty' are disavowing an alternative Marxist tradition which recognised 'the transformative force of *eros* and its implicit relationship to political desire' (Muñoz, *Cruising Utopia*, 30–1). Muñoz traces this tradition back through the Frankfurt school to Oscar Wilde, the 'ghost' that 'haunts [Ernst] Bloch's thinking' (ibid., 40). In fact, this tradition of *eros*-embracing socialism is older, and Wilde is but one late-blooming flower on a tree that Shelley helped plant.

Queer Socialism

Mullen coined the phrase 'queer socialism' (Mullen, *The Poor Bugger's Tool*, 30) as part of his brilliant analysis of Wilde's prose in *The Poor Bugger's Tool: Irish Modernism, Queer Labor, and Postcolonial History*. He uses it to denominate an alternative economic theory that he believes Oscar Wilde invented in 'The Portrait of W. H.' and 'The Soul of Man Under Socialism', in which 'homoerotic affect' becomes a 'value form' which circulates as an alternative currency, undermining the monopolistic power of capitalism's commodity value system (ibid., 30–5). Because he claims Wilde as a modernist, however, Mullen presents Wilde's queer socialism as *sui generis*, and does not consider whether it might have been related to the socialisms articulated by his Victorian contemporaries. Wilde's 'Soul of Man' certainly is forward-looking in its proto-Gramscian grasp of the way modes of production and ownership condition every aspect of lived experience and human subjectivity (Kuch, 'Wildean Politics', 373; Mullen, *The Poor Bugger's Tool*, 35). But Wilde's bid to 'redefine labor, and with it pleasure, by envisioning a kind of *creative* labor which places pleasure at the very foundation of society' (Lesjak, 'Utopia, Use, and the Everyday', 180) is also enabled by his 'engagement with contemporary social and political issues' (Kuch, 'Wildean Politics', 369). These included Morris's and Carpenter's socialism, which was founded on an idealist 'perception of the world' articulated by 'second-generation Romanticism' (Kirchhoff, *William Morris*, xi). I will therefore leave aside Mullen's definition of 'queer socialism', which is more a theoretical than a historical construct, and reconceptualise 'queer socialism' for our purposes as a discursive formation which developed out of Shelley's radical *eros*.

Because I am approaching queer socialism as a historical phenomenon, I must also diverge from Mullen on the vexed question of the relationship between the term 'queer' and homosexual identity. Signalling his alignment with a major shift in post-Sedgwick queer studies, Mullen deploys a conception of 'queer' which functions 'both as a capacious index for a series of non-normative desires, sexualities, people, politics, and cultural expressions and as a term that maintains specific relations, at times contradictory and elusive, with the homosexual and the homoerotic' (Mullen, *The Poor Bugger's Tool*, 6). But it is crucial, especially in this chapter, to remember that homosexual men who expressed their particular radical *eros* corporeally were exposed to, as Shaw put it, 'monstrously severe punishments' (Shaw, *Collected Letters*, 230). From my point of view, the chief attraction of the term 'queer socialism' is that it foregrounds the 'specific relations' that radical *eros* inaugurated between socialism and 'the homosexual and the homoerotic' – relations which were by no means 'elusive' in late Victorian London. As Sally Peters notes, 'most of the radical thinkers on sexuality' at this time 'were socialists and feminists, thereby linking political liberation for women with that of homosexuals' (Peters, *Bernard Shaw*, 168). Shelley's conception of the erotic as radical was an important link between Morris's anarchism and the sexual revolution that included not only Wilde and Carpenter but New Women like Florence Farr.

At the same time, as homosexuality was not clearly distinguishable, at this time, from gender fluidity – gender 'inversion' was the dominant scientific account of homosexuality, promulgated by Havelock Ellis and to some extent endorsed in Carpenter's conception of homosexuals as an 'intermediate sex' – and as nongenital sexual practices were still considered perverse *per se*, we will also need the more 'capacious' definition of 'queer'. Guided by Lee Edelman, I propose to narrow Mullen's 'capacious index' by substituting 'non-reproductive' for 'non-normative.' Fundamentally, what separates Shelley, Morris, Carpenter and Wilde from their contemporaries on the British left is their recognition of pleasure, rather than production, as both a mode of socialist praxis and the object of utopian desire.

The queer potential of Shelley's radical *eros* was legible to Carpenter, who emerged in the 1880s as a 'socialist prophet' and in the 1890s as one of England's first queer theorists. In an essay written for George Barnfield's *The Psychology of the Poet Shelley* (1925), Carpenter attributed Shelley's prophetic genius to his 'intermediate (or double) . . . character – *intermediate* as between the masculine and feminine and *double* as having that twofold outlook upon the world' (Carpenter, 'Introduction', 46). In Carpenter's reading, Shelley envisions the end of gender difference as a revolution which will succeed where violence has failed:

> [Shelley] saw that only a new type of human being combining the male and the female, could ultimately save the world – a being having the feminine insight and imagination to perceive the evil and the manly strength and courage to oppose and finally annihilate it. (Ibid., 19)

Ashton Nichols has argued that Shelley's fusion of sexual and social radicalism was generative for Morris, who replicated it in his influential 1890 utopian novel *News from Nowhere* (Nichols, 'Liberationist Sexuality', 21–5). John Ruskin inspired a generation of Victorian progressives with the faith that aesthetics and socialism were natural partners (Livesey, 'Morris, Carpenter, Wilde, 602); but it was Morris who '[located] aesthetics in the realm of the body via the pleasures of labor' (ibid., 606). Morris's and Carpenter's shared vision of the 'communal labor' (ibid., 603) through which man under socialism would find his bliss was radically different from labour as understood either in capitalist or Marxist terms, in that the value of labour inhered in the 'sensuous pleasure' (Morris quoted in ibid., 606) that the labourer derived from it. For Morris, it was of paramount importance that this transient bodily pleasure was materialised in the beauty of the product. Carpenter laid more stress on 'the aesthetic pleasures of the body itself', which would become 'the force for the transformation of society' (ibid., 610). For both of them, as for the 'ecstatic' (ibid., 603) crowds they inspired in the 1880s and 1890s, this ideology was in part a rejection of the prevailing conception that 'the ethical effect of the aesthetic – Arnold's "sweetness and light" – was a perquisite of the bourgeoisie' (ibid., 607).

Livesey argues that Carpenter transforms Morris's somatics into a 'biological idealism' which eroticises 'manliness' in the image of the 'potent naked body of the laboring man' (ibid., 613). Equally important to Carpenter, however, was Morris's assertion that socialism would transform masculinity emotionally, inaugurating new relations between men based on mutual love. Morris argues in 'The Socialist Ideal in Art' that it is precisely by divorcing production from human relationship that capitalism renders labor 'devoid of pleasure' (64). Carpenter's 'Transitions to Freedom' indicts the affective damage caused by capitalism, looking forward to a society based 'not on individual dread and anxiety, but on the common fullness of life and energy' (179). The key to this transition was the recovery of what Morris calls 'fellowship' and what Carpenter calls 'comrade love': the benevolent, affectionate, non-hierarchical relations between men which are precluded by the competition enforced by capitalism.[3] For Carpenter, socialism would usher in a queer-friendly world in which love was '[tied] to comradeship rather than reproduction' (Bevir, *Making of British Socialism*, 249).

Morris's socialism thus privileged not just the body's needs but its wants, desires and joys – and it recognised that these intangible necessities would inevitably be at odds with the claims of a state interested in forcing the greatest number to produce the greatest quantity. Morris's vigorous rejection of the strong centralised state was, from a queer point of view, one of the most attractive features of his socialism. Oscar Wilde's 'The Soul of Man Under Socialism' does not so much make Morris's socialism queer as reveal that it always was – by elaborating, in a code which is not too hard to crack, on the link between aesthetic socialism and queer desire.

For Carolyn Lesjak, Wilde's major innovation in 'Soul of Man' was 'to uncouple the concept of pleasure from sexuality *per se* and link it instead to a more expansive notion of use' (Lesjak, 'Utopia, Use, and the Everyday', 180), whereby pleasure ideally permeates all sensuous experience. Wilde's 'expansive' definitions of labour and pleasure are founded on his recognition of capitalist production as interdependent with, and mutually constitutive of, heteronormativity. The 'impatience with definition' that Peter Kuch identifies in 'Soul of Man' (Kuch, 'Wildean Politics', 369) – the speaker's refusal to discriminate amongst the myriad anticapitalist ideologies promoted by factions of London's progressive community – is one of the reasons that Wilde's essay has been dismissed *qua* political theory. But triviality, for Wilde, is a pose; and this disregard for ideological rigour is strategic. It dismisses the dogmatic points used to distinguish between socialism, anarchism, Communism, 'or whatever one wants to call it' (quoted in ibid.) as superficial features which obscure the only really *important* difference between any 'ism' and any other: its relationship to authority. Wilde implies here that the really salient feature of any anticapitalist ideology is whether it promises to liberate the individual from 'tyranny', either of private property or of a 'government armed with economic power' (Wilde, 'The Soul of Man Under Socialism', 6). 'If the Socialism is authoritarian', Wilde warns, 'then the last state of man will be worse than the first' (ibid.).

It is this consciousness of the antagonism between the state and queer pleasure that distinguishes Wilde's critique of authoritarian socialism in 'Soul of Man' from his contemporaries' critiques of it. In 'Soul of Man', the strong state is a problem not because it appropriates the individual's labour or his private property, but because it arrogates the power of determining *how* the individual is to work, and therefore how he should use his body. Wilde's redefinition of 'work' as 'activity of any kind' (ibid.) – as *anything* that a given individual might wish to do – openly challenges 'the productivist biases' (Lesjak, 'Utopia, Use, and the Everyday', 181) shared by capitalist and state-socialist ideologies. The soul can only achieve its full expression in a society that liberates the individual from the demand to produce.

The importance of specifically queer desire to Wilde's socialism is legible in his discussion of marriage and the family. It was common for socialists to argue that 'the abolition of private property' would render 'marriage in its present form' obsolete; but Wilde's assertion that '[s]ocialism annihilates family life' predicts an unusually radical disruption (Wilde, 'The Soul of Man Under Socialism', 13). Wilde offers a bridge across this chasm: 'Individualism accepts this and makes it fine. It converts the absence of legal restraint into a form of freedom that will help the full development of personality, and make the love of man and woman more wonderful, more beautiful, and more ennobling' (ibid.). Ironically, the criminalisation of homosexual desire ensures that homosexual love is carried on in 'the absence of legal restraint'; the British state can incarcerate queer men, but it has no power to regulate queer relationships. It can separate, punish and prevent; but it can neither compel two partners of the same gender to remain in a relationship with each other, nor dictate the terms according to which such a relationship can be dissolved. Having discovered the 'form of freedom' made possible by their exclusion from marriage, Wildean 'Individuals' can introduce the bewildered fragments of these 'annihilated' families to relationships based on unproductive pleasure rather than on the accumulation of children and property.

From Wilde's contribution to queer socialism, then, we see that Morris's conception of socialism, by protecting individualism from capitalism's demand for mass production and from the state's authority, would create a more liveable world for men whose sensuous pleasures depended on contact with the bodies of other men. One of the things that drew Wilde and Carpenter to socialism was its promise to create a world in which their desires would no longer consign them to social death. The era during which Morris's and Carpenter's socialist gospel found its largest and most enthusiastic audiences was also the era of the 1885 Criminal Amendment Act, popularly known as 'the blackmailer's charter', which gave the police and the courts greater latitude to enforce the prohibition on homosexual sex. Muñoz's observation that to be queer is to recognise that 'the here and now is a prison house' (Muñoz, *Cruising Utopia*, 1) was, for Wilde and Carpenter, true in a specific and concrete way.

Carpenter articulated the connection between sexual and socialist liberation more explicitly in *Homogenic Love*, printed in 1894 for private circulation by the Labour Press.[4] At the core of his argument for the social utility of homosexuality is the idea that the heterosexual family and the collective good are inevitably at odds. Acknowledging that the production of children is socially necessary, Carpenter reasons that 'another form of union is almost equally indispensable to supply the basis for social activities of other kinds', precisely because parents always put their own children first: '[I]t is not to be expected . . . that the man or woman who have dedicated themselves to each other and to family life should leave the care of their children . . . in order to perform social duties of a remote and less obvious, though may-be more arduous, character' (Carpenter, *Homogenic Love*, 43–4). Examples drawn from antiquity prefigure the great nineteenth-century struggle in which Carpenter is engaged, which will demand the same courage from its queer heroes:

> It may indeed be doubted whether the higher heroic and spiritual life of a nation is ever quite possible without the sanction of [same-sex love] in its institutions; and it is not unlikely that the markedly materialistic and commercial character of the last age of European civilised life is largely to be connected with the fact that the *only* form of love and love-union that it has recognised has been one founded on the ... comparatively materialistic basis of matrimonial sex-intercourse and child-breeding. (Ibid., 44–5)

Homosexuality is socially necessary not merely because it creates passionate attachments between members of different classes (ibid., 47), but because these attachments constitute part of a collective – a new 'institution of human solidarity' whose mission is to create a 'higher heroic and spiritual life' than the one currently produced in the factories and reproduced in the family.

Through their veneration of Shelley and their intimacy with Morris, all of Florence Farr's Irish playwrights were immersed in this queer socialism. Shaw was enormously attracted to this vision of the socialist future; but he was also well aware of the state's antagonism towards homosexuality, and the battle of Trafalgar Square taught him early on that open defiance of the state would be brutally punished. The history we are about to examine requires us to resist the temptation to allow Shaw's larger-than-life persona to obscure the fact that Shaw had a vulnerable body just like ours, and that this fact may have affected Shaw's decisions about what not to say and how not to say it.

The Playwright and The Police: Sexuality and Self-Suppression in *Widower's Houses*

Shaw positioned himself, at the beginning of the Ibsen revolution, as an anti-idealist. But Shaw's use of the terms 'idealism' and 'realism' in *The Quintessence of Ibsenism* is extremely misleading. The idealism that *Quintessence* attacks – the idealism Shaw believed Ibsen was smashing – was not romantic idealism, but its dessicated Victorian remnant. *Quintessence*, which began as part of a lecture series on 'Socialism in Contemporary Literature', opens by naming Shelley as a model for all visionary 'pioneers' who would lead 'the march to the plains of heaven' (Shaw, *Quintessence*, 1). 'The [Victorian] idealists did not call Shelley a cynic', Shaw notes; 'they called him a fiend' until they persuaded themselves that 'his ideals must be identical with those of Tennyson and Longfellow' (ibid., 28). The fact that 'idealism' is used to describe what Shaw sees as two entirely antithetical aesthetics creates a semantic trap that

Shaw recognises but can't escape. In the end, he invites confusion by redefining romantic idealism as realism. Believing, like Yeats, in the superiority of the ideal over the actual, Shaw insists that Shelley's visions were more 'real' than the Victorian illusions they shattered. 'If the term "realism" is objected to on account of some of its modern associations', he finally says, 'I can only recommend you, if you must associate it with something . . . to associate it, not with Zola and Maupassant, but with Plato' (ibid., 29). Any claim Shaw ever made about his relationship to idealism or realism has to be understood in the context of his identification of Shelley as a realist.

Quintessence is one of several early texts in which Shaw endorsed Shelley's synthesis of social and sexual radicalism. In 1892, the centenary of Shelley's birth, Shaw responded to the depoliticisation of his hero with 'Shaming the Devil about Shelley', in which he claimed Shelley as 'a radical of the most extreme type', insisting that if he were alive Shelley would be a 'Land nationaliser' and would be 'advocating Social-Democracy with a view to its development into the most democratic form of Communism practically attainable' (Shaw, 'Shaming', 118). 'Shaming' emphasises the revolutionary importance of Shelley's rejection of family structures and normative sexuality. Shaw argues that Shelley attacked the family as a 'doomed institution' (ibid., 119) shoring up an oppressive patriarchy:

> [Shelley] would not draw any distinction between the privilege of the king or priest and that of the father . . . His determination to impress on us that our fathers should be no more and no less to us than other men, is evident in every allusion of his to the subject, from the school curse to *The Cenci* . . . (Ibid.)

Shaw grasps the social importance of Shelley's attack on the family: the father's ability to dictate to his children is an image of the 'king or priest's' authority, and to challenge one is to undermine the other.

Shaw's own interpretation of revolutionary *eros*, however, expresses an ambivalence about queer socialism which I will suggest was linked to a sense of shame about his own masculinity which was exacerbated by his confrontation with state power. Shaw collaborated with Carpenter and knew other queer men, including Samuel Butler, whose work Shaw admired (Peters, *Bernard Shaw*, 191–2). The circles in which he and Yeats moved in London included many queer women.[5] As a journalist, Shaw was peripherally involved in the breaking of the Cleveland Street scandal of 1889, when a raid on a gay club exposed a number of aristocratic clients (Shaw, *Collected Letters*, 230). Shaw took a stand against the criminalisation of homosexuality in a letter submitted to *Truth*, in which he displayed his awareness of London's homosexual subculture and mocked other journalists for pretending that they had 'never heard of such things' (ibid., 231). It is an open secret, Shaw states, that homosexuality is 'constantly carried on by a small minority of people' (ibid., 23) of both genders.

Shaw's letter articulates Wilde's connection between individualism and sexual liberty: 'I appeal now to the champions of individual rights . . . to join me in a protest against a law by which two adult men can be sentenced to twenty years penal servitude for a private act, freely consented to and desired by both' (ibid., 231). He points out that homosexuality has been singled out from a range of anti-reproductive sexualities, noting 'all the practices, from the subterfuge of Onan [masturbation] to the peculiar continence of the Oneida Creek [celibacy], which might be persecuted as "abominations" with as much reason as the *poses plastiques* of Cleveland St.' (ibid., 232). At the same time, Shaw calls homosexuality 'abnormal', 'nasty' and 'unnatural' (ibid., 230–1), and refers to the Cleveland Street patrons as 'debauchées' (ibid., 232). Taking a stand, but protecting himself by disavowing and condemning homosexuality, Shaw is already struggling with the tension between his sense of justice and his need for safety. Ultimately, Shaw faced no consequences, as no newspaper would publish the letter.

That tension is buried at the heart of Shaw's first produced play, *Widowers' Houses*, in which he attempts to replicate Shelley's fusion of sexual and social. However, the radical *eros* of *Widowers' Houses* is so heavily encrypted, and so firmly fixed within a normalising frame, that without recourse to the archive it is illegible as either erotic or radical. The play is ostensibly an attack on slum landlordism in London. But Shaw protects himself by articulating its overt critique of systemic capitalism, which constituted a shocking innovation for London's theatregoers, within a plot which renders capitalism entirely unassailable. Similarly, Shaw's characterisation of Blanche Sartorius, the romantic heroine of *Widowers' Houses*, incorporates a potentially quite provocative representation of homoerotic desire which is all but buried under layers of self-protection.

Widower's Houses began as a Wagnerian dream in the mind of Shaw's friend and sparring partner, the Scottish drama critic William Archer. Its hero is Harry Trench, a young doctor in love with Blanche Sartorius, whose father is a wealthy slum landlord. Archer sketched out a prose scenario for a conventionally idealistic romance which ended with the hero 'throwing the tainted treasure of his father-in-law, metaphorically speaking, into the Rhine' (Archer quoted in Shaw, Preface to *Widowers' Houses*, 667). Shaw transformed Archer's scenario into realism using Ibsen's model: a development which would have been the resolution of well-made play (here, the hero's renunciation of dirty money) leads instead to a discussion scene which interrogates the characters' foundational beliefs. In Act III, Trench, having learned that his own income derives from a mortgage on Sartorius's slum properties, is forced to accept Sartorius's money and the marriage that comes with it.

Between Shaw's draft of the first two acts and his conception of the third – in which Trench accepts Sartorius's insistence that 'a better state of affairs' is impossible and agrees to join his corrupt development scheme – falls the shadow of Bloody Sunday. Shaw, having worked up dialogue for the scenario Archer had given him, wrote to Archer on 4 October 1887 to ask for more material: 'I think the story would bear four acts, but I have no idea how it is to proceed' (Shaw, *Collected Letters*, 176). Archer was not forthcoming. A few weeks later, Shaw found another source of inspiration on the way to Trafalgar Square. In a letter to William Morris, Shaw presents his account of Bloody Sunday in engagingly self-deprecating terms:

> The women were much in the way. The police charged us the moment they saw Mrs. Taylor. But you should have seen that high hearted host run. Running hardly expresses our collective action. We *skedaddled* [original emphasis], and never drew breath until we were safe on Hamsptead Heath or thereabouts. Tarleton found me paralysed with terror and brought me on to the Square, the police kindly letting me through in consideration of my genteel appearance. On the whole, I think it was the most abjectly disgraceful defeat ever suffered by a band of heroes outnumbering their foes a thousand to one. (Ibid., 177)

Shaw generously expands his self-indictment to include his fellow protestors, ironically naming their disordered retreat a 'collective action'. R. Cunninghame Graham, who was assaulted and arrested by police, later dubbed Shaw 'the first man to run away from Trafalgar Square on Bloody Sunday' (quoted in Peters, *Bernard Shaw*, 94), an epithet Peters claims he cheerfully accepted (ibid.). But Shaw's account acknowledges another, apparently more frightening, response: becoming 'paralysed with terror'.

I want to emphasise, before we go on, that Shaw is describing an involuntary physical response to an unprecedented threat. The actions taken by the police on Bloody Sunday were expressly intended to produce terror. To expect unarmed and unprotected human beings to be unafraid in a situation like the one the police created in and around Trafalgar Square that day is to deny the realities of embodiment – vulnerability, pain, fear, death – and cling instead to an imaginary construction of masculinity as heroically resistant and stoically indifferent to even the most brutal repression. That this heroism is occasionally manifested under such conditions should not seduce us into believing that it is the norm, or that it should be.

My point is not that Shaw *should* have been ashamed of his performance on Bloody Sunday, but that this letter clearly indicates that he *was*. Specifically, Shaw is disappointed with himself and his 'band of heroes' for failing to live up to his ideal of masculinity. Only a month earlier, Shaw was berating working-class men for failing to do the same: 'It is not our business to flatter [working men], but to point out that they are a disunited, faithless, servile crew who have only to unite, keep faith, and renounce all servility to make themselves men and citizens' (Shaw, *Collected Letters*, 176). Though he imparts his personal pungency to it, this exhortation to renounce 'servility' for manhood is a tactic deployed by liberation movements everywhere. Because strength, power and autonomy are core components of hegemonic masculinity, rebellion can be justified (for men) as the natural expression of an essential need for self-assertion against an oppressive power that seeks to emasculate or feminise them.[6] What is striking about Shaw's tough-love posture in this fragment of a letter is a total lack of acknowledgement of the damage inflicted by the oppressive structures that produce compliance. Shaw presents 'servility' as a choice which can be 'renounced', and economic oppression as the result, rather than the cause, of a broken working-class masculinity which could be repaired through a simple act of will. It is up to the 'proles' to 'make themselves men', after which the revolution should be simple enough to achieve.

Bloody Sunday appears to have changed Shaw's thinking on this point. On the evidence of his letter to Morris, Shaw's shame about his own incapacitation was amplified by his awareness that some of the women he marched with responded more confrontationally. Shaw's fellow-Fabian Annie Besant reached Trafalgar Square and presented herself to the police to be arrested; their mutual friend Eleanor Marx threw herself into the mêlée and 'shouted [her]self hoarse calling on the men to stand and show fight' (Peters, *Bernard Shaw*, 94). Shaw credits the socialist, suffragist and Ladies' Land Leaguer Helen Taylor with provoking the police charge, invoking her ironically as he shares his new-found wisdom about the pitfalls of provocation.[7] He no longer sees the point of publishing 'revolutionary' articles which will put their writers 'in gaol without doing any good' (Shaw, *Collected Letters*, 177):

> I object to a defiant policy altogether at present. If we persist in it, we shall be eaten bit by bit like an artichoke. They will provoke; we will defy; they will punish. I do not see the wisdom of that until we are at least strong enough to resist twenty policemen with the help of Heaven and Mrs. Taylor. (Ibid.)

We see here an explicit articulation of the relationship between Shaw's fear of state punishment and his embrace of gradualism. We also see resentment of the women whose militancy got 'in the way' of his own safety and self-regard, and a sudden distaste for masculine posturing: 'If Stead had not forced us to march on the Square a week too soon by his "Not one Sunday must be allowed to pass" nonsense, we should have been there now' (ibid., 178). He now disdains simple-minded appeals to a heroism which Bloody Sunday has exposed as a lie: 'It all comes from people trying to live down to fiction instead of up to facts' (ibid.).

Widowers' Houses lives up to the facts by representing defiance as misguided and futile. Trench's high-minded attempt to renounce Sartorius's tainted money is easily nullified by Sartorius's greater intelligence, stronger grasp of the facts and superior rhetorical skill. Once Sartorius demonstrates that Trench's own 'independent' income actually derives from Sartorius's own slum properties, and that by extension there is no such thing as 'clean' money, Trench accepts that he is 'powerless to alter the state of society' (Shaw, *Plays Unpleasant*, 72). Blanche's capricious refusal of the chastened Trench appears to offer him, at least, an escape from the Sartorius family. But in Act III, Lickcheese offers to let Sartorius in on a corrupt development scheme for which he will need Trench's help. Sartorius threatens to cut off Trench's income, then reopens the marriage question as a way of taking the sting out of the blackmail (ibid., 91–2). After reconciling with Blanche, Trench informs Sartorius of their engagement not by protesting his love or his happiness, but by agreeing to join the scheme: 'I'll stand in, compensation or no compensation' (ibid., 96).

Trench and Blanche's courtship is thus not so much a romance as a forced march through a well-made plot designed to produce the marriage that signifies Trench's permanent integration into Sartorius's empire. The 'well-made play' that dominated 'legitimate' drama in London during the late nineteenth century was imported from France. The pleasure of a 'well-made play' derived from the finesse with which the required elements were executed (Cardwell, 'The Well-Made Play', 878). Critics placed a high value on the ingenuity by which the individual scenes were linked in a clear and coherent causal chain (ibid., 879). The ideal *dénouement* was both astonishing and inevitable; the audience should 'not be able to put them together before the right moment', but should 'quickly recognise the logic of the situation once it is presented' (ibid., 881). 'Well-made' plots gave spectators the same pleasure anyone gets from observing the operation of a beautifully designed – or, to use the term Shaw sniffs at in his 1893 preface to *Widowers' Houses*, 'constructed' – machine.

In an 1896 letter, Shaw defined being a socialist playwright as 'mak[ing] people thoroughly uncomfortable whilst entertaining them artistically' (Shaw, *Collected Letters*, 632). Shaw's stroke of genius was to realise that the well-made plot could still produce pleasure even if he fed it 'uncomfortable' ideological content. It's precisely the artificiality of the 'well-made' plot – in which nothing is extraneous or irrelevant, and every mystery yields to explanation – that makes it compelling. In the well-made world, unlike the actual world, action is never without meaning.

Formally, then, *Widowers' Houses* owes more to its predecessors than Shaw's preface admits. What *is* novel is the way the play uses the romance plot to reveal private ownership of land as the basis for the 'logic of the situation' that compels the *dénouement* (Grene, *Bernard Shaw*, 160). But the play's construction confirms Sartorius's insistence that there is no escape from that logic; capitalism becomes a machine as elegant and inexorable as the plot. By forcing Trench into a relationship with Sartorius, the romance plot makes complicity a fact of life. While Shaw's writing *around* the play focuses on improving housing conditions, the play itself dramatises the futility of reform. In *Widowers' Houses*, neither Blue Books nor reforming politicians have any salutary effect; even government ownership merely creates opportunities for development schemes which enrich the capitalists, displace the poor, and chain Trench to a woman whose volatility counterbalances her charms.

Widowers' Houses does not reject the commercial formula, then, so much as re-engineer it, transforming a machine for the stimulation of pleasurable sensations into a trap for liberals. To read *Widowers' Houses* as a critique of capitalism, rather than a critique of the deluded fatuity of (Victorian) idealists like Trench, we have to see it as an attempt to infuriate spectators into clawing their way out of the trap. We must read the inescapability of the play's conclusion as a call for an alternative to capitalism – for the imagination of a socialist society in which the immutable economic laws that Sartorius wields like bludgeons would cease to function. Nobody inside the play ever articulates such an alternative. It is left to the spectator to imagine another world in which a better ending might be possible.

As part of this trap, Blanche's function is conventional; she represents capitalism as simultaneously irresistible and repellent. The only revolutionary thing about Blanche's character is her physicality. One of the original production's memorable moments was a sensational scene in which Blanche vents her frustration by grabbing her parlourmaid Annie by the throat and shaking her (Figure 1). The cast found this incident 'grotesque' and asked Shaw to eliminate it (Johnson, *Florence Farr*, 54). Shaw refused, though he did revise the scene for the play's republication in *Plays Unpleasant*. Nicholas Grene has described this scene as 'an almost open suggestion of sado-sexuality' (*Bernard Shaw*, 17), and the archive provides some confirmation.

In a 1926 essay, Shaw claimed that the parlourmaid scene was based on a real-life incident. Walking home one night through Wigmore Street, Shaw says, he saw two women engaged in a heated argument:

> The dominant one of the pair was in a black rage: the other was feebly trying to quiet her. The strained strong voice and the whimpering remonstrant one went on for some time. Then came the explosion. The angry one fell on the other, buffeting her, tearing at her hair, grasping at her neck. The victim, evidently used to it, cowered against the railings, covering herself as best she could, and imploring and remonstrating in a carefully subdued tone, dreading a police rescue more than the other's violence. Presently the two came on their way, the lioness silent, and the

Figure 1 Artist's sketches of Florence Farr in *Widowers' Houses*. Reproduced with permission from Josephine Johnson's *Florence Farr: Bernard Shaw's New Woman* (Gerards Cross: Colin Smythe, 1975).

lamb reproachful and rather emboldened by her sense of injury. (Shaw, 'How William Archer Impressed Bernard Shaw', 26)

Shaw's relation of this scene focuses the violence on the victim's hair and neck, both signifiers of her feminine vulnerability. His assumption that the victim is 'used to it' implies a relationship with her attacker, as does the fact that the 'lamb' leaves the scene with the 'lioness'. The fear of 'police rescue' that Shaw attributes to the victim suggests that she expects to be terrorised by the police rather than protected by them. Violence is *the* quintessentially male prerogative. In this context, at a time when masculinisation was considered indistinguishable from homosexuality in women, her violence marks the 'dominant one' as queer.

As this essay was written more than two decades after the fact, it is impossible to know whether any of this really happened. But whether it's *vero* or *ben trovato*, this anecdote re-presents the militancy demonstrated by Helen Taylor, Annie Besant, Eleanor Marx and other women at Trafalgar Square as a decontextualised fantasy in which a woman's violence has no clear explanation and no purpose other than, perhaps, to give pleasure to herself, to her masochistic partner, and/or to Shaw the voyeur. This fantasy segues into a slightly more family-friendly anecdote about the sexual assertiveness of New Women:

> I had about this time a friendship with a young independent professional woman ... As she was clever, goodnatured, and very goodloooking, all her men friends fell in love with her. This had occurred so often that she had lost all patience with the hesitating preliminaries of her less practiced adorers. Accordingly, when they clearly longed to kiss her, and she did not dislike them sufficiently to make their gratification too great a strain on her excessive goodnature, she would seize the stammering suitor firmly by the wrists, bring him into her arms by a smart pull, and saying, 'Let's get it over', allow the startled gentleman to have his kiss ... (Ibid., 27)

Blanche, he says, 'developed from my obliging but impatient friend in the first act to the fury of Wigmore Street in the second' (ibid.). What Shaw sees when he looks back at Blanche's journey from her management of the stammering Trench's proposal in Act I to her strangling Annie in Act II is a progression from the aspect of the New Woman's sexuality most attractive to straight men – an 'obliging' willingness to gratify their desires – to its most threatening aspect, the predatory lesbian desire represented by the masculinised 'fury'.

The 'friend' Shaw describes here is most likely Florence Farr, for whom Shaw created Blanche. Like Yeats, Shaw fell in love with Farr while she was rehearsing the role of Amaryllis in Todhunter's neoclassical verse play *A Sicilian Idyll*, which he produced at Bedford Park's private theatre in 1890. *A Sicilian Idyll* was part of Todhunter's attempt to establish a foothold for poetic drama in London's theatrical revolution. As an expression of Todhunter's infatuation with Farr, and as the origin of Yeats and Shaw's attraction to her, *A Sicilian Idyll* strongly suggests that Yeats, Todhunter and Shaw fell for Farr partly *because* they identified her as queer. They did not, of course, see her as exclusively lesbian – she had one failed marriage behind her, and for years she was romantically involved with Shaw – but *A Sicilian Idyll* suggests that Farr's bisexuality was, for them, one of her charms.

A Sicilian Idyll is loosely based on the *Idylls* of Theocritus, a Classical Greek poet known for his pastoral love lyrics. The work of John Addington Symons and Edward Carpenter established Greece as an origin point for male homosexuality; the word 'lesbian' derives from the Greek island of Lesbos, the ancient home of the poet Sappho, who was known for her passionate love lyrics to other women. In this neoclassical setting, the fact that Amaryllis is introduced as a man-hating virgin who is grieving the end of a passionate attachment to a younger woman who is just beginning to take an interest in men is enough to establish her as Sapphic. Amaryllis's description of her relationship to Thestylis passes quickly from kinship metaphors ('Hast thou not been the sister of my choice/ Dearer than one born of my father's blood?') to explicitly marital ones: 'Have we not vowed/ Our souls in maiden wedlock to each other/ And railed at love, the enemy of our vows!' (Todhunter, *Sicilian Idyll*, 13). Amaryllis grieves over Thestyllis's declaration that she is no longer an 'enemy' of heterosexual love as if it were an irrevocable loss, mourning the 'music' that she and Thestyllis once made together: 'O, what a secret glee/ Made vivid every sense when I could think/ My thoughts would soon wed thine!' (ibid., 14).

For those unwilling to infer a physical analogue for this thought-wedding, the staging offered some hints. A photograph of this scene shows Farr and Lily Linfield (Thestylis) seated together, Linfield parallel to the camera and Farr facing it (Figure 2). Farr, with one hand resting on Linfield's knee, gazes solemnly at Linfield; Linfield, her free hand resting on her own breast, turns her head towards the camera, lowering her eyes. Farr's unreturned gaze signifies unrequited longing, just as Linfield's averted eyes and passive posture suggest reluctance and guilt. No wonder, then, that Daphnis, the young swain who loves Amaryllis, is dying of despair. But none of this discourages Alcander, the man destined to claim Amaryllis for heterosexuality. He is attracted to her, not in spite of her preference for women, but *because* of it: 'A most unnatural maid, she hates all men,/ Therefore I love her! Nature, moulding her/ Disdained her common patterns; therefore I love her' (ibid., 22). For him, Amaryllis's Sapphism only makes her a more enticing target for masculine conquest; the greater the struggle, the greater the glory.

Shaw's restaging of his Wigmore Street encounter in the parlourmaid scene incorporates both the shaming memory of the furies of Trafalgar Square and the radical *eros* of his queer leading lady into his critique of private landownership. In this he emulates Shelley – but tentatively, obscurely and ineffectively. As the well-made plot insists on a heterosexual romance, Blanche's queer 'fury' can only appear as a momentary aberration. By making the 'lamb' Blanche's servant, Shaw encourages the casual spectator to misread the scene as the typically abusive behaviour of a callous and spoiled ownership class. This invocation of the New Woman's transgressive sexuality can only accentuate the unpleasantness of the system that has captured Trench, not help him escape or subvert it.

Widowers' Houses, then, checks both socialism and queer sexuality with a strongly repressive frame. The plot gives heterosexuality and capitalism absolute monopolies which Shaw knew neither had; compulsory heterosexuality was clearly being challenged in London, and capitalist progress was just as obviously being thwarted in Ireland by land agitation. The play's dramatic universe, however, excludes the possibility of revolution from below; *Widowers' Houses* critiques Sartorius's exploitation of his tenants but never questions his *ability* to exploit them. It deplores the landlord's ruthlessness while confirming his power and authority. *Widowers' Houses* is, in that sense, idealist – but it idealises capitalism, not the revolution or the revolutionary. The fact that

Figure 2 Thestylis (Lily Linfield), left, with Amaryllis (Florence Farr), right, in John Todhunter's *A Sicilian Idyll*.
Reproduced with permission from Josephine Johnson's *Florence Farr: Bernard Shaw's New Woman* (Gerards Cross: Colin Smythe, 1975).

Widowers' Houses established such a strong model for socially committed drama in England multiplies and extends the consequences of Shaw's act of self-suppression.

Farr's Avenue Theatre experiment brought Shaw into collaboration with two other Irish playwrights willing to embrace the more disruptive possibilities of radical *eros*. Participating in this venture, and witnessing the opening night catastrophe, resolved – for about a decade – the ambivalence about queer socialism that we can read in *Widowers' Houses*. The public response to Yeats and Todhunter's representations of desire between women demonstrated that coding was no longer sufficient protection against public outrage, and suggested to Shaw that even covert representations of queer femininity might expose him to punishment.

A Haunted Doll's House: Inside and Out in *Land of Heart's Desire*

Yeats was at least as fascinated by Farr as Shaw was, and she influenced *Land of Heart's Desire* just as she influenced *A Sicilian Idyll* and *Widowers' Houses*. This time, however, it was not in her capacity as muse, but in her capacity as producer. Farr asked Yeats to write something with a part that could be played by her eleven-year-old niece, Dorothy Paget (Johnson, *Florence Farr*, 60). Yeats complied by creating the 'fairy child' who tempts Maire into leaving her home in *Land of Heart's Desire*. Yeats would later confess himself 'uneasy' about this decision, and with good reason. By making the 'fairy child' the supernatural power that lures the mortal victim away from love, family, religion and the living world, Yeats was sending a girl to do what *Cathleen ni Houlihan*, *On Baile's Strand*, *At the Hawk's Well*, *The Only Jealousy of Emer* and really most of Yeats's plays suggest is a woman's job. Just as the fairy child fatally disrupts the Irish peasant cottage into which she is introduced, she disrupts the play, the performance and the opening night, making trouble everywhere she goes.

For one thing, the introduction of a fairy child into a play for grown-ups created some generic difficulties. The idea of Ireland as a place inhabited by fairies and other supernatural creatures was something that Yeats and Todhunter were assiduously cultivating. But Yeats's 'fairy plays' strove for a 'wild and mystical' ideal that was the antithesis of the crass materialism of the Victorian spectacular theatre with which London playgoers associated fairies. To rescue magic from the abjected fairyland of Victorian pantomime, Yeats excludes it from the stage space itself, internalising occult power in the bodies of the performers. The world from which the fairy child enters is evoked entirely by the people contained in the domestic interior. In *Land of Heart's Desire* as it was performed in 1894, the person who does most of that work is Maire, the 'new-married bride' who is beginning to tire of an unremarkable husband, a bossy mother-in-law, and a father-in-law who often seems to be hitting on her.[8] After using the book she's reading to let the audience know about the 'land of faery', Maire removes the props that materialise the domestic interior one by one, transferring each through the cottage door. The fact that these objects don't return with her confirms the 'reality' of the world outside the cottage without rendering it perceptible to the audience. The door that communicates between the cottage set and the offstage space serves as a visual barrier for the spectators, rescuing the land of faery from the vulgarity of visibility.

As Michael McAteer has shown, the strategy Yeats uses here – representing the 'land of heart's desire' as a real but not visible 'place' whose supernatural dimension has to be created by the performers – brings *Land of Heart's Desire* into close relationship with two important plays from the European avant-garde: Maurice Maeterlinck's symbolist drama *The Intruder* and Henrik Ibsen's realist *A Doll's House* (McAteer, *Yeats and European Drama*, 17–20). As McAteer points out, both plays are set in solidly bourgeois domestic interiors and each ends with the final exit of the young wife and mother confined in it. In *The Intruder* the mother dies just as an invisible and menacing supernatural presence enters the house; *A Doll's House* ends with Nora walking out of her home and her marriage. In spatial terms, what *Land of Heart's Desire* does is attach Maeterlinck's haunted outside to Ibsen's turbulent inside, thereby endowing the feminine discontent which was a favourite subject of Ibsenite realism with destructive occult powers. As McAteer puts it, in *Land of Heart's Desire* magic becomes the vehicle for 'the expression of Nora Helmer's revolt against bourgeois values' (ibid., 19).

By yoking together these two diametrically opposed avant-garde modes, however, *Land of Heart's Desire* creates possibilities not found in either. *A Doll's House* made the bourgeois wife the embodiment of existential discontent; the mysteries and seductions of symbolism's occult otherworld were also figured as female, in the ideal beauty of *Axel*'s Sara or Maeterlinck's Mélisande. Even the original title of *The Intruder*, *L'Intruse*, genders the sinister otherworldly power that infiltrates the house as feminine. *The Intruder*, however, never stages the encounter between the mortal woman and her occult double. *Land of Heart's Desire* puts its Nora figure into direct contact with her doppelganger, inaugurating a new version of the *Doll's House* plot in which the mortal figure who passes from the domestic interior into the wild green yonder is drawn there *by* someone who brings the otherworld and its seductions into the house.

The fact that the occult is not externalised as spectacle but internalised in the performers amplifies its erotic dimension. The most significant romantic relationships in Yeats's life were mediated by the occult, and he could never entirely separate magic from the erotic. Because Yeats is writing this play, and because the inspiration for Maire Bruin's character is Maud Gonne, the battle for Maire Bruin's soul is inevitably framed as an erotic competition. Maire's plea to be taken by the fairies emphasises the physical freedom she will enjoy in a landscape which seems to have been expressly designed for wanton abandonment: 'I would . . . run on the top of the dishevelled tide/ And dance upon the mountains like a flame' (Yeats, *Land of Heart's Desire*, 31). She longs for escape from John's attentions: 'I am right weary of . . . a kind tongue too full of drowsy love' (ibid.). When this speech rouses John to a surprisingly lyrical outburst, the prospect of more passionate love at home momentarily makes the fairy world less tempting. But the moment John is foolish enough to declare that 'there is not a power in heaven or hell or earth/ Can break the sacrament [sic] that made you mine' (ibid., 37), a voice is heard outside singing (ibid.). And then the challenger from the land of faery presents herself to both the onstage audience and the Avenue Theatre spectators as an eleven-year-old girl.

Precisely because the prospect of a child seducing an adult is so disturbing, it is very important that the audience knows that what has come to the door of this restless 'new-married bride' both is and is not a child. The fairy child claims to be older than 'the oldest thing upon the earth' (ibid., 59), but her face, voice and body are not adult. It is perhaps for that reason that Yeats risks generic pollution by giving Paget a recognisably fairy-like costume. As Clement Scott complained, the appearance of a 'pantomime fairy child' (Scott, 'The Playhouses', 412) ruined the tone Yeats was striving for – but the costume does warn the audience not to read Paget as an ordinary human child.

For the characters, however, the costume doesn't work that way. Maire is the only one who recognises the child as fairy. The others, as far as they know, react as they would to a human child – but at the same time, they also respond to the powerful attraction with which Yeats can't help investing his supernatural female figures. Paget's performance thus evokes all the ways in which people in Maire Bruin's world – and the larger culture of which this performance is a part – fail to differentiate between women and children. Ibsen's *A Doll's House* presents infantilisation as the primary expression of male erotic love. Nora has turned herself into a 'doll' because that's what Torvald wants. When she *really* needs something from Torvald, Nora promises to do exactly what Dorothy Paget was doing on stage at the Avenue Theatre: 'I'd pretend I was an elfin child and dance a moonlight dance for you' (41).

What pushes *Land of Heart's Desire* beyond the boundaries of Ibsen's critique of the bourgeois family, however, is the fairy child's effect on the Bruin family women. Bridget's first reaction to the fairy child is 'How pretty you are!' (Yeats, *Land of Heart's Desire*, 41); and, like the men, she wants to touch the fairy child, offering to 'chafe [her] poor chilled feet'. But Bridget also keeps feeding her – bread, honey and warm milk. Bridget's nurturing reveals her attraction to the child as maternal, just as Maire's gift of milk to the little queer people outside the door symbolically establishes her as their mother. At the same time, we're informed by Bridget that Maire's yearning after the fairy's land is antithetical to her real-life responsibilities as wife and mother. Father Hart's first speech assures us that motherhood domesticates women: 'Their hearts are wild/ As be the hearts of birds, till children come' (ibid., 9). Bridget and Maire's nursing of the fairies is thus put in tension with their prescribed roles as the bearers and nurturers of human children. When Dorothy Paget enters that set she is incorporated into conflicting semiotic systems. Bridget and Michael's eagerness to welcome the child suggests they read her as a harbinger of the human children that Father Hart has promised will settle Maire down; but the more Bridget mothers this child, the more danger Maire is in of being stolen from the home. Maire, who knows that this child is not a child, refuses to go near her; but the more she tries to evade the fairy's power, the more she looks like a bad mother. The play thus produces a split and conflicted maternity which is most unstable at the moment when the child announces herself as fairy. Still reading as a child, the fairy simultaneously becomes the anti-Child – an anti-reproductive force come to lure potential mothers into a timeless place where, since 'nobody gets old and crafty and wise', there is neither labour nor gestation nor development nor growth. Making a child the embodiment of the erotic power of the supernatural doesn't so much liberate Maire from maternity as render maternity itself terminally unstable. As soon as the fairy child enters that house, the 'good mother' role is no longer available. If Maire rejects the fairy child, she disavows the maternal instincts that Bridget shows in nurturing her; if Maire embraces the fairy child, she rejects any chance of becoming an actual mother.

Maire, who knows a thing or two about ambivalence, realises that the fairy child is not singular but multiple; she alone hears the echoes of other voices and steps when the fairy sings and dances (ibid., 47, 53). While Bridget, Michael and Father Hart cluster around the fairy child, Maire remains planted on the settle next to John until the fairy child comes to her. When the fairy child asks the older men if they love her, they immediately say yes; Maire, understanding how many different kinds of love might be implied in that question, demurs: 'I don't know' (ibid., 55). When the fairy child once again frames the crisis as a contest between marital love and physical passion – 'You love that great tall fellow over there/ Yet I could make you . . . [r]un on the top of the dishevelled tide' (ibid., 55–7) – Maire begs the Virgin Mary to protect her. Maire's ambivalent feelings about marriage, about heterosexual love *and* about childbearing are thus all staged simultaneously through her interaction with the fairy child. *Land of Heart's Desire* fuses its restless protagonist's rejection of the home, motherhood and the 'drowsy love' of mortal men into one unsettling image.

The Sketch printed four photographs from the production, all featuring Fraser and Paget. In the two photos of them together, the fairy child gazes at Maire while Maire avoids her eyes – a pose which evokes the image of Farr and

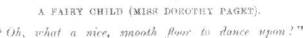

Figure 3 Maire Bruin (Winifred Fraser) and the Fairy Child (Dorothy Paget) in publicity photos for *Land of Heart's Desire* by Hills and Saunders. Published in *The Sketch* ('Some of the Folk of Land of Heart's Desire', 25 April 1894, 669). Copyright of and reproduced with the permission of *The Illustrated London News* Ltd/Mary Evans.

Linfield in *Sicilian Idyll*. In both photos the fairy child has her two hands on Maire's body. In the left photo, the fairy child's head is cocked as she studies Maire's averted face, as if assessing the effect of something she has just whispered to her, while Maire looks away (Figure 3). Because Maire is seated, their heads are on the same level, making them appear the same height. If this makes the fairy child's pose reminiscent of a lover imploring a reluctant mistress to take pity, she nevertheless also remains a child imploring her distracted mother to pay her some attention.

One of the things *Land of Heart's Desire* stages, then, is the complexity and fluidity of female desire. The maternal context the play creates for these desires, from which the fairy child's function as seducer can never be fully disentangled, renders that desire disruptive, taboo and unspeakable. The puzzled but generally not unkind reception of *Land of Heart's Desire*, however, suggests that whatever Yeats's deployment of the fairy child stirred up, the association of the 'fairy-play' with children's entertainment prevented critics from articulating any of it. A puff piece in the production's clipping file infantilises the play itself as 'pretty' and 'fanciful'.[9] Archer reads *Maire* as the fairy, 'a wild, elemental creature, tamed for a time by human love' who is 'drawn by an irresistible homesickness back to her native element' (Archer, *Theatrical 'World' of 1894*, 92). The assumption of childhood innocence protected spectators from recognising the play's adult aspects.

Unfortunately for all concerned, the most dangerous possibilities created by the fairy child's interactions with Maire were then made startlingly legible in *Comedy of Sighs*. Written in prose and set in a modern drawing room, *Comedy* takes place in a sexually charged environment defined by a much less subtextual erotic competition between a husband, wife and lover. It also includes a parallel romance involving the twenty-five-year-old wife and a teenage girl. Their flirtation is, of course, coded; but since it is coded partly through Todhunter's integration of supernatural elements into a realistic plot, *Comedy*'s representation of female desire resonates with *Land of Heart's Desire*'s in revealing ways. The fuse Yeats lit in *Land of Heart's Desire* thus detonated in *Comedy*; and though the spectators may not have remembered who struck the match, there could be no doubt about when the bomb went off.

Kiss The Good Fairy: Florence Farr's Gender Trouble

Comedy of Sighs presents itself as a realistic comedy featuring well-to-do characters engaging in witty banter while carrying on romantic intrigues. *Comedy* is set at the country estate of Sir Geoffrey Brandon, which he shares with his wife Lady Carmen Brandon and his cousin Lucy Vernon. Sir Geoffrey has invited Major and Mrs Chillingworth and the Reverend Horace Greenwell down to stay.[10] Carmen, while establishing her callous indifference to most of Sir Geoffrey's wants and needs, spends much of the play flirting with Major Chillingworth. The Reverend Greenwell is infatuated with the sweet-tempered and single Lucy. When Reverend Greenwell observes Major Chillingworth and Carmen kissing, he informs Mrs Chillingworth, who informs Sir Geoffrey. Sir Geoffrey confronts Carmen and tells her that she can either 'perform the duties of a wife decently' or they can part company. Thrilled by this assertion of masculine dominance, Carmen feels her love for Sir Geoffrey awaken, and promises to reform.[11]

Given the ubiquity of love triangles on the London stage, Carmen's nearly-platonic flirtation with a married man cannot account for the revulsion this play evidently inspired in the opening night audience. Todhunter suggested that it was provoked by Lady Carmen Brandon herself:

> The new play was received with inarticulate cries of horror by the critics ... Here was Ibsenism again – nay, worse than Ibsenism, Dodoism, Sarah-Grandism, Keynotism, rampant on the English stage! For had I not

most impudently exhibited *The Modern Woman* upon it? And although there was no tragedy this time, but beautiful reconciliation, and return to her Duty at the fall of the curtain, was she not there, the Abomination of Desolation? (Todhunter, *Comedy of* Sighs, vii–viii)

The references to 'Ibsenism', 'Keynotism' and 'Sarah-Grandism' suggest that this is just another hysterical outcry at the appearance on stage of yet another New Woman.[12] But by 1894, everyone in that theatre must have already encountered the 'Modern Woman'. Indeed, Todhunter had been lavishly praised for exhibiting one on stage only a year earlier in the Independent Theatre's production of his play *The Black Cat*. William Archer went so far as to identify *The Black Cat*'s favourable reception as evidence of a cultural shift: '[C]ritics, who would at one time have had nothing but contumely for *The Black Cat*, now treat it with courtesy, and almost with enthusiasm' (Archer, *Theatrical 'World' of 1893*, 285).[13] Farr's performance somehow provoked the first-night audience to mutiny at a time when even the most hidebound London critics were resigning themselves to the New Woman as the new normal.

Todhunter's vocabulary – 'horror', 'abomination', 'desolation' – suggests that the play evoked visceral hatred. Yeats characterises the opening night crowd as 'almost as violent as that Synge met in January 1907, and certainly more brutal, for the Abbey audience had no hatred for the players, and I think but little for Synge himself' (Yeats, *Autobiography*, 238). The comparison implies that the audience was attacking Farr and Todhunter personally. Shaw certainly seemed to have identified Farr as the lightning rod. With the opening night catastrophe fresh in his mind, Shaw denounced Farr's Carmen in a letter to the actress Elizabeth Robins: 'Oh my Saint Elizabeth, holy and consoling, have you ever seen so horrible a portent on the stage as this transformation of an amiable, clever sort of woman into a nightmare, a Medusa, a cold, loathly, terrifying, gray, callous, sexless devil?' (Shaw quoted in Johnson, *Florence Farr*, 61). Shaw was given to hyperbole when haranguing actresses; but even by his standards this is a striking concatenation of epithets. Though Archer's description of Farr as 'panic-stricken' (Archer, *Theatrical 'World' of 1894*, 93) suggests that she might simply have been unprepared, Shaw seems to have thought it lucky for all concerned that this 'panic' mitigated the incendiary power of Farr's performance. 'Had she been able to give full effect to herself', he told Robins, 'the audience would have torn her to pieces' (Shaw quoted in Johnson, *Florence Farr*, 61). Shaw's first reaction was to push Farr out of the limelight. Instead of allowing Farr to replace *Comedy* with *Widowers' Houses* – in which she would have played the parlourmaid-throttling Blanche – he talked her into waiting for him to finish *Arms and the Man* (Shaw, *Bernard Shaw: The Diaries*, vol. 1, 1023). He then fired off a letter to Alma Murray asking her to play the heroine and bluntly stating, 'I want Miss Farr to play, *not* the heroine, but the servant' (Shaw, *Collected Letters*, 422).

What exactly *was* it that Farr summoned up on the stage of the Avenue Theatre? Todhunter may be right when he identifies his 'exhibition' of the 'modern woman' as the problem; but it might have been less of a problem if his play hadn't been following Yeats's. Like *Land of Heart's Desire*, *Comedy of Sighs* fuses two fundamental anxieties evoked by the New Woman: the fear that she would reject motherhood, and the fear that she would reject heterosexuality. Todhunter had touched on both topics in *The Black Cat*; but *A Comedy of Sighs* was the first time Todhunter had to follow a curtain-raiser in which the New Woman's rejection of motherhood and men was dramatised through her interactions with a magical feminine figure presented as both a child *and* a lover. *Comedy of Sighs* also evokes *A Sicilian Idyll* by casting Florence Farr in the lead and pairing her with a much younger actress (Farr's character was twenty-five, but she herself would have been thirty-four) whose character executes the kind of 'Greek dance' that earned *A Sicilian Idyll* a lot of positive attention. In so doing, Todhunter echoed the fairy child's seduction of Maire, foregrounding the exchange of erotic desire between an experienced New Woman and an ingénue who finds her fascinating – and all in the context of a plot that staged the New Woman's repudiation of maternity.

Since *Comedy* is a realistic play with a contemporary setting, Greece functions as a *signifier* of same-sex love but not as a screen for it. Carmen is only too modern; and it is therefore much harder to conceal the fact that while seducing the married Major Chillingworth, she is also flirting with Lucy Vernon. Both flirtations begin during Carmen's first appearance, which establishes her as both masculinised and irresistible to men. Lucy's conventional femininity – she makes her first entrance carrying a basket of fresh flowers and peaches – is contrasted with the dramatically unconventional Carmen, who makes *her* first entrance carrying a fishing rod and a basket of dead trout which she has caught on a bet, as proof that she 'can kill when other people can't'. This opposition, however, is immediately complicated after Carmen's unladylike declaration that she's 'starving':

> LUCY I've got some peaches for you, Carmen. (*Shows basket*)
> LADY B What beauties! O, you good little thing! (*Kisses LUCY savagely*) (I.5)

The adverb 'savagely' suggests the kind of erotic ferocity to which the men who fawn over Carmen respond. Major Chillingworth confirms this:

> MAJOR May we come and see you eat those peaches, Lady Brandon? I like to see a woman eating fruit. It brings out all the fine sensuality of her nature. (I.5)

In addition to offering her peaches up to be consumed by Carmen's 'sensuality', Lucy is the first to express a desire to see Carmen's 'Spanish dance':

> LUCY I wish Carmen would do her Spanish dance – it must be wonderful.
> SIR G She won't – unless *you* persuade her to be good.
> LUCY I'll try. O, here she comes! (I.4)

In *A Doll's House*, Nora's 'turn' as the Neapolitan fisher girl who dances the tarantella establishes dance as a way of making the erotic public. Carmen's name and 'Spanish' costume also evoke Bizet's opera *Carmen*. Dance in *Comedy of Sighs* is thus presented a means of arousing male sexual desire; but, as in *Land of Heart's Desire*, it is also a means by which desire circulates between women.

Carmen never performs her 'Spanish dance' on stage. Before she and Chillingworth have their love scene, however, Lucy begs her to dance, and Carmen offers her a deal:

> LADY B I'll tell you what I'll do: if *you*'ll dance for *me*, now and here, *I'll* dance for *you* afterwards in my own room. Is it a bargain? (II.5)

Lucy agrees. Carmen, meanwhile, allows the Major the pleasure of being titillated by her Spanish costume – 'Merely to see you in that dress is a revelation of splendid possibilities!' (II.9) – but reserves the dance itself for Lucy's private delectation.

Lucy's Greek dance pushes the Sapphic subtext close enough to the surface to make it legible. It also entangles Carmen's attraction to Lucy with her fear and loathing of motherhood. Earlier in the play, Carmen looks into a 'magic crystal' and is horrified by what she sees. When Chillingworth asks if it's 'something terrible', she says, 'Not to another woman, perhaps, but to me' (I.21). Later, Carmen gets Lucy to look into the crystal: 'I wonder if I could make you see what I saw' (II.3). What happens next is worth quoting in full:

> LUCY Oh, I begin to see something now – like a milky cloud! Now it opens, and a little naked child comes out, holding jewels – rubies, in its two hands. Was that what you saw?
> LADY B Not exactly – it means the same thing.
> LUCY But a little child's not horrid?
> LADY B It is, when it's not wanted.
> LUCY Oh?
> LADY B (*Going to the window*) Let's kill flies!
> LUCY But that's cruel!
> LADY B Why is it cruel? Don't you know that flies carry disgusting diseases, and fertilise us with them, as bees fertilise flowers with pollen?

I always kill flies when I'm bored. I wish they were *men* sometimes. (II.3–4)

In *Land of Heart's Desire*, the supernatural elements obscure the more troubling aspects of female desire. Todhunter uses the occult elements of *his* play to clarify them. By introducing a symbolic child for Carmen, the vision allows her to make her horror of motherhood – if you will – crystal clear, while Lucy demonstrates a psychic connection with Carmen which stands in for the physical intimacy at which this scene hints. After Carmen's declaration that any children the gods send her would be 'unwanted', her apparent non sequitur – 'Let's kill flies!' – fuses an urge towards abortion and/or infanticide with the ferocity Carmen has demonstrated towards the men who love her. 'Killing flies' becomes a metaphor in which the termination of pregnancies – the 'disgusting diseases' with which vermin 'fertilise' women – is indistinguishable from killing the men who would engender them. Carmen fuses Amaryllis's man-hatred – now more obviously the corollary of an attraction to women, who don't 'bore' her – with infanticidal rage and despair . . . right before promising to dance for Lucy in her bedroom.

This scene, then, reveals some of what Yeats encoded in *Land of Heart's Desire*. Like the fairy child, Lucy performs a dance which seduces both men and women in the onstage audience. Carmen's stage-managing, however, implicates the Avenue Theatre audience by framing Lucy's dance as a performance calculated to arouse the spectators. While waiting for Lucy to get into costume, Reverend Greenwell admits that arousal is part of the appeal of popular theatre: 'Oh, it's the poetry of motion is a skirt-dance!' (II. 9) The Avenue Theatre audience cannot, therefore, avoid acknowledging the erotic aspect of their own enjoyment of Lucy's dance.

The reconciliation that Todhunter scripts between Carmen and Sir Geoffrey does nothing to stabilise anything that Lucy's dance has disrupted. For one thing, it is preceded by a knock-down drag-out between Carmen and Sir Geoffrey in which Carmen's performance of gender is at its least normative. It's in this scene that Carmen adopts the provocatively masculine habit of swearing. Clement Scott's declaration that 'the swearing woman is a very objectionable stage novelty' and that 'the ordinary man gets a shock when swear-words come from the mouth of his idolised woman' is only to be expected (Scott, 'The Playhouses', 412). More surprising is Shaw's equally traumatised response to Farr's delivery of Carmen's mild expletives: 'Did you hear those damns and devils, meant to be pretty – did they not sound like the blasphemes of a fiend?' (Shaw quoted in Johnson, *Florence Farr*, 61). For both of these men – so far apart ideologically and aesthetically – what shocks about Farr's performance is the way it masculinises both Carmen's character *and* the actress who's refusing to make her 'pretty'.

Farr's refusal of 'prettiness' went beyond her line delivery. Baron Stepniak complained to Todhunter that although Farr's performance was excellent she 'does not make herself beautiful enough for the part and does not dress well' (Stepniak, Letter, 580). An unsigned commentary on *Comedy of Sighs* in the *Westminster Review* confirms that the 'inarticulate horror' of which Todhunter complained was inspired in part by Farr's refusal of 'beauty':

> Women of the *Dodo* type, women who are loveless . . . such women are repulsive, and they become hateful when represented, as Miss Farr did, without one atom of charm and with an absolute unconsciousness of the humour which the author had put into the character. ('The Drama', *Westminster Review*, 589)

Dodo was the central character of a sensational New Woman novel of 1894, Edward Benson's *Dodo, a Detail of the Day*. Like Todhunter's Amaryllis, Benson's Dodo identifies herself initially as an enemy of love: 'It isn't my fault I'm made like this. I want to know what love is; and I can't' (Benson, *Dodo*, 32). As both *Dodo* and the anonymous *Westminster Review* piece suggest, the 'loveless' woman is tolerated when and only when she is willing to 'charm' the men she refuses to gratify. The lack of 'humour' in Farr's performance was both a refusal to entertain her male spectators and a refusal to allow them to turn the 'loveless woman' into a joke. Even Carmen's feminising 'Spanish' costume is a signifier of lesbian desire; and by swearing in it, Farr forces the 'ordinary men' in the audience to confront her as simultaneously masculine and feminine.

Just before responding to Sir Geoffrey's ultimatum, then, Carmen's character achieves peak gender trouble; and the resolution can't undo the damage. Carmen claims that Sir Geoffrey's anger has inspired real love; but not only can she not stop acting, she can't stop talking about the fact that she's acting. She puts on the jewellery that signifies both prettiness and Sir Geoffrey's marital ownership of her because she recognises it as an important prop: '[T]hat's part of my scene' (IV.13). The reconciliation scene thus offers no guarantee that Carmen will or can engage in heterosexuality except as a performance.

Even though Carmen has agreed to marriage and to motherhood, her involvement with Lucy is not resolved. Not only does Lucy refuse the conventional resolution for the ingénue's storyline by turning down Greenwell's proposal, but she is interpolated by Carmen into the reconciliation. Insisting that Lucy should be 'in at the death' (IV.13) of the 'old Carmen', Carmen sends Lucy into the 'inner room' from which Greenwell witnessed her scene with the Major before Sir Geoffrey comes in to confront her. As soon as Lucy thinks their scene is over, she strikes up the wedding march from Mendelssohn's music for *A Midsummer Night's Dream*. Carmen, offended by this musical cliché, hales Lucy out from behind the curtain:

> LADY B I've caught the eavesdropper this time. You wretched little girl, if we *must* have music, let us have something strong and splendid! I want Beethoven, I want Wagner – something symphonic and orchestral! The last band is burst! Kiss her, Geoffrey, she is the good Fairy who has freed us from enchantment. (IV.15)

Carmen's demands for 'strong and splendid' (IV.15) romantic music may be an attempt to persuade her audience of the intensity of her new feelings. But if Todhunter's own intention was to convince an audience that had just seen *Land of Heart's Desire* that Lucy would cause no further trouble for this newly-symbolically-remarried bride . . . then he probably shouldn't have had Carmen call Lucy a fairy.

Instead of containing Carmen's transgressions, then, the reconciliation resonates more strongly than ever with *Land of Heart's Desire*'s subtext. The reaction is thus produced not just by *Comedy* itself but by the interaction between the two plays. The double bill was a large-scale demonstration of the explosive potential of the interaction between the 'ancient idealism' that Yeats and Todhunter found in Irish folklore with the modern debates about women and sexuality that were circulating in London. Though neither *Land of Heart's Desire* or *Comedy of Sighs* are unambiguously queer-positive or feminist, they do indicate that Yeats's and Todhunter's shared attitude towards this fascinatingly protean female desire separated the winner of the Avenue experiment from the losers. In sending the fairy child and everything that had come in with her back to Ireland, the Avenue Theatre spectators and critics repudiated two Irishmen who were willing to acknowledge a range of gender and sexual possibilities that ran from the queer to the merely strange.

With all this in mind, let us look back at Shaw's letter to Elizabeth Robins:

> . . . this transformation of an amiable, clever sort of woman into a nightmare, a Medusa, a cold, loathly, terrifying, gray, callous, sexless devil? What madness led Todhunter to write her a part like that? – What idiocy has led me to do virtually the same thing in the play which I have written to help her in this hellish enterprise? (Shaw quoted in Johnson, *Florence Farr*, 61)

It's unclear whether Shaw is talking about Farr's transformation or Carmen's. Whoever she is, though, she's monstrous, frigid, repulsive and unsexed. In Farr as Carmen, Shaw perceives and rejects the same masculinisation, and the same implied sexual inversion, that was such a turn-off to Scott, Stepniak and the *Westminster* reviewer. Clearly the shock of witnessing it is already leading him to reassess Farr herself as well as his decision to participate in her 'hellish enterprise'. Shaw ended his romantic relationship with Farr a few months later, in November 1894 (Shaw, *Bernard Shaw: The Diaries*, 5).

Looking at *Arms and the Man* in light of what we have learned from restoring *Comedy of Sighs* to the picture, we see a new story emerging about what it meant – both for the future of British drama and for the future of Shaw's relations with an Irish dramatic movement heavily influenced by Yeats – that *Arms and the Man* was both the sole survivor of the Avenue catastrophe and the play that launched Shaw's London career. Shaw sought to present the Bulgarian setting as arbitrary (Tchaprazov, 'The Bulgarians', 71), but the more his readers know about Eastern Europe and/or nineteenth-century Ireland, the less disposed they are to believe him. McAteer has argued that nineteenth-century Anglo-Irish writers 'recognised' a number of things about Eastern Europe's geopolitical situation that made it a convenient proxy setting for stories about Ireland ('Representations of Eastern Europe', 209–16). McAteer notes that Shaw's use of this setting diverges from LeFanu's use of it in *Carmilla* and Bram Stoker's in *Dracula* in its attitude towards the Gothic. LeFanu and Stoker discover in Eastern Europe a 'hidden world of cryptic meaning, artistic mystery, and illicit desire' (ibid., 211); by contrast, Shaw's plot stages the clearing-away of these ruins by the pragmatic Swiss hero, Bluntschli, through whom Shaw represents the urge to skedaddle as sympathetic rather than shameful. LeFanu's and Stoker's Anglo-Irish Gothic vampire tales use the supernatural, as Yeats and Todhunter used it, to smuggle in erotic possibilities that would draw more fire if they were represented in a mode as ostensibly transparent as realism. In *Carmilla*, the vampire and her victim are both beautiful adolescent girls; *Dracula*'s engagement with decadent/deviant sexualities is too rich and varied to summarise here, though one might begin by noting the ease with which Stoker's model of vampirism produces allegories of polyamory. In light of the *Comedy* crash, it is significant that one of the things Shaw accomplished by expelling the Gothic was the purging from both his proxy-Ireland and from his own oeuvre of the 'illicit desires' encoded in *Land of Heart's Desire* and displayed in *Comedy of Sighs*.

The same history suggests that we should read Raina, the character Shaw originally created for Farr, in relationship with Louka, the character in whom Shaw sought to confine the 'sexless devil' he had seen Farr become. In light of what Shaw used *Arms and the Man* to contain, we can see that the Sergius/Louka romance is more than just a send-up of the sentimental idealisation of heterosexual love. It is also a manoeuvre whereby, while apparently challenging conventional notions about class, Shaw actually draws on class ideologies to confirm both heterosexuality and masculine superiority as 'real'.

From Shaw's letter to Robins we can conclude that his change in casting was more than a demotion for incompetence. Seeing Farr as Carmen brings home to him the fact that by creating Raina with Farr in mind he has done 'virtually the same thing' that Todhunter did by creating Carmen for her. Shaw's letter shows him regretting the 'madness' that once drove him to release Blanche's fury. How much this revulsion of feeling affected the text of the play is difficult to determine. What we can see is that by replacing Farr with Alma Murray, Shaw sought to give Raina a foundation of *real* idealism which would emerge after her false idealism was stripped away. Murray played Beatrice in *The Cenci*, where Shaw had been impressed by her 'remarkable power' (*Drama Observed* I, 61). Pitching the role to Murray, Shaw presents Raina as having more in common with the Romantic heroines he admired in Shelley's work than with either Todhunter's 'modern woman' or his own. He is careful to let her know that Raina will be untainted by Blanche and Carmen's most provocatively masculinising traits:

> The lady does not swear, nor does she throttle the servant like the heroine in my other play. She has to make herself a little ridiculous (unconsciously) once or twice; but for the most part she has to be romantically beautiful or else amusing in a bearably dignified way. (Shaw, *Collected Letters*, 422)

What mattered to Shaw, then, was that Murray would endow Raina with the *real* beauty and dignity that was inseparable from the *real* idealism promoted by his hero Shelley. A few weeks into the run, when Shaw felt that Raina's 'ridiculous' side had taken over, he wrote to chastise her: 'Where's the poetry gone – the tenderness – the sincerity of the noble attitude and the thrilling voice? Where is the beauty of the dream about Sergius, the genuine heart stir and sympathy of the attempt to encourage the strange man when he breaks down?' (ibid., 435). Dukore identifies this letter as a playful 'Rainaesque' exhortation (Dukore, in *Arms and the Man*, xxiii); but Murray's response shows she took it very seriously (Shaw, *Collected Letters*, 435–6). Shaw's histrionic reaction to the loss of Raina's 'sincerity' – he ends the letter with a drawing of his heart 'stuck full of swords by your cruel hands' (ibid., 435) – testifies to its importance to him. Murray's job is to convince spectators of Raina's 'romantically beautiful' essence – an essence which has been obscured and perverted by the pseudo-idealism she has consumed, but which finds its fullest expression in her 'tenderness' and 'sympathy' towards the man whose honest admission of his own cowardice makes him worthy of the 'poetry' of her nature.

Farr, meanwhile, is given the job of rescuing Sergius from an emasculating pseudo-idealism which requires him to deny the existence of any such thing as carnal desire and forces him to sublimate it by performing deeds of physical courage on the battlefield. His flirtation with Louka compensates for the loss of the romantic ideal by reassuring the spectators of both his sexual orientation and his sexual drive. Moments after Raina exits he confesses to Louka that the 'higher love' is a 'very fatiguing thing to keep up for any length of time. One feels the need for some relief after it' (Shaw, *Plays Pleasant*, 50). A sex drive which is so 'fatiguing' to deny and which, when blocked, builds up so much pressure that it creates such a 'need' for immediate and indiscriminate 'relief' must be fairly robust; and though Sergius's internalisation of the romantic ideal has led him to dissociate from his sexuality – it becomes one of the 'half dozen Sergiuses that keep popping in and out of this handsome figure of mine' (ibid.) – Louka's primary purpose is to confirm that heterosexual desire is the bedrock of whichever Sergius is the 'real man' (ibid., 51).

Shaw seeks to confirm this by restoring the violence he witnessed in the women of Trafalgar Square and Wigmore Street to its rightful gender. Blanche's abuse of her parlourmaid is repeated in Sergius's violent response to Louka's insinuation that his love for Raina is not real: 'I know the difference between the sort of manner you and she put on for one another and the real manner' (ibid., 52). His attempt to crush this truth – he grabs Louka by the arms so hard that he leaves visible bruises – only confirms it: '[N]ow I've found out that whatever clay I'm made of, you're made of the same' (ibid., 53). Her 'recognition' of Sergius destabilises class hierarchies by establishing that there is no material difference between the flesh of a noble and the flesh of a servant.

The violence that marks Sergius as 'clay', however, also produces a material sign of his uncontainable heterosexual desires. Louka refuses to allow him to become a 'gentleman' again by apologising, and refuses to let him reassert his class superiority by offering her money. Instead, she shows him that the only way he can make her 'well' is to acknowledge the link between masculine violence and masculine sexuality by kissing the bruise. Sergius's refusal is another failed disavowal of arousal, which Louka then deliberately baits by wearing her sleeve looped up 'with a broad gilt bracelet covering the bruise' (ibid., 69). By concealing the bruise she eroticises it; the next time Sergius touches her, it's to remove the bracelet (ibid., 72). Now no longer curable, the bruise is the visible sign of an irresistible sexual urge which distinguishes Sergius's 'real' desire for Louka from his concocted 'higher love' for Raina. The bruise that affirms Sergius's essential masculinity also ensures masculine dominance; the visible proof that Sergius has already touched her, it is also a sign that she 'belong[s]' to him (ibid., 75). In his rush to affirm heterosexuality, gender difference and masculine dominance, Shaw undermines his own critique of war by making violence – sexual and martial – the sign of 'real' masculinity.

Conclusion

Both Yeats and Todhunter perceived Shaw's triumph at the opening night of *Arms and the Man* as the victory of a pugilistic masculinity which was alien to them. In Yeats's account, *Comedy* failed because Todhunter wasn't tough enough to take on the audience: '[N]othing could arouse the fighting instincts of that melancholy man' (Yeats, *Autobiography*, 239). Shaw, on the other hand, by successfully defeating a lone opening-night heckler, instantly 'became the most formidable man in modern letters' (ibid.). In his preface to *The Black Cat*, Todhunter ironically cast himself as a feminised Arnoldian Celt who went forth to battle though doomed to fall: 'The *Comedy of Sighs* was slain, waving its tiny flag in the van of a forlorn hope; and over its dead body "Arms and the Man", its machine-guns volleying pellets of satire, marched to victory' (Todhunter, *The Black Cat*, viii). Todhunter's metaphor captures the fact that one of the things at stake was the question of which of these Irish playwrights – and which of their visions of Ireland – would occupy the London stage. And, like Yeats's frustration with Todhunter's 'melancholy', Todhunter's figures of speech suggest that it was the best man who won. *Arms and the Man* succeeded because its 'anti-idealist' and anti-military mandate was significantly compromised by Shaw's determination to restore heteronormativity to his own dramatic universe.

By dividing Farr's three Irish playwrights into winners and losers, the London audiences who attended the Avenue Theatre productions ejected the hybridisation of 'ancient idealism' and modern social politics produced by Yeats in *Land of Heart's Desire* and Todhunter in *Comedy of Sighs* from legitimate drama in London. Less easily discouraged (and less brutally savaged) than Todhunter, Yeats continued to pursue that ancient idealism in Dublin. The founding of the Irish Literary Theatre in 1897 was, in part, Yeats's attempt to continue Farr's experiment in a more hospitable environment. We can now see this intention in the mission statement:

> We hope to find in Ireland an uncorrupted and imaginative audience trained to listen by its passion for oratory, and believe that our desire to bring upon the stage the deeper thoughts and emotions of Ireland will ensure for us a tolerant welcome, and that freedom to experiment which is not found in theatres of England, and without which no new movement in art or literature can succeed.

Yeats and friends are 'hoping to find' in Ireland precisely what Yeats did *not* find in London in 1894: an audience willing to 'listen' to poetic speech and eager for 'deeper thoughts and emotions' instead of superficial spectacle; a 'tolerant welcome' for 'imaginative' work; and most of all, 'freedom to experiment'. When the Irish Literary Theatre produced his *Countess Cathleen* in 1899, one of Yeats's first 'experiments' was to cast Florence Farr as the Countess's love interest, the bard Aleel. The explanation for this has always been that Yeats loved the way Farr spoke verse. But casting Farr as a man in love with a woman could also have been a deliberate, even defiant response to the audiences that had howled Lady Carmen Brandon off the stage, and a reproach to Shaw for his repudiation of a woman they had both loved. By casting Farr in a male role, Yeats once again staged a dance of desire at the edge of the otherworld, acted out by two female performers. The English dramatic revival built on Shaw's foundations might not have room for such things; but *The Countess Cathleen* sent the signal that the *Irish* dramatic revival would. The influence of Irish nationalist performers, press and audiences had its own impact on the cartography of the land of heart's desire. By the time Shaw started work on *John Bull's Other Island* in 1904, a stable horizon of expectations was beginning to form around the Ireland that can be seen emerging in *Land of Heart's Desire*.

Because it derived in part from Shelley, Shaw could never fully relinquish queer socialism; but because its adherents were vulnerable to the kind of homophobic punishment dealt out at the Avenue Theatre, Shaw remained unwilling to publicly embrace it. During the ten years following the Avenue Theatre experiment, Shaw would deny and disavow utopian desire, and cultivate a fear and loathing of the corporeal and the erotic which peaks, as we will see, in his 1903 play *Man and Superman*. But writing a play set in Ireland allowed Shaw to experiment again with the fluidity, ambiguity and ambivalence that had become the antithesis of the 'brilliance' Shaw was celebrated for in *Arms and the Man*. Because, by 1904, dreaming itself had become Irish, *John Bull's Other Island* also allowed Shaw to confront his own ambivalence about the kind of left theatre that he had helped establish. In the next chapter, we will see how Shaw's first Irish play stages Shaw's struggle not only with the kind of place that Ireland has become, but with dreaming itself.

Notes

1. The change from *Comedy* to *Arms* appears on the programme for 21 April. This and other programmes for the 1894 shows are preserved in the Avenue Theatre, 1894 file in the Theatre and Performance Collection of the Victoria and Albert Museum.
2. The earliest programme listing *The Man in the Street* is from 5 May.
3. On the importance of 'fellowship' in Morris, see McCarthy, *William Morris*, 547–9; on its importance to Carpenter, see Bevir, *Making of British Socialism*, 249.
4. *Homogenic Love* was later incorporated into Carpenter's *The Intermediate Sex* as 'The Homogenic Attachment'.
5. See Cullingford, *Gender and History in Yeats's Love Poetry*, 74; Jennings, *A Lesbian History of Britain*, 64–73.
6. For a discussion of this point in a nineteenth-century Irish context, see Valente's *The Myth of Manliness*.
7. Shaw identifies her only as 'Mrs. Taylor'. Molly Housego and Neil R. Storey's *The Woman's Suffrage Movement* reproduces an illustration of police seizing the flag on Bloody Sunday, identifying the woman holding it as Helen Taylor.
8. Yeats revised *Land of Heart's Desire* several times, and changed some of the characters' names. Using the manuscript materials edition of the play, I cite the text closest to what would have been actually performed at the Avenue Theatre.
9. Avenue Theatre, 1894 folder held in the Theatre and Performance Collection of the Victoria and Albert Museum. The squib is untitled and publication information has not been preserved; it is dated 29 March 1894.

10. Chillingworth's name is borrowed from Nathaniel Hawthorne's *The Scarlet Letter*. Todhunter also cast Farr in his dramatic adaptation of Hawthorne's story 'Rappacini's Daughter', *The Poison Flower*.
11. I thank the University of Reading Special Collections for their permission to cite the typescript of *Comedy of Sighs*, which is held in the Todhunter papers. Each act is a separate booklet and the page numbering is not continuous, so I will cite by booklet and page number.
12. *Keynotes* was a collection of stories published by the Irish New Woman George Egerton in 1893; Sarah Grand was a New Woman novelist and author of *The Heavenly Twins* (1894). Carmen Brandon bears a superficial resemblance to Gypsy, the protagonist of the opening story of *Keynotes*.
13. Johnson represents *The Black Cat* as a failure, but period sources indicate that it was a success. Archer and Scott see it as a promising start for a new playwright. Possibly Johnson was confused by the fact that most of Archer's review of *The Black Cat* is a mock-review in which Archer imagines all the horrible things Scott *would* have said about *The Black Cat* if it had premiered a few years earlier. Johnson cites part of this embedded mock-review on p. 60 as if it were a representation of Archer's own reaction.

2

ARRESTED DEVELOPMENT: UTOPIAN DESIRES, DESIGNS AND DEFERRALS IN *MAN AND SUPERMAN* AND *JOHN BULL'S OTHER ISLAND*

Introduction

In 1912, Shaw prepared a special edition of *John Bull's Other Island* with a new preface conclusively demonstrating the inevitability of Home Rule in Ireland. A draft preserved in the British Library shows Shaw assuring his readers that everyone in Ireland *really* wants Home Rule. When he finally acknowledges the existence of militant unionists, Shaw disables sympathy for them by conflating political orientation with sexual orientation:

> There are, I know, men and women who are political perverts by nature. The supreme misfortune of being born with one's natural instincts turned against nature by a freak of nature is a phenomenon that occurs politically as well as physiologically. There are Poles who are devoted with all their soul to Russia and the maintenance of Russian rule in Poland ... [and] Indians and Egyptians who are ready to sacrifice all they possess for England and English rule. And it is not to be denied that among these are persons of high character and remarkable ability, comparing very favorably with the dregs of the nationalist movements, which, just because they are national and normal, are made up of all sorts ... [...] Even in more personal relations, natural passion cannot pretend to inspire more intense devotion than perverted passion. But when all is said, the pervert, however magnificently he may conduct his campaign against nature,

remains abhorrent. (Shaw, 'Preface to the Home Rule Edition', ADD 50615, 21/6)

Superficially this may look like an ordinary instance of Victorian homophobia: Shaw deploys the 'perversion' trope to render militant unionism loathsome and wrong. By aligning it with heterosexuality, Shaw seeks to render Home Rule inevitable – as inevitable as what Malthus called 'passion between the sexes' and what Lee Edelman calls 'reproductive futurism'.

But this analogy also shows how strongly the rhetoric of inversion and perversion generated by the sexual revolution we examined in the previous chapter conditioned Shaw's ambivalence about Ireland's alterity. We perceive in this passage a certain shame about the way the paradox of militant unionism – a physical-force resistance movement whose members assert their loyalty to England by threatening to rebel against it, and their political autonomy by fighting *not* to be free – queers the campaign for Home Rule, which could otherwise present as 'national and normal'. And yet, we also see Shaw revelling in his status as an Irish outsider in London as he shames Ireland's unionist minority by taking pride in his own political perversity:

> I think that if I as a Home Ruler (and many less orthodox things) can live in England and hold my own in a minority which on some very sensitive points reaches the odds of about 1 to 48,000,000, an Ulster Orangeman should be able to face Home Rule without his knees knocking shamefully in the face of a contemptuous England which despises him none the less because his cowardice seems to serve its own turn. (Ibid., 21 5/6)

By presenting himself as more marginalised than these other Irish Protestants – as an Irishman and Home Ruler, but also as a champion of 'less orthodox' social politics – Shaw shows them how an embattled minority *should* conduct itself. *He* is immune to the 'cowardice' that leads militant unionists to imagine that they cannot survive Home Rule without the help of a foreign state; *he* has the fortitude to be a revolution of one. His analogy between political and sexual deviance betrays both pride and shame in his own perversity.

As I will argue, the turn to Ireland in *John Bull's Other Island* – in which Home Rule politics provide just enough 'national and normal' cover for his cautious embrace of Ireland's alterity – enabled Shaw to revisit a political orientation that he had disavowed with increasing stridency in the years following the Avenue Theatre experiment. *John Bull*'s ideological and formal confusions are in part generated by its covert return to the idealistic socialism that he had rejected over its association with 'perverted passion'. It's partly because *John Bull's Other Island* engages – obscurely, and in very conflicted ways – with the utopian dreams of queer socialism that it has been recognised as more complicated, ambiguous and inconclusive than nearly any other play in Shaw's oeuvre.[1]

As I will argue, Shaw can entertain the impossible dream of capitalism's end in *John Bull* partly because Ireland's colonial past renders its future unusually uncertain. The mere existence of that Home Rule edition of *John Bull's Other Island* is a testament to how unpredictable Ireland's future was – at least to him. Shaw's decision to produce a popular edition for the 'Home Rule year' of 1912, to declare confidently in its preface that Home Rule as a live political issue 'is to be disposed of this year' (ibid., 17/2), and to assert that the Irish can now be 'confident that their battle is won' (ibid., 18/3) show him failing to foresee the failure of the 1912 bill and the eventual pre-emption of Home Rule by the 1916 Easter Rising. But in *John Bull*, Shaw does recognise Ireland as a place where the relationship between cause and effect cannot be taken for granted, and the future does not evolve from the present so much as explode out of it. For that reason, the play's Irish setting allows him to imagine – albeit ambivalently – the kind of future that the eternal capitalist present seeks to render unthinkable.

We will begin by situating *John Bull's Other Island* in the context of Shaw's attempt to reposition himself politically and artistically in the early twentieth century.[2] After publicly repudiating his former socialist politics (and colleagues) in his 1903 *Man and Superman*, Shaw finds in Ireland in 1904 a place from which he can reclaim the utopian desires which he had rejected. *John Bull*, I argue, is not a progression from but a reaction against *Man and Superman*, and especially against *Man and Superman*'s fervent embrace of the developmental logic that undergirds evolutionary theory, reproductive sexuality and capitalist growth. Because *John Bull* challenges this developmental logic, construction – literal and literary – is one of its major problems. Yeats and Gregory had many reasons not to include *John Bull* in the Abbey's inaugural season; but the deciding factor was the play's punishing length.[3] After Yeats saw the Court Theatre production in London, he reported to Lady Greogry that it 'acts very much better than one could have forseen, but is immensely long', adding with typical Yeatsian tact that it seemed 'fundamentally ugly and shapeless' (Yeats, *Collected Letters*, 666).

I will approach these interrelated formal and ideological questions through *John Bull*'s explicit engagement with a specific manifestation of utopian socialism in England: Ebenezer Howard's Garden City scheme. Referred to briefly in Broadbent's initial conversation with the stage-Irish Tim Haffigan, the Garden City movement was sparked by Howard's 1898 book *To-Morrow: A Peaceful Path to Reform*, in which he set forth a scheme for transitioning from private to public ownership of land without uprisings or revolutions. In the published text of *John Bull's Other Island*, Broadbent's initial reference to the Garden City is never followed up, and appears to have been introduced 'rather irrelevantly' (Beevers, *Garden City Utopia*, 78) into a critique of stage-Irishness. It appears irrelevant, however, only because of cuts made during production, which eliminated much of the dialogue that developed the play's treatment of the Garden City and of socialism. When we look at the typescript sent to Yeats and Gregory for evaluation, the Garden City scheme becomes a passage into the subterranean ambiguities that undermine *John Bull*'s dialectics, warp its structure and inflate its size. The Garden City scheme was an attempt to synthesise radical utopian desire with the pragmatic gradualism that Shaw felt it was safer to advocate. Howard's text also demonstrates an ardent faith in the power of design which resonated strongly with William Morris's aesthetic socialism. For both reasons, the Garden City scheme fascinated a Shaw who was disillusioned with socialist practices and yet ambivalent about the new gospel with which he had attempted to replace them. *John Bull*'s 'shapelessness' is partly an expression of Shaw's profound ambivalence about grand designs – including, and especially, his own.

Reproductive Futurism, Queer Futurity and Victorian Utopias

Queer theory can help us understand how Shaw's ambivalence about normativity complicated his relationship to utopian desire. During the first decade of the twenty-first century, as the move towards marriage equality began to normalise same-sex partnerships, the opposition between homosexuality and normativity, which was one of queer theory's foundational premises, appeared to be dematerialising. The desire to be both inside and outside came to preoccupy queer thinkers and activists seeking to keep homosexuality strange without relegating it to the unliveable space outside society. In response to a brave new world in which 'homonormativity' (Muñoz, *Cruising Utopia*, 21) was possible, queer theory elaborated two antagonistic paradigms of futurity which – partly because of their genealogical connections to Shaw's own context – can help map the conflicts that structure Shaw's relationship to utopian desire.

For Lee Edelman, the most provocative recent proponent of an 'antirelational mode of queer theory' inaugurated by Leo Bersani (ibid., 10–11), to be queer is to be beyond the pale; anyone who enters the social or political sphere is perforce going straight. Edelman identifies 'reproductive futurism' as the force that has always-already captured the social, and will always-and-forever exclude an anti-productive queer desire powered by a Freudian death drive and inhabiting the self-annihilating present of Lacanian *jouissance*. Edelman presents the reproductive imperative as the quintessence of totalitarianism: the call to reproduce is a universal and irresistible demand with which every member of any society must in some way comply. Edelman thus parlays the inescapability of biological reproduction into a vision of the future as the enforced replication of existing norms. Sexuality may be in flux; but reproduction is as permanent as capitalism, linked to it by a shared need for growth, development and production.

Edelman's insistence on the absolute futility of activism – from Edelman's perspective, as Jack Halberstam points out, 'material political concerns' are always-already 'a part of the conjuring of futurity that his project must foreclose' (Halberstam, *Queer Art of Failure*, 107) – has, on the other hand, challenged queer theorists to articulate strategies which resist assimilation without rejecting liveability as a goal. In search of an escape from 'heteronormative maps of the present where futurity is indeed the province of normative reproduction' (Muñoz, *Cruising Utopia*, 28), José Muñoz turns to the 'German idealist philosophy' that informed Shelley's radicalism. From the premise that both the queer and the utopian are defined by the 'rejection of a here and now and an insistence on potentiality or concrete possibility for another world' (ibid., 1), Muñoz extrapolates the construct of 'queer futurity' – a future which is a necessary alternative to an inadequate present, and which can never become normative because it will never be fully realised. Conceding the 'here and now' to normativity, Muñoz orients queer desire towards an imagined 'there and then' which – because it is always *just about* to happen – cannot be captured by the reproductive imperative.

The practical utility of a future that is eternally deferred is, of course, open to question; but the concept of utopia as 'potentiality' – 'a thing that is present but not actually existing in the present tense' (ibid., 6) – is a major improvement over a concept of utopian desire that reduces it, as Matthew Yde's does, to either a 'blueprint' for totalitarian 'social engineering' or a vague and ineffective intention to '[work] toward a better world' (Yde, *Bernard Shaw and Totalitarianism*, 7). From Muñoz's point of view, the fact that the queer future does not arrive is not a bug, but a feature. Instead of being captured by 'straight time', queer futurity is perpetual alterity; it is always what *should* happen, but never what's happening now (Muñoz, *Cruising Utopia*, 22).[4] This 'potentiality' leaves footprints in the present in the shape of queer communities determined by a *potential* collectivity which, unlike the identity politics defined by existing oppressions, will allow for 'multiple forms of belonging-in-difference' (ibid., 20). Queer futurity thus merges 'desire for larger semiabstractions such as a better world and freedom' with a desire for 'better relations with the social that include better sex and more pleasure' (ibid., 30). The difference between queer futurity and reproductive futurism, in a sense, is the difference between a future too good to be true and a future too true to be good.

These two antithetical paradigms can help us distinguish between the antithetical modes of utopian futurity that dominated Victorian socialism.[5] The vital differences between a future that *must* happen and a future that *should* happen were amply illustrated for Shaw and his contemporaries by two enormously influential utopian novels: the American Edward Bellamy's 1887 *Looking Backward* and William Morris's 1890 'riposte' to it (McCarthy, *William Morris*, 584), *News from Nowhere*. Bellamy and Morris use the same conceit: a nineteenth-century narrator falls asleep and awakens in the twenty-first century, where he discovers that capitalism is dead and society's problems are solved. But Bellamy's future, in which a powerful central government has a monopoly on production, is the state-socialism yin to *News from Nowhere*'s anarchist yang. In both utopias, universal heterosexuality is taken for granted. Nevertheless, Bellamy's ideology grounds his utopia in reproductive futurism, whereas Morris's yearns towards queer futurity.

We see the contrast in the way each novel negotiates the transition from the protagonist's 'here and now' to the desired future. The preface that frames Julian West's narrative in *Looking Backward* is dated 26 December 2000. It interpellates the nineteenth-century reader as a twenty-first-century citizen for whom the dominance of socialism is 'so simple and logical that it seems but the triumph of common sense' (Bellamy, *Looking Backward*, iii). This future already *has* happened, and therefore always *had* to happen. Bellamy asserts in an afterword that *Looking Backward* is 'intended ... as a forecast, in accordance with the principles of evolution, of the next stage in the industrial and social development of humanity' (ibid., 334). The evolutionary paradigm presents *Looking Backward*'s future as an extension of Bellamy's present: 'The epoch of [capitalist] trusts had ended in The Great Trust' (ibid., 56).

Though set in the future, then, *Looking Backward* is contiguous with Bellamy's own 'here and now', and thus part of 'straight time'. Socialism supersedes capitalism as a hegemony which remains dependent on reproductive futurism. Sex matters in *Looking Backward* only in terms of reproduction. Dr Leete's claim that all marriages are 'love matches' simply means that 'the principle of sexual selection ... has unhindered operation' (ibid., 267). The identification of desire as pernicious is foundational to Bellamy's vision of a planned economy. The idea of citizens establishing a black market for the gratification of irrational consumer desires is as foreign to Dr Leete as the idea of citizens engaging in sex outside of marriage. Leete describes his society's compulsory labour system as 'a codification of the law of nature – the edict of Eden' (ibid., 116), invoking heterosexuality's origin myth to naturalise state power (ibid.). Reproduction and production are irresistible demands made by an all-powerful state whose needs always trump individual desires.

News from Nowhere, by contrast, dispenses with straight time. Morris's utopian future is generated, not by evolution, but by irrepressible desire. The England of the future emerges when a frustrated anarchist, unable to articulate his vision, cries out, 'If I could but see a day of it!' (Morris, *News from Nowhere*, 2). In place of the string of mundane incidents that naturalise Julian West's historical displacement, William Guest's portal to the future opens, like one of Coleridge's or Shelley's visions, when his perception of beauty causes his 'discontent and trouble' to fall away (ibid.). Guest's vision is offered to readers as a potentiality which might enable 'future collectivity' (Muñoz, *Cruising Utopia*, 25): '[I]f others can see it as I have seen it, then it may be called a vision rather than a dream' (Morris, *News from Nowhere*, 238).[6]

News from Nowhere identifies the conditional mode of queer futurity as appropriate for any utopia in which pleasure trumps production. Nichols suggests that Morris's treatment of human sexuality is rooted in Shelley's rejection of 'sexual tyranny' in *Queen Mab* and *Laon and Cythna* (Nichols, 'Liberationist Sexuality', 22); and through *News from Nowhere* we can see some of the queer applications of Shelley's radical *eros*. While he assumes heterosexual attraction as 'natural', Hammond is keen to impress on Guest that sex is no longer regulated: '[T]here is no unvarying conventional set of rules by which people are judged; no bed of Procrustes to stretch or cramp their minds and lives' (Morris, *News from Nowhere*, 64). The future dreamed in *News from Nowhere* is founded not on the demand for production but on the desire for pleasure; work is as voluntary, unregulated and desire-driven as sex is. Morris imagines this future as a radical break with the present; it will be achieved, not through evolution, but through violent struggle inspired by 'a longing for freedom and equality, akin if you please to the unreasonable passion of the lover' (Morris, *News from* Nowehere, 116).

We also see Muñoz's queer futurity prefigured in Edward Carpenter's contribution to the 1897 anthology *Forecasts of the Coming Century*, which collects a range of futures imagined by British socialists (including Shaw's anti-utopian essay 'Illusions of Socialism'). In 'Transitions to Freedom', Carpenter celebrates the 'potentiality' of the future he imagines:

> [I]t has to be remembered – and Bernard Shaw has consumed a great many valuable pages of this book in showing it – that there is not the smallest chance of any 'ideal', pure & simple, of society being at any time absolutely realized . . . So that while we can see plainly enough the communistic direction in which society is trending, we may both hope and fairly expect that the resulting form will . . . be broad enough and large enough to include an immense diversity of institutions and habits as well as a considerable survival of the social forms of to-day. (Carpenter, 'Transitions to Freedom', 191)

It is precisely because ideals cannot be realised that the *actual* future inspired by them will be 'large enough' for everyone who has to live in it. Queer futurity's impossibility precludes the imposition of a single ideology on an 'immense diversity'.

Shaw was, as his inclusion in Carpenter's *Forecasts of the Coming Century* indicates, attracted to *both* modes of utopian socialism: he contributed to Carpenter's utopian project, but offered a piece in which he represented himself as the one socialist in London hard-headed enough to do without the utopian 'Illusions' motivating everyone around him. Over the next several years, however, Shaw abandoned socialism altogether for a vision of the future which elevated the demand for reproduction to the status of categorical imperative.

THE MEANS OF REPRODUCTION: EVOLUTION AND STRAIGHT TIME IN *MAN AND SUPERMAN*

The influence of Nietzsche on Shaw's *Man and Superman* is well known; and it has been suggested by many before me that *Man and Superman* is an expression of Shaw's terminal frustration with the British left organisations to which he had dedicated so much time and energy. Published in 1903 but not produced until 1905, *Man and Superman* rejects the activism of his previous decade wholesale in favour of a new gospel preaching the omnipotence of the Life Force, an irresistible creative power which compels humans to reproduce.

In a 1903 letter to John Burns, Shaw acknowledged this shift from the means of production to the means of *re*production as strategic. Having concluded that Marxist theory 'doesn't interest the working man', Shaw says, he took a leaf out of Burns's book:

> I have since seen you achieve success after success by appealing to the workers' pride of citizenship and pride of manhood. Very well then: I am a teachable man; and I take my money off surplus value and put it on pride of manhood. (Shaw, *Collected Letters*, 368)

Abandoning the focus on property ownership that defined *Widowers' Houses*, *Man and Superman* stakes everything on evolution – as Shaw conceives of it.

Perhaps no figure in Anglophone literary history has embraced reproductive futurism with greater zeal than Jack Tanner, the gentleman radical who becomes the unwilling hero of *Man and Superman*'s primary romance. From Tanner's point of view, women – whose purpose is to produce offspring – are the chief agents of the Life Force on earth. Men obey the reproductive imperative only after they have been trapped by their self-appointed mates. When the terrified Jack is forced to accept marriage to Ann Whitefield – a woman viewed by Tanner as a man-eating tigress hell-bent on using mankind to fulfil her reproductive function – he insists that pleasure is the *last* thing he expects from it: 'What we have both done this afternoon [by becoming engaged] is to renounce happiness, renounce freedom, renounce tranquility, above all, renounce the romance of an unknown future, for the cares of a household and a family' (Shaw, *Man and Superman*, 174).

The Life Force, by compelling reproduction, protects Jack Tanner from *eros* and its problems. Shaw's preface explains that his 'Don Juan play', precisely because it is about sex, is *not* about desire. Shaw insists on a stark opposition between plots built on *eros* – the love/adultery/romance plots of the well-made play – and the 'modern English [play]' he is writing, 'in which the natural attraction of the sexes is made the mainspring of the action' (ibid., vii). Denominating 'sexual attraction' as a 'social substance', Shaw promises a treatment purged of the sensual as well as the sentimental: 'I do not adulterate the product with aphrodisiacs nor dilute it with romance and water' (ibid., xiv). '[T]he serious business of sex' is not the gratification of desire but the production of offspring (ibid., xvi). His Don Juan's marriage is acceptable only because Jack and Ann's attraction is above mere pleasure; to trap Jack, Ann must 'claim him by natural right for a purpose that far transcends their mortal personal purposes' (ibid., xvii).

Shaw's rejection of *eros* is so vehement, in fact, that he even denies its evolutionary function. *Man and Superman*'s reproductive ideology is grounded not on Darwin's theory of sexual selection, but on the anti-Darwinian evolutionary theory of Samuel Butler. Shaw reviewed Butler's *Luck, or Cunning as the Main Means of Organic Modification?* in 1887, and Butler is widely recognised as an influence on the doctrine of Creative Evolution that Shaw unveiled in his 1921 'pentateuch' *Back to Methuselah* (Grene, *Bernard Shaw*, 56; Yde, *Bernard Shaw and Totalitarianism*, 28). Though they are often lumped together, however, the evolutionary gospel preached by Tanner in *Man and Superman* differs substantially from the one laid out in *Back to Methuselah*, which seeks to eliminate sex entirely from human evolution. *Man and Superman* accepts the link between reproduction and evolutionary change. At the same time, *Man and Superman* also strives to incorporate Butler's idea of evolution as a process of 'design' (Butler, *Luck*, 1).

Butler, whose intention is to reconcile the process of evolution with the existence of God (ibid., 317), argues that organisms 'design themselves' (ibid., 80). Chance (luck) creates variations, but these do not confer any advantage until the organisms, over many generations, have by careful husbandry (cunning) 'accumulated' enough variations to create complex adaptations. The better a species gets at managing its 'luck,' the more likely it is to survive. Butler's theory of evolution can be construed as queer in its rejection of sexual selection. It diverges from the premises of queer socialism, however, in that it denies the power of *eros*, instead attributing progress to the quintessentially Protestant values of thrift and hard work. Shaw underlined this in a 1901 letter to H. G. Wells about *Luck, or Cunning*:

> A man who cannot see that the fundamental way for a camelopard to lengthen his neck is to want it longer, and to want it hard enough, and who explains the camelopard by a farfetched fiction of an accidentally long necked Romeo of the herd meeting an accidentally longnecked Juliet, and browsing on foliage which the other Montagues and Capulets could not reach, ought really to be locked up! (Shaw, *Collected Letters*, 246)

Shaw's satirical deployment of *Romeo and Juliet* repudiates erotic desire in favour of a productive will. The camelopard who works 'hard' at wanting a long neck will be rewarded for his industry, whereas to assume that mere *eros* might achieve anything material is tantamount to insanity.

Butler's insistence on the power of 'application, energy, effort, industry, and good sense' (Butler, *Luck*, 124) naturalises and indeed sanctifies the core values of capitalism and Protestant theology. The saved are distinguished from the damned by their superior 'thrift' (ibid., 72–3). Darwin's mistake was his failure to internalise capitalist 'common sense' – being, instead, mad enough to believe that adaptation (imagined by Butler as a 'sustained accumulation of bodily wealth') could take place 'unless sustained experience, watchfulness, and good sense preside' over evolution, as they must in the accumulation of 'wealth of any other kind' (ibid., 7–8). For Butler, 'what applies to property applies to organism also' (ibid., 127):

> The body is property carried to the bitter end ... [T]he expression 'organic wealth' is not figurative; none other is so apt and accurate [...] [T]he laws that govern the development of wealth generally are supposed to govern the particular form of health and wealth which comes most closely home to us – I mean that of our bodily implements or organs. What is the stomach but a living sack, or purse of untanned leather, wherein we keep our means of subsistence? (Ibid., 128)

Butler's idea of 'bodily form' as a vast fortune 'formed by accumulated millionths of farthings' (ibid., 316) eliminates *eros* by turning flesh into money. Among *successful* organisms, desire is always productive: the body, like property, only wants to grow, to accumulate, to yield ever greater return on investment.

Economic inequality is not the only form of oppression that Butler's paradigm naturalises. For evidence that evolution rewards merit and not blind luck, Butler turns to the newspapers for a topical example:

> [T]ake, for example, the following extract from a letter in the *Times* of the day on which I am writing (February 8, 1866): 'You may pass along a road which divides a settlement of Irish Celts from one of Germans. They all came to the country equally without money, and have had to fight their way in the forest, but the difference in their condition is very remarkable; on the German side there is comfort, thrift, peace, but on the other side the spectacle is very different.' (Ibid., 123)

The reappearance within that *Times* quotation of Butler's 'thrift' reminds us that in adopting Butler's paradigm, Shaw embraced a view of the world that roots all good things in a trait which the Irish were famous for not possessing. Shaw's gravitation towards Butler's evolutionary theory testifies to the extent to which the Protestant values that formed him survived his apostasy; but it also reveals that, for Shaw, pleasure is shameful not just because it is queer, but because – in its denial of the claims of industry and thrift – it is Irish.

Shaw's internalisation of the capitalist logic of Butler's evolutionary paradigm appears in the relationship that Shaw articulates in *Man and Superman*'s preface between Irishness and re/productivity. *Man and Superman*'s preface associates Irishness with unproductive desire, forcing it beyond the boundaries of both evolutionary success and normative heterosexuality. The London marriage market is founded on evolutionary principles: 'Money means nourishment and marriage means children; and that men should put nourishment first and women children first is . . . the law of Nature' (Shaw, *Man and Superman*, xv). Arguing that the 'prosaic man's' success in life is due to 'the simplicity with which he pursues these ends', whereas the artistic man fails by 'stray[ing] in all directions after secondary ideals', Shaw maps the prosaic/artistic binary onto the English/Irish divide: 'From the first day I set foot on this foreign soil I knew the value of the prosaic qualities of which the Irish teach the English to be ashamed as well as I knew the vanity of the poetic qualities of which Englishmen teach Irishmen to be proud' (ibid.). The English are superior in 'acquisitiveness, combativeness, and fecundity'; the Irish may nevertheless appropriate the fruits of English labour due to 'superior . . . imagination' (ibid., xvi). Even as he insists on socialism as a higher stage of development than the English have achieved (ibid.), Shaw – by defining 'fecundity', productivity, acquisitiveness, and 'vitality' as un-Irish – replicates Butler's insinuation that the Irish are too queer for evolutionary success, just as socialism is too queer for the 'prosaic' English mind.

Man and Superman's aggressive boosting of the 'fecundity' and 'vitality' that Shaw's preface denies to the Irish can thus be read as the continuing expression of the defensive panic evoked in Shaw by the work of his Irish collaborators a decade earlier. It certainly continues the rebuke of Farr that began in *Arms and the Man*. Since critiquing *Man and Superman* from a feminist perspective is like shooting fish in a barrel – it's not that entertaining, and people feel bad for the fish – I will content myself with noting that in its insistence on defining 'Woman' in terms of her reproductive function, its insistence that women are responsible for male sexual behaviour, and its terror of female sexuality, Jack Tanner's 'revolutionary' doctrine differs from the reactionary idealism of either Catholicism or Puritanism only in its rejection of the sanctity of marriage. *The Revolutionist's Handbook*, published as an appendix to the play and purportedly 'written' by Jack Tanner, shows him eager to appropriate the bodies of women for the fulfilment of his ideological vision. In a 1904 letter to Farr, Shaw enjoyed relaying the impact that *Man and Superman* had on one of his feminist fellow-Fabians, who was firmly persuaded that my views on the production of the Superman involve the forcible coercion by the State of selected women to breed with selected men ... she, being a good-looking and a clever person, very likely to be selected under such a scheme, fears the worst. (Bax, *Florence Farr*, 28)

Shaw is joking; but he is also letting Farr know that, in the world imagined by his alter ego, good-looking and clever women such as herself would not be free to choose – or reject – their own sexual partners.

Man and Superman also protects Shaw from the dangers of activism, much more effectively than *Widower's Houses* did. In *The Revolutionist's Handbook*, reproduction becomes the *sole* mechanism of change. Once man accepts that his paramount duty is to enable the Superman to be 'born of Woman by Man's intentional and well-considered contrivance', all obstacles to progress will melt away:

> Even Property and Marriage, which laugh at the laborer's petty complaint that he is defrauded of 'surplus value,' and at the domestic miseries of the slaves of the wedding ring, will themselves be laughed aside as the lightest of trifles if they cross this conception when it becomes a fully realised vital purpose of the race. (Shaw, *Man and Superman*, 185)

Tanner is not the first revolutionist to decide that it is easier to regulate women's bodies than to effect any other kind of change. But by exhorting revolutionaries to 'give up the idea that Man as he exists is capable of net progress' (ibid., 206), *The Revolutionist's Handbook* absolves Tanner's comrades of any duty to risk life or limb by opposing the state. Their job is simply to propagate a revolutionary idea – an activity which, in a liberal democracy, typically does not elicit police brutality or lead to a prison term. By throwing over 'the Socialist's dream of "the socialization of the means of production and exchange"' (ibid., 218) in favour of 'the socialization of the selective breeding of man' (ibid., 219), Tanner rescues middle-class revolutionaries everywhere from praxis and its dangers. *Contra* Frederick Douglass, power will be conceded without a struggle – or at least with only one struggle, in which the only bodies put at risk are women's.

Shocking as Tanner's rhetoric is, the effect of substituting the womb for land and property as the site and source of social progress is to re-present utopian desire as normative. This is apparent in the Act III dream scene, where the aesthetics of queer socialism are expounded by the Devil himself:

> THE DEVIL: It is true the world cannot get on without me; but it never gives me credit for that; in its heart it mistrusts and hates me. Its sympathies are all with misery, with poverty, with starvation of the body and of the heart. I call on it to sympathize with joy, with happiness, with beauty –

DON JUAN: [*nauseated*] Excuse me: I am going. You know I cannot stand this. (Ibid., 98)

The Devil's performance of queer socialism's 'sympathy with love and joy' (ibid.) never fails to evoke disgust from Tanner's über-heterosexual alter ego. The Devil's complaint that Don Juan no longer makes music elicits homosexual panic: 'You talk like a hysterical woman fawning on a fiddler' (ibid., 100). Sensual pleasure is consigned to Hell, 'the home of the unreal and the seekers after happiness', along with its Wildean prince. Don Juan escapes Hell by realising that he hates everything that once attracted him to it. His real home is heaven, where he can 'live and work instead of playing and pretending' (ibid., 104).

But *Man and Superman* also represents the limitations of a universe in which there is no longer room for queer socialism. Shaw's satirical presentation of his progressive colleagues as a band of highwaymen demonstrates how little room there is in Tanner's universe for deviance; even a token attempt to act on socialist principles puts the brigands outside the law. *Man and Superman*'s principal characters cannot even *get* outside of normativity. Anyone who tries is pulled back in by another well-made plot. Though *Man and Superman*'s Don Juan in Hell episode is, as Levitas notes, a significant break with dramatic convention (Levitas, 'These Islands' Others', 20), as theatre *Man and Superman* is less innovative than it appears. Grene notes the play's debts to stock comic characters and plots, arguing that it only 'superficially resembles' either literary modernism or avant-garde theatre (Grene, *Bernard Shaw*, 60). Even in a dream – even in Hell – the play retains its Shavian 'cohesiveness and cogency of argument' (ibid.). Shaw always expected that the Hell episode would be cut in performance, as it originally was (Yde, *Bernard Shaw and Totalitarianism*, 67); and without it *Man and Superman* is a well-made play. Motorcars notwithstanding, Tanner, like Trench, is trapped by a marriage plot whose power is now augmented by the Life Force. Tanner's frothing about how marriage will mean his annihilation is a confession of the central failure of a revolutionary gospel based on reproductive futurism: by making the Ultimate Sacrifice prescribed by his own doctrine, all the revolutionary can achieve is his own assimilation into the 'here and now'.

Other apparent challenges to the institutional power of marriage prove to be complications generated by miscommunication. In Act I, Ann's pregnant sister Violet appears to have rebelled against marriage's monopoly on sex and reproduction; but only because she has chosen to conceal her marriage to the American millionaire Hector Malone. Hector's Act IV conversation with his father raises the possibility of polyandry, but only because Malone Sr thinks that Violet is married to someone else. Once everyone knows that Hector is

Violet's husband, her behaviour is revealed to be in full compliance with her society's norms.

At the same time, the B plot offers a slim possibility of escape by suggesting that Tanner's world – the world for which Shaw's new gospel was designed – may not include Ireland. The only thing that brings socialism *nearly* into the open in *Man and Superman* is the land question. The Jewish brigand Mendoza and the Irish millionaire Malone are diasporic wanderers connected by the dream of nationalism to homelands in which they were never at home. Mendoza looks forward to the day 'when the Zionists need a leader to reassemble our race on the historic soil of Palestine' (Shaw, *Man and Superman*, 76); Malone wants not return but revenge. 'English rule drove me and mine out of Ireland', he tells Violet. 'Well, you can keep Ireland. I and my like are coming back to buy England' (ibid., 150). Malone the capitalist can make his dream a reality, whereas Mendoza's Zionist future is comically unattainable. But Malone's boast also implies limits to the power of capital by conceding that the English can in fact 'keep Ireland'. England is for sale; Ireland is not. English rule, though it starved Malone's ancestors, has accomplished one miracle: by prioritising sectarianism, bigotry and the other irrationalities that sustain colonial oppression, it made Ireland a place where the markets are not free, and capitalism is not supreme.

Paradoxical as it may seem, that was precisely the situation of late-Victorian Ireland. Irish land agitation was driven by a conception of land ownership which had no basis in British law. Barred by the penal laws from owning land, Irish farmers upheld instead a construct called 'tenant-right', according to which a tenant earned, by working his holding, some of the rights usually conferred by ownership (Warwick-Haller, *William O'Brien*, 23).[7] Sara Maurer has argued that Irish land agitation was hailed by some English observers as proof that the 'native right to property' which the encroaching state had wiped out in England remained 'perfectly preserved in the hearts of the Irish' (Maurer, *The Dispossessed State*, 7). Marxist historian Barbara Solow has shown that land agitation in Ireland was 'a struggle between two conceptions of property' – and that, thanks to 'organised tenant coercion', it was the landlords' conception that lost (Solow, 'The Irish Land Question', 77). The threat of violence that prevented landlords from raising their rents or evicting nonpaying tenants prevented Ireland from completing the 'shift from . . . pre-capitalist villages to market economies' that enables, according to Marxist theory, the 'the transition from feudalism to capitalism' (ibid., 73, 76–7). Land agitation marked Ireland as simultaneously revolutionary in its opposition to the state, and conservative in its resistance to economic 'progress'.

Man and Superman, then, gestures towards Ireland's economic alterity, offering a glimpse of Ireland as a place which might not be fully subject to the normativity that gathers up Tanner and presses him to its rigid breast. Shaw, however, is unwilling to explore that place until after the Irish Players have come twice to London to stage it. Shaw was away for the Irish Players' first visit in May 1903, but caught the return trip in 1904, which 'provided the impulse to write *John Bull*' (Levitas 'These Islands' Others', 19). The Ireland staged by the Players had been, of course, impregnated by the Yeatsian blend of magic and eroticism which Shaw had repudiated in 1894; but it was also the site of a new Irish realism which challenged the evolutionary doctrine that had swallowed up Shaw's revolutionary politics. The repertoire that the Irish Players brought to London in 1903–4 suggested that in addition to resisting the transition to capitalism, Ireland had also resisted the reproductive imperative.

Yeats's *Cathleen ni Houlihan*, featured on the 1903 tour, shows a young man rejecting marriage to a fertile woman to die for an old hag. The poet-protagonist of *The King's Threshold*, which featured on the 1904 programme, rejects acquisition and nutrition to die for things intangible. The 1904 tour also introduced London to J. M. Synge. In *In the Shadow of the Glen*, Nora's marriage to Dan produces no offspring, and the closest thing the play offers to a happy ending is Nora's rejection of the money and the home that should have nourished and protected her children. In *Riders to the Sea*, Maurya's obedience to the reproductive imperative is catastrophic; the more children she bears, the more she multiplies her own agony as her sons are fed to the insatiable sea. Ireland as Yeats and Synge were staging it in 1903–4 appears to be in the grip of a death drive strong enough to defeat anything the Life Force could throw at it. As for thrift, neither Yeats's and Gregory's *The Pot of Broth*, whose poet-protagonist swindles a stingy housewife out of a chicken, nor Padraic Colum's *Broken Soil*, whose fiddler protagonist cannot embrace a sedentary life dedicated to the accumulation of property, suggest that there is much room for it in Ireland.

Counter-Evolutions

Just after Shaw's socialist apostasy, then, the Irish Players offered him an Ireland where the ideologies he had articulated in *Man and Superman* would never wield the totalitarian power which Tanner attributes to them. At the same time, they offered Ireland as a place which might not have been entirely colonised by the 'here and now'. Though Martyn had departed the scene, the Irish Players were still driven by Yeats's and Gregory's conception of Ireland as 'the home of an ancient idealism' – a place where materialism's triumph was not assured, and where the spiritual/supernatural could coexist even with a naturalism as stark and bleak as Synge's. That this continued to define Yeats's and Gregory's project even after the demise of the Irish Literary Theatre is amply demonstrated by A. B. Walkley, the *Times* drama critic to whom Shaw addressed *Man and Superman*'s preface. In his review of the 1903 visit, Walkley pointed out that, unlike Continental naturalism, the naturalism he perceives in the Irish Players promises access to transcendent meaning: '[W]hile the French enterprise was an artistic adventure and nothing else, the Irish theatre is that and something more. It is part of a national movement, it is designed to express the spirit of the race, the "virtue" of it, in the medium of acted drama' (Walkley, 'The Drama', 146). Even when confining themselves to 'real life', as in Lady Gregory's play *Twenty-Five*, the players give the audience access to an immanent and immaterial 'spirit' or 'virtue'. The 'something more' guaranteed by the players' cultural and political mission expands Irish naturalism beyond the materialist boundaries of Zola's naturalism.

The 'something more' with which the Ireland of *John Bull's Other Island* tantalises its characters, however, is not nationalism *per se*. It is much more akin to the queer futurity imagined in Morris's *News from Nowhere*: a maddeningly intangible and incomplete vision of a world beyond the 'here and now' which is most vividly presented through the play's realisation of Ireland as a natural environment. Larry's Act I monologue prepares us for an Ireland whose beauty generates a longing for some immaterial not-yet-here: 'You've no such colors in the sky, no such lure in the distances, no such sadness in the evenings' (Shaw, *John Bull's Other Island*, 18).

Unlike Carpenter, Larry Doyle professes to see no value in a future that cannot arrive. For Larry, desire for another world can only be a source of shame. To follow the 'lure' that Ireland's environment makes visible is simply to give oneself over to 'torturing, heartscalding, never satisfying dreaming' (ibid.). The vehemence of his tirade, however, betrays the extent to which he still finds the alternative made perceptible by Ireland's peculiar 'climate' compelling. Larry accuses Ireland's 'dreamers' of becoming Impossibilists:

> At last you get that you can bear nothing real at all: youd rather starve than cook a meal; youd rather go shabby and dirty than set your mind to take care of your clothes and wash yourself; you nag and squabble at home because your wife isnt an angel, and she despises you because youre not a hero; and you hate the whole lot round you because theyre only poor slovenly useless devils like yourself. (Ibid.)

Larry's use of the second person implies that all this dreaming belongs to someone else, but also prevents Larry from fully disavowing it. Larry's description of himself as a 'slovenly useless devil' conveys his shame at belonging to the country of the unproductive, the unthrifty and the damned. His description of the laughter produced by this contempt for reality as 'fouling and staining' (ibid., 19) renders 'ancient idealism' excremental. Larry perceives dreaming as emasculation; he has been 'made a man of ... by England' because it has worked the dreams out of him. '[I]t is by living with you and working in double harness with you', he tells Broadbent, that he has learned – as Don Juan eventually does – 'to live in a real world and not in an imaginary one' (ibid., 20–1).

Act II 'apparently belies the blast of Doyle's sardonic memory' by introducing us to the play's other dreamer, the ex-priest Peter Keegan, who acts out a 'gentler and more playful' (Levitas, 'These Islands' Others', 19) expression of utopian desire. The 'whimsicality' (ibid.) of the grasshopper, however, does not disguise Keegan's confirmation that the 'something more' impregnating this Irish landscape is a constant source of 'torment' and 'punishment' for those capable of perceiving it (Shaw, *John Bull's Other Island*, 32). What makes Ireland so difficult is that the alternative to the 'here and now' is neither fully present nor fully absent. 'You can only look at Heaven from here', Keegan tells the grasshopper; 'you cant reach it' (ibid., 32).

Shaw wanted to support Keegan's perspective with a set that offered the spectators the same glimpse of 'something more' than realism. As Meisel points out, Shaw's lampooning of 'Irish romance' in *John Bull's Other Island*'s plot is at variance with his much less ironic treatment of Ireland as a setting; he may mock Broadbent for his susceptibility to Ireland's beauty, but all the same he demands that beauty from his 'scene makers' (Meisel, *Shaw and the Nineteenth-Century Theatre*, 284).[8] Ironically, Shaw's desire to idealise Ireland – to create a set that would serve, like Keegan's sunset, as a portal through which the spectators could see beyond the 'here and now' – helped keep the play out of the real Ireland. On 31 August 1904, while Yeats was still considering producing *John Bull* at the Abbey, Shaw wrote with some questions about staging:

> Is there any modern machinery in the I. L. Theatre? Is there, for instance, a hydraulic bridge? There is an extremely awkward change of scene in my second act, and again in my fourth; and I should like to know what I can depend on in the way of modern appliances, if any. It seems to me that as you will deal in fairy plays you may have indulged yourself with hydraulic bridges. (Shaw, *Collected Letters*, 452)

A hydraulic bridge is a pair of pillars housed below the stage floor and used to raise, sink or tilt sections of the playing surface. Often multiple bridges were installed under the same stage so that the whole playing area could be manipulated. Instead of merely replacing one set with another, hydraulic bridges transformed the stage itself.

Even if by some miracle Annie Horniman had been willing to subsidise an enormous and expensive piece of machinery normally found at gigantic commercial playhouses, there would have been nowhere to put it. Offstage space at the Abbey Theatre was legendarily insufficient (Cave, 'On the Siting', 96–7). Our only hint as to why Shaw would entertain the possibility that the Abbey Theatre might 'indulge' in a hydraulic bridge is in Shaw's assumption that Yeats and company 'will deal in fairy plays'. Shaw is thinking here not of Yeats's mythological drama but of the fairy extravaganza of Victorian spectacular theatre and its climactic 'transformation scene'. Conventionally, a fairy extravaganza ended with the good fairy waving a wand and transforming the onstage environment, with the help of hydraulic lifts and other invisible machinery, into 'a spectacular scene representing joy and happiness' (quoted in Davis, 'Do You Believe', 71n).

As a critic, Shaw had assisted at fairy extravaganzas, pantomimes and other spectacles; and although he deplored them, they infiltrated his consciousness. In an 1893 letter to Farr, for instance, he complains that 'you wave your arms about like a fairy in a transformation scene' (Shaw, *Collected Letters*, 12). The transformation scene is also remembered in Edward Carpenter's 'Transitions to Freedom', where it is a metaphor for the arrival of the utopian future: 'It is this general rise in well-being due to the next few years of collectivist development which will, I believe, play the part of the good fairy in the transformation-scene of modern society' (Carpenter, 'Transitions to Freedom', 189). Shaw's desire to set *John Bull* on a stage that could be transformed testifies to his desire to render Ireland's environment susceptible to radical change – a place in which the 'here and now' might reconfigure itself at any moment to reveal another world.

Despite the lack of hydraulics at either the Abbey or the Court, Shaw's set descriptions insist on transformation. Both of the 'awkward' scene changes involve the 'hillside' set described at the beginning of Act II. Getting into and out of that set might have been less 'awkward' if Shaw had not plunked an enormous boulder smack in the middle of it:

> *Roscullen. A hillside of granite rock and heather, sloping across the prospect from north to south with a huge stone on it in a naturally impossible place, a little south of half way as if it had been tossed up there by a giant. Over the brow, in the desolate valley beyond, is a round tower. A lonely white high road trending away westward past the tower loses itself at the foot of the far mountains. It is evening; and there are great breadths of silken green in the Irish sky.* (Shaw, *John Bull's Other Island*, typescript, vol. II, 5)[9]

Lauren Ramert sees in this description an opposition between the materialistic London, where life 'revolves around business and politics', and a 'a splendid Irish landscape' which 'establish[es] that Ireland is to be valued for its natural, almost supernatural, beauty' (Ramert, 'Lessons from the Land', 47). Her slippage from 'natural' to 'almost supernatural' reveals how this description links Ireland's beauty to powerful but invisible transformative forces. As evidence of these now-vanished 'giants', the boulder materialises Shaw's sense that there was 'something unreal about Ireland' (Yde, *Bernard Shaw and Totalitarianism*, 93). It situates Shaw's 'other island' in the 'impossible' borderland between actuality and fairyland, within which one cannot be entirely certain that dreams will not come true.

Shaw was, of course, aware that Ireland's landscape had been transformed by more material forces. The dark side of this landscape's malleability – its responsiveness to invisible powers, its openness to not-yet-here alternatives – is its 'vulnerability' (Saddlemyer, '*John Bull's Other Island*', 232) to foreign threats, represented in *John Bull* by Broadbent's shadowy Land Development Syndicate. But the set warns us that even that invasion narrative is not straightforward. Precisely because these scene changes are 'awkward' – in other words, they can be neither fully concealed from the audience nor seamlessly incorporated into the dramatic illusion – they present the Irish landscape to the spectators as *both* impressionable *and* intractable: you *can* change this landscape, but not without a fight.

The turn to Ireland, by sensitising Shaw to the importance of setting (Grene, *Bernard Shaw*, 69), thus enables his return to socialist concerns about land use and land ownership which were, in *Man and Superman*, overwritten by Tanner's evolutionary gospel. The play's treatment of these questions is complicated by a deeply conflicted presentation of utopian desire. The joke on Larry is meant to be that the 'prosaic' Englishman whose efficiency has 'made a man' of him becomes, when he gets to Ireland, a thousand times more romantic than the 'slovenly useless devils' who dream their lives away there. But casting Broadbent as a dreamer is more than just a reversal of stereotypical notions about national character, or a demonstration of the effect of the Irish 'climate' on even the most phlegmatic of temperaments. It is precisely because Broadbent *wasn't* raised in Ireland and therefore doesn't have Larry's baggage – because he hasn't been shamed for his Irish unthriftiness – that he is a force through which utopian desire might (for better or for worse) do some transformative work in Ireland.

The City on the Edge of Tomorrow

Tim Haffigan's performance of stage-Irishness effectively distracts both spectators and critics from the content of his Act I conversation with Broadbent. This is worth rectifying, because this conversation is about Broadbent's reasons for travelling to Ireland, and therefore ought to be foundational to the plot. Broadbent wants Haffigan as a native guide, of course, but he is recruiting him for a specific expedition. Broadbent plans to use his role as a member of the Land Development Syndicate, and the opportunity created by their foreclosure on Nick Legrange's estate, to extend into Ireland a utopian land reform scheme which has recently established a foothold in England's 'here and now': the Garden City movement catalysed by Ebenezer Howard's book *To-Morrow: A Peaceful Path to Reform*.

For years, the Garden City Association had been searching for investors among the British liberals and progressives that made up the Court's core audience. The pitch Broadbent makes to Haffigan, during which he hands him a copy of Howard's book, would have been painfully familiar to many in the audience who would have been tapped when the GCA was raising money to build the first Garden City, Letchworth, which opened in 1903. There is a slight twist at the closing, however. Broadbent winds up with the apparently rhetorical question, 'Why not start a Garden City in Ireland?' and Tim Haffigan 'defiantly' responds, 'Tell me why not' (Shaw, *John Bull's Other Island*, 9).

Answering that question requires a bit of excavation. Because the Garden City movement is well known to historians of architecture but not to literary critics, Shaw's use of it is poorly understood. Ann Saddlemyer and Matthew Yde, for instance, both identify *Major Barbara*'s Perivale St Andrews as a version of the 'Garden City concept' (Saddlemyer, '*John Bull's Other Island*', 220) introduced in *John Bull*; but neither indicates any awareness that the Garden City existed outside of Shaw's own mind. Those who *do* know about the Garden City movement are apt to read Shaw's use of it as a straightforward metaphor for British imperialism.[10] But the Garden City movement was a complex phenomenon arising from a murky ideological background. It was, in fact, the compromised, adulterated, yet still idealistic nature of the Garden City project that made it a powerful analogue for Shaw's own ambivalence about utopian desire.

Because it explicitly responds to the Irish Land Act of 1903, land reform has long been recognised as one of *John Bull*'s preoccupations (Grene, *Bernard Shaw*, 71). The play's Irish context, however, has obscured the importance of the land question in Shaw's formation as a socialist. *Widowers' Houses* emerged from an obsession with the economics of rent which may have had its roots in Shaw's stint as a rent collector in Ireland (Levitas, 'These Islands' Others', 16), but was also fuelled by his contact with a London movement seeking to end private ownership of land. Shaw was attracted to the Fabians in part because of their interest in the problem of rent (Bevir, *Making of British Socialism*, 133–45). Shaw maintained that he was 'converted' to socialism at a lecture given by Henry George, the American prophet of land nationalisation (ibid., 156).

Henry George's London appearances turned a middle-class issue into a mass movement (Buder, *Visionaries and Planners*, 15). The 'Land Question' so urgently raised by Irish land agitation coincided with English concerns about a massive urban migration which promoted in London's slums the kind of rack-renting that had long been a fact of life in Ireland (ibid., 20). Morris's inner circle included Alfred Russell Wallace, one of the chief English proponents of land nationalisation, who advocated 'government acquisition and nationalization of all land' (ibid., 20) to liberate the poor from the greed of landlords. After Bloody Sunday, however, it became clear that the 'here and now' was inhospitable to the collaboration between Irish nationalism and British socialism that emerged around land nationalisation; and the Fabians lost some of their enthusiasm for it. 'After 1890', Bevir notes, 'rent played an increasingly minor role in Fabian socialism' (Bevir, *Making of British Socialism*, 145).

For other socialists, on the other hand, the end of landlordism only became more important during the decade in which Shaw was making his reputation as a playwright. The goal of land nationalisation, while utopian in its 'splendid magnitude', was believed by many to be achievable *without* revolution, via the establishment of cooperative communities built on collectively owned land. As these alternative communities succeeded, they would proliferate, and eventually render private landownership obsolete.

Wallace articulates the state-socialism version of land nationalisation in his *Forecasts* essay, 'Re-Occupation of the Land'. London's urban housing crisis was a corollary of the depopulation of the countryside from which these new Londoners had migrated. Wallace proposed to rectify both situations by establishing 'colonies' – modelled on 'Labour Colonies' in the Netherlands – which would support themselves economically through agriculture and manufacturing. Undeveloped land would be bought by the county government, or perhaps 'paid for [by the colony] by means of a terminable rental, similar to that by which Irish tenants have been enabled to purchase their farms' (Wallace, 'Re-Occupation of the Land', 22). Surpluses would return to the community and 'all profits would go to increasing the comfort of the colonists' (ibid., 23).

If the colony appealed powerfully to state-socialists as a pathway to land nationalisation, the self-sustaining autonomous collective appealed just as strongly to the adherents of queer socialism. As the events of 1887 put revolution further out of reach, the 1890s saw a proliferation of 'new anarchist' communes (Bevir, *Making of British Socialism*, 270–5). These were typically established on underutilised land collectively owned by the founders, and in each community a shared vision of the utopian future was implemented on a small scale. Many of these communes rejected both capitalist structures of ownership and existing family structures, so that the new anarchism overlapped with nascent sexual liberation movements (ibid., 270–2). Russian expatriate Peter Kropotkin inspired many of these communes; but so did Morris and Carpenter, each of whom made his own home the hub of an informal socialist collective (ibid., 271, 275).

It is the nature of queer futurity not to arrive; and these communes failed. But in 1898, Ebenezer Howard's book launched one of the few millenarian utopian projects to have a major impact on twentieth-century land use. *To-Morrow* combines ideas borrowed from socialist and anarchist thinkers – including Bellamy, Wallace, Morris and Kropotkin – with spiritualism, romanticism and political economy, producing a highly idiosyncratic vision (Hall et al., 'Commentators' Introduction', 2–5). *To-Morrow* proposed to solve the twin problems of urban overcrowding and rural depopulation through the establishment of collectively-owned developments which would combine agriculture, industry and a city centre in a community more attractive than either the city or the country. It is important to understand that the Garden City was not conceived of as 'suburban' (Miller, 'Exporting the Garden City'). The country would not provide refuge from the city, but embrace it, infiltrate it and transform it. Howard named his new 'smokeless cities' (Howard, *To-Morrow: A Peaceful Path to Reform*, 156) Garden Cities.

Compared to the sources on which it drew, Howard's plan attracted a much higher level of financial support from much less radical people. Historians of urban planning suggest three main reasons for Howard's unlikely breakout success. First, *To-Morrow* presents itself as an alternative to binaristic thinking. Howard's scheme synthesised ideas, concepts and styles that more doctrinaire socialists, more hard-headed materialists, more cynical industrialists and more idealistic visionaries considered incompatible (Hall et al., 'Commentators' Introduction', 5). Instead of accepting the town/country opposition, Howard promises that in the Garden City, 'all the advantages of the most energetic and active town life, with all the beauty and delight of the country, may be secured in perfect combination' (Howard, *To-Morrow: A Peaceful Path to Reform*, 7). The Garden City also spanned the state-socialism/anarchism divide, 'provid[ing] a bridge between a radical tradition seeking small voluntary experiments in community and mutual aid and early twentieth-century modes of reform, looking toward government' to lead the way (Buder, *Visionaries and Planners*, 5).

Wallace and the Land Nationalisation Society recognised the Garden City's kinship to the labour colony, and actively supported the Garden City Association when it formed in 1899 (Beevers, *Garden City Utopia*, 71). But Howard presents his imagined future in visionary rather than pragmatic terms:

> The town is the symbol of society – of mutual help and friendly co-operation, of fatherhood, motherhood, brotherhood, sisterhood, of wide relations between man and man – of broad, expanding sympathies – of science, art, culture, religion. And the country! The country is the symbol of God's love and care for man ... Its beauty is the inspiration of art, of music, of poetry ... Town and country *must be married*, and out of this joyous union will spring a new hope, a new life, a new civilization. (Howard, *To-Morrow: A Peaceful Path to Reform*, 9–10)

Like Bellamy, whose *Looking Backward* was one of Howard's models (Hall et al., 'Commentators' Introduction', 4), Howard uses heterosexual metaphors to naturalise his utopian vision. Unlike Bellamy's utopia, however, the Garden City is generated by desire. One of the most frequently reproduced images from Howard's *To-Morrow* is his 'Three Magnets' diagram, showing three magnets ('Town', 'Country', and 'Town-Country') competing for a bar of iron labelled 'The People', and asking the question, 'Where will they go?'

To-Morrow's second distinctive feature was its attempt to integrate a collectivist future into a capitalist present. *To-Morrow* devotes whole chapters to calculations proving that the Garden City is economically viable in the 'here and now'. Industrial capitalists were to 'act as chief agents in the process' of establishing Garden Cities, which were to inaugurate 'a third socio-economic system, superior both to Victorian capitalism and to bureaucratic centralised socialism' (ibid., 5–7). In *To-Morrow*, Howard imagines that the Garden City land will be 'legally vested in the names of four Gentlemen of responsible position and of undoubted probity and honour, who hold it in trust ... for the people' (Howard, *To-Morrow: A Peaceful Path to Reform*, 12–13). Rent will be paid to the trustees; as development raises land values, rents increase, enabling the trustees to pay off start-up costs. After that, all revenue generated by rent will 'pass back to the community' (Hall et al., 'Commentators' Introduction', 25) to fund public works.

Howard never saw the Garden City as a for-profit venture (Beevers, *Garden City Utopia*, 85–7). The trusteeship plan was compromise which acknowledged that the 'here and now' was not structured so as to enable truly collective ownership (ibid., 74). But concentrating land in the hands of a cadre of 'Gentlemen' risked reducing the Garden City to the kind of 'model village' designed by industrial magnates to house their own workers (Creese, *The Search for Environment*, 15). George Cadbury, who built Bournville for his employees in 1895, was one of Howard's early backers. Cadbury was typical of a group of industrialists who shared Morris's revulsion against the ugliness produced by industrial rapacity. The sensual impoverishment characterising the typical mid-century industrial town – the 'shortage of the ambient qualities of beauty in the whole environment' (ibid., 2) – was the product of capitalist indifference to everything but profit: lack of intentionality manifested as lack of design. The model village was an attempt to rectify this by imposing the coherent vision of a single man – in this case, the factory owner – on an entire town. As sole owner of the 'model village', Salt or Akroyd or Cadbury or Lever could create his own work of art on a scale of which Morris could only dream.

Already, then, in 1898, a segment of the ownership class was primed to appreciate *To-Morrow*'s third distinctive feature: its faith in the power of design. Howard's real legacy is his impact on twentieth-century urban space. *To-Morrow* became 'without question the most important single work in the history of modern town planning' (Hall et al., 'Commentators' Introduction', 1). It was certainly a major improvement over earlier efforts like the Public Health Act of 1875, which attempted to bring 'light, air, and mobility' (Creese, *The Search for Environment*, 76) to overcrowded neighbourhoods. This was accomplished by carving up working-class areas with 'bye-law streets' – 'straight, wide, continuous' roads lined on both sides with identical houses (ibid.). The bye-law street did improve 'municipal health and efficiency' – but at the price of creating a landscape 'so cold and impersonal' that it 'aggravate[d] the original loss of identity and personal locus which the town and factory had brought at the outset of the industrial revolution' (ibid., 82).

Howard planned the Garden City along different lines. Long, wide streets do enter into it, but as 'six magnificent boulevards' – all lined by trees – which radiate from a central hub like spokes from a wheel, connecting a series of concentric circles which contain the residential areas (Howard, *To-Morrow: A Peaceful Path to Reform*, 14). In keeping with Howard's belief in the human need for enrichment, diversion and society, the arts are literally central: the public library, theatre and art gallery occupy the innermost ring which encircles the garden at the city's heart. The cultural ring is surrounded by a circular Central Park which is ringed by the Crystal Palace, a covered 'glass corridor' dedicated to recreational shopping, whose 'bright shelter' encourages Garden Citizens to make use of the central park 'even in the most doubtful of weathers' (ibid.).[11] Factories would be located in the outermost ring, linked by a circular railroad which cuts through the surrounding farms.

Howard's geometry was dictated by his personal blend of mysticism and materialism. The concentric organisation ensures that inhabitants will be roughly equidistant from the green spaces and the cultural/entertainment facilities, and is thus an expression of Howard's socialist and anarchist influences (ibid., 15). Spiritualism's influence is apparent in Howard's most futuristic diagram, which imagines a network of six new Garden Cities sprung from the roots of the original model. Howard based it on a diagram he found in a prophetic text by the Anglo-Irish mystic Gideon Jasper Ouseley (Hall et al., 'Commentators' Introduction', 159). Its elegant deployment of the mystical number seven, to say nothing of its wheel-like design and its incorporation of cities which are themselves widening gyres, would have gladdened the heart of Yeats himself.

Like everything else about it, *To-Morrow*'s designs were double-faced. Edward Pease, laying down the Fabian critique of *To-Morrow*, mocked its 'pretty plans, nicely designed with a ruler and compass' (quoted in Beevers, *Garden City Utopia*, 71). These plans are in fact an odd combination of the beautiful and the sinister. The romanticism of the warm tints and archaic lettering only partially softens the severe abstraction of the figures. Their pleasing geometrical perfection betrays an apparently total indifference to existing topography, which conflicts with the text's veneration of nature; they suggest a space station more readily than they suggest a terrestrial city. The treatment of an inhabited space as a blank canvas on which to impose an abstract, rationalised design is characteristic not only of the kind of totalitarian social engineering so vigorously anathematised by Yde, but of a tradition of imperialist cartography which treats the to-be-colonised space as tabula rasa.

Howard's 'pretty plans' nevertheless captured the imaginations of Morris's followers in the Arts and Crafts movement, for whom the 'indispensability of beauty' (Creese, *The Search for Environment*, 171) was the foundational principle of design. The two architects hired by the first Garden City Company, Barry Parker and Raymond Unwin, were 'attracted to the garden city movement . . . for the message of social reform it proclaimed' (ibid.). They approached their work on the Garden City from an Arts and Crafts ethos strongly influenced by Morris's medievalism; their stress on the village as an *organic* whole, like their emphasis on 'mutual relations' (quoted in ibid., 100), pulls the Garden City away from *Looking Backward* and towards *News from Nowhere*. Unwin found in Morris support for his own 'reaction against urban anonymity, rootlessness, and harshness' (ibid., 172); his appreciation for Howard's 'ruler and compass' designs was softened and nuanced by his internalisation of Morris's ideals (ibid., 175–6).

Unwin's political formation, meanwhile, was deeply influenced by his friendship with Edward Carpenter. As Unwin began to apprehend 'the overwhelming complexity and urgency of the social problem' (Unwin, 'Edward Carpenter', 234), he started visiting Carpenter at Millthorpe. In a 1931 essay, Unwin describes how Carpenter's epic visionary poem *Towards Democracy* enabled his own 'escape from an intolerable sheath of unreality and social superstition' (ibid., 235). Nearly fifty years after reading it, Unwin remained impressed by the way *Towards Democracy* links sensual pleasure with social politics. It was by offering a vision of 'a new understanding, relation, and unity to be realised between the spirit of man and his body, the animal man no longer a beast to be ridden, but an equal friend to be loved', that Carpenter made possible 'a new sense of equality and freedom in all human intercourse' (ibid.). Creese suggests that Carpenter's identification of nature as more 'real' than industrial civilisation shaped Unwin's approach to green space (Creese, *The Search for Environment*, 164); Unwin suggests that his designs were influenced by Carpenter's revolutionary 'acceptance of bodily needs and imperfections' (Unwin, 'Edward Carpenter', 239).

Though the Garden City's financial foundations may have been capitalist, then, its realisation was entrusted to an architectural team whose sensibilities were formed by queer socialism. From one point of view, Parker's and Unwin's implementation of Morris's and Carpenter's ideals through their architectural work merely highlights the deterioration of a once-robust radical movement; revolutionary socialism dwindles into innovative design. At the same time, the Garden City project reveals an unexpectedly bright side of the environmental determinism that produced late nineteenth-century naturalism. For Howard, Morris, Carpenter, Parker and Unwin, the determining power of the environment was an inescapable given – but the environment itself was not. If an ugly, polluted, inhumane environment generated human misery, then a beautiful, undefiled, hand-designed and lovingly-built environment could eradicate it.

Walter Beevers describes Shaw's relationship to the Garden City movement as 'strangely ambivalent' (Beevers, *Garden City Utopia*, 69). Ambivalent it certainly was. Critical of the Garden City project in public, Shaw nevertheless invested a significant amount of money in each Garden City (ibid., 78). Though his decision to make an Englishman the ambassador of the Garden City in Ireland does suggest, as Miller argues, Shaw's awareness of 'shifts in imperial policy' through which development was replacing military conquest (Miller, 'Exporting the Garden City'), Shaw also saw the Garden City project in the context of a tradition of utopian attempts at collective landownership and communal living which Shaw had been following with interest 'ever since I plunged into Socialism' (Shaw, letter to Neville, ff. 248).[12]

But it should be clear by now that ambivalence about a utopian project with strong ties to queer socialism was not, for Shaw, strange at all. If the Garden City 'continued to fascinate Shaw' (Beevers, *Garden City Utopia*, 78) long after Letchworth had demonstrated the corrosive effects of the 'here and now' on Howard's dream and on Parker's and Unwin's plans, that is perhaps because Shaw recognised in it the ambivalence that complicated his own politics. Socialist and capitalist, spiritualist and materialist, visionary and pragmatic, linear and circular, abstract and concrete, ideal and real, Morrisian and Bellamistic, productive and pleasant, crank and corporate, designed by queer socialism but built in straight time, the Garden City promised to reconcile many of the tensions that we have observed in Shaw's own relationship to utopian desire.

Tell Me Why Not

We are now ready to take up the question of what it would mean to build, or *not* to build, a Garden City in Ireland. We will not, however, find our answer in the published text, which gives us very little idea of how Shaw planned to deploy Howard's scheme. In the typescript sent to Yeats and Gregory, Broadbent's initial pitch makes the Garden City's utopian origins much more evident:

> BROAD   Have you ever heard of Garden City?
> TIM   Garden City? What part of Ireland is that in, now?
> BROAD   No part. It has not been built yet.
> TIM   Ah. Praps that's why I've never been in it.
> BROAD   It is as yet only an ideal.
> TIM   Dye mane Heaven?
> BROAD   No: at least not a heaven in the skies, but a heaven on earth.
> (Typescript, 6–7)

The 'ideal' Garden City is named here as both *u-topia* (no place) and *eu-topia* (good place). By the time *John Bull* opened, however, Letchworth was open for business; and Broadbent's response to Tim's 'D'ye mane Heaven?' becomes the comically prosaic 'Heaven! No: it's near Hitchin' (Shaw, *John Bull's Other Island*, 8).

The typescript's stronger references to paradise more clearly present Broadbent's Garden City as the 'here and now' twin of the futurity for which Peter Keegan longs. What distinguishes Keegan from Larry is not that his dreams of another world are any less 'heartscalding', but that he embraces them without shame. Keegan, whose status as an ex-priest enables him to remain celibate without inviting speculation, does not share Larry's disabling desire to conform to the 'prosaic' model of productive masculinity. Keegan's 'nature' is defined in a stage direction by a rejection of the 'here and now', which belongs to Broadbent and his like:

> KEEGAN   You feel at home in the world, then?
> BROAD   Of course. Don't you?
> KEEGAN [*from the very depths of his nature*]   No. (Ibid., 90)

But despite his worldliness, Broadbent is less rigidly wedded than Larry is to 'straight time', precisely because Englishness authorises him to dream without shame. Broadbent recognises that Keegan's vision of the cosmos has its roots not only in the Catholic Church or in Indian spirituality but also in the romanticism that inspired the British left: 'It reminds me of poor Ruskin – a great man, you know. I sympathise. Believe me, I'm on your side. Don't sneer, Larry: I used to read a lot of Shelley years ago. Let us be faithful to the dreams of our youth' (ibid., 113). Larry, in contrast, disclaims any knowledge of heaven and dismisses Keegan's vision as sentimental 'drivel' which is no use to 'men with serious practical business in hand' (ibid., 115). As we have seen, however, the Garden City was a dream of a better world which was expressed as 'serious practical business'. Through Broadbent, the Garden City is offered as an alternative to the all-or-nothing thinking to which Larry is so violently addicted. Anything Broadbent can support can't, of course, be radical; but it was precisely by infiltrating the consciousnesses of people like Broadbent that the Garden City scheme changed the shape of reality.

Broadbent's original mission to Ireland was thus once presented as something more complicated than an outright land-grab. To those familiar with the history of nineteenth-century socialism, in fact, it would have appeared as an ironic modern reprise of a well-known episode in which another English adventurer travelled to Ireland to found a commune using the unpaid labour of the 'warm-hearted Irish race'. In 1830, as a wave of agrarian violence swept across County Clare, an Irish landlord named John Scott Vandeleur contacted the Manchester-born socialist Edward Thomas Craig and asked him to come help him turn his 618-acre estate into a cooperative farm (Ellis, *History*, 91). Vandeleur wanted to save his land and his skin, of course; but he was also an admirer of Robert Owen, a Welsh radical lionised by Shaw as one of the 'three great Utopians' of socialist tradition ('Socialism, Utopian and Scientific', 7). Owenite communes founded in Indiana and Scotland failed within two years. The commune Craig established at Ralahine, however, was a galloping success. Craig was initially 'treated with deep suspicion' by Vandeleur's Irish-speaking tenants – Broadbent recruits Tim Haffigan precisely because he foresees a similar reception – but he learned Irish, gained their trust and had the commune up and running by November 1831. Agrarian violence around Ralahine dropped. Governed by a democratically elected committee according to a constitution that guaranteed freedom of religion and speech as well as female suffrage, the Ralahine cooperative became a 'Mecca for social reformers' and a 'model commune' (ibid., 91–4).

The Garden City mission thus connects Broadbent, albeit ironically, to a tradition of British reform that goes well beyond liberalism, and which once provided effective support to socialists in Ireland. Broadbent also represents the naïve but inspiring optimism that led Howard to attempt the synthesis of all of those opposing forces; and in the pre-production Act I, Broadbent made the case for the fusion of capitalism and socialism that Howard attempted in *To-Morrow*. In a conversation cut from the published text, Broadbent suggests that it is only through being co-opted that socialism can change the environment:

> BROAD I shall do my duty as a landlord – on behalf of the syndicate, of course. I'm going to try the Garden City dodge in Rosscullen.
> LARRY Turned Socialist, have you?
> BROAD Not a bit. Let me give you a valuable business wrinkle, Larry. Say what you will mere sordid money grubbing doesn't pay when you have a big land scheme to develop. There's such a deuce of a lot to be done, that if you have to pay for all the work, you never get your money back.
> LARRY Well, if the scheme won't pay, you must let it alone, that's all.
> BROAD Now that shews the danger of not keeping your eyes open and your mind open. Look here. Do you realize what an enormous force social enthusiasm is in the world – what a huge, thumping, solid money value it has? [. . .] I tell you, Larry, one of the greatest commercial discoveries of the age is the lot of work you can get out of people for nothing under the influence of philanthropic ideas – call them socialistic if you like. I learnt that in Mexico on my first engineering job. (Typescript, Act I, 16)

Briefly, Broadbent's first job was to finish a canal that had been dug by volunteers who were under the erroneous impression that they were living in a 'Socialist colony'. Social enthusiasm gets the canal to within a hundred yards of the sea; but when Broadbent completes it, they discover that the socialists 'dug the canal deeper at the sea end than at the head' (Typescript, Act I, 16), rendering it useless.

The punchline of Broadbent's anecdote does not, however, cancel his appreciation for utopian desire as an agent of material change – as, in fact, a 'bigger force' than the technology mobilised in the service of capitalism:

> That was a lesson to me that Ive never forgotten. Ive never sneered at Socialism since. It's a force – a real force – a bigger force than steam or electricity – lying there ready for any capitalist with brains enough to organise it. Well, why not organise it in Rosscullen? Why not create a Garden City there, not by paid labour, but by the enthusiasm of an imaginative, warmhearted race? (Typescript, Act I, 16)

Broadbent's Garden City 'dodge' is thus an expression of ambivalence about the future of socialism. Broadbent's cold-blooded intention to harness and exploit the unpaid labour of radicals coincides with the Fabian critique of the Garden City as a capitalist ruse siphoning money and effort away from *real* socialism (Miller, 'Exporting the Garden City'). Broadbent's praise of 'social enthusiasm' as an 'enormous force' with 'huge, thumping, solid money value', however, complicates this. While it presents this 'enthusiasm' as vulnerable to cooptation, it also rescues utopian desire from futility. Broadbent's belief that he can build a better estate with the volunteer labour of such enthusiasts than he can through 'sordid money grubbing' identifies dreaming as perhaps the only means of achieving environmental transformation.

Broadbent's imagination of socialism crying out to be 'organised' by the right capitalist is the kind of English bull we've come to expect from him; but it is also strongly reminiscent of a letter that Shaw drafted about the Garden City movement for former MP Ralph Neville. Shaw expresses reservations about the partnership with capital through a dramatic monologue delivered by an imaginary industrialist to the Garden City Association.[13] 'You have made us and all the world a present of your idea', says the industrialist, 'which contains absolutely nothing new except the recognition, denied by former Utopists, that the whole scheme depends absolutely on our own co-operation'. Having captured the project, this Machiavelli of the mills dictates the role that the progressives who invented it will play in its execution:

> Now, gentlemen, we will tell you what you *can* do for us. You can advertise us, you can think out the plan of our city for us; and you can get us a great deal of Kudos and much gratuitous aid both in work and in money

from your enthusiastic friends, and possibly important assistance from the Government. We admit that all this has a considerable money value, and we quite recognize the fact that it can only be realized on condition that we give reasonable guarantees of a higher 'moral minimum' of open space, sanitation, education, workmen's houses, and a lower 'moral minimum' of rent for workmen's houses, of hours of labor, etc. etc., than the existing law prescribes. (Quoted in Beevers, *Garden City Utopia*, 75)

It is Howard's 'recognition' of the necessity for capitalist partnership that is the source of Shaw's ambivalence. Capitalist influence limits the scheme's transformative power; but partnership with capital is nevertheless necessary to get even so much as a 'higher "moral minimum"'. Like Bellamy, Shaw seems here to have accepted the idea that state socialism can only grow out of its closest 'here and now' analogue, the capitalist trust. Shaw begins the letter by asserting, in his own voice, that no transformative scheme could succeed *without* this structure. 'I am not hostile to a trust', Shaw insists; in fact, he remained aloof from earlier socialist proposals along these lines only because '[t]hey could only have been carried out by a big and broadminded capitalistic trust, and the time was not then ripe for such trusts' (Shaw, draft letter to Richard Neville, ADD 50615, 248/2).

Like Bellamy in *Looking Backward*, Shaw imagines here that the end of private landownership must come about through the evolution of a capitalist syndicate. At the same time, the example of Ralahine validates Shaw's scepticism about the long-term survival of a project based on a gentleman's agreement between tenants and trustees. Regarding the actual ownership of the land, Vandeleur and the members of the 'Ralahine Agricultural and Manufacturing Co-operative Association' entered into an agreement that anticipated Howard's plan for financing the Garden City: Vandeleur was to retain ownership of the estate until the commune had enough revenue to buy it, when it would become 'the joint property of the society' (quoted in Ellis, *History*, 93). The Ralahine commune had just reached the crucial two-year mark when Vandeleur fled Ireland to escape his gambling debts, and the estate was seized by Vandeleur's creditors (ibid., 94). Craig's history of the commune reports that when informed that the commune would be disbanded, the tenants began keening (ibid.).

The Garden City thus appears in Broadbent's exchange with Doyle as a representation of what utopian desire has to become in order to enter the 'here and now'. If Broadbent's Mexican canal anecdote represents socialists as naïve and ineffective, it also establishes the indispensability of socialism in any attempt at environmental change. If Broadbent preaches the supremacy of capitalism, he also acknowledges the limitations of 'money grubbing', which discourages the cooperation necessary for large-scale projects. As Larry says, under capitalism as we understand it, if a project 'won't pay, you must let it alone' (Typescript, Act I, 15).

This exchange also suggests that, *contra* Larry, *resistance* to dreaming may be the source of Ireland's troubles. Larry dismisses Broadbent's plan not because it is intrinsically flawed, or because he sees in it a thinly veneered attempt at enslavement, but because 'social enthusiasm' is a raw material in which Ireland is not rich: 'The Irish are not socialists. They're too clever to help one another' (Typescript, Act I, 17). Broadbent then contemplates a Plan B:

> BROADBENT Well, will they borrow money if they get the chance?
> DOYLE Yes.
> BROADBENT Good. Then I think I see my way. (Typescript, Act I, 17)

What this passage emphasises is that the banal and straightforwardly exploitative golf hotel scheme discussed by Broadbent, Larry and Keegan in the play's final scene is the devolution of a more visionary plan for Ireland's transformation. The Garden City project might have offered a real-world alternative which would foster collectivity more effectively than either the Syndicate's golf hotel or the petty landlordism that Larry excoriates in his Act III outburst.

Larry's disgust with the joyless 'industry' of Mat and his fellow tenants-turned-landowners is the only protest he allows himself against his own fetishisation of hard work. Acutely aware of Ireland's colonial history, Larry recognises Ireland as a place where industry is *not* productive and thrift impoverishes both community and individual. Larry's attempt to articulate an alternative, however, disintegrates quickly into an affirmation of capitalism as the only force capable of changing Ireland: 'If we cant have men with ability, let us at least have men with capital' (Shaw, *John Bull's Other Island*, 65). The Garden City 'dodge', even led by Broadbent and his Land Development Syndicate, appears as a compromise between the atomisation Larry fears and the exploitation historically inflicted upon Ireland by English 'men with capital'. For all its flaws, the Garden City movement was still defined by Howard's goal of collective landownership. In it, a diluted and adulterated version of land nationalisation survived.

That idea had not survived Irish land reform. For Michael Davitt, the leader of the Irish Land League, 'the land of Ireland for the people of Ireland' had a quite concrete meaning: he, like Shaw, had been 'converted' by Henry George to the idea of land nationalisation (Moody 522). For the tenant farmers who made up the movement, however, 'the land of Ireland for the people of Ireland' meant 'occupying ownership' – the right to control the land they farmed (Moody 522). Davitt's commitment to ending private land ownership in Ireland had more support among English radicals than among Irish farmers (Moody, *Davitt and Irish Revolution*, 521). The Land Act of 1903 offered not public landownership but a path to occupying ownership; and Larry's despair over this devolution is the strongest evidence we have of his disavowed utopian dreams.

When Aunt Judy predicts the result Davitt had hoped for – 'theres harly any landlords left, and there'll soon be none at all' – Larry retorts that 'On the contrary, therll soon be nothing else' (Shaw, *John Bull's Other Island*, 56). If 'men of capital' succeeded in establishing a Garden City in Ireland, they would at least be creating something beautiful and shared out of land which would otherwise be parcelled up into units like Matt Haffigan's 'dirty little podato patch' (ibid., 68). If the Irish weren't 'too clever to help each other', their 'social enthusiasm' – even exploited by Broadbent – might nevertheless transform Ireland's landscape more beneficially than the individual 'industry' (ibid., 55) of individual tenants-cum-landowners.

But this reading is hopelessly entangled with the play's darker view of the Garden City project as utopian socialism's deal with the devil. When Broadbent, in the final scene, claims that he will 'make a Garden city of Rosscullen' yet (ibid., 110), Keegan tasks him with making the same mistake about which Shaw warned Neville: wasting 'all his virtues – his efficiency, as you call it – in doing the will of his greedy masters instead of doing the will of Heaven that is in himself' (ibid., 111). Just as Ireland divides its inhabitants into 'saints and traitors' (ibid.), it is finally hostile to the synthesis Howard attempted in *To-Morrow*; and through Keegan Broadbent's Garden City 'dodge' is revealed to be a mere swindle.

Nevertheless, Ireland, which fosters 'strange perfection' (ibid.), becomes the place from which Shaw can at last allow himself to make the case *against* possibilism. Keegan is tragically faithful to an unrealisable 'there and then' which he persists in calling 'Heaven', and which he describes in Catholic cadences (Saddlemyer, '*John Bull's Other Island*', 229), but which is also explicitly the utopia of queer socialism: 'a commonwealth in which work is play and play is life' (Shaw, *John Bull's Other Island*, 116). Keegan's vision positions him, and by extension the Irish landscape through which this dream was born, in direct opposition to the *Man and Superman* universe, where between the heaven of work and the hell of play there is a great gulf fixed. To the crushing certainty of *Man and Superman*'s reproductive futurism, Keegan opposes the undecidability of queer futurity.

Losing the Plot

By going back to his 'Round Tower' and 'dreaming of Heaven', Keegan leaves Broadbent and Doyle in possession of the stage, apparently conceding the fight. Most readings take it for granted that Broadbent's vision of Rosscullen's future will come to pass – that in fact this is the play's central irony.[14] But now that we know that the future is what has always been at stake in *John Bull's Other Island*, perhaps we should think twice about the fact that Broadbent's triumph is deferred. When the play ends, Broadbent is engaged to Nora but not married to her; he's running for Parliament but he's not elected; he's choosing the site for his golf hotel, but he doesn't yet own the land on which he imagines building it. And our impression that Broadbent's victory is inevitable – that it will evolve naturally and continuously from the play's enacted present – depends largely on the prophet of queer futurity.

It is Keegan who predicts Broadbent's election to Parliament in language reminiscent of Butler's evolutionary theory: 'You will get into parliament because you want to get into it badly enough' (ibid., 87). It is Keegan who responds to the news of Broadbent's engagement by hailing him as

> The conquering Englishman, sir. Within 24 hours of your arrival you have carried off our only heiress, and practically secured the parliamentary seat. And you have promised me that when I come here in the evenings to meditate on my madness; to watch the shadow of the Round Tower lengthening in the sunset; to break my heart uselessly in the curtained gloaming over the dead heart and blinded soul of the island of the saints, you will comfort me with the bustle of a great hotel, and the sight of the little children carrying the golf clubs of your tourists as a preparation for the life to come. (Ibid., 106)

The power of Keegan's prophecy is only intensified for contemporary readers by its uncannily accurate prediction of a 'future' that is now part of Ireland's recent past.

But once we understand Keegan as the advocate of utopian futurity, we can see that the battle is just beginning. Even if Keegan's predictions come true, Broadbent's triumph merely confirms Keegan's privileged knowledge of the future. This, in turn, authorises the predictions Keegan makes of a 'there and then' *beyond* Broadbent's triumph: 'For four wicked centuries the world has dreamed this foolish dream of efficiency; and the end is not yet. But the end will come' (ibid., 113). Because it ratifies Keegan's ability to see the future, the short-term success of Broadbent's capitalism only lends authority to Keegan's belief in the ephemerality of the 'here and now'. The more enthusiastically 'straight time' embraces Broadbent, the more certain it becomes that straight time will ultimately pass away.

But the play's deep structure gives us reason to doubt that Broadbent's vision will *ever* be realised. The inevitability of 'straight time' is guaranteed by evolution's developmental logic, which presumes a future that progresses incrementally from existing conditions. The logic governing the well-made plot, whose coherence is produced by the clarity of the causal chain that links the events, mimics that inevitability. *John Bull* does not possess the kind of elegance that produces inevitability. It is, remember, 'fundamentally ugly and shapeless' – because its plot is very badly made.[15]

We see this most clearly in the play's unusually weak romance. Role-reversal comedy can account for the fact that Broadbent's first proposal to Nora is comically unprepared; but the second proposal scene is both less funny and more arbitrary. Nora accepts Broadbent, not because of the great love growing in her heart, but because Broadbent happened to come upon her while she was crying over her breakup with Larry: 'I let you be kind to me, and cried in your arms, because I was too wretched to think of anything but the comfort of it. And how could I let any other man touch me after that?' (ibid., 100). Logic and causation have little to do with their engagement, which appears to depend on an obscure code of 'Irish delicacy' (ibid., 99) which dictates that a woman becomes the property of the first man upon whose breast her tears shall fall. Broadbent and Nora don't share a 'plot' so much as a loose collection of chance encounters.

Broadbent's second proposal confirms Shaw's identification of 'fecundity' and the Life Force with the English. In an inversion of Ann's conquest of Tanner, Broadbent's vitality and 'strength' entrap a resistant Nora. Nora doesn't so much accept Broadbent's proposal as mourn her inability to refuse it: 'I could never marry anybody but you now' (ibid.). But Broadbent's electioneering violates the very delicacy that prompted her to accept him: 'Oh, how could you drag me all round the place like that, telling everybody that we're going to be married, and introjoocing me to the lowest of the low, and letting them shake hans with me' (ibid., 103). The sparks that fly during Nora's final confrontation with Larry indicate that her feelings towards him are stronger than any Broadbent has evoked. We cannot, therefore, take it for granted that we can see the future of this relationship.

Unlike Blanche and Trench's, Nora and Broadbent's romance is too weak to serve as a skeleton supporting and shaping the play's dialectical meat. The only other structure that might have given the play a spine is the development plot. Before the cuts made to Act I, the pitch meeting with Tim Haffigan and Broadbent's conversation with Doyle about the 'Garden City dodge' served as the anchor for an ironic quest narrative. Like other deluded English progressives before him, Broadbent sets out to bring the revolution to Ireland; but the lack of 'social enthusiasm' frustrates his ambitions, and in the end all he can do with the 'ideals of [his] youth' is pillage and steal like the others before him. With Howard's vision as its starting point and the golf hotel as the end point, the development plot would have a clear downward trajectory. Cornelius's borrowing money from Broadbent at the beginning of Act IV (92–3) would mark the abandonment of the 'Garden City dodge' and the shift to Plan B ('Will they borrow money if they get the chance?'). The line that initiates Broadbent's final discussion of his development scheme – 'I begin to see my way' (ibid., 106) – would chime, with satisfying and ominous irony, with his Act I line, 'I think I see my way.'

It is here that we see how the sheer complexity of Shaw's identity position vexes his first Irish play.[16] It is no wonder that when Shaw needed something to cut, the Garden City was the first to go. Its function is so ambiguous and so complex that it would not have 'read' to audiences in either of this play's intended venues. Nevertheless, exploring his own ambivalence about utopian socialism was a major part of Shaw's motivation in turning to Ireland; and cutting most of the explicit *discussion* of the Garden City project doesn't remove it from the *structure*. The Garden City and its ambiguities are preserved in the play's situation; the Garden City project is the reason, for instance, that Broadbent and Doyle are a pair of up-and-coming young architects like Parker and Unwin, instead of belonging to another profession equally appropriate for the development plot. Apart from Nora, the Garden City project is the only thing mentioned in Act I that still appears to be relevant in Act IV.

Cutting the Act I discussion merely destabilises the play's foundation by obscuring Broadbent's motives. As performed, Act I drops the development language as soon as Tim Haffigan leaves; Broadbent's only comment on his motives is that 'I had to foreclose [on Nick Lestrange's estate] on behalf of the Syndicate. So I'm off to Rosscullen to look after the property myself.' This is immediately dropped to explore Larry's ambivalence about Ireland. The development plot is so diminished by the removal of the Garden City discussion that one critic of the Court production was under the impression that Broadbent and Doyle went off to Ireland on 'holiday' ('Mr. Shaw's Play').

We cannot, however, blame the obscurity of the development plot entirely on the loss of its Act I anchor. Starting with Broadbent's scene with Tim Haffigan, Shaw seems to have been bent on obscuring the development story under a more 'national and normal' comedy about Englishness and Irishness. On arrival in Ireland, Broadbent appears to have forgotten why he came. His original motive is further buried under an avalanche of 'freewheeling comedy' (Grene, *Bernard Shaw*, 76) generated by Broadbent's enthusiastic pursuit of various shiny objects. A substitute purpose is provided for Broadbent when he finds Nora at the round tower; but as soon as the romance starts up, a Parliamentary seat pops up out of nowhere. Broadbent can't move the election plot forward without being swept up in a tragicomic set piece denouncing cruelty to animals. Just as it appears that Larry might develop the romance plot by complicating it, Keegan's arrival wrenches us back to the development plot, which dissolves into something that Shaw called 'no ending at all' (Shaw, *Collected Letters*, 444).[17]

The lack of a clear motive for Broadbent's journey wrecks the coherence of the well-made plot. Frederick George Bettany, while detecting a vestigial 'semblance of unity' in the play's focus on Doyle and Broadbent, announced that *John Bull's Other Island* 'is not a play ... but a series of loosely connected, almost disconnected scenes' (Bettany, 'The Playhouses', 643). But we can see considerable room for hope in the fact that none of Broadbent's plots is allowed to develop. Shaw's conviction that it was only in Ireland – a place 'like no other place under heaven' (Shaw, *John Bull's Other Island*, 111) – that he could risk the exploration of his submerged utopian desires introduced into *John Bull's Other Island* so many entangled issues that he could neither weave them into a seamless whole nor rip any of them out. The result was the destruction of the developmental structure that underlies the forms of normativity that Shaw had heretofore embraced: Tanner's reproductive futurism, Butler's capitalist evolutionary theory, Fabian gradualism. The play's 'ugly' shape even rebukes the ruthless disregard for organic irregularity manifested in the austere abstraction of the 'pretty plans' that attracted Shaw to *To-Morrow*.

In Broadbent's final vision, the town-country synthesis that Howard imagined for the Garden City has come apart. He now sees the future as a choice between two mutually exclusive types of development: 'Yes, Mr. Keegan, this place may have an industrial future, or it may have a residential future' (ibid., 108). But Keegan challenges Broadbent's assumption that Ireland runs on straight time, and that its present must yield to a foreseeable future. '[Ireland] may have no future at all', Keegan says. 'Have you thought of that?' (ibid., 112). Broadbent hasn't; but that is just another way in which he fails to understand his own situation. *John Bull*'s dialogue is full of invective indicting Ireland's backwardness and belatedness. But *John Bull*'s structure locates Ireland's best hope precisely in its refusal to develop, and in its resistance to design.

John Bull's Other Island is itself an anti-development. It temporarily thwarts Shaw's own progress towards the authoritarianism of his later work.[18] It offers a glimpse of the value of a utopian socialism that would be displaced in the century to come by noisier, harder, more muscular versions of left ideology and left masculinity. By refusing to choose a future, *John Bull* maintains room for doubt, ambiguity, ambivalence – for desire and for the dream of a place which has for the time being escaped the tyranny of development. Deferral, in *John Bull*, is finally not a source of existential despair but a way of keeping utopian futurity alive.

Conclusion

Ann Saddlemyer sees *John Bull's Other Island* as 'part of a trilogy which began with *Man and Superman* and culminated in *Major Barbara*', arguing that *Major Barbara* 'offers a clearer direction for Keegan's dream: Barbara (power spiritual) unites with Cusins (the future philosopher-king, power material) promising a synthesis of these two opposites, where Superman (God of war and commerce) would no longer be necessary' (Saddlemyer, '*John Bull's Other Island*', 219).[19] But recovering the Garden City subtext makes it clear that what *Major Barbara* stages is in fact the annihilation of Keegan's dream.

In Undershaft's company town, the Garden City has been wholly captured by capitalism. Re-presented as the *'almost* smokeless town' (emphasis added) of Perivale St Andrews, the new Garden City is 'beautifully situated and beautiful in itself' (Shaw, *John Bull's Other Island and Major Barbara*, 268) – but utterly dependent on and controlled by the most destructive of industries. Beauty and design no longer challenge the power of capitalism. The ambiguities have been resolved. Through Cusins, Shaw allows himself a moment to mourn the final assimilation of Howard's vision: 'Not a ray of hope. Everything perfect, wonderful, real. [Perivale St Andrews] only needs a cathedral to be a heavenly city instead of a hellish one' (ibid., 269). Undershaft gloats that it does contain a William Morris 'labor church'; Cusins howls in dismay. Morris's socialism has been finally assimilated into capitalism. There will be no more dreaming. Only violence now offers access to 'reality and ... power' (ibid., 289). Cusins believes that 'the way of life lies through the factory of death' (ibid., 292). There is no such thing as a peaceful path to reform. From now on, change comes from the barrel of a gun.

In that sense, *Major Barbara*'s prediction of the future is, if vastly more depressing, also more accurate than *John Bull*'s. When the revolution came, it looked very different from anything imagined by the socialists we have been discussing. In part this is due to the rise of a newly militant international labour movement which played a leading role in both the Irish revolution that began with the Dublin Lockout in 1913 and the Russian Revolution of 1917. The organisation of the state around labour councils (or, as the Russians called them, 'soviets'), the cult of *zakal* ('steeliness') that derived from the exaltation of the factory worker and his strength, and the dictatorship of the proletariat were things that had no place in the socialism that Morris, Carpenter and Wilde derived from Shelley. Queer socialism, by virtue of its anti-productive stance and its emphasis on individual desire, imagined a 'there and then' without organised labour. In *News from Nowhere* labour is the opposite of organised: decentralised, casual and spontaneous. For Carpenter, industrial labour separates the body from desire and thereby inflicts a wound that must be healed, preferably through sensual engagement with the natural world. Wilde envisions a world where machines have rendered physical labour unnecessary.

Shaw greeted the workers' revolution in Russia with 'an enthusiasm which ... never died' (Ormond, Preface, ix); but this enthusiasm did not extend to the workers themselves. One thing Shaw retained from his exposure to queer socialism was its indifference to labour as a force for revolutionary change. The working-class men who enter his pre-1917 drama – Lickcheese, Straker, Hodgson – are fish out of water whose jobs bind them closely to their bourgeois employers. When we finally get inside a factory in *Major Barbara*, we are assured that Undershaft's workers will never organise, as long as Perivale

St Andrews keeps them contented. After the Bolshevik revolution, Yde argues, Shaw's contempt for 'the masses' only intensified (Yde, *Bernard Shaw and Totalitarianism*, 192), and his dramatisations of the post-revolutionary world remained obsessed with the evolution of an elite whose superiority to pre-revolutionary humanity was measured by its increasing disengagement from the corporeal world of pleasure and work.[20]

During the revolutionary period, then, Shaw's vision of socialism became increasingly remote from socialism's incarnations in the 'here and now' – in Russia, but also in Ireland, where attempts to organise workers in Ireland's major cities led, in the summer of 1913, to class warfare openly waged in the streets of Dublin. It would fall to other playwrights to grapple with Ireland's revolutionary period and the role that left politics played in it. In the next chapter, we will move away from Shaw and his milieu and into revolutionary Ireland as we investigate the representation of radical labour at the Abbey.

Notes

1. Nicholas Grene says *John Bull* offers a higher degree of 'emotional ambiguity and uncertainty' (Grene, *Bernard Shaw*, 72); Ben Levitas detects in *John Bull* unusual 'ambivalence' regarding Irish nationalism and Fabian socialism (Levitas, 'These Islands' Others', 20–4).
2. For a description of the role *John Bull* played in the launching of Vedrenne and Barker's experimental seasons at the Court and the English dramatic revival in general, see Levitas, 'These Islands' Others'.
3. Shaw's claim that the play was commissioned by the Abbey and then rejected for ideological reasons has been debunked. Shaw's intention to write an Irish play predates negotiations with Yeats and Gregory; it was guaranteed production at the Court; and the play's size and technical complexity were at least as problematic for Yeats and Gregory as its politics. See Laurence and Grene, *Shaw*, x–xii; Levitas, 'These Islands' Others', 15–20. In his 'Instructions to Producers' Shaw hopes that 'with smart work in striking and changing' *John Bull's* running time could be reduced to '3 ¼ hours' (Shaw, 'Instructions to Producers', ADD 50615, 2).
4. Muñoz's concept of 'straight time' is based on Judith Halberstam's work on queer temporality (Muñoz, *Cruising Utopia*, 17).
5. Matthew Yde devotes *Bernard Shaw and Totalitarianism* to the state-socialism version of 'utopian longing'.
6. Morris betrays his romantic influences with echoes of Samuel Taylor Coleridge's *Kubla Khan*.
7. 'Tenant-right' meant the right to sell the tenancy to a new occupant, the right to remain on the land, and the right to a 'fair rent'. See Warwick-Haller, *William O'Brien*, 23–5.
8. Levitas makes the same point in 'These Islands' Others'.
9. I thank the Society of Authors on behalf of the Bernard Shaw Estate and the Henry W. and Albert A. Berg Collection of English and American Literature, New York Public Library, Astor, Lennox and Tilden Foundations, for permission to quote from this early typescript of *John Bull's Other Island*. Each act is in a separate booklet and the page numbering is not continuous, so I will cite by act number and page number.
10. See C. Brooke Miller's 'Exporting the Garden City', one of the only extant arti-

cles focusing on the Garden City reference. Saddlemyer notes the existence of an 'uncut' Act I but relies on Dukore's summary of it, which treats the Garden City scheme as a straightforward scam (Saddlemyer, '*John Bull's Other Island*', 220 n7).
11. These elements were inspired by Manhattan's Central Park and the Crystal Palace designed for the Great Exhibition of 1851.
12. *The Revolutionist's Handbook* includes a laudatory discussion of the utopian Oneida Community, whose inspiration was religious rather than socialist, but who practised common ownership and 'common marriage'.
13. Beevers identifies this imaginary industrialist as a prototype of *Major Barbara*'s Andrew Undershaft.
14. C. Brooke Miller's assumption that 'Broadbent's plans for Rosscullen moves forward unimpeded' by any of Keegan's concerns is typical.
15. The play's 'plotlessness' was complained of by London critics (Grene, *Bernard Shaw*, 75). To demonstrate that *John Bull* possesses unity and coherence, Saddlemyer has to define them in terms radically different from those understood by Shaw's contemporaries. Miller notes the 'poverty' of the plot.
16. The third instalment in the *Back to Methuselah* Pentateuch, *Tragedy of an Elderly Gentleman*, is also set in Ireland, in a very distant future.
17. Saddlemyer argues that neither *John Bull* nor *Major Barbara* provides a 'conventional ending' ('*John Bull's Other Island*', 219).
18. Matthew Yde documents this in chapters 4–6 of *Bernard Shaw and Totalitarianism*.
19. Yde agrees that *John Bull* is one term in a trilogy 'straining toward unity and utopian reality' (*Bernard Shaw and Totalitarianism*, 87), but reads it as a 'dead end' from which *Major Barbara* rescues Shaw (ibid., 95).
20. On Shaw's hatred of the body, see chapters 4 and 6 of Matthew Yde's *Bernard Shaw and Totalitarianism*.

3

WE'LL KEEP THE RED FLAG FLYING HERE: SYNDICALISM, JIM LARKIN AND IRISH MASCULINITY AT THE ABBEY THEATRE, 1911–1919

INTRODUCTION

'Next to a war', observed *The Irish Times* theatre critic on 4 November 1914, 'it is probable that nothing holds so much that is tragic and dramatic as a strike' ('Abbey Theatre. A Powerful Strike Play', 6). So soon after the Great Lockout of 1913, he could not have found many Dubliners willing to argue with him. In summer of 1913, the Irish Transport and General Workers' Union (ITGWU), under the leadership of the Liverpool-born labour leader James Larkin, began organising employees of the Dublin United Tramways Company (Yeates, *Lockout*, 5). The company owner, William Martin Murphy, was the head of the Dublin Employers' Federation and a fierce opponent of organised labour. Murphy's efforts at retaliation prompted the ITGWU to call a tramworkers' strike, which began on 26 August (ibid., 1–15). Other Dublin employers responded by retaliating against ITGWU workers (ibid., 27). Soon the ITGWU was engaged in a battle with Dublin capitalists which lasted until February 1914 and kept tens of thousands of Dublin's poorest citizens out of work.

The Great Lockout of 1913 was more than a labour dispute. As Dublin historian Padraig Yeates puts it, the Lockout was a form of 'street theatre' through which Dublin's rich and poor staged a 'public debate' about 'the type of society people wanted under home rule' (Yeates, *A City in Wartime*, 6). It dramatised the desperation of Dublin's unskilled workers and their capacity for collective action. It dragged into the light of day the shame of Dublin's failure to provide humane housing for its poor. It offered local media a compelling protagonist (or villain, depending on the ownership of the paper) in the figure of Jim Larkin, the charismatic organiser who led the ITGWU through the Lockout. It is thus not surprising that when A. Patrick Wilson staged his Lockout play, *The Slough*, at the Abbey Theatre in 1914, even *The Irish Times* reviewer confessed himself fascinated by it.

But the Lockout was only one incident in a revolution that had been unfolding internationally since the beginning of the century. What made strikes particularly 'tragic and dramatic' during the first two decades of the twentieth century was the rise of a radical labour movement known as syndicalism. The formation of the Industrial Workers of the World (IWW) in the United States in 1905 was one of its more vivid manifestations; but syndicalism was rooted in the French radical left, and spread rapidly in Spain and Italy as well (Darlington, *Syndicalism*, 1). Syndicalism appealed to its working-class adherents as an alternative to 'bureaucratic socialism' (O'Connor, *Syndicalism in Ireland*, 4) – the political structures established by the first wave of trade unionism. Syndicalism 'insisted that society's revolutionary transformation necessarily had to come *from below*, to be the work of the majority, the product of workers' own self-activity and self-organization at the point of production' (Darlington, *Syndicalism*, 2). Because of their commitment to the flexibility and spontaneity created by this bottom-up structure, syndicalists cultivated indifference or even hostility to doctrine and theory; syndicalism 'needs to be understood not only in terms of *ideological* doctrine, but as a mode of action, a *practical* social movement engaged in working class struggle' (ibid., 7). Syndicalism therefore adopted different organisational structures and different tactics in different locations, something which makes the movement hard to define ideologically. Irish syndicalism, for instance, shared with its American cousin the dream of organising the entire working class into 'One Big Union' (ibid., 43) – a single army which could do battle with the employers – which was not as persuasive in other areas.

Despite this 'lack of theoretical clarity', however, syndicalism was defined by its conception of the union as a revolutionary force. Syndicalism's primary tactic was to engage union members in 'direct action', a range of anti-employer activity that included 'conventional strikes, intermittent strikes, passive resistance, working to rule, sabotage, and the general strike' (ibid., 33). In addition to extracting concessions from individual employers, constant engagement in direct action would create the necessary conditions for total revolution. Syndicalists envisioned that, if direct action kept the pressure on long enough, 'a full-blown general strike would break out at an unpredictable moment', and 'act as the spark that set the revolution aflame' (ibid., 40).

Irish drama offers us an excellent vantage point from which to observe the political and cultural impact of the syndicalist movement. In Ireland, syndicalism did not have to compete with an established political left. Partly because Ireland had comparatively little industry, Irish politics 'never developed a socialist tradition' like those of Britain, France and Germany (Lane and Ó Drisceoil, *Politics and the Irish Working Class*, 1–2). The closest thing Ireland had to an industrial centre was Belfast, 'where religious sectarianism grounded in political beliefs militated against class unity' (ibid., 1–2). Partly for that reason, however, 'workers and their organisations played a more significant role in the political and social developments that shaped modern Ireland than is generally acknowledged' (ibid., 1). In Irish cities with large concentrations of industrial workers – chiefly Belfast, Cork and Dublin – conditions were desperate, and workers were ready for radical solutions. Irish historians like Padraig Yeates and Roy Foster have recently begun to recover the impact of radical labour on the republican revolutions that followed the Lockout – the 1916 Rising, the War of Independence and the Civil War.

In this chapter, then, we turn to revolutionary Ireland to continue our investigation of the interrelationship between internationalism, sexual politics and socialism by examining three attempts to bring the drama of syndicalism to the Abbey stage. Each was inspired by an industrial strike led in one of Ireland's hotbeds of labour agitation in the years before the Rising. St. John Ervine's *Mixed Marriage*, inspired by the 1907 Belfast dockers' strike, was first staged at the Abbey in 1911. A. Patrick Wilson, who knew Larkin and who was involved in the ITGWU's cultural activities, staged his Lockout drama *The Slough* at the Abbey in 1914. In 1917, Daniel Corkery, inspired by Larkin's organising efforts in Cork, wrote *The Labour Leader*; it was produced by Lennox Robinson at the Abbey in 1919.

This chapter will *not* focus on the work of the most famous playwright to emerge from Ireland's syndicalist era, who is of course Sean O'Casey. O'Casey served as the secretary for the Irish Citizen Army and was a frequent contributor to Larkin's paper *The Irish Worker (and People's Advocate)*. Robert Lowery identifies the Lockout as O'Casey's formative political experience ('The Development of Sean O'Casey's *Weltanschaung*', 63–4). Ben Levitas and Stephen Burch have established *Juno and the Paycock*'s link to A. Patrick Wilson's *The Slough*.[1] O'Casey made three attempts to dramatise the Lockout, none of which was initially produced at the Abbey. We will investigate two of these plays, one in Chapter 5 and one in the epilogue.

This chapter focuses on the period *before* O'Casey's emergence in order to recover a story that was overwritten when O'Casey became the voice of the Irish urban poor. This is the story of syndicalism's impact on Irish masculinity and Irish drama, and its consequences for dramatic representations of the working-class family. Genealogically, I will argue, the formula that O'Casey deployed to such devastating effect in *Juno and the Paycock* was counter-revolutionary, arising out of St. John Ervine and A. Patrick Wilson's anxieties about the more excessive aspects of Larkin's performance of left masculinity. Both playwrights embraced the family plot partly as a defence against the disruptive potential they saw in syndicalism, which was vividly incarnated for them in Larkin. In contrast, Daniel Corkery's nearly-forgotten play *The Labour Leader* acknowledges and incorporates Larkin's excesses, dispensing with the family plot and instead producing a sophisticated dramatisation of syndicalism's revolutionary potential. *The Labour Leader* embraces Larkin's volatility, his passions and his romanticism, making the case for syndicalism's 'irrationalism' (O'Connor, *Syndicalism in Ireland*, 1) as the foundation not so much of labour politics as of modern drama, and rejecting the cerebral mode of socially conscious drama which was so firmly established by Shaw.

Lovers and Fighters: Larkin, Connolly and Queer Socialism

Syndicalism announced its arrival Ireland in 1907, when Jim Larkin was sent by the Liverpool-based National Union of Dock Labourers (NUDL) to organise the dockers of Belfast. The result was a strike which lasted for weeks, involved several trades, nearly led to a police mutiny, and alarmed the NUDL leadership. The NUDL suspended Larkin in 1908; in 1909, Larkin founded the ITGWU (O'Connor, 'Labour and Politics', 33). The ITGWU's first rule book represented the establishment of an *Irish* industrial union as an important rite of passage: 'Ireland has politically reached her manhood' (quoted in ibid.).

As the Lockout was more than a labour dispute, syndicalism was more than a theory. It was an embodied practice which transformed the lives of its adherents on every level. Syndicalism's reliance on agitation demanded much from the rank and file, who were frequently called on to expose themselves to economic hardship, employer retaliation and police brutality. These demands required a reconception of the role of emotion in labour politics. Irish syndicalism embraced a philosophy of 'normative irrationalism' – the 'belief that behaviour should be governed by ethics, sentiment, and natural impulse' rather than the calculated pragmatism associated with party politics (O'Connor, *Syndicalism in Ireland* 1). Dethroning rational self-interest, syndicalism established passion as the driving force in a radical movement which sought not just to change working conditions, but to transform the power relationship between the ownership class and the working class. To inspire that kind of commitment, syndicalism had to cultivate in the working poor a wide range of intense emotions and passionate attachments. To unsympathetic observers, the affective revolution catalysed by syndicalism represented chaos, anarchy and tyranny on the part of Larkin, who was so thoroughly identified with syndicalism in Ireland that the employer-controlled press referred to it as 'Larkinism'.[2]

The centrality of Larkin's personality to a movement which – despite its inclusion of women and children – was and still is almost always represented as a mass of working-class *men* underscored the homosocial aspect of labour politics during the syndicalist era.³ The labour leader, in journalism and in drama as well as actuality, typically appeared as a man speaking to men.⁴ The gender politics of theatre history helped ensure that the 'worker', in left theatre, was usually male, while women more commonly appeared as love interests or dependents. James Connolly helped organise a linenworkers' strike in Belfast in 1911; but it was not until the formation of the all-female Charabanc Theatre Company in 1983 that anyone tried to write a play about it.

While James Connolly hammered out his own revolutionary theories in a series of influential books and pamphlets, Jim Larkin employed his more gregarious gifts in his agitational speeches and his paper, *The Irish Worker*. *The Irish Worker* was one of many ways in which Larkin perpetuated and transformed the legacy of queer socialism. Larkin's leadership style and his speaking style placed him firmly in the romantic tradition of Shelley and Morris, whose work he knew well. In Larkin's editorial 'Revolution!', published on the eve of the Lockout, he describes retreating after a long day to refresh himself with 'a cheap copy of Morris's *News from Nowhere* and *The Dream of John Ball*' (Larkin, 'Revolution!', 2). Larkin shared queer socialism's faith in fellowship and in the power of beauty, and was generous with the *Irish Worker*'s space when it came to arts and culture. Though neither Yeats nor Gregory went as far in supporting the Lockout as their colleague AE, they shared Larkin's hatred of commercialism – especially when it was incarnated in Larkin's nemesis William Martin Murphy, who opposed funding a gallery for the Lane pictures as much as he opposed allowing the ITGWU to organise his employees. Contributors to the *Worker* included Sean O'Casey (writing as 'S. Ó Cathasaigh'), A. Patrick Wilson (writing as 'Euchan') and Delia Larkin (founder of the Irish Workers' Dramatic Company).

Larkin's self-dramatisation blended the aesthetics and the fellowship of queer socialism with a more conventionally masculine capacity for violence. Larkin's voice also resonates with the cadences of a Christian evangelism that would have repelled Shelley and Carpenter. The title of Wilson's *The Slough* derives from a *Pilgrim's Progress* reference which turned up a few times in Larkin's speeches during 1911:

> We are going to rouse the working classes out of their slough of despond – out of the mire of poverty and misery – and lift them a plane higher. If it is good for the employer to have clean clothing and good food, and books and music, and pictures, so it is good that the people should have these things also . . . (Larkin, 'Workers' Victory, Sunday Meeting')

Giving these utopian yearnings a specifically Christian form increased queer socialism's appeal to an Irish rank and file whose lives had been defined by religious affiliation.

Nevertheless, Larkin's assimilation of some aspects of queer socialism distinguishes him from Connolly, who had no use for it whatsoever. Romanticism, to Connolly, simply represented an era in which 'Socialism was the fad of the rich instead of the faith of the poor' (*Labour in Irish History*, 105). Connolly's *Labour in Irish History* (1910) delineates an Irish socialist tradition which has little intercourse with Shelley, Morris, Carpenter or Wilde. In Connolly's narrative, Irish socialism is always-already militant, having arisen as resistance to the violent imposition by the British of an alien and exploitative economic system. While socialists elsewhere were dreaming of an ideal world, according to Connolly, Ireland's misery produced instead a grim recognition of 'the political and social subjection of labour as the worst evil of society' and an abhorrence of 'the disastrous consequences to political freedom of the presence in society of a wealthy class' (ibid., 90–1). Nineteenth-century English socialists were only intimidated by 'the Irish workers' impatience of compromise and eagerness for action' (ibid., 134). *Labour in Irish History* claims nearly every insurrection in Irish history as a socialist uprising, and insists that most failed because their leaders were less eager for military action than the working-class rank and file were (ibid., 42–58). Connolly's Irish socialism was for fighters, not for lovers.

We can see the contrast to Larkin's approach in Connolly's 'Tram Strike,' published in the *Irish Worker* on 30 August 1913:

> The fault of the Transport Union! What is it? Let us tell it in plain language. Its fault is this, that it found the labourers of Ireland on their knees, and has striven to raise them to the erect position of manhood; it found them with all the vices of slavery in their souls, and it strove to eradicate these vices and replace them with some of the virtues of free men; it found them with no other weapons of defence than the arts of the liar, the lickspittle, and the toady, and it combined them and taught them to abhor those arts and rely proudly on the defensive power of combination; it, in short ... out of ... the labourers of Dublin, the Transport Union has created an army of intelligent self-reliant men ... (Connolly, 'Tram Strike', 2)

Whereas Larkin is wont to range widely, this passage displays a single-minded focus on syndicalism's power to 'raise' Ireland's 'degraded' workers to 'the erect position of manhood', enabling them to reject deceit, flattery and manipulation – 'arts' which are feminising precisely because they are the last resort of those incapable of physically resisting their oppressors.

A. Patrick Wilson admired this 'plain language':

> The [*Irish*] *Worker* is straight; it is clear; it is to the point. Its virility is astonishing, and it 'gets there' every time. That is why some people don't

like it – it is too straight for them; it catches them on the hop. In other words, to use a vulgar expression, now almost obsolete, 'it catches them bending'. (Wilson, 'Some Casual Comments on Rolling Stones and Other Things', 1)

The use of 'straight' to mean 'heterosexual' is in the future; but that meaning did not arise arbitrarily. 'Virility' *is* straightforward: assertive, pithy, laconic. 'Straight', in this context, is the opposite of feminine; but it is also the opposite of the crooked employer, whose deviousness allows him to defraud *real* men and thereby accumulate the economic power that compensates for his feminising avoidance of physical labour. Virility is also antagonistic to those who are *not* straight, something perhaps implied in Wilson's cryptically 'vulgar' reference to the *Worker* 'catching' its bourgeois critics 'bending'.

But syndicalism's 'virility' could not eradicate the legacy of queer socialism, because some of it was preserved in syndicalism's conception of direct action. The ideal syndicalist union was an expandable organisation spreading promiscuously in all directions to incorporate all the workers it could absorb. Syndicalism strove to scale up Morris and Carpenter's ideal of male 'fellowship', transmuting comrade love into fraternal solidarity. The ideal of workers everywhere feeling *for* and *with* each other is implicit in the syndicalist concept of 'sympathetic' action. Sympathetic action included walking out simultaneously with workers at another shop who had come out on strike; it also extended to boycotting 'tainted' goods, so that even if an employer kept production going, he could not get the product to market. Syndicalism staked everything on the workers feeling so closely connected to each other that they would act as if, in the words of the IWW slogan, 'An injury to one is an injury to all.'

This infinite network of relations between workers was, of course, the antithesis of the kinship model foundational to most capitalist states, where property ownership is regulated through the biological and marital relationships that define the family unit. As perpetual agitation meant keeping workers in a nearly-constant state of arousal, syndicalism also had to find some way of mobilising the *eros* that defined queer socialism. Larkin made arrestingly obvious the ways in which the labour leader's job – like the actor's – depended on his ability to persuade large numbers of working-class men to share his own passions. The mass meetings, marches and assemblies that made up syndicalist 'street theater' (Yeates, *A City in Wartime*, 6) helped produce the workers' sense of themselves as a community through their shared emotional response to Larkin. O'Connor argues that Larkin's self-dramatisation was important in enabling Dublin's beleaguered poor to identify with their idealised perception of him: 'As an agitator, [Larkin] associated the workers with his heroic style and gave them a sense of moral purpose by presenting himself as the embodiment of moral resurrection' (O'Connor, *Syndicalism in Ireland*, 9).

While it was crucial to his success as an organiser, however, Larkin's theatricality also hurt the movement. It created massive interpersonal conflicts, especially with Connolly, and antagonised British trades' unions, whose frustration with Larkin accelerated the ITGWU's final defeat (Yeates, *Lockout*, 496–538). Larkin's pungent anti-employer invective made employers unwilling to negotiate, and his love of the limelight made him a rich target for his opposition. Larkin's theatricality is continually satirised in Arnold Wright's 1914 book *Disturbed Dublin: The Story of the Great Strike of 1913–14*, a tendentious 'history' of the Lockout subsidised by Dublin employers. Wright draws attention to the theatrical nature of syndicalist agitation in an attempt to neutralise the movement's political content by reducing it to entertainment. Wright implies that the poor who flocked to the ITGWU's events were merely seeking sensory stimulation:

> To most of the slum denizens the intrusion into their lives of a labour movement of the more strenuous kind – with its marchings and its countermarchings, its shouting and cheering, and its periodic thrills – is a welcome change from the drab monotony of ordinary existence in which the normal excitement is provided by a wedding or a funeral or a drunken brawl on Saturday night. (Wright, *Disturbed Dublin*, 42–3)

Wright was not wrong about Larkin's entertainment value. Larkin's fidelity to the style of queer socialism ensured that every speech he gave was a continuation of war that Morris, Carpenter, Wilde, Howard, Parker and Unwin had waged against the 'drab monotony' produced by industrial capitalism. But when Wright draws attention to the 'thrills' electrifying the bodies of the marching and cheering spectators, it is to de-intellectualise them, analogising the spectators' affective responses to the 'excitement' of a 'drunken brawl' and rendering Larkin's performance degrading rather than uplifting.

This happens again in Wright's treatment of the Lockout's own 'Bloody Sunday'. Larkin had promised to speak in Sackville Street on 31 August, but the meeting was banned. Under a fake name, Larkin reserved a suite with a balcony at the Murphy-owned Imperial Hotel. Two Abbey actors helped make up Larkin as 'a respectable elderly gentleman'; thus disguised, he checked in, attained his suite, and rushed to the window for his balcony scene. When the crowd responded, the police blocked it in and baton-charged it, wounding hundreds (Yeates, *Lockout*, 61–8). To exonerate the police, Wright returns in his description of this event to the image of Larkin as a master thespian manipulating impressionable audiences:

> A dramatic – it may even be said a melodramatic – touch never fails to appeal to a popular Irish audience ... Therefore, though he knew that the club men and the society people, and even the business men, would

smile contemptuously at his theatrical ruse, the people he cared for – his followers – would discover in it a heaven-sent inspiration and would be bound closer to him accordingly. (Wright, *Disturbed* Dublin, 139–40)

Wright deftly replaces 'dramatic' with 'melodramatic', associating syndicalist street theatre with the overblown histrionics, overt sensationalism and crude oversimplifications of the mode that realism and its truths have supposedly displaced. He also denigrates the 'popular Irish audience' whose 'impressionable' natures render them susceptible to melodrama's 'theatrical ruse[s]' – which evidently have no power over the more sophisticated 'business men'. Larkin's theatricality becomes proof of his insincerity, rendering him a charlatan whose only motivation is to line his pockets with money taken from his credulous audiences. At the same time, this passage betrays the fear and bewilderment with which Larkin's success inspired his opponents, who cannot account for the intense response to a performance so flamboyant that it *should not* have been effective.

Larkin's theatricality was a source of both inspiration and anxiety to all of the playwrights under consideration here. St. John Ervine chose to deal with it, in *Mixed Marriage*, precisely by *not* representing Larkin – or at least, by representing him as something other than a complete man. Though inspired by Larkin's first appearance in the role of labour leader, *Mixed Marriage* goes to great lengths to prevent any single character from exerting that kind of dramatic power. Instead, Ervine adopts a divide and conquer approach, splitting Larkin into two different male characters and then using the family plot to undermine and contain both.

Bigger than the World: Mixed Marriage, Irrationalism and the Family Plot

A Protestant born and raised in Belfast, St. John Ervine was, in 1911, a socialist, a Fabian and a devoted follower of George Bernard Shaw. *Mixed Marriage* is set during a strike in Belfast and 'looked back to 1907' (Levitas, *The Theatre of Nation*, 186–7); but it is not identified as a dramatisation of the NUDL strike. Indeed, Ervine keeps the strike as generic as possible. The union is not identified; we don't know which trades are involved; the strike's objective is mentioned only twice. Larkin is never named. Ervine cannot have been unaware of Larkin's impact on the Belfast labour movement; his later writing shows not only that he followed Larkin's career but that he retained considerable knowledge of working-class conditions in Belfast at the time of the 1907 strike (Ervine, *Sir Edward Carson*, 116–19). Larkin's absence from *Mixed Marriage* was therefore not a simple reflection of actuality; it was intentional, and it is worth interrogating.

Mixed Marriage is set in the home of the working-class and Protestant

Rainey family. We don't know where John Rainey and his sons Hugh and Tom work, though Rainey's status and the family's relative prosperity suggest the shipyards. Hugh, who is courting the Catholic Nora, is also friendly with the Catholic Michael O'Hara, a member of the socialist Independent Labour Party. O'Hara asks John Rainey to speak to his Protestant comrades about the importance of overcoming sectarianism and cooperating with Catholic workers during the strike. Despite his anti-Catholic prejudices, Rainey agrees, and seems quite happy in his new role until he discovers that Hugh is engaged to Nora. Rainey publicly denounces the strike as a Papist plot. Days later, the Rainey house is besieged by an angry Protestant mob. When police threaten to fire on the crowd, Nora rushes out and offers herself as a sacrificial victim: 'It wus my fault, a tell ye' (Ervine, *Mixed Marriage*, 54). She is shot by the soldiers and dies in Hugh's arms.

The doomed romance between Hugh and Nora has historically been treated as more important than the labour dispute. For Joe Cleary, *Mixed Marriage* is a domestic tragedy about the North; the strike matters because it engages the structural foundations of bigotry, complicating what might otherwise be a 'banal ethical or moral critique of individualised sectarianism' (Cleary, *Outrageous Fortune*, 240). Structurally, however, the play supports Levitas's assessment of it as a 'complex treatment of labor relations' worked out through 'the prism of domestic conflict' (Levitas, 'Plumbing the Depths', 139). The strike plot is established first; the romance is a complication. The fact that, in 1911, Dublin was undergoing its own dockers' strike would have foregrounded the strike plot (Levitas, *The Theatre of Nation*, 186–7). Like Cleary, however, Levitas sees the play as engaging labour in the service of national allegory: 'The generational conflict between father and son emphasised that a Young Ireland, free of prejudice, could be waiting in the wings' (Levitas, 'Plumbing the Depths', 140).

Without disputing the importance of sectarian and national politics, I argue that *Mixed Marriage*'s plot was also shaped by Ervine's anxiety about the potential for radical change represented by syndicalism. *Mixed Marriage* shifts the strike play's focus from interpersonal conflict between two male figures – the labour leader and the captain of industry – to the strike's effect on a single working-class family.[5] By looking at *Mixed Marriage* as a strike play, we can see this shift as a Fabian's defensive reaction against a revolutionary movement that threatened to make gradualism impossible. In particular, *Mixed Marriage*'s representation of the working-class family expresses fear of Larkin's signature strategy: the excitement of emotion in large groups of working-class men.

Systemic employment discrimination in Belfast consigned most Catholic workers to the ranks of unskilled labour, reserving skilled work for Protestants. But the split between unskilled and skilled labour in Belfast did not align neatly with the sectarian divide. Though most Catholics were unskilled workers, most unskilled workers were Protestant (Gray, *City in Revolt*, 23). The desperate conditions that made unskilled labour susceptible to syndicalism affected Protestants as well as Catholics. The disruptive potential of Larkin's particular brand of excitement thus appeared even greater than the threat of sectarian violence with which Ervine, like any other Belfast native, was familiar. In *Mixed Marriage* Ervine seeks to limit the destabilising effect of Larkin's contagious discontent by subordinating homosocial relationships – which threatened to proliferate uncontrollably among an ever-expanding group of strikers – to heterosexual ones bounded by the romantic dyad and/or the nuclear family unit. By highlighting the heterosexual 'mixing' named in the play's title, the play strives to suppress the more daunting possibility of a revolutionary 'mixing' of Catholic and Protestant working men.

Before 1907, the Belfast labour movement was dominated by skilled labour – a well paid and overwhelmingly Protestant 'artisan elite' whose craft unions cultivated cozy relations with paternalistic employers (ibid., 47–52). The stranglehold that the National Question had on Belfast electoral politics, meanwhile, made it impossible to establish a robust Labour party. Unlike most of his NUDL colleagues, Larkin took the syndicalist view of organising – as a 'necessary prerequisite for the revolutionary transformation of society' (ibid., 2–3). Larkin thus brought a revolutionary vision to a place where gradualism had mellowed into stagnation. To Belfast's unskilled workers – all underpaid, underemployed and very poorly served by parliamentary politics – Larkin endeared himself with his signature blend of anti-employer invective, pugnacity and 'optimism' (ibid., 57) about the struggle. Within a few months, Larkin had ignited a firestorm of working-class discontent that spread far beyond the NUDL.

Despite the 'spontaneous and non-sectarian mobilization' of public support (ibid., 205), the strike ended in defeat. John Gray blames NUDL general secretary James Sexton, who was desperate to resolve the strike before it bankrupted the union (ibid., 100–2). Another factor was the near-mutiny of the overextended Belfast police. On 19 July, the suspension of Constable William Barrett led to a mass demonstration involving more than half the police force (ibid., 115–22). Belfast and Dublin authorities mobilised 2,500 troops to Belfast (ibid., 129). The presence of the army inflamed sectarian animosity, and on 11 August a two-day battle broke out between residents of the Catholic/nationalist Falls Road area and the police. This created a 'new atmosphere' of sectarian mistrust which eroded popular support for the strike (ibid., 169). After the strike failed, defeated Protestant workers vented their frustration in sustained and brutal persecution of their Catholic colleagues, especially in the shipyards.

When he invents the fictional strike of *Mixed Marriage*, Ervine makes inflamed sectarian tensions the cause, rather than a consequence, of the strike's failure. Larkin's ability to recruit Protestant and Catholic workers for the same cause is not represented. The closest thing *Mixed Marriage* offers us to a labour leader is Michael; but his role is strangely ambiguous. His relationship to the union is unclear. Michael's Catholicism hampers his efforts in a way that Larkin's did not. Cleary argues that Catholics in Northern drama 'share many of the constraints that usually apply to women characters', and one is that Michael cannot act in the public sphere except by manipulating someone else (Cleary, *Outrageous Fortune*, 250). Michael is thus forced to recruit Rainey for the most important and dangerous aspect of the labour leader's role: speaking to 'the men'. Rainey is given Larkin's ability to share his passions with other working-class men, while Michael becomes a photographic negative of Larkin's public persona: mild-mannered, self-effacing and pacifist, with all the charisma of a damp rag. Michael resembles Larkin only in his vision of a utopian world full of 'happy men an' weemen ... an' the childher runnin' about in the sun' (ibid., 12).

Mixed Marriage, then, doesn't exclude Larkin so much as disassemble him, splitting his role between Michael and Rainey. This separation of ideology from efficacy manages a not unreasonable anxiety about the potential effect of a revolutionary labour movement on a city where sectarianism was a built-in mechanism for escalation, and Protestant extremists routinely used violence to end political challenges to the unionist establishment (Gray, *City in Revolt*, 17, 33, 47–52). Given the already low threshold for political violence in Belfast, it is not surprising that Ervine's attitude towards revolution was even more conservative than Shaw's: 'Bloody revolutions ... are expensive and incalculable things, likely at any moment to end in the violent death of those who begin them' (Ervine, *Sir Edward Carson*, 59). Splitting up Larkin doesn't prevent bloodshed, but it does make revolution impossible. Michael, without Rainey's power, is incapable of conducting the strike; and Rainey, without Michael's vision, cannot start a revolution – only another sectarian riot which will be put down like all the others.

By assigning Larkin's gift for oratory to Rainey, Ervine conflates the irrationalism of syndicalism with the fearmongering of unionism. The ideal of masculine 'fellowship' which syndicalism sought to mobilise is, in *Mixed Marriage*, always-already subordinated to its evil twin, a toxic homosocial collective whose members are united not by shared love but by shared hatred. This is, of course, the Orange Order, represented in *Mixed Marriage* as the brutal enforcer of patriarchal authority. Like Shaw's, Ervine's critique of patriarchy is founded on the resentment of the son rather than on sympathy for wives and daughters. The Orange Order – from which, as Mrs Rainey complains, women are excluded (Ervine, *Mixed Marriage*, 42) – confers on Rainey an annihilating masculinity which his sons cannot challenge. Amplified by the passions of his fellow Orangemen, Rainey's determination to impose his will on his son becomes political when Hugh is beaten on the Customs House steps for speaking against him (ibid., 51). Even the police function, symbolically, as an extension of Rainey's patriarchal authority; by killing Nora during the riot, they give Rainey what he wished for. But the son's resentment of the father's authority is always complicated by his knowledge that it will one day be his own; and Ervine will not or cannot imagine a universe which the father does not control. In this dramatic universe, as Cleary notes, 'social transformation can only be accomplished if the father lends it his support' (*Outrageous Fortune*, 239). Rainey's tragedy is not that his patriarchal privilege is destroyed, but that it is unassailable.

Associating irrationalism with sectarian politics renders it tremendously destructive. However, Ervine's move also protects one of Fabianism's core principles from the challenge that syndicalism represented. Like Shaw's, Ervine's support for Home Rule was based on belief in a binary opposition between the rational politics of class and the irrational politics of nation and religion. It's precisely because 'real politics' – i.e., social politics – are temporarily obscured in Ireland by bogus nationalist and sectarian conflicts that, from Ervine's point of view, Irish politics are so embarrassingly aberrant (Ervine, *Sir Edward Carson*, 27). Ervine saw the Irish political landscape as a perverse collage of 'false unities and false cleavages' generated by the unresolved national question (ibid.). Once Home Rule failed to justify their apocalyptic predictions, Carson and all his kind would simply melt away in the pure light of reason beaming from the risen Home Rule sun. Like Shaw, Ervine justified this fantasy by defining 'industry and thrift' (ibid., 21–2) as essential Protestant attributes which must inevitably lead even the most misguided bigot to a rational politics based on economic self-interest. *Sir Edward Carson* makes this point by naming land reform as the *real* 'revolution proceeding in Ireland', which will transform it 'from an incoherent, unorganised, poverty-stricken nation into one which is united and planned and prosperous' (ibid., 43–4). Prosperity is the only legitimate goal of any revolution – a goal to which Carson has contributed 'absolutely nothing' (ibid.).

The startling effectiveness of Larkin's oratory threatened that opposition between socialist and sectarian politics by suggesting that socialist politics also had an emotional dimension. Separating irrationalism from Michael preserves that binary division between reason and feeling, while also separating class politics from violence. Michael is concerned that 'the workers may get led astray be religious rancour' (Ervine, *Mixed Marriage*, 9), but not that the strike itself might generate class warfare. Violence is always and only a tool used to undermine solidarity:

> They set the Cathliks agin the Prodesans, an' the Prodesans agin the Cathliks, so's ye can't git the two to work thegither for good o' their

class. Look at the way it is in the shipyards. Ye git men workin' thegither peaceably all year til the Twelfth o' July, an' then they start batin' wan another fur the love o' God. (Ibid., 11)

Belfast employers certainly did exploit sectarian hatred for their own ends. My point is that in this speech, Michael presumes a stable opposition between violence – always incited for spurious national and sectarian reasons – and labour action, which always manifests as peaceful cooperation. When violence threatens in *Mixed Marriage* it always has a clear sectarian and/or nationalist origin. Michael is beaten for stopping some 'wee lads' from 'singin' a party tune, an' cursin' the Pope' (ibid., 28). The mob that besieges the Rainey house in Act IV is yelling for 'Fenians' (ibid., 46). When Michael intervenes in the riot, he is met with 'shouts of "Fenian" and "To hell with the Pope"' (ibid., 50). The troops that kill Nora are not breaking a strike, but putting down a sectarian riot.

This representation of labour politics as above and outside of violence was a fantasy. Many of the early gains in the 1907 Belfast strike resulted from the strikers' intimidation of replacement workers (Gray, *City in Revolt*, 62–72). Larkin, far from crusading against anti-employer and/or anti-scab violence, fuelled it with inflammatory invective, approved the strikers' decision to go around 'armed with staves' (ibid., 138) and participated in an altercation between union members and a replacement worker (ibid., 66–8). It is unlikely that Ervine was unaware of all this, since in *Sir Edward Carson* he deplores 'acts of sabotage and personal violence with which workmen in Belfast have from time to time conducted strikes' (19).

Because anti-Larkin propaganda dwelled so luridly on the incitement question, it is difficult to discuss this aspect of Larkin's organising objectively. It is nevertheless undeniable that Larkin advocated a militant response to the violence visited on striking workers. In Ireland, by 1913, both the unionists and the nationalists had organised their own militias (the Ulster Volunteer Force and the Irish Volunteers, respectively), and political factions across the spectrum were busily romancing the gun. Yeates, for instance, cites a Lockout speech in which, after noting that Carson has called on 'the men of Ulster' to arm themselves, Larkin calls on his listeners to do likewise for the coming showdown with police, recommending that 'whenever one of your men is shot, shoot two of theirs' (Yeates, *Lockout*, 21). Larkin's support for the intimidation of replacement workers testifies to a tension in syndicalism between an idealistic conception of solidarity as universal, spontaneous, inclusive and loving, and a more pragmatic and limited understanding of solidarity as a weapon. If we refuse to acknowledge that incendiary speech was a Larkin signature trait, or that he considered aggression part of the syndicalist toolkit, we cannot understand the anxiety that his activism provoked – in the employer class, or in the hearts of socialists like Ervine who wanted economic justice but feared 'real, red terror' (Ervine, *Sir Edward Carson*, 59).

Identifying Larkin's oratory with bigotry, and identifying syndicalism's irrationalism with sectarianism, allows Ervine to present socialism as ethically pure, leaving Michael the satisfaction of occupying the high ground. But by depriving Michael of Larkin's problematic passions, Ervine purges Michael's socialism of *eros*. In fact, Michael is put in direct opposition to *eros*, which proves to be an indefensible position. In a last-ditch attempt to regain Rainey's allegiance, Michael calls on Nora to put the collective good ahead of her desires and refuse to marry Hugh. Mrs Rainey upbraids him:

> MRS. RAINEY: Ye're wrong til be suggestin' partin' til them. Can't ye see, they're doin' the very thing ye want Irelan' t' do. It's Cathlik an' Prodesan joinin' han's thegither. It's quare ye should be wantin' til separate them.
> MICHAEL: It's acause a want a bigger joinin' o han's. It's not enough fur a man an' a wumman til join han's. A want til see the whole wurl' at peace.
> MRS. RAINEY: Ye'll only git that be men an' weemen bein' at peace. Him an' her, Mickie, are bigger than the wurl', if ye on'y knew it.
> (Ervine, *Mixed Marriage*, 40)

Michael's vision of 'the whole wurl' at peace' references not the goal of 'national unity' (Cleary, *Outrageous Fortune*, 244) but the universal fellowship dreamed of by Morris and Carpenter and assimilated by syndicalism. Since his initial appearance, Michael has been driven by the conviction that the only way to pursue this goal is to persuade *men* to join hands with each other. Michael is opposing the affectionate, anti-competitive comradeship promoted by queer socialism to the 'one man and one woman' model of marriage – only to be told by Mrs Rainey that the heterosexual dyad is 'bigger than the wurl''.

This exchange thus stages the defeat of comrade love by heterosexual love. When Mrs Rainey names the heterosexual family unit as an antidote to the poisonous passions nurtured in 'churches an' Or'nge Lodges' (ibid.) and the seed from which any better future must spring, she is supported by realism's obsession with the family, by hundreds of years of dramatic marriage plots, and by the play's naturalisation of heterosexuality and gender difference. The only support Ervine allows Michael is an unexpected burst of misogyny: 'Whinivir a man come near deliverin' Irelan', a wumman's stepped in an' destroyed him... There'll be no salvation fur Irelan' til a man is born that dussen care a God's curse fur weemen' (ibid.). In addition to rather nervously assuring us that no such men yet exist, Michael's invocation of the Kitty O'Shea debacle associates him with the blinkered Catholic hierarchy that brought down Parnell.

By looking at *Mixed Marriage* in its labour context, then, we can see that the working-class family home and the individual family did not emerge inevitably as the template for Irish working-class drama. Nor does the working-class mother's universalising humanism; nor does the identification of a passive and negative pacifism as the only responsible form of socialist practice. All of these things arise from Ervine's fear of syndicalism's irrationalism. The formula that Ervine concocts in *Mixed Marriage* is in part a defence against Larkin's disruptive potential, and a strategic suppression of a competing model of affiliation based on class rather than genealogy, and structured by homosocial rather than heterosexual love.

It is no surprise that this suppression is achieved through the imposition of reactionary gender politics. With Ervine so protective of the father's authority, no alternative to Rainey's bigotry can emerge from the play's men, who are trapped in a patriarchal order in which everyone is either an emasculated son or an invincible father. The alternative emerges instead from the women, who – because their subordination to patriarchal authority is taken for granted – are disqualified from dominance games. Femininity in *Mixed Marriage* is wholly identified with the nurturing which is painfully absent from relations between men. Mrs Rainey makes it clear to Nora that her religious affiliation is far less important than her ability to continue caring for Hugh: 'A wud be very angry if ye wurn't able til luk after him' (ibid., 19). 'What differs does it make what religion [Nora] is', Mrs Rainey shouts at her husband, 's'long as she's a good wife til him. D'ye think if A cudden cook yer dinner fur ye an' keep the house clane an' bring yer childher up, it 'ud be any consolation t'ye that A wus a Prodesan' (ibid., 35).

Mrs Rainey's insistence on the importance of nurturing undermines Rainey's bigotry by putting the Catholic/Protestant opposition in conflict with the all-important gender binary. There are two problems introduced by this tactic which will bedevil left realism for decades to come. One is that the working-class mother is so completely defined by her nurturing function that she is forced to oppose anything that interferes with it, including the labour movement. 'There ought to be some other way o' settlin' these things nor stracks', Mrs. Rainey insists, complaining that '[y]ou men don't have to face the rent agent an' the grocer wi' no money' (ibid., 6). The other is the infantilisation of working-class men as 'big childher' (20) who can't survive without female nurturing. Rainey literally can't tie his own shoes; Act II ends with Mrs Rainey kneeling down to help him take his boots off (ibid., 24). In a society where Rainey can always augment his own power by calling in the Orange Order, infantilising the father does not actually strip him of agency. But when this model is taken up by Wilson in *The Slough*, the loss of the Belfast context universalises the gender politics of *Mixed Marriage*, representing the working-class father as so weak that not even syndicalism can save him.

My Daddy's on Strike: Larkin, Family Values and The Slough

In 1911, a Scottish actor named Andrew P. Wilson came to Dublin as part of a 'third-rate theatrical company' and got stranded (Wilson quoted in Burch, *Andrew P. Wilson*, 53). Restyling himself A. Patrick Wilson in order to pass as Irish, he joined the Abbey Theatre's second company while working as a freelance journalist (ibid., 54). He found his way to Liberty Hall and joined the Irish Workers' Dramatic Company (Levitas, 'Plumbing the Depths', 141), churning out columns for the *Irish Worker* while ingratiating himself at the Abbey. In 1914, Wilson was appointed to replace Lennox Robinson as the Abbey's managing director. He produced *The Slough* at the Abbey in November, with himself in the role of Jim Larkin – or rather, 'Jake Allen' (Levitas, 'Plumbing the Depths', 142–3).

The Slough begins on the eve of a strike led by 'Jake Allen's General Union'. It opens in tenement rooms occupied by the Hanlons, a poor Catholic family headed by the alcoholic Peter Hanlon and his wife Mary. There are three Hanlon children: the self-absorbed Jack; the cynical Peg; and the consumptive Anne, who is in love with Tom Robinson, a skilled worker in the General Union. Act II is set in the General Union's committee room, where Jake Allen conducts union business while waiting for the result of the strike vote. By the time Peter Hanlon arrives, he has been expelled from the union. After the drunk and belligerent Hanlon is ejected, Allen opens the window so he can announce that the union has voted overwhelmingly to strike, 'in spite of all the scabs in Ireland' (Wilson, *The Slough*, Act II, 54). Act III jumps to the end of the strike, after 'the men are beaten' (Wilson, *The Slough*, Act III, 57).[6] The situation is strongly reminiscent of the final act of *Mixed Marriage*: Tom and the Hanlon family are huddled inside the Hanlons' tenement as a mob of strikers surrounds it. When one of the ringleaders calls Tom a scab, Tom rushes out to confront him, and is arrested. The shock causes Anne to expire.

The aliases fooled nobody; even the not-overbright Joseph Holloway had no difficulty in recognising Allen as Jim Larkin, or in detecting the influence of *Mixed Marriage* (Holloway, *Abbey Theatre*, 167). As in *Mixed Marriage*, the conflict is driven by the father's hostility towards the union. As in *Mixed Marriage*, a fragile Catholic heroine is involved in a doomed romance which is blocked by the father figure, and whose consummation is postponed until after the strike. As in *Mixed Marriage*, the father's betrayal of the union leads to a mob attack on the family home, which leads to a police action, which claims the life of the heroine.

Wilson's adaptation of Ervine's structure was in part a means of coping with the special problems that the working-class family posed for a syndicalist union. Syndicalism diverged from queer socialism in that it accepted production and reproduction as givens; the goal was not to end work as we know it or to redefine sex and gender, but to ensure a better future for workers and their children. The history of the Lockout, as we will see, supports Lee Edelman's contention that reproductive futurism is a trap. It is a trap, however, that no organisation dedicated to addressing economic inequality can easily or ethically avoid.

During Larkin's tenure, the ITGWU was bedeviled by the tragic disjunction between the symbolic power of the Child and the extreme disenfranchisement of its members' actual children. Dublin's unskilled labourers were the victims of an urban housing crisis even more horrific than the one that inspired *Widowers' Houses*. In 1913 'Dublin had the worst housing of any city in the United Kingdom' (Yeates, *A City in Wartime*, 9). Overcrowding, poor sanitation and neglect made slum tenements particularly noxious for infants – Dublin's infant mortality rate was also the worst in the UK (Kearns, *Dublin Tenement Life*, 12) – and children. To make a better future imaginable, the ITGWU had to promise some means of creating an environment that would not kill and/or blight the next generation of workers. The ITGWU invested in this promise by purchasing Croydon Park as a safe, green, healthy place in which the members' children could play (Wilson, 'The Jovial Revolution'). Shortly before the Lockout began, the *Irish Worker* ran a front-page column in which Wilson announced that 'The Social Revolution, so far as Ireland is concerned, was ushered in last Monday ... with a picnic' (ibid.). The 'fuller and more enjoyable life' that queer socialism demanded for adults is justified here by the needs of their children: 'We wanted a place for them to play, and we wanted a place for their fathers and mothers to learn to play also' (ibid.).

But embracing the politics of the Child carries its own risk. Because direct action usually meant loss of income, any attempt to ameliorate the working conditions that contribute to poverty and infant mortality could be re-presented by the employers and their sympathisers as anti-Child. The double bind in which the Child puts labour was realised in startlingly concrete form in October 1913 during the backlash against Dora Montefiore's 'Dublin Kiddies Scheme'. Montefiore had recruited families in England to house, feed and clothe the children of some of the striking Dublin families during the conflict. The idea of Irish children being parented by English socialists so inflamed the Catholic right that priests led mobs down to the boats and prevented them from embarking, defending the Child's symbolic value as the future of a Gaelic and Catholic Ireland at the expense of actual Irish children (Yeates, *Lockout*, 258–72).

Even before the Lockout began, Larkin took aim at the employers' attempts to blame the union for the suffering of children. In a February 1913 editorial, Larkin waxes poetic on the irony of employers shaming the union:

> Fancy William Martin Murphy sympathizing with a hungry child, the Ghoul, the creature who swated [sic] and starved a whole country side

during the strike of the railway slaves in Clare, the ghoul who has sacked hundreds of men for trivial complaints, knowing that such dismissal meant actual starvation for these dismissed men's children. (Larkin, 'My Daddy's on Strike')

Though he could not rise to such rhetorical heights, Wilson recognised the threat represented by this kind of propaganda (Wilson, 'A Procession and its Banners', 1). He tackled the Child problem head-on in his one-act play *Victims*, staged at Liberty Hall in 1912 by the Irish Workers' Dramatic Club (Levitas, 'Plumbing the Depths', 141–2).

In *Victims*, the infant child of mechanic Jack and seamstress Annie is 'dying of hunger' (Wilson, *Victims*, 7) because Jack has been blacklisted for his union activities (ibid., 10). Nobody in *Victims* refers to this infant by name; it is simply 'the child' (ibid., 8). The child is not a character, but the embodiment of a problem that syndicalism has to solve: the fact that the fight for the future threatens to destroy those who should inherit it. *Victims* tries to make capital's responsibility for the child's suffering visible by bringing representatives of the ownership class into the tenement; but that doesn't solve the problem of how to get to the utopian future without rendering the toxic present positively lethal. Jack tells the rent collector who has come to evict them that 'To-morrow can look after itself . . . to-night the place is mine' (ibid., 14). Moments later, Jack discovers that the child is dead. Tomorrow can't look after itself; the future won't arrive unless the workers agitate for it. And the here and now doesn't belong to Jack; it belongs to the employers who have starved his child out of it.

Mixed Marriage, as a model, offered Wilson a way out of this bind. *Mixed Marriage*'s plot represents the working-class family's struggle, but does not hold the union responsible for the family's disintegration. In this respect it was superior to the strongest model that British drama had to offer: John Galsworthy's strike play *Strife* (1909), of which Wilson wrote a glowing review for the *Worker* (Wilson, 'Strife'). Galsworthy's *Strife* focuses on the conflict between worker-agitator David Roberts and company owner John Anthony. Roberts and Anthony are commanding presences whose forceful oratory and personal magnetism dominate lesser men; both are such paragons of virility, in fact, that they have to be deposed by their followers before the strike can be resolved. *Strife* is set during the starvation phase of the strike, and Galsworthy mines the workers' suffering for pathos. Roberts's inflexibility causes his wife to perish of hunger and cold, and the other working-class women harass their husbands with increasing stridency as they try to avoid a similar fate.

Wilson had long admired *Strife*, but seeing it in Dublin he felt that syndicalism had rendered it 'out of date' (Wilson, 'Strife'). As a model for Wilson, *Mixed Marriage* was superior in that the bigotry plot absolves the union itself of responsibility for the tragic outcome. The suffering of the workers' children never even comes up in *Mixed Marriage*; thanks to the Orange Order, the strike in *Mixed Marriage* doesn't survive sectarianism long enough to starve anyone. However, transposing this plot to Dublin significantly adds to the father's troubles. First, Hanlon's masculinity is not protected, as Rainey's is, by his membership in a violent homosocial collective with a privileged relationship to state authority. Second, Hanlon's hostility towards the union, which is required by the *Mixed Marriage* plot, cannot be motivated by religious bigotry; the union's leadership and membership are overwhelmingly Catholic, and so is Hanlon. Wilson has to substitute another motive, and his choice reopens some of the questions that Ervine so carefully excluded. Hanlon is hated and hateful not for being a Catholic or a Protestant, but for being a scab.

Though technically a member of the union when the play opens, Peter Hanlon is identified as a scab by Jake Allen because he worked during the union's previous strike. For Allen, 'scab' is as stable an identity position as Catholic and Protestant were for Rainey; a man who's 'scabbed before' will 'scab again' (Wilson, *The Slough*, Act II, 39). Hanlon's scabhood motivates everything that was motivated by Rainey's bigotry in *Mixed Marriage*: the blocking of the marriage (Hanlon forbids the marriage only after he comes to believe that Tom is spreading rumours about him being a scab), the failure of the strike ('If it hadn't been for scabs like Peter Hanlon going in', Edward complains, 'the strike would have been won easily' (ibid., Act III, 58)), the violent siege of the working-class home (which begins as an attack on scab workers by 'a few of the boys' (ibid., Act III, 70)) and the death of the romantic heroine (Tom is called a 'scab' only because he's been visiting Hanlon's home to see Anne).

Wilson did not share Ervine's embarrassment about syndicalism's irrationalism, and neither did Larkin. The *Irish Worker* appears to have gone out of its way to cultivate in its readers a visceral disgust for the scab. The *Irish Worker* attacked the scab through every medium: ballads and poetry ('St. Peter and the Scab'), Larkin's editorials and speeches ('Why This Strike?'), parody and satire (Wilson's 'Lyres and Liars!'), and propaganda ('Shellback's' 'Few Remarks on Settlements of Labor Disputes'). This was not directed solely against individual workers. The larger problem was the proliferation of 'scab unions' – spurious unions established by employers for the purpose of competing with the ITGWU. Many of these were led by 'a small but intensely vocal group of Larkin's opponents within the labor movement' (Yeates, *Lockout*, 10–11). If the length and the intensity of the committee's debate over Hanlon's expulsion in Act II seem vastly out of proportion to his individual importance it's because Hanlon stands in for 'all the scabs in Ireland' (Wilson, *The Slough*, Act II).

Though the bigot and the scab serve the same structural function in this family plot, they have diametrically opposed relationships to masculinity. The bigot is *too much* of a man; the scab is not a man at all. 'Craobh na nDealg' exhorts readers not to scab with a bracing cry of 'Men, be men!' ('Craobh na nDealg', '"Independent" and "Herald notes"'). Anti-scab diatribes routinely question the scab's masculinity.[7] Scabs don't use violence, they fear it and 'skulk' like cowards in the shadows, lest better men give them what they deserve ('Description of a Scab', *Irish Worker*). 'Shellback' compares scabs to 'rats' fleeing 'to their lairs in the drains and sewers of civilization' once the employers' protection is withdrawn ('Shellback', 'The Crime of Blacklegging', 1). The scab is the Other of the ideal union man, who proudly gathers with 'sturdy sons of Labour' to parade through the streets demanding respect (Larkin, 'May Day Demonstration').

By substituting the scab for the bigot, Wilson replaces a working-class father who is too strong for his own good with a working-class father who is too weak for everyone's good. Unlike Rainey, Hanlon is so apathetic about his own patriarchal privileges that when Tom informs Hanlon of his engagement to Anne, he asks, 'And what's that got to do with me?' (Wilson, *The Slough*, Act I, 26). Hanlon is as dependent on Mary as Rainey is on his wife, but unlike him can't command anyone's respect or obedience. As in the *Worker*, the scab's lack of these masculine attributes emphasises the idealised masculinity embodied by the union man – especially Jake Allen himself.

In his eagerness to respond to the criticism of Larkin that followed the Lockout's failure, Wilson makes Allen an idealised and sanitised character, depriving him of some of the sources of Larkin's power.[8] In particular, Wilson strips him of the theatricality that made Larkin such an effective organiser – and which had recently been used by the employer-controlled press as a stick with which to beat him. 'Jacques's' glowing review of *The Slough* in the *Irish Independent* appeared only two pages away from an equally glowing review of Wright's *Distressed Dublin*. Wilson tones Larkin down by keeping literary allusions, rhetorical flowers and evangelical cadences out of Jake Allen's dialogue, reducing Larkin's style to something closer to Connolly's 'plain language'. Allen's dialogue rises towards richness only in the one speech singled out by Levitas, which analogises the scab to a 'blood-poisoned' finger that has to be amputated lest it infect the rest of the body (quoted in Levitas, 'Plumbing the Depths', 144–5). But even that speech is prefaced by Allen's sober and reasonable defence of his decision:

> I recognise your point of view, and though you said you weren't a speaker, you've put your case very clearly, but you're letting your private sympathy for Hanlon run away with your discretion as a trade-unionist. I recognise fully that there hardly ever was a scab yet that went scabbing because he liked it. They are as much a product of a rotten social state as a trade unionist himself, but the very existence of the working class depends upon keeping them under. (Wilson, *The Slough*, 42)

Larkin rarely wrote about scabs in language so temperate. Allen's characterisation is thus not 'realistic' either in the sense of being accurate or in the sense of belonging to that dramatic mode. The same could be said of Act II in general, which is built around an event which most likely never took place. Yeates, whose history of the Lockout is more sympathetic to Larkin than many another, concludes that there never was a strike vote, and that the 'fatal decision' to bring out the tramworkers was 'made by Larkin alone' (Yeates, *Lockout*, 9, 14–15). Wilson counters the perception of Larkin as a demagogue with an autocratic 'leadership style' (ibid., 14) by making a strike vote the main business of Act II – and reporting the results as 17,104 in favour to 462 against (Wilson, *The Slough*, Act II, 49).

Levitas claims that the move to the union hall and the inclusion of a 'chorus' of workers signal a 'shift out of realism that hints at an epic dimension' (Levitas, 'Plumbing the Depths', 145). It's a tempting argument. Wilson was frustrated with realism and its obsession with actuality (Wilson, 'The Drama – Old and New'). Including the union hall setting and the 'chorus' (Wilson's Act II set description specifies about a dozen) of workers does depart significantly from the *Mixed Marriage* model. However, similar 'choruses' appear in earlier realistic strike plays. George Moore's 1893 play *The Strike at Arlingford* rather improbably imports a deputation of striking workers into Lady Anne's drawing room to serve as an onstage audience for that play's labour leader figure, John Reid. *Strife* incorporates an open-air meeting at which Roberts holds forth, interrupted by interjections from the onstage audience of striking workers. These attempts at 'lend[ing] the necessary sense of scale to the proceedings' and 'dramatizing the social forces that constitute the union itself' (Levitas, 'Plumbing the Depths', 145) were received as realism; and so was *The Slough*'s committee meeting.[9]

To the extent that Jake Allen seems 'larger than life' (ibid.), I would suggest it is not because (as Levitas argues) he prefigures Brecht's Azdak (ibid.), but because his lack of complexity, his concern for women and children, and his preservation of the ideal balance between 'strong passions' and 'vigilant rational self-control' that defined the Victorian 'ideal of manhood' (Valente, *The Myth of Manliness*, 3) call back to the pre-Shavian days of the idealist hero. Like the strike vote, much of Jake Allen's behaviour in Act II defends Larkin's heroism against charges levelled against him during and after the Lockout. Like Larkin, Allen is contemptuous of procedure, cavalier about money, and partial to men who are at least as loyal to him as they are to the union. But where Azdak's justice is achieved through the ironic inversion of audience preconceptions, *The Slough* turns Larkin's foibles into proof that he shared the spectators' family values.

The first thing we see Allen do is forgive the debts of a member who fell behind in his dues while caring for his sick wife. When Crocker protests, Allen excoriates him for devaluing the natural feelings of a husband and father: 'This man has been practically victimised through the callous action of one of the Union's officials, and when I right the wrong a Member of this Committee asks if it's in order. What sort of men are you?' (Wilson, *The Slough*, Act II, 37). Crocker tries to stop Allen from putting Tom on the committee by accusing Tom of being a scab: '[H]e's blooming fond of the company of scabs anyway. He's never out of Hanlon's house, and what's he doing there if he's straight?' (ibid., Act III, 47). Crocker's concern would, according to the *Irish Worker*, seem to be justified; the first thing union men are always exhorted to do with a scab is shun him. And yet, Allen denounces Crocker's accusation as 'the meanest thing I ever did hear anywhere' (ibid.). Allen's defence of Tom corrects Michael O'Hara's mistake by implying that it's unreasonable to expect this 'type of healthy manhood' (Jacques in Irish Independent, 'A Powerful Play') to put his trade union ahead of heterosexual passion. Allen's sensitivity to the family man's needs makes Hanlon's irresponsible neglect of his own family all the more damning. Having translated the scab's treachery to his class into a form even the most bourgeois spectator can recognise and deplore, Wilson can now allow Allen to expel Hanlon with impunity.

Wilson, then, manages Larkin's scab problem by aligning Allen with the Victorian 'ideal of manhood' (Valente, *The Myth of Manliness*, 3). Crocker's suspicion of Tom is presented as political manoeuvering unworthy of the 'straight' union man; and when the crowd supports Crocker, Allen quashes it with a classic display of masculine dominance: 'Shut up, damn you! Are you a lot of wild beasts or what?' (Wilson, *The Slough*, Act II, 52). Similarly, Act II frames anti-scab violence as the triumph of virility over scurrility. When Allen tries to protect Hanlon from the wrath of the other members – 'For heaven's sake, leave him alone, Bill, the man's drunk' – Hanlon takes a swing at Allen, who 'catches at his wrist, and doubling his arm throws Hanlon over the table' (ibid., Act II, 54). By subduing Hanlon, Allen establishes his superior masculinity while presenting anti-scab violence as self-defence. A perfect balance between passion and self-restraint is achieved in Allen's next line: 'Take him out of here, for God's sake, before I do him an injury' (ibid.).

Despite Allen's expulsion of him, Hanlon's corrupted masculinity does poison the union; scabbing scuttles the strike, transforming Jake Allen's good union men into a mob no less violent than the one that surrounds the Rainey house. *Mixed Marriage*'s structure still protects socialism to some extent by making the angry mob a product of the strike's *failure*, not a constituent of its success. Ultimately, however, the play's final image endorses the employers' critique of the union as anti-Child: the strike destroys the working-class family, killing the daughter who should have inherited the better world for which this battle was supposedly fought.

You're on the Wrong Side:
Masculinity and Metatheater in The Labour Leader

Mixed Marriage and *The Slough* reinforce each other, consolidating a set of realistic conventions about the urban working-class family: the irresponsible father figure, the apolitical mother figure, the doomed younger generation and the family's inevitable destruction by the struggle itself. Violence is defined not as a tool of the struggle but as a premonition and/or a symptom of its failure. The emotional revolution that syndicalist agitation catalysed among the working poor in Larkin's theatres of action does not transfigure these working-class men; with Ervine defending his dramatic universe against Larkin, and Wilson defending Larkin against his antagonists, neither play is willing to consider the question of how Larkin made the men he spoke to feel, or how that might have changed what it meant to be a man.

Daniel Corkery's *The Labour Leader*, on the other hand, is fascinated by both questions. Consequently, *The Labour Leader* avoids the domestic environment entirely; the first two acts are set in the committee room of the fictional Quaymen's Union and the third is set backstage at the Atheneum Hall. Both are masculine spaces which women enter only briefly. The officers of the Quaymen's Union are grappling, not with the problem of the Child, but with the problem of Larkin himself, this time disguised as the Quaymen's Union's charismatic general secretary David 'Davna' Lombard. The Quaymen's Union is on strike, and trying to persuade the railwaymen – skilled workers with higher status – to engage in sympathetic action. While Davna is off haranguing the railwaymen, the union's sectional officers – Clarke, Dempsey and Murphy – decide that they need to rein Davna in by assigning him a personal secretary. In Act II, the rank and file are up in arms because the new secretary, O'Sullivan, had a member named Tobin arrested for leading an attack on scab workers. Davna proposes to free Tobin by organising an ambush on the police van that will transport him.[10] Davna's right-hand man Phil is so alarmed by this that he tips off the police. Clarke and Dempsey appoint Phil to Davna's position. Act III is set backstage at the hall where Clarke and Dempsey plan to introduce Phil to the members as their new leader. Davna, with a retinue of cudgel-wielding followers, forces himself backstage and calls Phil a scab. A boxing match between Davna and Phil ends in stalemate. On the other side of the partition, the assembled workers sing 'The Red Flag'. 'Don't you see, old men and little men', Davna cries. 'It is not given to you to lead *them*!' Phil agrees, promises to be loyal to Davna 'to the end', and goes with him through the door to greet the unseen crowd, while 'Dempsey, Clarke, and O'Sullivan remain on the stage, silent and defeated' (Corkery, *The Labour Leader*, 134).

The Labour Leader is deeply concerned with relations between men, and especially with the charismatic Davna's ability to inspire other men with passionate devotion. Much of the conflict stems from the union officers' fear, not only of Davna's power and popularity but of the fact that the members' love for him is so often mediated through violence. Unlike Ervine, Corkery acknowledges violence as part of class struggle; unlike Wilson, he does not make violence a marker of the strike's failure. The rank and file see the intimidation of scab workers as an indispensible tactic and object to being deprived of it. When Dempsey defends O'Sullivan on the grounds that arresting Tobin prevented 'riot and bloodshed', one of the workers complains that it was 'at our expense'; another says bluntly, 'What are we organised for?' (ibid., 46–7).

The Labour Leader offers the most sophisticated consideration we have yet seen of what Larkin's relationship with unskilled labour might reveal about the emotional landscape of working-class masculinity. Corkery presents Larkin's fidelity to both the substance and style of queer socialism as enriching a masculinity which the militarisation of revolutionary Ireland threatens to impoverish. Corkery's fascination with Larkin as performer is absorbed into the play's form, which becomes a critique of the Shavian model of left theater. *The Labour Leader* is not, as Levitas claims, yet another example of the conventions of 'classical naturalism' preventing the dramatisation of social forces (Levitas, 'Plumbing the Depths', 147). Instead, I will argue, *The Labour Leader* twists the conventions of realism until syndicalism's irrationalism manifests through them as the foundation of revolutionary theatre.

Unlike Ervine and Wilson, Corkery was Catholic. He wrote primarily about his native rural Cork, in which he discerned (as he argued in *Hidden Ireland*) the survival of a Gaelic and Catholic culture that had been forced underground during the eighteenth century. Though now known primarily for his fiction, Corkery co-founded the Cork Dramatic Society in 1909 and produced several of his plays there. Patrick Maume has argued that *The Labour Leader* is a crypto-republican play, in which the strike becomes 'an allegory of the struggle between constitutionalism and physical force' (Maume, '*Life that is Exile*', 63). *The Labour Leader* was written in 1917, produced at the Abbey by Lennox Robinson in 1919 and published in 1920; the War of Independence is as much a part of its context as the Lockout was, or the strikes in Cork on which the plot is based. *The Labour Leader* allowed Corkery to write a 'three-act play in praise of revolutionary enthusiasm' (ibid.) which – because it dealt with a revolution that was supposedly dead – would not provoke censorship.

The play's labour setting, however, is not incidental; nor is it as out of character as it might seem. The Lockout was not the end of radical labour in Dublin. The ITGWU survived, with Connolly in charge; Connolly led the Irish Citizen Army into the 1916 Easter Rising, and was executed in Kilmainham Gaol after it failed. We are now familiar with the contemporary critique of Connolly's participation in the Rising as a fatal misstep that subordinated labour's revolutionary agenda to a bourgeois nationalist movement.[11] This subordination continued into the 1918 general election, which Labour sat out in order to leave Sinn Féin a clear field (O'Connor, 'Labour and Politics', 34).

As Irish labour historians have argued, however, electoral politics have never been a good gauge of the strength of the Irish left. ITGWU membership exploded during the years following the Easter Rising, jumping from 5,000 in 1916 to 120,000 in 1920 (ibid.). Labour cooperated with Sinn Féin in a number of strikes that took place in 1919 and 1920, which O'Connor suggests were driven by 'pressure within the labour movement' and 'used to provide a safe outlet for rank-and-file militancy' (ibid., 35). Meanwhile, Helga Woggon argues, Connolly's rising importance forced Sinn Féin to the left. Nationalists could no longer repudiate the martyred Connolly's socialism; instead, Sinn Féin sought to expand its base by 'facilitating the incorporation of the labour movement into the national revolution' (Woggon, 'Interpreting James Connolly', 175). When the Dáil Éireann met for the first time, they unanimously adopted an agenda '[d]rafted by the Labour leader, Thomas Johnson' (Kiberd and Mathews, *Handbook*, 107) which asserted, among other things, that 'all right to private property must be subordinated to the public right and welfare' (reprinted in ibid., 106–7).

A less official index of this shift was Sinn Féin's flirtation with Bolshevism. The Russian Revolution of 1917 inspired in Ireland 'an element of enthusiasm that led to a series of workplace occupations, styling themselves 'soviets', during the War of Independence' (Woggon, 'Interpreting James Connolly', 176). Sinn Féin thereafter had to cope with 'a discernible sympathy among workers with the Bolshevik revolution' (ibid., 180). It was during 1919, when power relations and property ownership were in flux, that Irish Bolshevism reached its peak (O'Connor, *Reds*, 1–3). We can see the effects of the 'mind-confusing euphoria' (Woggon, 'Interpreting James Connolly', 181) of Yeats's least favourite year in the republican propagandist Aodh de Blacam's 1919 tract *Towards the Republic: A Study of New Ireland's Social and Political Aims*. In it, de Blacam claims that Bolshevism was 'born in Ireland', appropriates syndicalism's concept of the One Big Union for nationalist purposes, and 'equat[es] Connolly's concept of a workers' republic with a Gaelic state, Catholic social policy, the communist republic of Russia and the *Civitas Dei* of St. Augustine' (Woggon, 'Interpreting James Connolly', 180).

Strange as it may seem, then, in 1919 it made a certain amount of sense for an Irish writer with republican sympathies who was also personally dedicated to recovering a lost native Gaelic culture – i.e., Daniel Corkery – to take an interest in syndicalism. De Blacam's attempted synthesis of Bolshevism and Irish nationalism was based on a strain of Irish revolutionary writing that constructed Gaelic culture as a precapitalist and communal society whose values and structures were not unlike those championed by utopian socialists. Connolly's *Labour in Irish History* was part of that tradition; so were George

Russell's *The National Being* and Darrell Figgis's *The Gaelic State* (de Blacam, *Towards the Republic*, 66). In 1916, de Blacam says, the 'Worker's Republic' might have seemed 'a vague and even perilous ambition', but the 'new conditions' established by the War of Independence reveal it as an inevitable part of 'Gaelic evolution' (ibid., xiii). Communism, according to this logic, was part of what was hidden in that lost Gaelic Ireland.

According to Lionel Pilkington, 1919 was also the culmination of the Abbey Theatre's *rapprochement* with Sinn Féin (Pilkington, *Theatre*, 81–5). In 1919, when Yeats and Gregory had no idea how serious Sinn Féin was about making common cause with labour, the decision to produce *The Labour Leader* would have been in line with their goal of maintaining a 'scrupulous balance between the broadly progressive sinn affiliations of its directors ... and the political and publicity needs of Sinn Féin' (ibid., 84). Ironically, it was James Connolly who made it possible for Jim Larkin to finally possess the Abbey stage in the full blaze of his glory.

There is yet a third revolution going on in *The Labour Leader*, this one dramatic. Though they name no names, the prefaces Corkery wrote for *The Labour Leader* and *The Yellow Bittern and Other Plays* in 1920 are obviously shots fired in the direction of George Bernard Shaw. *The Yellow Bittern*'s preface questions the usefulness of 'page-long' stage directions (Corkery, *The Yellow Bittern*, vii); *The Labour Leader*'s takes on 'the lengthy preface' (Corkery, *The Labour Leader*, vii). Corkery argues that the sole purpose of these techniques is to 'bring the author between us and his play', preventing performers and spectators from engaging it directly (Corkery, *The Yellow Bittern*, x–xi). This desire for control is linked to the playwright's intellectual pretensions. Corkery imagines him cherishing 'his preface of a hundred pages', and gloating over the spectators' naiveté: 'The fools, they ought to know that here I am not to be found in my fullness, that indeed this business of foot-lights ... is only a penny-gaff advertisement for my book' (Corkery, *The Labour Leader*, viii).

Corkery rejects the Shavian mode as both anti-democratic and anti-dramatic: 'Sometimes one wonders if these prefaces are intended to be the prose of the matter ... the play, the poetry of the matter, the heart of it. But then one reads the plays' (ibid., x). He also implies that Shaw's effect on modern drama has been counter-revolutionary. 'It is curious to reflect', he observes, that 'that this new style of stage direction, the "narrow limits" style, has come upon the world at the very time we were seeking a way of mounting drama that should have something of vision and breadth' (Corkery, *The Yellow Bittern*, xi). Again, though he speaks of 'the world', Corkery is referencing the Abbey Theatre, which had recently witnessed the second coming of George Bernard Shaw.

A. Patrick Wilson was fired as Abbey manager in 1915. According to

Holloway, he made the mistake of telling Yeats and Gregory that it wasn't fair to the players to keep producing Synge when 'there was no money' in it (quoted in Burch, *Andrew P. Wilson*, 63). A memo by Yeats corroborates this, but suggests that the real problem was that Wilson was still playing Larkin behind the scenes:

> Some two months ago, Wilson made a sort of strike speech to the Company, trying to stir them up against us and against unprofitable artistic plays. The speech failed, and taking it to be a sign of excitability, rather than of any very settled policy, we continued him in his post for the time being, though giving him to understand that we would not keep him permanently. [handwritten] The company has petitioned us not to dismiss him. He got them to do so. (Yeats, 'Reasons for Dismissal of Manager')

The casting-out of A. Patrick Wilson was not just a defence of the Abbey's literary tradition, but the quashing of what looked to Yeats like labour agitation. This action soon found its reaction in the dramatic termination of Wilson's replacement, St. John Ervine, who was forced out by an actors' boycott shortly after the Easter Rising.

Yeats and Gregory replaced Ervine with J. Augustus Keough. He promptly swamped the Abbey in a 'deluge of deferred Shavianism', including the first Abbey productions of *Arms and the Man*, *Widowers' Houses*, *John Bull's Other Island* and *Man and Superman* (Welch, *The Abbey Theatre*, 70). The fact that Shaw's plays were used to help put down a workers' rebellion at the Abbey is only superficially ironic. As we have seen, Shaw's dramatic universe does not include the possibility of revolution from below. It is as impossible to imagine Andrew Undershaft's workers joining a syndicalist union as it is to imagine Sartorius's tenants organising a rent strike. *The Labour Leader* is thus framed by its preface as a strike against the dramatic counter-revolution Shaw was leading at the Abbey. We should recognise the conflict taking place in *The Labour Leader* as a fusion of all these revolutions: the national one, the syndicalist one and the dramatic one. All of these revolutions are driven by the sensations, needs and impulses incarnated in the labour leader's 'flesh and blood' (Corkery, *The Labour Leader*, 70).

Corkery was deeply impressed by Larkin when he came to organise in Cork in 1909. Writing for *The Leader*, Corkery presented Larkin as having been transported, through his love for literature, to a plane to which his colleagues don't know enough to aspire:

> ... [B]y dint of reading, it was his custom to quote poetry as freely as I would myself if I had more courage; by brooding and thinking on problems that for his companions must practically have had no existence – he

had raised himself so much above his fellows that he deceived himself if he dreamed he could find lieutenants in their ranks. Here is a drama for any Ibsen that cares to write it – the failure of a leader of the democracy to find lieutenants. (Quoted in Maume, *Life that is Exile*, 11)

Of all the labour leaders we have yet encountered, Davna owes the most to Shelley. Davna aspires to 'read all the poetry that was ever written' (Corkery, *The Labour Leader*, 107), and describes himself as '[l]ike a poet who has a hundred misty thoughts fluttering around in his crainum' waiting for the 'touch of fire' to 'fuse them all into one poem' (ibid., 113).

The union officers, however, fail to grasp either the appeal or the transforming power of romanticism. Tim Murphy – the only officer always loyal to Davna – defends the vital importance of the literary trimmings that Davna's opponents reject as irrelevant:

And if ye give him a secretary his job will be to cut Davna off when he's giving us the history of Ireland in the tenth century, or giving us Shelley: 'Rise like lions after slumber': 'Shake your manes like thunder!'; 'Ye are many, they are few!' He was a great lad – a great lad, that Shelley, and he only a poor sheep of an Englishman and all. And what would we know about him only for Davna? Or about the Red Flag? Or about anything at all. (Ibid., 26)

Murphy recognises the political functions of Davna's apparently spontaneous flourishes. Davna's broad range of references – ancient Irish history, an English romantic poet, a poem written by an Irish socialist during a British docker's strike but now sung by labour movements around the world – demonstrate to his listeners that as members of an international labour movement, Irish workers are more powerful than they might imagine themselves to be. Davna's misquotation of Shelley's *The Mask of Anarchy* has the salutary effect of persuading a group of people who are used to being called 'lice' or 'vermin' to think of themselves as lions.[12] Davna considers this transformation *more* important than the outcome of the strike. When Dempsey complains that the railwaymen might have come out if Davna hadn't yelled at them, Davna responds, 'Do you see they might have come out and never known at all that compared with them the Seven Sleepers of Ephesus were forty winkers! But now they know it, whether they'll come out or not' (ibid., 32).

Corkery's 1909 reference to Larkin's 'courage' sheds some light on *The Labour Leader*'s complicated deployment of queer socialism. Davna's climactic outburst at the end of Act III demonstrates intimate knowledge of this aspect of socialist culture. 'Why, it is all for the future I work', he declares, evoking core concerns of queer socialism's founding figures: Morris's aestheticism ('I want an education [for the workers] that will be surrounded by golden fields, by pictures and music, and buttressed by decent homes'), Carpenter's nature-worship ('I'll implore them to tell me how often in the year they lay their eyes on a wide sweep of landscape'), and Wilde's hope for the elimination of physical labour by machines:

> DAVNA. ... And the education must be kept up until no man will be found debased enough to use his back for bagging corn, or his bleeding shoulder blades for flinging deals about.
> PHIL. And will you say that to the boys outside?
> DAVNA. Of course I will.
> CLARKE. Somebody must fling the deals about.
> DAVNA. Nobody must fling deals about with his bleeding shoulder blades. What have we machinery for? Let machinery fling them about.
> PHIL. Will you say that to the meeting outside?
> DAVNA. Certainly! I am going to educate them.
> PHIL. They are against machinery.
> DAVNA. Why wouldn't they – at present – when they can hardly compete with it – at its lowest? But I work for the future, when society will be wise enough to reserve its mankind for doing such work as machinery cannot do. (Ibid., 117)

The veiled threats – 'Will you say that to the boys outside?' – imply that it might be dangerous to espouse queer socialism in front of a crowd of working-class men who, from Phil's point of view, will read all this poetry as a failure of masculinity which calls for violent punishment.

But just as Davna's queer socialism enriches, softens and complicates prevailing conceptions of working-class masculinity, his capacity for violence recuperates queer socialism by making it manly. In Davna and in *The Labour Leader*, militancy and queer socialism rescue each other. We see this especially in Davna's relationship with Phil Kennedy, who is cast both as Ferdia and as the Young Man to Davna's Cuchulain.[13] Agonising over his betrayal, Phil remembers not Davna's rage but his tenderness: 'I'll break down in my speech if I suddenly remember certain nights I spent with Davna – certain things he said to me' (ibid., 104). Corkery protects the love between these two men from homophobic condemnation by staging it as violence. They repair their romance by touching each other – not as lovers, but as fighters.

The extended boxing match between Davna and Phil certainly justifies Levitas's complaint that Davna 'loses sight of the political' while he indulges in his 'celebrations of violence' (Levitas, 'Plumbing the Depths', 146). The play itself, however, provides us with a metatheatrical frame which incorporates the fight back into the political. The fistfight forms the climax of Act III, the portion of the play dedicated to accomplishing *The Labour Leader*'s third revolution: the exaltation of 'flesh and blood' theatricality over Shavian realism. Davna's theatricality is constantly derided, in Acts I and II, as evidence of his selfishness and vanity; and in the first two acts Davna often justifies that perception. As Davna is always 'on', it is impossible to detect his authentic self. Corkery even deprives Davna of a domestic interior in which he might suspend his public performance and reveal a private core that could be presented to the audience as authentic. Though Larkin was married with children, Corkery's Davna doesn't appear to have a private home or private life; at the end of Act I he starts bedding down for the night in the union hall. The answer to the question 'Who's Davna when he's at home?' is 'Nobody knows.'

The Labour Leader, then, deliberately runs the risk of confirming the accusations of insincerity and inauthenticity levelled at Larkin by representing Davna as a character whose performance of himself does *not* have an authentic origin – who has been so fully absorbed into his public persona that he cannot manifest the 'depth' that defines realistic characterisation. But Davna's theatricality, while depriving him of an essence, allows him to question everyone else's. Act III assists him by putting *all* the characters into a theatre. As the union officers are revealed to be just as dependent on theatricality as Davna has ever been, Davna pushes his audiences to confront the violence in working-class masculinity – and to ask where that violence actually comes from and whose work it does.

When Davna announces his ambush scheme in Act II, Phil snaps, 'This isn't the time for dramatic side shows: we're not a film company' (Corkery, *The Labour Leader*, 80). At that moment, he aligns himself with the union officers, who see Davna's irrationalism as the opposite of their own pragmatism. What Act III of *The Labour Leader* demonstrates, however, is that neither the union officers, nor the play in which they are contained, nor the theatre in which that play is being staged, can thrive without irrationalism. Davna has always insisted that the only way to reach unskilled workers is to share the irrationalism produced by their embodied experience. 'That's where we have the power over all the other parties, if we only knew it', Davna says; '[w]e are in touch with flesh and blood' (ibid., 77).

But Davna's understanding of embodiment is influenced by his awareness of himself as an actor, which gives him a rudimentary grasp of performativity. He is the first character in any of these plays to hint that the working-class man's 'capacity for violence' might not be essential. In Act III, when Davna forces his way backstage, Davna launches into a soliloquy about the relationship between violence and unskilled labour:

> That's our name all right. Brute force! Bless you, there's no art, no skill in us. We labour without implements. Those of the bronze age, the stone age, would do us all right. We're lower than machinery at its lowest – a drag, a winch, a pile-driver is not so low as we are – we, mere bodies,

mere drags, mere winches! Implements of no skill! Only implements of violence! (Ibid., 110)

The skill with which Davna shapes this monologue ironises his insistence that 'there's no art, no skill in us'; if the unskilled workers are 'lower than machinery at its lowest', it's not because they're unfit for anything higher. If they are named as 'brute force', it's because they've been denied the tools that would allow them to dispense with it. 'That violence which is in us', he implies, has been driven into them as their bodies repeat the motions enforced on them by industrial capitalism:

> ... [A]ll the days of our lives we, unskilled labourers, must be violent to live: our week's wages depends on it: the more capable of violence we are, the more efficient we are. We must drag and tug ... and swing and wrench, and shove and drive – but when we're on strike, all that violence which is in us, our fortune – all that we must close down, must bottle up ... The very time, the only time we have leisure to brood upon our terrible lives – then we must be as astral bodies, mute and uncomplaining! (Ibid., 110–11)

The 'violence in us' originates with capitalism's appropriation of the worker's strength, and is rewarded as long as it is economically productive. It is condemned only when the workers have the 'leisure' to consider turning this violence against the infernal machine that created it.

Just as capitalism cannot do without violence, politics cannnot do without drama. Theatre, we learn in Act III, is the only medium through which anyone becomes a leader of men. The Act III set turns the Abbey's stage into a narrow strip trapping the performers between two audience spaces: the darkened house in which the Abbey's actual spectators sit, and the the imaginary house of the imaginary Atheneum Hall, located behind the partition that serves as the rear wall of the set. Two doors in the rear wall allow passage between the visible stage area – in the world of the play, the *backstage* area – and the unseen stage of the imaginary hall, on the other side of which sits an invisible but increasingly noisy crowd of Quaymen's Union members. While the actors put on their show for the Abbey audience, the characters they're playing are rehearsing the show they intend to present to the union members on the other side of the partition. It's intimidating for everyone involved. Given the times that are in it and the Abbey's history of riots, the actors are not necessarily safe with the real audience. Their characters cannot be confident about their reception from the imaginary audience; they are about to tell them that it will be the understudy performing, instead of the star they came to see. At the same time, the Abbey audience is confronting not just the actors and their characters but a shadow version of itself as a crowd of rowdy working-class men.

This set-up turns the Abbey Theatre into a *mise en abîme*, playing merry hell with the actual/theatrical binary and converting realism into metatheatre. Characters and spectators alike are oriented in the space by the never-named Caretaker, who brings out the props the union officers will need and schools them on stage management (ibid., 100). The union officers' fear of failing to please the menacing unseen audience reveals the supposedly pragmatic and realistic decisions that led them here as risky and desperate. Acknowledging that it's not just Davna who craves adulation – 'Everybody likes a big crowd' – Clarke and Dempsey reassure each other about Phil's performance: 'He has his speech very well arranged; if he can bring it off just as he intends, it ought to make a great impression' (ibid., 97). Phil is as nervous as an actor making his debut: 'Hope I don't get stage fright' (ibid., 103).

By calling so much attention to the theatrical setting, the characters make the Abbey spectators aware of themselves *as* spectators – as the counterpart to the audience that so terrifies Clarke, Dempsey and Phil – right before Davna's forced entrance triggers a cascade of increasingly sensationalistic events. What they see in Act III becomes both 'unreal', in that they cannot escape the knowledge that this is all being performed by actors on a stage, and 'real', in that what they see is presented within the world of the play as precisely that which is *not* on stage: the authentic 'behind the scenes' actuality to which the union audience does not have access. Phil and Davna's fistfight is, like all stage combat, 'play' in that nobody is actually being hurt. Within the world of the play, of course, Phil and Davna are really hitting each other; but as the other characters treat this fight as a boxing match, as Davna seems to think that he and Phil are role-playing Cuchulain and Ferdia, and as the prize for which they're fighting is the right to go out on stage and put on a show for the 'other' audience, there is no point at which the characters' reality is uninfected by performativity. On one level, Act III's violence is the spontaneous eruption of authentic emotion; but Act III is never for a moment contained by that one level.

The Act III set also raises the question of who this violence is *for*. As the fight begins, the imaginary audience behind the partition starts stamping their feet and whistling. In the world of the play, this is not a response to the fight – which the union members can't see – but an expression of impatience at *their* show's delayed opening. As Davna says, 'they want the curtain up'. But the Abbey spectators can't help correlating the 'noises off' with the onstage action, so that the 'other' audience becomes a sensational mirror of their *own* arousal as they watch two men fight each other for their entertainment. It's the Abbey spectators who paid for their ringside seats; it's the Abbey spectators who are consuming the show 'Phil' and 'Davna' are putting on; it's the Abbey spectators who came to *The Labour Leader*, as one reviewer put it, hoping for 'refreshing sidelights on present-day industrial problems' ('Davena's Diatribes'). This display of working-class violence is *for them*.

If being mirrored by the working-class audience is unsettling for the Abbey spectators, things get even hairier when it becomes apparent that the *real* show is behind the partition. Shortly after the fistfight, for no reason that anyone can see, 'there is a sudden and sustained burst of applause' from the union audience (ibid., 131). This marks the entrance of the railway workers into the hall. Getting the railwaymen to join them is the goal for which all the characters have been working; it was fear that Davna would make this impossible that prompted Clarke and Dempsey to turn on him in the first place. This goal has now been accomplished by the rank and file, while the officers were busy with their backstage shenangians. All this time, the Abbey spectators have been under the impression that they're the ones watching the *real* action; but in fact, the revolution has been going on without them, in the spaces the spectators can't see.

Act III thus subverts a number of conventions which typically serve the needs of the bourgeois spectator. Corkery denies the Abbey spectators the exalted position that naturalism normally offers them; from their position, the spectators cannot observe the working-class crowd like a bug under glass. Naturalism's promise of 'total visibility' (Chaudhuri, *Staging Place*) is retracted. What's behind that partition is certainly important – it may in fact actually be the elusive truth about the working class which naturalism keeps promising to exhibit – but the Abbey spectators never see it. This in itself is frustrating. At the same time, however, the partition is there to remind them that if this barrier *does* come down, they might have bigger problems. Like *Mixed Marriage* and *The Slough*, *The Labour Leader* ends with a house under siege; but it's not the working-class family's house. It's the Abbey's.

Even more threatening is the implication that the building has already been taken. Everything that's 'off stage' from the Abbey spectators' point of view is, from the union audience's point of view, *on* stage. It's impossible for that mob to be 'outside' the house; both the visible and the invisible spaces are 'houses'. The mob is already inside the theatre. As Victor Hugo tells us: when a mob goes into a theatre, it becomes a people. It is a people, however, from which the Abbey spectators are excluded.

By turning the theatre around, Act III decentres the spectators, consigning them to the now-dead liminal space inhabited by the defeated moderates. At the moment of his triumph, Davna turns his back on the Abbey spectators and disappears. Everyone in the 'other' house knows the words and the tune to 'The Red Flag'; this is may or may not be true for the Abbey spectators, who in any case are warned by the blank wall and by theatre etiquette not to join in. The real show, it transpires, is *not* for them; they perceive its power, but they are excluded from sensational pleasure being shared by Davna, Phil and the male chorus.

In the end, the violence that is supposedly essential to these unskilled labourers is revealed to be ephemeral, created as much in the minds of the spectators as in the actions of the performers. As international socialist anthems go, 'The Red Flag' is relatively gentle. It is typically sung to the tune of 'O Tannenbaum', and the lyrics stress 'the people's' stoicism in the face of adversity rather than their thirst for blood. Indeed, the first stanza lays so much stress on *self*-sacrifice that the uninitiated might easily mistake it for a republican hymn:

> The people's flag is deepest red;
> It shrouded oft our martyred dead.
> And ere their limbs grew stiff and cold,
> Their hearts' blood dyed its every fold.

Through Davna, play-acting – which the union officers are always afraid will lead to 'riot and bloodshed' – is ultimately revealed as a peaceful path to reform. This is precisely what Davna claims throughout Act III: that all he's ever tried to do is to draw 'society's' attention to 'that mass of uneducated violence that is in its midst' (Corkery, *The Labour Leader*, 115). Theatre is a way to stage that attention-getting violence without doing harm. It is, or could be, a means of 'snapping at' society to 'force it to begin' the process of reform. But that is true only if it is allowed to contain the irrationalism which conducts emotion from the performers' 'flesh and blood' to the spectators'.

'The Red Flag' even points towards a role that the Abbey Theatre could have in the revolution to come. The workers behind the partition don't pledge to kill or die; they don't even threaten to arise. The only promises made in 'The Red Flag' are promises that theatre can keep:

> Though cowards flinch and traitors sneer,
> We'll keep the red flag flying here.
> ....
> With heads uncovered swear we all
> To bear it onward till we fall;
> Come dungeons dark or gallows grim,
> This song shall be our parting hymn.

While it's on the Abbey stage, *The Labour Leader* keeps the red flag flying in the city where the Lockout failed; it bears that flag 'onward' into the unfolding national revolution; and for the two audiences divided by the blank wall, 'The Red Flag' will be their parting hymn.

Where *Mixed Marriage* and *The Slough* are – from very different perspectives – obsessed with explaining the failure of the revolution, *The Labour Leader* continues it – not on the streets, but in the only way that theatre can. It becomes something more than realism, but yet not very much like the 'epic' theare which would soon emerge on the German stage. Most of *The Labour*

Leader looks, sounds and behaves like realism, and reviews show that that's how it was received. The only innovative thing about it is the way Corkery, in an attempt to do justice to Larkin's theatrical intelligence, exploits the awareness of the theatrical situation that is always latent in spectators, whether the illusion presented to them is 'realistic' or not. Corkery also exploits the ways in which political action mirrors that situation – whether it's the labour leader himself thrilling his listeners, or the members' performance of sympathy by singing 'The Red Flag'. And it also insists that all of our performances, in all of these spaces, are driven by what's felt in 'flesh and blood'.

The most positive review *The Labour Leader* received was also the one that most clearly recognised and appreciated Corkery's departure from the Shavian model:

> 'The Labour Leader' is a welcome relief from the type of 'serious' play in which repertory theatres – not excluding the Abbey – delight to specialise. Even the most long-suffering theatre-goer has grown weary of the interminable discussions in which the characters hurl chunks of undigested blue books at one another's heads, and are so occupied in saying the right thing philosophically that they forget to say or do anything that matters dramatically. ('The Labour Leader')

The Labour Leader does for left drama what Larkin did for left politics: it makes the case for flesh and blood, for the irrational, for the argument that as frightening and threatening as our human bodies may become, they must be incorporated into any revolution attempting to solve any of the problems defined by socialism.

Conclusion

All of these plays have vanished. *The Slough* was never performed at the Abbey again after Wilson's departure, and Wilson never published it; it was thought lost until Ben Levitas found a copy in the Examiner of Plays archives at the British Library. *The Labour Leader* was never produced at the Abbey again; it was published, but as Corkery is now studied and taught for his prose, hardly anyone looks for it. *Mixed Marriage* held the Abbey stage until about 1924, when Sean O'Casey produced a realistic play about the Irish working-class family called *Juno and the Paycock*. As nearly everyone who reads *The Slough* immediately realises, *Juno* is built on the model that Wilson adapted from Ervine. *Juno*'s success knocked *Mixed Marriage* out of its niche. Between 1911 and 1924, *Mixed Marriage* had ninety-one performances at the Abbey (not counting tours); after 1924, it had thirty-two performances there, dropping out of the repertoire in 1940. Ervine's strike play about a working-class family was displaced by a play about a working-class family that happens to have a strike in it. Larkin never appears in *Juno*, or in the rest of O'Casey's Dublin trilogy.

Most of us would not trade *Juno and the Paycock* for a hundred *Mixed Marriage*s or a thousand *Slough*s. So why should we care that O'Casey's anointing as the Abbey's one and only socialist playwright helped bury the story of Irish syndicalism? For one thing, our investigation shows that Larkin's absence from the modern Irish dramatic canon is not a simple reflection of the historical failure of the Lockout. The displacement by *Juno* of the socialist drama which, as Levitas has shown, paved the way for it represented the triumph of a plot whose original form was counter-revolutionary. With *Juno*'s triumph, the story of labour receded so far behind the domestic tragedy that it became almost invisible. The destructive father figure who was once a warning about the dangers of irrationalism, who was transformed by Wilson into a warning about the importance of solidarity, re-emerges in *Juno* as an entertaining blowhard whose refusal to work has been emptied of political content and simply becomes proof of his own laziness. The anti-union working-class mother, whose drive to nurture prevents her from grasping the importance of class struggle, is glorified even more vigorously in Juno than she was in Mrs Rainey. A set of strategies and structures which accreted around the problem of dramatising a radical labour movement becomes, in *Juno*, a 'realistic' depiction of the working-class family as inherently fragmented, working-class masculinity as inherently dysfunctional, and the labour movement (represented in *Juno* by Jerry Devine) as incapable of bringing about change.

With *The Labour Leader*, we lost the best demonstration the Abbey ever gave us of syndicalism's transformative power for the men who adhered to it – and a compelling argument for the possibility that this power might remain at work in Ireland even after the revolution had ostensibly failed. We lost an unusually complex treatment of Irish masculinity, in which the capacity for violence is acknowledged but not essentialised, and in which the unorthodox feelings that drove queer socialism are at least temporarily incorporated into a working-class masculinity which is at least nominally heterosexual. We lost *The Labour Leader*'s challenge to a word-driven Irish dramatic tradition, and its argument about how theatre can – and cannot – continue a revolution by other means.

Most important, perhaps, we lost a story about the relationship between theory and practice. Like syndicalism itself, these three plays are about what happens when the rubber meets the road. As artistically imperfect as they all are, they remind us that the situation with which O'Casey's Dublin trilogy characters are coping was created in part by an extended attempt to make revolution real. The despair that envelops *Juno* and so many of the plays that have imitated it did not arise as a mimetic reflection of an always-already reality. It was created in part by the very ambition of syndicalism's project. It was generated by the obstacles and impasses that syndicalism encountered in its attempt to produce revolutionary change. If we lose our memory of that vision and of those obstacles, then all we can do, when presented with post-revolutionary despair, is assume that it was always like this.

Wilson's *The Slough* contains a coded version of this lesson. Each act of *The Slough* has its own subtitle, drawn from the episode of *Pilgrim's Progress* from which Larkin took the metaphor. Act II's is 'The Mending of the Slough'. Allen's performance at the Act II union meeting, we might assume, is a vision of the revolution as it *should* be – a movement whose goal is not just to alleviate the workers' suffering, but to change the environment that traps them. In Act III, when Edward cites Larkin's formula about lifting the workers out of the slough, Tom Robinson complains that 'when we have exerted every tissue, fibre and muscle in the lifting process, we'll still see the toilers wallowing, sinking, struggling, choking in that Slough!' (Wilson, *The Slough*, Act III, 58–9). We might take this as a lament about the futility of the struggle; but *Pilgrim's Progress* suggests a more specific interpretation. When Christian falls into the Slough of Despond, and Help comes to get him out, the dreaming narrator asks why the local authorities haven't fixed such an obvious hazard. The answer is that the slough can't be mended because it is created *by* the struggle. As soon as a soul awakens to the need to be saved, 'there arise in his soul many fears and doubts, and discouraging apprehensions'; those fears all run down into the same spot, creating the slough (Bunyan, *Pilgrim's Progress*, 47). The more souls awaken – the better the evangelists are – the farther the good news reaches – the worse the slough gets. To give up the struggle is unthinkable; to repair the slough is impossible. Theatre can't change that. Scholarship can't change that. One thing they *can* do is remind us that the murkier the slough has become, the brighter the stars once burned.

Notes

1. See Ben Levitas, 'Plumbing the Depths' and Stephen Dedalus Burch, *Andrew P. Wilson*, 70.
2. See Wright's *Disturbed Dublin* and Wilson's 'Larkinism!'.
3. The Irish Women Workers' Union, led by Delia Larkin, was 'technically independent but in reality a section of the ITGWU' (Yeates, *Lockout*, 152). In 1911, the ITGWU organised Dublin's newsboys, some of whom were girls (ibid., 8–9). However, syndicalism and the left in general were preoccupied with male workers (Darlington, *Syndicalism*, 104–11).
4. This is true in George Moore's *The Strike at Arlingford* (1893), John Galsworthy's *Strife* (1909), all three plays under discussion here, Ernest Hutchison's *The Right to Strike* (1920), Alfred Maltz's *The Black Pit* and Clifford Odets's *Waiting for Lefty* (1935).
5. Earlier strike plays built around interpersonal conflict include George Moore's *The Strike at Arlingford* and John Galsworthy's *Strife*.
6. I am citing the copy of *The Slough* submitted to the Examiner of Plays for performance in Liverpool. Page numbering is not consecutive, so I include the act number and page number.
7. 'The phrase [Tyranny Hall] has emanated from men—should I say men?—who

have dodged about Liberty Hall . . .' (Wilson, 'Some Casual Comments on Rolling Stones and Other Things'), 'Imagine for a moment that these three specimens of man's degradation . . .' (Wilson, 'Lyres and Liars!'), 'the good fellows had to work alongside imported scabs . . . who took the place of MEN' (Larkin, 'Why This Strike?').
8. Ben Levitas recognises Allen as a heroic and antirealistic character in 'Plumbing the Depths'.
9. It was singled out for its 'downright realism' in the *Irish Independent* ('A Powerful Play: *The Slough* at the Abbey', 2 November 1914, 6). Joseph Holloway compared Act II favourably to ensemble scenes in other realistic plays (Holloway, *Abbey Theatre*, 167). Holloway also noted the 'startlingly realistic effect' of the breaking of the Hanlons' windows (Holloway, *Diaries of Joseph Holloway*, microfilm, 837).
10. Davna admits he got the idea from the Manchester Martyrs (Corkery, *The Labour Leader*, 84).
11. This is the argument made in Jamie O'Neill's *At Swim, Two Boys*, for instance, and Roddy Doyle's *A Star Called Henry*.
12. The refrain of *Mask of Anarchy* runs: 'Rise like lions after slumber/ In unvanquishable number./ Shake your chains to earth like dew . . . Ye are many, they are few.'
13. During the fistfight Davna calls Phil 'Ferdia' and refers to the 'gae bulg', the weapon with which Cuchulain defeats his son.

4

MOBILISING MAURYA:
J. M. SYNGE, BERTOLT BRECHT AND THE REVOLUTIONARY MOTHER

INTRODUCTION

The emergence of a Communist state had a transformative effect on left politics and left culture around the world. Within the Soviet Union, the radical break with the past catalysed an explosion of experimental art and literature, including a vibrant avant-garde theatre movement whose influence was felt throughout Europe and in the United States (Carter, *The New Theatre*, v). Outside the Soviet Union, the real-world existence of an 'other place' where capitalism's writ did not run changed both the content and the formal expression of utopian desire. The Soviet Union became a real destination towards which that desire could yearn; it promised, much more persuasively than experiments like the Garden City could, that socialism was a functional alternative to a capitalism whose days appeared to be numbered. It promised that the hoped-for utopian future was no longer queer; that it could be, and had been, realised in straight time.

Straight time has its privileges; and it has its price. With the establishment of the Communist International in 1919 (also known as the Third International or Comintern), the Soviet Union began its bid for ideological and tactical control of an international workers' movement of which the Communist Party had until then been only one iteration. Though it was a long, chaotic and incomplete process, the establishment of the Comintern was the beginning of the end for syndicalism. Between a wave of repressive measures taken against them by capitalist governments and the Comintern's efforts to co-opt, infiltrate, merge with, or eradicate them, most national syndicalist organisations had withered away to irrelevance by the end of the 1920s (Darlington, *Syndicalism*, 3). The one exception to this trend was Spain, where the anarcho-syndicalist Confederacion General del Trabajo (National Confederation of Labor, or CNT), remained a thorn in the side of their Marxist and Communist competitors and a major obstacle to Soviet hegemony – from the establishment of Spain's republican government in 1931, to the very bitter end of the Spanish Civil War in 1939.

The survival of anarcho-syndicalism and other non-Communist and anti-Communist left organisations in Spain helped make it one of the most dramatic, compelling and tragic subjects for left writers during the 1930s. In 1936, a military uprising against the Second Republic – a left coalition government that had been democratically elected in 1931 – triggered a civil war that pitted the left and the right (and the left and the left) against each other. The Spanish Civil War became a proxy battle between Communist and fascist powers, as the Soviet Union sent tanks and troops to support the republican government and Hitler and Mussolini supported Franco's army. The Comintern used its network of national Communist Parties – including the 'very small Communist Party' of Ireland (O'Riordan, *The Connolly Column*, 55) – to recruit thousands of fighters for the famed International Brigades. Ultimately, the republican resistance disintegrated and Franco emerged victorious in 1939.

Soviet propaganda presented the Spanish Civil War as a battle for the survival of democracy against fascist aggression; and for a long time, that's how it was remembered. For American and European left intellectuals who came of age during the 1930s, Spain was 'the symbol for what was later to be spoken of as "the good fight"' (Radosh et al., *Spain Betrayed*, xv). For Russians who lived through the terror of the 1930s, supporting the Spanish republican government against fascism became the one bright spot of a hideous decade – a 'cherished memory' of participation in 'an idealistic struggle ... of which all Soviets could be proud' (Payne, *The Spanish Civil War*, 317). As Payne observes, '[t]he myth of the Spanish Republic ... retained its power to enlist the sympathy of later generations' (ibid., 290), including a number of postwar playwrights (among them John Osborne, Brian Friel and Frank McGuinness).

That was then. To enter into the history of the Spanish Civil War in the post-Soviet era is to step onto a battlefield still pitted with land mines. Paul Johnson observed in the 1980s that 'no episode in the 1930s has been more lied about than this one' (quoted in Radosh et al., *Spain Betrayed*, xvi); and that was before anyone even knew what was in the Soviet archives. Access to those documents has fatally complicated the 'good fight' narrative. Stanley G. Payne now argues that the Spanish democracy everyone was dying to defend was a fiction generated for propaganda purposes – that it was the disintegration of the Second Republic that triggered the war in the first place (Payne, *The Spanish Civil War*, 290), and that from that point on the shared objective of the Comintern, the Soviet Union and the Spanish Communists was to establish a Soviet-style socialist republic. Radosh et al. concur that 'Stalin sought from the very beginning to control events in Spain and to manage or prevent the spread of actual social revolution' (Radosh et al., *Spain Betrayed*, xviii), which involved crushing Spanish left parties and organisations which were resistant to Communist control. Gerald Howson discovered that the Soviet Union cold-bloodedly 'swindled the Republic out of several hundred million dollars in arms deals' (ibid., xvii). Apart from the gold and the geopolitical games, Payne argues, Stalin was interested in Spain primarily because, during a period 'when totalitarianism was at its most extreme and naked within the Soviet Union', the 'Popular Front banner of antifascism' that rallied liberals and radicals to the Spanish cause 'restored the appearance of progressivism and created much stronger moral standing for the Soviet Union' (Payne, *The Spanish Civil War*, 145).

The Soviet Union raised that banner in the cultural arena as well, including in the workers' theatres that proliferated internationally during the 1920s and 1930s. These were amateur organisations, founded and staffed by people with working-class jobs, which often had close ties to trade unions and were sometimes financially supported by local Communist parties. Their initial mission was to radicalise the workers who participated in these productions, as well as those who saw them. During the 1920s, workers' theatre delivered primarily confrontational agitprop; but the 1930s, when the Comintern developed the 'popular front' goal of recruiting progressive and liberal allies for the fight against fascism, saw the establishment of organisations like New York City's Theatre Union and London's Unity Theatre, whose goal was to promote Communist ideology through more sophisticated productions using techniques more in line with the expectations of middlebrow spectators.

Because of the interactions between Irish national politics and Soviet geopolitics, the story of Irish playwrights and workers' theatre takes place largely outside of Ireland. Whereas the 'popular front' campaign of the 1930s was tremendously successful in Britain and the United States, in Ireland interest in the Bolshevik revolution peaked much earlier, during the War of Independence (Kostick, 'Labour Militancy', 187; Woggon, 'Interpreting James Connolly', 179–81). Indeed, in 1922, IRA leaders met secretly with Comintern representatives and 'signed an agreement providing for the transformation of Sinn Féin into a new republican party with a socialist programme' in exchange for the Comintern's promise of weapons (O'Connor, *Reds*, 1). This came to very little; but the temporal coincidence of the Irish and Russian revolutions meant that Russia functioned for Irish socialists and republicans as an inspiration, as a model, and as a prediction – just as it served as a source of anxiety, terror and foreboding for other Irish observers. The radicalising effects of Ireland's own liberation war and civil war meant that the Irish political climate remained 'tolerant of communism' well into the 1920s (ibid., 2).

But the Spanish Civil War exacerbated the antagonism between the Soviet Union and the Catholic Church. The election in 1932 of De Valera's Fianna Fáil government generated a right-wing backlash that produced Ireland's own fascist paramilitary organisation, the Blueshirts, led by Eoin O'Duffy. O'Duffy organised a pro-Franco Irish Brigade; they fought in Spain for the first few months of 1937 but left in disgrace after the nationalists got fed up with O'Duffy's erratic leadership and the drunkenness, volatility and insubordination of his men (McGarry, *Irish Politics*, 17–47). On the political side, the Spanish Civil War spawned the pro-Franco Irish Christian Front (Keogh, *Ireland and the Vatican*, 127). Catholic groups circulated antirepublican atrocity propaganda which inflamed Catholic opinion (O'Riordan, *The Connolly Column*, 9). Though more sympathetic to the republic than to Franco, De Valera was also deeply invested in Catholic hegemony, and the new Irish constitution which passed in 1937 included language establishing a 'special position' in the Republic of Ireland for the Catholic Church. As church and state fused into a single entity, the 'pink decade' became, in Ireland, an era of extreme reaction *against* Communism (O'Connor, *Reds*, 2–3). There was no Irish equivalent of the Unity Theatre, or the Theatre Union.

Nevertheless, Irish revival drama did play a role in the propaganda battles fought over the Spanish Civil War between 1936 and 1939, albeit in an indirect and somewhat astonishing way. In 1936, the German playwright Bertolt Brecht was asked by the Bulgarian director Slatan Dudow to write a short play about the Spanish Civil War which he could stage in support of Spain's republican government.[1] The result was *Gewehre der Frau Carrar* (*Señora Carrar's Rifles*), first produced by Dudow's group Die Laterne on 18 October 1937 in Paris, then remounted in Copenhagen in 1938 by a workers' theatre directed by Ruth Berlau.[2] Brecht's note to the published play indicated that it was 'partly based on an idea by J. M. Synge'. The credit line understates his debt; *Señora Carrar's Rifles* is an adaptation – albeit an unfaithful one – of Synge's classic one-act tragedy, *Riders to the Sea*.[3]

Señora Carrar's Rifles may have been written in a hurry, but it nevertheless represents a major transition in Brecht's dramatic theory and practice, and that is what we will be investigating in this chapter. To understand the role that *Riders* played in the development of Brecht's drama during what Brecht called 'the dark times', we must broaden the scope of our investigation both geographically and methodologically. When Kleinstück introduced Syngeians to *Señora Carrar* in 1972, he was outraged by Brecht's attempt to reinvent Synge as a 'communist or social reformer' (Kleinstück, 'Synge in Germany', 275–6). I offer the perhaps equally enraging argument that Brecht was not terribly invested in Synge himself. Brecht's interest in *Riders* had much more to do with the fact that in the late 1930s there were many forces pushing Brecht back towards realism, none of which had much to do with the Irish literary revival. These included Hitler's rise to power in 1933, the flight of the cultural left from Germany, and the designation of 'socialist realism' as the official mode of Soviet literature. Unable to buck all of these trends, Brecht nevertheless remained convinced of realism's inadequacy. *Riders*, I will argue, appealed to Brecht as a model that might help him solve a pressing formal and practical problem: how to stage the radicalisation of the working-class mother in the context of a realistic production. By asking how and why *Riders* helped Brecht do this – and by taking a closer look at the results of this experiment – we gain new insight not only into Synge's *Riders to the Sea*, but into Brecht's deployment of gender and the maternal in his drama, and into the vexed question of how the spectators' emotions function in Brecht's epic theatre.

This chapter is intended in part as a contribution to the robust tradition of feminist engagement with Brechtian theory which has developed in Anglophone scholarship over the past forty years – a tradition from which *Señora Carrar's Rifles* has been almost entirely absent. Critics of Brecht's gender politics are drawn to *The Mother*'s Pelagea Vlassova, whose transformation from distressed mother to revolutionary activist reveals a 'typical Marxian blindness toward gender relations' (Diamond, *Unmaking Mimesis*, 44) in Brecht's work.[4] Feminists arguing for the liberating possibilities of Brechtian dramaturgy are usually attracted to Brecht's self-subverting Mother Courage or the fractured hero/ine of *The Good Person of Szechwan*.[5] *Señora Carrar's Rifles* has something to contribute to these investigations, since it is the chronological and methodological link connecting the sexless, selfless, 'moral mother' (Cima, *Performing Women*, 109) of *The Mother* (1932) to the more complex protagonists of *Courage*, *Szechwan* and *Caucasian*. But apart from a brief mention in Sara Lennox's 1978 essay, *Señora Carrar's Rifles* was not alluded to in many of the foundational feminist studies of Brecht's work.[6] Even Claire Gleitman, who contrasts Mother Courage with Maurya from *Riders to the Sea*, does not mention the play that mediated between them ('All in the Family', 167).

Much of this can be explained by *Señora Carrar*'s formal similarity to *Riders*, which makes the play seem like an embarrassing regression for Brecht. As I will show, however, Brecht's assimilation of *Riders* as a model during the period between *The Mother* and *Mother Courage* was crucial in helping him negotiate some of the contradictions embedded in his conception of epic theatre. In particular, Brecht saw in *Riders* a means of creating the emotional pleasures associated with realism without sacrificing the benefits of alienation. We will then turn to Brecht's response to his own experiment, suggesting some of the ways in which his engagement with Synge's peculiar brand of realism might have complicated his understanding of the relationships between theatre, realism and reality.

THE MOTHER LOSES MANHATTAN

Señora Carrar's Rifles is well known to German scholars because it was a mainstay of the Berliner Ensemble. In Anglophone scholarship, it is well-nigh invisible. When it does crop up there, it is often because a Synge scholar has (re)discovered the play's connection to *Riders*, become fascinated by it, and attempted to extract meaning from it. This has often proved a risky operation. Part of the problem is a tendency to treat Brecht's play primarily as an opportunity to enhance Synge's legacy. Initially, this took the form of chastising Brecht for daring to sully Synge's tragic masterpiece with his filthy Marxist paws. Sidney Poger, for example, accuses Brecht of assuming that 'being a writer during the Irish literary renaissance made Synge automatically a member of the IRA' (Poger, 'Brecht's *Señora*', 42). In these latter days of the 'global turn', however, Brecht's interest in Synge is gratefully seized upon as evidence that the Irish literary revival had international roots and international impact. Anthony Roche frames his 2004 article 'Synge, Brecht, and the Hiberno-German Connection' as a response to the critique of the Irish revival as insular and anti-modern (9). Ben Levitas, who has dubbed Synge 'the anticipator of Bertolt Brecht' ('Censorship', 285), cites the plays' 'shared debt to Marx' ('J. M. Synge: European Contexts', 88) in support of his claim that Synge was 'intimately connected to the development of modern drama in Europe' (ibid., 77).

It is fair to say that *Señora Carrar's Rifles* extended Synge's influence into regions Yeats would never have dreamed of penetrating. *Señora Carrar's Rifles* was produced by left-wing theatre groups around the globe (Willett and Manheim, 'Introduction', xii) – including London's Unity Theatre, whose 1938 production made *Señora Carrar's Rifles* the first Brecht play staged in England. But if we see the growth of Synge's cultural capital as the only important outcome of this exchange, we miss most of its significance. If we want to understand Brecht's engagement with *Riders*, we cannot insist on making Synge the key term in this equation – or even on making Synge one side of a bilateral exchange. To do so is to make Ireland and the Irish dramatic revival more important to Brecht than they were, and thus to misunderstand the context in which this extraordinary encounter took place.

Looking at *Señora Carrar's Rifles* from a Hibernocentric point of view, for instance, tempts us to assume that *Señora Carrar's Rifles* links the Irish republican cause to the Spanish republican cause. Many Irish republicans did see such a connection, and joined the 'Connolly Column' of the International Brigade (O'Riordan, *The Connolly Column*, 55). But if Brecht knew that, he didn't think it worth mentioning. Brecht has the International Brigade actually march past Teresa Carrar's cottage. As they go by, we hear the fighting songs of the Germans, the French, the Poles, the Italians, the Americans and the Spanish; but we wait in vain for the Irish. Claiming kinship with Irish republicans was evidently not part of this play's agenda. Brecht's non-dramatic writing does not suggest any sustained interest in Irish politics. To the extent that *Riders*'s setting mattered to Brecht it was not because it was Irish, but because it was rural, poor, Catholic and part of a distinctive regional culture – characteristics which Synge's desperate Aran family shared with the Basque family that *Señora Carrar* originally intended to represent.

Spain's Basque region had its own identity – Catholic, bourgeois and comparatively centrist (Payne, *The Spanish Civil War*, 137) – and its own politics, and was never completely integrated into any of the revolutionary movements that swept the country during the 1920s and 1930s. The inclusion of Basque nationalists in the governments formed during the Spanish Civil War provided a semblance of political diversity and helped present the conflict as a 'national-revolutionary war' whose object was to protect the autonomy of regions like Catalonia and the Basque country from fascist encroachment (ibid., 143). However, the fall of Bilbao in 1937 forced Brecht to move the setting to a region where the republicans were still holding out (Willett and Manheim, 'Introduction'). Brecht chose Andalusia, another Catholic region with a distinctive regional tradition which had been popularised in Federico Garcia Lorca's 1933 play *Blood Wedding* – which, according to Levitas, was also a loose adaptation of *Riders to the Sea* (Gibson, *Performing Women*, 339–41; Levitas, 'J. M. Synge: European Contexts', 89). Even in Andalusia, as a Catholic mother who rejects the naïve consolation offered by the unnamed 'young priest' in favour of the hard material truths of life on the islands, Maurya had a lot to offer Brecht – if he could only get her mobilised.

It is not clear how Brecht first discovered *Riders to the Sea*. Brecht's first mention of Synge in a diary entry from 1920 does not indicate what exactly he was reading or where he found it (Roche, 'Synge, Brecht, and the Hiberno-German Connection', 25–6, Levitas, 'J. M. Synge: European Contexts', 88). Apart from the acknowledgment, Synge's name never comes up again in Brecht's writing about *Señora Carrar's Rifles* (Allen, '*Señora Carrar's Rifles*', 156). Complicating the picture is the fact that *Señora Carrar's Rifles* was written and produced in collaboration with the three women Brecht was involved with at the time. These were Brecht's wife, the German actress Helene Weigel; his lover, the actress and playwright Margarete Steffin; and his soon-to-be lover Ruth Berlau, the Danish actress/director who produced *Señora Carrar* in Copenhagen.[7] It is possible that Brecht was introduced to *Riders* by one of them; but he could have encountered it on his own. *Riders to the Sea* was translated into German by Werner Wolff in 1935 (Casey, 'German Productions', 166; Roche, 'Synge, Brecht, and the Hiberno-German Connection', 25), and by the time he wrote *Señora Carrar's Rifles* Brecht knew

English well enough to read the original. He could also have discovered it through *Blood Wedding*.

The more baffling question is *why* Brecht was drawn to a play that appears to compress into one short act everything Brecht hated about conventional drama. Brecht's notes on *The Mother* open with a useful encapsulation of his critique of 'Aristotelian' drama:

> [*The Mother*'s] dramaturgy is anti-metaphysical, materialistic and NON-ARISTOTELIAN. Thus it declines to assist the spectator in *surrendering himself to empathy* [original emphasis] in the unthinking fashion of the Aristotelian dramaturgy; and it relates to certain psychic effects, as for instance catharsis, in an essentially different manner: In the same way as it refuses to tacitly hand over its heroes to the world as though to an inalterable destiny, it also has no intention of handing over the spectator to a 'suggestive' theater experience. Rather its concern is to teach the spectator a most definitely practical conduct that is intended to change the world, and for this reason must be afforded a fundamentally different attitude in the theater from that to which he is accustomed. (Brecht, *The Mother*, 133)

What Brecht objects to about 'Aristotelian' drama is not that the spectator *feels* emotion but that he *surrenders himself* to it – specifically, that he 'surrenders' his ability to question the 'unalterable destiny' that forces the tragic ending. Once he identifies with and shares the protagonist's emotions, or so goes the theory, the spectator becomes so involved in the protagonist's suffering that he can no longer ask himself *why* he is suffering or *how* this suffering might have been prevented. It is precisely by trying to imagine circumstances under which this suffering would no longer be necessary that the spectator asks himself the questions that will lead him to 'change the world.' Brecht's desire to prompt the spectator to imagine these alternatives motivates his rejection of illusionistic theatre; a fully-realised and sensually captivating stage environment renders the world of the play so 'real' that no other seems possible.

One might be forgiven for thinking that anyone trying *not* to 'hand over [the play's] heroes . . . as though to an inalterable destiny' would be well advised to stay away from *Riders*. In addition to being Synge's most Aristotelian play, *Riders* is notorious for the relentless foreshadowing that renders Bartley's death inevitable.[8] The original production of *Riders* remains legendary for the lengths to which everyone involved went to replicate the Aran Islands actuality in all their sensory detail, from the antique spinning wheel to the (stinking) pampooties to the flannel of the drowned Michael's shirt.[9] To anyone approaching this misalliance from Brecht's side of the family, the obvious explanation would be that Brecht was using *Riders* as a Trojan horse, insinuating himself into it in order to bring down Aristotelian tragedy from within.

Keith Dickson advanced this argument in 1978 when he identified *Señora Carrar* as a 'counter-project' (Dickson, *Towards Utopia*, 107) – an attempt to critique *Riders* by deconstructing it. Anthony Roche, who has produced the best English-language treatment of *Riders* and *Señora Carrar* to date, concurs, concluding that *Señora Carrar* stands in 'dialectical relationship' to *Riders* with 'the ending of one ... deliberately antithetical to the ending of the other' (Roche, 'Synge, Brecht, and the Hiberno-German Connection', 28).[10]

The 'counter-project' hypothesis, however, remains persuasive only if we ignore the circumstances in which *Señora Carrar* was conceived, written and produced. Brecht's correspondence with Dudow about *Señora Carrar* explicitly identifies it as 'realism' (Brecht, *Letters*, 258) and a note published with the play labels it 'Aristotelian empathy-drama' (Brecht, *Collected Plays*, IV, iii, 161). This, along with the fact that Brecht later described *Señora Carrar* as 'opportunistic' (Brecht, *Bertolt Brecht Journals*, 23), suggests that *Señora Carrar* was not so much a critique of *Riders'* form as an exploitation of it (Esslin, *Brecht*, 69). To understand why, in 1937, Brecht would be willing to give 'empathy-drama' another try, we have to consider not only the practical limitations imposed on Brecht by his exile, but the brutal lessons Brecht learned from the disastrous production of *The Mother (Die Mutter)* in New York in 1935.

Die Mutter, which premiered at the Theatre Am Schiffbauerdamm in Berlin in 1932, was Brecht's first attempt to dramatise the coming to political consciousness of a working-class mother. Brecht remained preoccupied with this problem for years, and he was not alone. Brecht wrote *Die Mutter* at a time when German Communists were making a concerted effort to recruit women (Baxandall, 'Introduction', 28); a poster in the theatre auditorium quoted Lenin's declaration that 'without the women there can be no genuine mass movement' (Brecht, *The Mother*, 137). Brecht was aware that the movement attracted its share of young working women; he was involved with several of them. But *The Mother* reflects widespread concern among men on the left about the recalcitrance of older women.

Walter Benjamin's review of *The Mother* gives some indication of what was at stake in this attempt to 'revolutionise the mother':

> Of these [family relations], it is clear that none is more important than the relationship between mother and child. Furthermore, the mother, among all family members, is the most unequivocally determined as to her social function: she produces the next generation. The question raised by Brecht's play is: can this social function become a revolutionary one, and how? ... The doubly exploited childbearer represents the exploited people in their most extreme oppression. If the mothers are revolutionised, there is nothing left to revolutionise. (Benjamin, *Understanding Brecht*, 33–4)

The last line of that passage hovers between hailing the mother as foundational to the revolution and naming her as its most formidable obstacle. Neither Benjamin nor Brecht was interested redefining the mother's role. For Brecht, the foundational characteristic of maternity was the mother's 'willingness to be instrumentalised serving others' (Lennox, 'Women in Brecht's Works', 86). Sue-Ellen Case agrees that throughout Brecht's career his definition of maternity remains 'restrictive' and 'patriarchal': 'Child-rearing is still assigned to women, which centers their action upon issues of kinship and nurturing' ('Brecht and Women', 66). Baxandall claims that Brecht saw mothers as naturally committed to the collective good; it is because Brecht sees 'maternal' as 'synonymous with "moral" or "useful to human needs and potential"' that he uses mothers to illustrate the unbearable conflict that capitalism creates between commitment to the welfare of others and the desperate struggle for individual survival (Baxandall, 'Introduction', 13–15).

Brecht's efforts to radicalise the mother are thus complicated first and foremost by his unwillingness to radicalise motherhood itself. From a feminist point of view, the problem is that Brecht assumes a '"natural" alliance ... between women and motherliness' (Lennox, 'Women in Brecht's Works', 91–2). From a Marxist perspective, the problem is that the same ideologies that demand the mother's sacrifice for the collective also limit the mother's 'collective' to the members of her nuclear family. Brecht flags this problem with a quote from Lenin projected during Scene 9 of *The Mother*: 'THE SOCIAL INVOLVEMENT OF WOMEN IS TO BE SOUGHT, SO THEY WILL LAY ASIDE THEIR PHILISTINE HOME-AND-FAMILY PSYCHOLOGY' (Brecht, *The Mother*, 136; Brecht's capitalisation).

As we saw in the previous chapter, it was precisely by defining the mother as nurturer that Ervine defined her as apolitical, anti-struggle and anti-union. The working-class mother figure established by these strike plays and popularised by *Juno* prioritises the interests of her children above all else, which is precisely why she is so often presented as a threat to solidarity. Realism accentuates this conflict by giving it a rigidly gendered spatial dimension; the places of masculine struggle – the factory floor, the union hall, the street – are in opposition to the home presided over by the mother. The worker's resistance to capitalist exploitation manifests as a threat to the mother, either through the economic hardship that makes it impossible for her to feed her children or through strike-related violence that threatens to destroy her home. While young unmarried women are sometimes portrayed as politically aware and sympathetic, mother figures are often either unable to grasp the ideological context of their family's struggle or openly hostile to the union and its leaders. Confined to, as Ben Levitas puts it, the 'small-minded domesticity' ('Plumbing the Depths', 145) enclosed by the kitchen set, the working-class mother is not allowed to see the big picture. Afraid of what collective action will cost her children, she clings to the little she has rather than risk it to fight for more.

Brecht's first approach to this problem in *Die Mutter* (1932) eliminates the father entirely and focuses on teaching the mother that it is capitalism, not labour, that takes the food off her table. Sara Lennox's division of Brecht's mothers into 'true' mothers who care for all children and 'false' mothers who care only for their own is useful here but somewhat misleading. All of Brecht's mother-protagonists are initially motivated by concern for their own children. The altruistic Shen Te of *The Good Person of Szechwan* promises her unborn child that she will become 'a tiger, a savage beast/ To others' to protect him (Brecht, *The Good Person of Szechwan*, 82–3). In *The Caucasian Chalk Circle*, Grusha cares for a child who is not biologically hers; but her willingness to make sacrifices for him is linked to her sense that Michael is her 'own' child in every other way, a conviction that Adzak's judgement ratifies. Before the working-class mother can 'consider the welfare of all children' (Lennox, 'Women in Brecht's Works', 86), she must learn that she will never be able to care for her *own* children until the revolution comes.

The Mother begins with Pelagea Vlassova, 'widow of a worker and mother of a worker', complaining to the audience that since her son's wages have been cut she can no longer feed him properly (Brecht, *The Mother*, 37).[11] A revolutionary chorus then breaks in to explain to her that as things stand now, her ingenuity and industry can only exhaust her without helping her child: 'If the kopeks are lacking your work is not enough' (ibid., 39). It is only by getting outside her home and involving herself in the struggle that Vlassova can fulfil her domestic duties: 'The meat not there in your kitchen/ Won't get there if you stay in your kitchen!' (ibid.). Accordingly, the Berlin production of *Die Mutter* broke down the spatial barriers separating the working-class mother from the struggle. Moving doors and canvas backdrops mounted on iron pipes continually redivided a stage space whose boundaries were never fixed (Brecht, *Brecht on Theatre*, 57). While standing in her kitchen, Vlassova could communicate with both the proletarian audience in the theatre and the 'chorus of revolutionary workers' who analysed her predicament. Images and slogans projected on screens kept the play's ideological dimension visible even during intimate scenes between mother and son. By the third episode Vlassova has made it to the factory yard, from there she takes it to the streets, and by the final scene Vlassova has become, in the admiring words of Walter Benjamin, 'praxis incarnate' (*Understanding Brecht*, 35).

Brecht's notes on *Die Mutter* hold up the original Berlin production as a sterling example of what epic theatre is when it works. But in 1934, when Brecht fled Nazi Germany and went into exile in Denmark, he lost access to his audiences and to many of the performers who had helped him realise his ideas. To get his work produced, Brecht turned to the international network of workers' theatres.¹² Workers' theatre was a haven for displaced professionals who, like Brecht, were part of the left diaspora generated by the Fascist revolutions; but workers' theatre also relied heavily on committed amateurs. Brecht would later describe Die Laterne, who mounted *Señora Carrar's* first production, as 'a tiny group of German exiles' who were 'widely varied in background, training, and talents' (Brecht, *Messingkauf*, 71). In terms of content, of course, Brecht's plays were eminently appropriate for these 'left-wing amateurs' (Willett in Brecht, *Letters*, 161–2). Form was another matter entirely. In 1935, as the Theatre Union prepared to produce *The Mother* in New York, Brecht was confident that epic theatre could work for any working-class audience and that 'all sorts of actors, the most famous stars as well as proletarian agitprop performers', could execute it (Brecht, *Letters*, 217).¹³ By the time he started work on *Señora Carrar's Rifles*, the Theatre Union had taught him how wrong he was.

Appalled by the 'translation' sent to him by the Theatre Union's Paul Peters, who had rewritten the play as a realistic family drama, Brecht travelled to America, involved himself aggressively in rehearsals, and dragged the cast kicking and screaming back to his original conception. The resulting show was a legendary disaster whose juicy details have long fascinated theatre historians. Laura Bradley calls the Theatre Union production 'a clear example of failed cultural transference' (Bradley, *Brecht and Political Theatre*, 17). American working-class audiences were not radicalised to the same extent or in the same way as working-class audiences in Germany; and *The Mother* 'scarcely could have proved less apt' for an ensemble dedicated to the 'popular front' strategy (Baxandall, 'Introduction', 11) of drawing support from all classes.¹⁴ It did not help that the slide projector broke down, that the actors hated the play, or that the musicians (having been the target of Brecht's rage and hatred in rehearsal) sabotaged the performances.¹⁵

If Brecht was not aware of these issues before he arrived, he certainly was by the time the play folded. In a critique intended for *New Masses*, Brecht notes that everyone involved in the production was 'unfamiliar' with epic theatre, and finally acknowledges that his technique 'requires special kinds of political knowledge and artistic capabilities' (*Brecht on Theatre*, 81). Critical and popular reception of the Theatre Union production were shaped by the cast's ambivalence and by the spectators' expectations. The anti-illusionistic elements that Brecht managed to preserve read to the uninitiated as technical mistakes.¹⁶ Thomas R. Dash and several other critics complained that the production should evoke 'more feeling' and that 'the onlooker, no matter how sympathetic, fails to become emotionally overpowered'; many compared the play unfavourably to earlier Theatre Union productions that delivered more 'excitement'.¹⁷ Stanley Burnshaw's positive response, on the other hand, was undoubtedly shaped by his familiarity with Brecht's conception of epic theatre, which he explained at some length in his review ('The Theater Union', 27–8).

But while in general these reviews confirm the importance of framing, they also reveal one important way in which this production *did* escape the horizon of expectations. The only aspect of the production which pleased almost everyone was Helen Henry's performance as Vlassova. Even reviewers hostile to the play's experimental form and/or didactic content identified Henry's performance as the most engaging aspect of the production. John Anderson praised 'the literal, sensitively wrought, admirably imagined portrait of the old woman, done in ordinary theatre terms by Helen Henry'.[18] Burns Mantle, who felt 'cheated' out of his emotional 'thrills', praised Henry's Vlassova as 'a gentle, soft-spoken, appealing soul'. Dash also singled out Henry's performance as 'outstanding'. Robert Garland gushed that Henry was 'sincerely simple, and simply sincere'; and John Whitney, while attacking the production's Stalinism, exonerated Henry: 'Her playing brings much to the play that is needed, but not enough, and the fault is not hers. The fault is in the play.'[19]

At first glance, this is not surprising. Maternal anguish has long been a reliable source of histrionics, and it makes perfect sense that an audience accustomed to the 'thrills' generated by melodrama and realism would respond to the Mother. Henry had worked successfully in the commercial theare and no doubt knew how to bring a house down. Strangely, however, the actress credited with moving the play's audiences is repeatedly praised for her *lack* of affect – for playing 'with little variety of expression but with a nice restraint' (Barnes, 'The Theaters') in a 'sober, subdued key' (Dash, 'Mother'), and for knowing 'what to do and when not to do it' (Garland, '"Mother"'). Brecht praised Henry for modelling the 'correct way of speaking' in Vlassova's sickbed scene, where she delivered her lines – as epic actors should – not with the passion of immediate suffering but 'with the same sense of responsibility as a statement made for the record in a court of law' (Brecht, *Brecht on Theater*, 83). Henry succeeded in moving these critics precisely by remaining unmoved.

The only reviewer who pauses over this paradox is Burnshaw, who argues that Henry's performance in Vlassova's reunion with her son challenges Brecht's assumptions about the emotional relationship between performer and spectator:

> According to the 'epic' principle, this [episode] calls for no display of emotion for that would 'entangle' the audience; and as this scene is performed the mother and son hew to the 'epic' line. But that hardly leaves the audience emotionally unentangled – in fact, the very restraint of the mother and son becomes an understatement a thousand times more emotionally stirring than realistic surrender to impulses (a la Bertha Kalisch and the school of hysterics) could ever be. (Burnshaw, 'The Theater Union', 28)

Here, then, is one insight Brecht could take away from this debacle. An 'epic' performance of maternal anguish could be *more* emotionally potent than a 'realistic' one – even for spectators who were ignorant of or hostile to Brecht's ideology and/or methodology. Burnshaw recognised Henry's performance as epic; but Henry's performance also moved those reviewers who interpreted it, as Anderson did, in 'ordinary theatre terms'.

In suggesting that Henry's performance contradicts Brecht's 'whole theory about channelizing emotion away from the players' (ibid.), Burnshaw appears to be making what contemporary Brechtians would consider a rookie mistake. Brecht repeatedly insisted that he was not against emotion in the theatre, but specifically against the 'empathy' produced by identification with the protagonist. Brecht is inconsistent in his application of the term 'empathy', and sometimes 'equates the terms 'Aristotelian' and 'empathetic' (Dickson quoted in Allen, '*Señora Carrar's Rifles*', 161). Ideologically, what he rejects when he rejects 'empathy' is neither Aristotle's conception of *cartharsis* as the purgation of pity and fear, nor the more generalised modern understanding of 'catharsis' as the eruption of powerful emotion, but 'the modern empathy with the individual' promoted by art in 'the era of fully developed capitalism' (ibid., 162). But in the context of theatrical performance, Brecht's conception of 'empathy' is so specific as to be almost technical.

When illustrating the pernicious effects of empathy on the spectator, Brecht typically cites situations in which the spectator shares the feelings of the performers, so that the spectator's emotion mirrors the actors' expressions. In 'Theatre of Pleasure or Theatre for Instruction', the 'dramatic theatre's spectator' says, 'I weep when [the actors] weep, I laugh when they laugh' (*Brecht on Theatre*, 71). In his 1929 'Dialogue on Acting' Brecht denounces realistic acting as a form of 'hypnosis' in which the players 'go into a trance and take the audience with them' (ibid., 26). In 'Conversation about Being Forced into Empathy', Brecht condemns as 'barbaric' Horace's advice to actors about how to produce this mirroring effect: 'So, if you want me to weep/ First show me your own eyes full of tears' (ibid., 270). Brecht seems to have conceived of this mirroring as an involuntary, almost physiological reaction which no spectator can resist. Brecht's problem with 'empathy' is that it is passive; and he identifies it as passive because it is a reflection.

The Helen Henry Effect would actually seem to be consistent with Brecht's ideas about 'channelizing emotion', in that what Henry evokes is *not* empathy as Brecht understands it. Emotionally 'entangling' as it may be, the spectators' response to Helen Henry's 'underaccentuation' (Garland, '"Mother"') of Vlassova's vicissitudes is not reflective. Confronted with a grieving mother who does *not* express suffering by exhibiting the symptoms of grief, these spectators cannot passively share in her emotions. Primed with the idea that a mother *must* grieve upon being parted from her son, the spectators read Henry's affect not as an *absence* of feeling but as a *suppression* of it. This impression is so strong that instead of identifying, these spectators project: unable to share the performer's feelings, they generate their own feelings to replace the 'missing' ones. Their emotional response to Henry's distressed mother is 'a thousand times' stronger, as Burnshaw puts it, than their response to a more 'realistic' portrayal precisely because it is *not* 'borrowed' from the performer. Instead, the spectators lend their own feelings to her.

Brecht would make divergence between the performer's expressions and the spectator's feelings foundational to the alienation effect when he first introduced it in his 1936 essay 'Alienation Effects in Chinese Acting'. As is well known, Brecht's *Verfremdungseffect* is an approximation of the Russian term *ostranenie*, or 'making strange', to which Brecht was exposed during his 1935 trip to the Soviet Union. It is worth pointing out that on the same trip he met some of the leading lights in Soviet cinema, and that Kuleshov's experiments with montage in film had already demonstrated that spectators could be primed by contextual cues to project different emotions onto the same impassive face (Stam, *Film Theory*, 38–9).

In 'Alienation Effects', Brecht identifies the 'automatic transfer of emotions to the spectator' from the actor as an 'emotional infection' (Brecht, *Brecht on Theatre*, 94) to be resisted at all costs. The alienation effect cures the infection because it 'intervenes, not in the form of absence of emotion, but in the form of emotions which need not correspond to those of the character portrayed' (ibid.):

> On seeing worry the spectator may feel a sensation of joy; on seeing anger, one of disgust. When we speak of exhibiting the outer signs of emotion we do not mean such an exhibition and such a choice of signs that the emotional transference does in fact take place because the actor has managed to infect himself with the emotions portrayed, by exhibiting the outer signs . . . In such a case of course the [alienation] effect does not occur. But it does occur if the actor at a particular point unexpectedly shows a completely white face, which he has produced mechanically by holding his face in his hands with some white make-up on them. (Ibid., 94–5)

To execute this technique, the actor need not feel or feign fear; his white face does not so much express fear as allude to it. If the spectator then feels afraid, it is because he interprets the sign, not because he has caught the infection. The objective of this kind of 'quoted' performance, according to Jameson, is not simply to create the distance necessary for rational analysis, but to reveal identification as impossible by marking the 'radical absence of the self' with which the spectator desires to merge (Jameson, *Brecht and Method*, 53).

But these 'outer signs of emotion' – the 'mechanical' effects that substitute for the performer's emotional symptoms – are crucial in part because they mark the actor's performance as 'strange', and cue the spectator to treat it as antirealistic. In the absence of 'mechanical' cues, how could a perfomer evoke emotion without becoming contagious? How would the spectators know that his 'signs of emotion' were 'outer' and not inner, quoted rather than felt? Jameson identifies this as one of the most frequent objections raised by Brecht's critics: '[H]ow can we tell ... whether Olivier is quoting Shylock, acting the role out with genuine feeling, or simply hamming it up?' (ibid., 55). Jameson solves the problem by side-stepping it: 'Perhaps in this instance, however, the actor is more important than the spectator, and we ought to begin by thinking of this Brechtian "method" as a kind of ethos' (ibid.). In other words, Brechtian 'quotation' is a 'symbolic ethical practice' that matters because it transforms the actors, even if its effects are invisible to the spectator (ibid., 56).

Helen Henry's reception, however, demonstrated that a performer trained (however reluctantly) in this 'symbolic ethical practice' could produce what Brecht seems to have wanted – a powerful but not 'empathetic' emotional response – even in spectators who misrecognised her performance as realistic. This supports Jameson's implication that third-person acting 'works' even when spectators can't distinguish it from realistic acting. But the Helen Henry effect also suggests that third-person acting works best when the 'radical absence' of the player's emotions becomes so intolerable that the spectator is compelled to fill it. The difference between Henry's reception and the play's reception also suggests that spectators find the 'radical absence' of feeling supremely and perhaps uniquely intolerable in a mother. The working-class mother thus emerges from this production as a figure through whom it might be possible to negotiate a compromise between his own convictions, his actors' abilities, and his spectators' expectations. If the exiled Brecht, after the Theatre Union disaster, had to give up on epic drama as technically beyond the reach of the groups available to him, could the grieving mother still help him achieve some of his 'non-Aristotelian' goals?

We can best understand Brecht's use of *Riders* in *Señora Carrar's Rifles* as an attempt to answer that question. In *Señora Carrar's Rifles*, Brecht strives to achieve the goal he set himself in *The Mother* – the dramatisation of a working-class mother's coming to political consciousness – without recourse to the antinaturalist techniques that had, for the Theatre Union cast, crew and audiences, proved to be alienating in a *bad* way. *Riders* provided Synge with an Aristotelian framework on which to build, and a stripped-down mise-en-scène that was economically and ideologically appropriate for workers' theatre. But just as important, *Riders* turns a mother's *refusal* to express the anguish that realism would seem to require into the climax of a realistic play. *Riders* thus modelled a way of preserving realistic conventions and generating audience excitement *without* replicating what Brecht considered most debilitating about empathy: the spectator's involuntary reproduction of the performers' emotions.

By adopting *Riders*'s realism, then, Brecht succeeds in 'tailoring' the play 'to the needs and limitations' of those destined to perform it (Willett in Brecht, *Letters*, 161–2). But Brecht's framing of the play as 'empathy-drama' is to some extent strategic. The play was designed with 'non-professional' (ibid., 278) actors in mind, and most of the cast is not asked to go beyond the boundaries of realism. But Brecht always conceived of Teresa Carrar as a part for an epic performer – or rather, *the* epic performer. Brecht acknowledged that *Señora Carrar* was written 'in such a way that it would only work' with Helene Weigel in the lead (ibid., 283). His writing about the play in performance assumes that the actress playing Teresa must '[dispense] with empathy in portraying the character, and . . . [allow] the audience to dispense with it too' (Brecht, *Collected Plays*, IV, iii, 162). Weigel originated the role of Vlassova, and ever since had become the 'embodiment of epic style' (Hanssen, 'Brecht and Weigel', 181) for Brecht. But since Brecht knew that Weigel would be – as the saying goes – surrounded by amateurs, Brecht could not support her with an epic apparatus. Teresa would have to reach her radicalising epiphany without any help from projected slogans, didactic songs, anti-illusionistic production techniques, or choruses of revolutionary workers. It was Maurya who showed Brecht how to get her there.

Maurya's Revolution

J. M. Synge's *Riders to the Sea* is set in a cottage in the Aran Islands inhabited by the widowed Maurya, who has lost a husband, a father-in-law and six sons to the sea. As the play opens, the family is still waiting to hear what became of Maurya's son Michael, who was lost at sea nine days earlier. Maurya is desperate to prevent her last surviving son, Bartley, from going to sea; he ignores her pleas, and is dead before he reaches the boat. Just as Maurya's daughters, Cathleen and Nora, finally tell her that Michael's body was found and buried in Galway, Bartley's body is brought back to their house by the neighbours. The neighbours' keen becomes the background for Maurya's final speech, which concludes with one of the best-known lines in the Irish dramatic canon: 'No man at all can be living forever; and we must be satisfied.'

In *Señora Carrar's Rifles* Brecht moves the time to April 1937, the month in which Franco's army bombed the Basque city of Guernica, and the place to the cottage of a poor Andalusian family whose surviving members are the widowed Teresa Carrar and her sons, Juan and José. It is night-time, and Teresa is baking a loaf of bread for Juan, who is out fishing. José is at the window keeping an eye on the light from Juan's boat. Virtually all the men in Teresa's village are with the republican forces defending the city of Motril; gunfire is audible throughout the play. Teresa's husband Carlos was killed in the workers' uprising at Asturias two years earlier. She is determined not to lose her sons, though by keeping them at home she has made them the target of community harassment. Teresa's brother Pedro arrives. While Teresa is out, Pedro tells José that he has come to find a stash of rifles hidden in the house which once belonged to Carlos and which Pedro wants to take to the republican militia. Before they can find them, Teresa returns with the parish priest. Lengthy political arguments ensue, during which Teresa rips up a red flag that once belonged to her husband. A confrontation over the rifles ends when Teresa realises that Juan's light has gone out. Assuming that Juan has joined the republicans, Teresa curses him. Teresa's neighbours enter the house. While the women begin 'murmuring an Ave Maria', two fishermen carry in Juan's corpse, which is lying on a plank and wrapped in a bloodstained sail. Juan, they report, was shot by one of Franco's patrols while he was fishing. Teresa denounces the fascists as inhuman, orders the neighbours out of her house, and observes that the bloodstained sail is an apt replacement for the torn red flag. As gunfire proclaims that the fascists have broken through at Motril, Teresa takes the bread out of the oven, grabs the rifles, and runs off to the front lines with her brother and son to fight fascism 'for Juan'.

As Roche points out, Synge 'purists' are 'outraged' by Brecht's hideous betrayal of *Riders*'s content (Roche, 'Synge, Brecht, and the Hiberno-German Connection', 27); but Brecht purists have been equally distressed by the play's scandalous fidelity to *Riders*'s form (Allen, '*Señora Carrar's Rifles*', 156–7). Though he crams a considerable amount of incident into it, Brecht preserves the structural elements of Synge's plot, including the recurrences that foreshadow Bartley's death (Poger, 'Brecht's *Señora*', 38; Roche, 'Synge, Brecht, and the Hiberno-German Connection', 26–7). He also reproduces the play's most striking visual effects, including the entrance of the neighbours with the son's corpse (ibid., 26). It is precisely this disjunction between Syngean form and Brechtian content that makes Teresa's final decision hard to swallow. How could Brecht expect to achieve Teresa's conversion to militant resistance using the same structures that produced Maurya's acceptance of inexorable fate?[20]

Maurya would in any case appear an unlikely candidate for radicalisation. She never develops a recognisable political consciousness; and even if she had a bunch of rifles hidden under her floorboards they would be no more help to her in her battle with the sea than Cuchulain's sword ever was to him. But Maurya, like Wlassowa, is a mother in extremis, a mother whose ability to care for her children has been severely compromised by her economic circumstances. Before Bartley leaves, Maurya's dialogue betrays desires and anxieties that are painfully contradictory. Bartley is her last remaining economic support, and when she imagines his loss she puts it in terms of his material value: 'What way will I live, and the girls with me, and I an old woman looking for the grave?' (Synge, *Complete Plays*, 87). But if Maurya succeeds in 'holding him from the sea' (ibid.), she limits Bartley's earning power. Either she stops Bartley from going to sea and thereby starves her two daughters, or she lets her only surviving son risk death. The painful conflict between her fear of becoming even poorer and her fear of losing Bartley explodes in her agonised appeal to him: 'If it was a hundred horses, or a thousand horses you had itself, what is the price of a thousand horses against a son when there is one son only?' (ibid., 86) Desperately affirming Bartley's pricelessness to her as her child over his economic value as a provider, Maurya simultaneously conveys with that 'if' her sharp awareness that they *don't* have a hundred horses or a thousand horses; they don't have anything that would buy her the luxury of keeping all her children safe.

Even before the play begins, then, Maurya has arrived at the point where she should be ripe for revolution. She understands that as things are, it is impossible to do her job. If she were in *The Mother*, she'd never be far from a helpful Communist who could explain that the solution is to change the world, as Masha does for Vlassova in the 'The Song of What to Do':

> If you have an empty plate,
> how do you expect to sup?
> It's up to you to take the state
> and turn it over, bottoms up,
> till you have filled your plate.
> Help yourself, no need to wait! (Brecht, *Mother*, 42)

In Synge's dramatic universe, Maurya is cut off not only from this kind of metatheatrical intervention, and not only from this kind of explicit ideological discourse, but even from the experience that would allow her to grasp the metaphor that illustrates the alternative. 'The state' is invisible in *Riders*; not only has Maurya never dreamed of turning it over, she wouldn't know where to find it.

So instead of the song of what to do, Maurya responds to her maternal crisis with the song of what she *won't* do:

> I'll have no call now to be up crying and praying . . . I'll have no call now to be going down and getting holy water in the long dark nights after Samhain, and I won't care what way the sea is when the other women will be keening . . . It's a great rest I'll have now, and great sleeping in the long nights after Samhain, if it's only a bit of wet flour we do have to eat, and maybe a fish that would be stinking. (Synge, *Complete Plays*, 96)

In most ways this seems 'antithetical' (Roche, 'Synge, Brecht, and the Hiberno-German Connection', 28) to Teresa's final declaration: instead of taking action Maurya renounces it. But we should take another look at what Maurya is actually renouncing. She is letting go of the 'crying and praying', the 'keening', the repeated trips down to the well in the dead of night for holy water that does not seem to be protecting her family. She is saying goodbye to all the exhausting, repetitive, futile things she used to do for her sons because there was no material way to help them. She is giving up the excruciating anxiety born of her realisation that the work of keeping her family alive also inevitably destroys it. When she welcomes the 'great sleeping' – the end of that anxiety – along with the death of her son and the hunger facing her and her daughters that is not necessarily resignation. It is also refusal and rebellion: refusal to continue trying to *be* a mother under these conditions, rebellion against the demand that she fight for her family's survival when that fight guarantees her family's destruction. Whatever happens to Nora and Cathleen, Maurya will not lose sleep over it. She may still have two children living; she may still love them; but she's done with being a mother.

Looking at *Riders* from Brecht's perspective, then, we can see how strange its conclusion really is. Motherhood is a job that no woman is supposed to quit. But that is essentially what Maurya does when she refuses to mourn Bartley as she mourned her other children or to prolong her unbearable anxiety by worrying about how to feed her daughters. One might object that Maurya can't quit because she's been fired. Having lost all her children – or, in this reading, all the children who matter to her – Maurya cannot choose to continue the struggle to save them, and therefore cannot choose to end it. But freedom, in Synge's plays, usually is unchosen. Nora Burke walks out of her house in the shadow of the glen because Dan won't let her stay. Christy Mahon returns home triumphant with his defeated father because Pegeen and the villagers have run him out of town. Deirdre ensures heroic death and undying glory for herself and Naisi because she knows that beauty and love cannot survive the passage of time and the weakness of the human body. The only 'choice' these characters make is to extract from whatever harsh fate they've been forced into the possibility of liberation. As for so many of Synge's other protagonists, Maurya's agency lies not so much in choosing an action as in choosing the words that describe the action she is forced to take.

In this final scene, then, Synge does what Brecht knows he needs to do: he creates a revolutionary *change* in his mother figure without using revolutionary technique. As in the Theatre Union *Mother*, the spectators' presumption of Maurya's anguish helps Synge break with the norms that prescribe maternal behaviour without being attacked for perpetrating an unrealistic portrayal of Irish women (as he had been for *In the Shadow of the Glen* and would be for *Playboy of the Western World*). Maurya's dialogue introduces these spectators to the radical possibility that a mother might choose *not* to feel that anguish – might choose, instead, a less 'realistic' but more liberating response to a beloved child's death. But it is precisely in response to that dialogue that the spectators grieve not so much *with* Maurya as *in her place* – producing for themselves and each other the feelings so unnaturally and painfully absent from her. Synge thus appears to achieve, without any violations of Aristotelian theory or illusionistic practice, the result that Helen Henry stumbled upon: a powerful climax in which the spectator is an active rather than a passive participant, generating emotions which are both intense and widely divergent from those of the performer who evokes them.

With this in mind, the ending of *Señora Carrar's Rifles* presents itself not as a dialectic antithesis of *Riders*'s climax, but as a replication of it. The two endings *look* antithetical because of their diametrically opposed content. If Maurya's final speech is revolution masquerading as resignation, Teresa's decision is resignation masquerading as revolution. By taking up the gun, Teresa is conceding defeat – abandoning her pacifism and accepting militancy as unavoidable. But at the moment that the son's body appears, both mothers experience the same insight. Each finally accepts the truth that she has been battling all along: that the world being as it is, no amount of mothering can protect her children. And in each case, that moment of acceptance is marked by the character's sudden refusal of the expected emotional response to her son's death.

If the resemblance between these two endings seemed stronger to Brecht than it does to most of his critics, that may be because Brecht was working without the benefit of the context that that has shaped nearly every influential reading of *Riders* since its first production in 1904. Brecht had most likely never seen *Riders* performed.[21] He had no deep knowledge of Ireland. He could not possibly have grasped, based on the play's text alone, how the keening women affect the audience in the final scene. Synge's first description of the 'the wild keen, or crying for the dead' in *The Aran Islands* presents it as a shocking eruption of the 'passionate rage that lurks somewhere in every native of the island' (Synge, *The Aran Islands* III, 52). As the keeners 'shriek with pitiable despair before the horror of the fate to which they are all doomed', they manifest all the 'external signs' of intense emotion:

> Each old woman, as she took her turn in the leading recitative, seemed possessed for the moment with a profound ecstasy of grief, swaying to and fro, and bending her forehead to the stone before her, while she called out to the dead with a perpetually recurring chant of sobs ... I could see the faces near me stiff and drawn with emotion. (Ibid., 51)

Synge's vision of the keen was apparently realised by the play's original cast. At least on Joseph Holloway – the Irish dramatic revival's most famous bourgeois spectator – their keen produced a 'gruesome and harrowing' effect: 'The thoroughly in-earnest playing of the company made the terribly depressing wake episode so realistic and weirdly doleful that some of the audience could not stand the painful horror of the scene, and had to leave' (Holloway, *Abbey Theatre*, 35). The keen thus performs the 'barbaric' operation prescribed by Horace, as the actors embody the 'depressing' grief that deprives spectators of their power to applaud. The spectators' emotions do diverge from those expressed in Maurya's dialogue; but that is precisely because the explosion of grief in the keen produces the involuntary 'empathy' that Brecht wanted to avoid. The spectators do not mirror Maurya because they are mirroring the keeners, who embody the emotions that Maurya has elected not to feel. Synge's stage directions, however, are deceptively understated: 'The women are keening softly and swaying themselves with a slow movement . . . [Maurya] pauses, and the keen rises a little more loudly from the women, then sinks away' (Synge, *The Aran Islands* I, 51). A reader who knew nothing about keening could hardly infer, from these lines, the intense emotional and physical energy generated in that first production.

Roche points out that the conflict between pagan and Christian beliefs in *Riders* is reworked in *Señora Carrar* as a conflict between 'Catholicism and the disruptive effect of Marxist revolution' (Roche, 'Synge, Brecht, and the Hiberno-German Connection', 28). Brecht seems to have misunderstood which side the keen was on. Irish grieving traditions being unknown to him, Brecht focuses on what he does recognise: the kneeling, the sign of the cross, the holy water, and Maurya's 'saying prayers under her breath' (Synge, *The Aran Islands* I, 50). Whereas the original staging emphasised the ironic contrast that Synge observed between the 'words of atonement and Catholic belief' and the 'cries of pagan desperation' (Synge, *The Aran Islands* III, 52) in the keen, Brecht renders the neighbour women's lament as stereotypically Catholic: 'Murmuring is heard outside the door, then the door opens and three women come in, hands folded over their breasts, murmuring an Ave Maria' (Brecht, *Collected Plays*, IV, iii, 122).

Turning the keen into an 'Ave Maria' which is 'murmured' by women with their hands decorously 'folded over their breasts' radically reduces its sensational impact. By making the keen Catholic, Brecht identifies the neighbour women as part of the oppressive apparatus that Teresa is called to fight; as Teresa kneels by the body of her son, 'the murmur of the praying women' merges with 'the muffled roar of the cannon in the distance' (ibid., 123). In fact, this trio of neighbours has less in common with the keeners of *Riders* than with the three women who come to condole with Vlassova for her son's death in *The Mother*. The 'consolation' these women offer along with their Bible epitomises a feminised, sentimental, oppressive Christianity from which Vlassova strives in vain to liberate them; the scene ends with a brawl in which the Bible is ripped to shreds. The praying women serve a similar function in *Señora Carrar*, though Teresa (constrained by realism) merely 'politely' orders them out of her house (ibid.). In the company of her silent brother and younger son – both firmly committed to the republican cause – Teresa covers her Juan's body with the red sailcloth: 'A minute ago, I tore up a flag. Now they've brought me a new one' (ibid.). Like Vlassova, she refuses consolation; like Maurya, she refuses grief. With the neighbours cleared away, the audience has no mirror, apart from this tableau of steely resolve. Whatever grief they feel, they must produce themselves.

Instead of 'harrowing' the audience, then, Teresa's neighbours simply provide an opportunity for Teresa to mark her conversion by rejecting Catholicism. Brecht increases the shock of this conversion by giving her an old-fashioned 'hysterical' outburst just *before* her son's body is brought in. In a displaced version of Maurya's refusal to give Bartley her blessing, Teresa lavishly curses her son for, as she believes, running off to the front:

> If he has done this to me and joined the militia I'm going to curse him. Let them hit him with their bombs! Let them crush him with their tanks! To show him that you can't make a mockery of God. And that a poor man can't beat the generals. I didn't bring him into the world to ambush his fellow men behind a machine gun ... When he comes back telling me he's defeated the generals, it's not going to make me open the door to him. I'll tell him from behind the door that I won't have a man in my house who has stained himself with blood. I'll cut him off like a bad leg. I will. I've already had one brought back to me ... They that take the sword shall perish with the sword. (Ibid., 122)

The emotional intensity of this speech is heightened by Teresa's demonstration of the tragic irony of motherlove under capitalism: the mother's desire to protect her own son at the expense of everyone else's forces her to will his destruction.

The arrival of the body immediately reveals this speech as materially impotent. Teresa's curse is a self-subverting mashup of two contradictory fantasies: one in which 'a poor man can't defeat the generals', and one in which a poor man *does* defeat the generals. Teresa is wrong about what has happened to Juan. Teresa is wrong to believe that only those who 'take the sword' will 'perish by the sword'. Teresa is wrong even when she predicts her own behaviour; when Juan is brought home, she will 'have in [her] house a man who has stained himself with blood'. This is the point at which, in *Riders*, Maurya's description of Patch's death is enacted by the neighbours, creating the irresistible impression that Maurya's words are shaping the characters' reality. By giving that description to José and placing it much earlier, Brecht deprives Teresa of Maurya's uncanny power; what materialises instead is the proof that Teresa has no control over her own universe. Maurya's refusal to bless is tragically efficacious; Teresa's curse is tragically futile.

Brecht's placement of the curse emphasises exactly what critics reject as most 'unrealistic' about this play: the sudden, radical and unexpected transformation of Teresa's world view. But this is perhaps the single most important thing Brecht adopted from Synge's model. Despite their different destinations, Brecht goes to considerable effort to ensure that the *structure* of Teresa's journey conforms to that of Maurya's. Roche retells an anecdote about a rehearsal for a 1952 Berliner Ensemble production during which Brecht's colleagues complained that Teresa's conversion was not credible. Weigel, who was playing Teresa, was asked to change her initial interpretation, in which she 'gave way' a little under each attack until she 'crumbles in the face of her son's death', to get 'closer to that followed in the Syngean version, whereby Teresa became increasingly more stoic in the face of each successive blow, with the son's death providing the catalyst for her break down' (Roche, 'Synge, Brecht, and the Hiberno-German Connection', 28). Roche leaves out the moment at which they are interrupted by Weigel, who cannot understand why they refuse to accept Teresa's conversion as the outcome of the pounding she takes: 'She suffers one blow after another, yet nobody believes they have an effect' (Brecht, *Collected Plays*, IV, iii, 169). Brecht asks her to repeat herself, and an acolyte has an epiphany: 'It's that one-thing-after-another that weakens it' (ibid.). It is at that moment that Brecht rediscovers what for him was distinctive about the realism of *Riders*.

Elin Diamond argues that Ibsenite realism was built around the Freudian construct of hysteria, depending for its truth effects not only on the histrionics of the female lead but on structures of knowledge borrowed from the methods of psychoanalysis (Diamond, *Unmaking*, 4). What Diamond refers to as the hysteric's 'confession' – the climactic breakdown during which the protagonist performs the symptoms that confirm the spectator's diagnosis of her repressed 'truth' (ibid., 14) – has to be authorised by a process of investigation which slowly brings to light the buried trauma or guilty secret. Like the well-made play, hysterical realism requires the kind of structure that Brecht dismisses as 'that one-thing-after-another' – the ratcheting up of tensions by means of questions and confrontations, the placement of clues pointing the spectator towards the revelation. Unless it is the culmination of a clearly marked and logical progression, the emotional climax is liable to be rejected as 'unprepared'.

Riders does without the structures of 'hysterical realism'. There is no long-repressed trauma; since the past continually recurs in the present, it cannot be buried and requires no excavation. In place of the cathartic explosion that we expect as the destination of her therapeutic 'journey', we are given Maurya's *lack* of feeling. This rupture of Maurya's 'character arc' generates for the audience a shock that resonates with Maurya's; and it is precisely that shock that Brecht identifies as the key to selling Teresa's conversion. Accordingly, he directs Weigel to replicate that change of direction: she is 'to [play] the way Carrar steeled herself after each blow had devastated her, then all of a sudden collapsed' (Brecht, *Collected Plays*, IV, iii, 169). Weigel replies, 'Yes, that's how I played it in Copenhagen [in 1938] . . . and it worked there' (ibid.).

Weigel's casual observation that the interpretation Brecht has just arrived at with such difficulty is the one she developed under the direction of his Danish lover fifteen years earlier testifies to the pivotal role that her role as Brecht's wife, as the mother of his children, and as his leading actress played in the initial success of *Señora Carrar's Rifles* – and in the development of his dramatic theory and practice. The Berliner Ensemble anecdote derives from one of several short pieces – many of them unpublished until long after the fact – in which Brecht attempts to account for the extraordinary power of Weigel's performance as Teresa. The difficulties he encountered were instructive for him, as they will be for us, as he struggled to redefine the relationships between theatre, reality and realism in the postwar world.

Weigel's Props

Despite Brecht's artistic and erotic liaisons with Berlau, Steffin and others, Brecht's fascination with Helene Weigel as a *performer* never waned during their exile. Hanssen quotes Brecht's assessment of the 1937 Paris premiere:

> [Weigel's] play was the best and most pure epic theater that hitherto (up to now) could have been seen anywhere. She played an Andalusian fisherwoman, and it was interesting how the usual contrast between realistic and cultivated acting could be completely done away with.[22]

The experiment was a success: 'Weigel had succeeded in combining an epic style of presentation with Aristotelian theater' (Hanssen, 'Brecht and Weigel', 185). As in *Riders to the Sea*, the mother's reversal was authenticated by the realistic setting without being fully naturalised. Weigel sold Teresa's conversion without marking the 'contrast between realistic and cultivated acting'. And best of all, though *Señora Carrar's Rifles* presented as realism, it produced the effects of 'pure epic theater'.

The problem was that, according to Brecht, these happy results could not be achieved by anyone *but* Weigel. While Weigel played Teresa in the German-language production mounted by Ruth Berlau's workers' theatre in Copenhagen in 1938, Berlau simultaneously mounted a Danish-language production starring Dagmar Andreassen, a cleaning woman with no formal training in theatre (Berlau, *Living for Brecht*, 34). According to Brecht,

> Andreassen's performance didn't make the story sufficiently interesting, and as a result one missed – as one did not with Weigel – any chance to empathise with the character and participate strongly and effectively in her emotions. One actually missed any use of those hypnotic powers which one is normally able to feel in the theatre. (Brecht, *Collected Plays*, IV, iii, 163)

No only was Andreassen no Helene Weigel, she was no Helen Henry. But Berlau tells a different story, noting that Andreassen had earlier impressed Brecht as a 'truly epic' performer in *The Mother*, and insisting that the

Danish-language production 'turned out wonderfully' (Berlau, *Living for Brecht*, 33–5). If Berlau's evaluation of her own production is open to challenge, so is Brecht's evaluation of his own wife's acting. When Brecht presents Weigel's performance of Teresa as a peerless example of epic technique, he never explains *how* Weigel did what she did. Maybe he wouldn't; but maybe he couldn't. Or, more precisely: maybe Weigel as Teresa was uniquely impressive – at least to Brecht – not only because she was a great actress, but because she was Helene Weigel.

From *Der Messingkauf*, which Brecht worked on in 1939–40, it appears that Brecht's perception of Weigel as the exemplary epic performer was so strong that nothing she did on stage could shake it – even when she 'burst into tears':

> In one play she took the part of a peasant woman in the Spanish civil war and had to curse her son and wish him dead . . . The civil war was still being fought when this performance took place. It is not clear whether the war had taken an unfavorable turn for the oppressed that day or Weigel had some other reason for being in a specially sensitive mood, but anyway that day as she spoke her curse against the murdered man the tears began to flow. She wasn't weeping as a peasant, but as a performer and for the peasant. I see that as a mistake, but I don't see any offence against my rules. (Brecht, *Messingkauf*, 71)

Grace Allen questions whether spectators could ever perceive the difference between Weigel weeping *over* Teresa and Weigel weeping *as* Teresa ('*Señora Carrar's Rifles*', 167). Nevertheless, unwilling to believe that Weigel might have committed the cardinal sin of being 'wholly absorbed in [her] part' – because, perhaps, that would require him to admit that Weigel did not always obey his 'rules' – Brecht insists that Weigel was *not* 'acting', but expressing her own feelings (Brecht, *Messingkauf*, 71). At a moment when spectators *other* than Brecht would see the tears of the fisherman's wife, Brecht sees only the tears of his own.

Brecht's speculations about where Weigel's emotion might have come from raise the question of the status of Weigel's, and/or Brecht's, investment in the cause itself. The opening of *Señora Carrar's Rifles* in Paris in October 1937 coincided with the retaking of Teruel by republican forces, which touched off a brief rally for the republic which ended at around the same time that Berlau staged *Señora Carrar* in Copenhagen in Feburary 1938 (Brecht, *Letters*, 274–6; Payne, *The Spanish Civil War*, 248). But by that point, it was clear that all was not well with the republican government. In May 1937, the same paranoia that led Stalin to purge his own ranks prompted him to force out Largo Caballero, the republican prime minister, and replace him with the more cooperative Juan Negrín (ibid., 213–21). Negrín promptly set about crushing the non-Communist Spanish left (ibid., 227). At Stalin's instigation, Negrín had Andreu Nín, leader of the rival Partido Obrero de Unificación Marxista (POUM), abducted and assassinated (ibid., 228). Defeat for the republic meant victory for fascists; but victory for the republic would mean the expansion of a paranoid regime whose purges had claimed some of Brecht's close friends (Willett and Manheim, 'Introduction', viii). In cursing the son she loves, Teresa wishes for the victory of the fascists she hates – because no matter how often people tell her that this is a fight for her liberation, Teresa can only experience it as oppression. There are many things that might bring tears to Weigel's eyes at a moment like this, and they don't all involve empathy. They might, for instance, involve rage or frustration at the way the world has suddenly narrowed, as they forge deeper into the 'dark times', until it no longer contains any outcome she could want.

The experience of seeing Weigel through Teresa seems to have brought theatre and actuality into a newly complex relationship for Brecht – partly, perhaps, because of how *Riders* materialises its environment. The poverty that Synge strives to recreate in *Riders* manifests as a minimalism which is both justified by verisimilitude and practically suited to the fledgling Irish National Theatre Society's limited resources. As I am hardly the first to note, the spareness of *Riders*'s setting enriches the significance of each object contained in it. The props the characters use are 'everyday Aran household items which persuade us that the action is naturalistic, but as the play unfolds they become charged with enormous symbolic voltage' (Benson, qtd. in Boeninger, '*Submarine Roots*', 50). Though this symbolism is often interpreted in cultural or mythical terms, it can also be read socially. When Bartley asks for 'the bit of new rope was bought in Connemara', and Maurya tells him they'll need it to lower Michael into his grave, that underlines Maurya's economic predicament: if Bartley stops 'going to sea', this family soon will not have *anything*.

Synge's use of props is one element of *Riders*'s realism that Brecht reproduces very carefully. Brecht imports many of the objects that appear in *Riders* – the bread, the plank on which the son's body is carried, the red sail that reappears as both the tattered red flag wrapped around the rifles and the blood-soaked sail wrapped around Juan's body, the net mentioned in *Riders*'s initial stage direction – and replicates Synge's dual use of props as both the anchors of the play's 'reality' and the foci around which the play's subtexts condense. The fishing net that Teresa mends, for instance, confirms the Andalusian setting while materialising Teresa's determination to remain enmeshed in the snares that have been set for her.

That net reappears in Brecht's poems about Weigel-as-Teresa, in which he becomes fascinated by the multivalent function of stage props. In 'The Actress in Exile', he describes Weigel preparing for the role backstage, highlighting the objects that she will use to create her character:

> Now she puts on her makeup. In the white cell
> She sits bowed on the simple stool
> With light movements
> She applies the makeup in the mirror.
> Carefully she washes away from her face
> All that is particular: the gentlest sensation
> Will transform it. From time to time
> She lets her frail and noble shoulders
> Fall forward, like those who have to
> Work hard. She already has on the rough blouse
> With patches at the sleeves. The bast shoes
> Stand on the makeup table.
> When she's ready
> She asks eagerly if the drum has arrived
> On which the thunder of the guns will be made, and
> And if the big net is
> Already hanging ... (Brecht, *Love Poems*, 74)[23]

While 'The Actress in Exile' holds Weigel up as the exemplar of epic acting – she walks on stage not to become Teresa Carrar, but to 'represent/ The struggle of the Andalusian fisherman's wife/ Against the generals' – it also merges Weigel's reality with Teresa's. Weigel's own environment is as dilapidated as Teresa's patched-up costume. When Weigel 'lets her frail and noble shoulders/ Fall forward', the posture she deliberately adopts for the war-weary Teresa echoes her earlier 'bowed' posture on the stool as she began her own hard work.

Brecht tried to articulate the significance of Weigel's 'eager' interest in the humble tools of her trade in two poems titled 'Weigel's Props', an epigram written in 1940 and a longer poem included in *Der Messingkauf* in 1950 (Willett in Brecht, *Poems*, 598). In the 1940 poem, Brecht juxtaposes the tools Weigel uses as an actress with the tools she used during their exile as wife and mother:

> See here the stool and the old mirror
> In front of which she sat, her lines upon her lap.
> See the stick of make-up, the tiny pot of grease-paint.
> And the net she made as fisherwoman.
>
> But also see, from the time of flight,
> The five-ore piece with the hole in it, the worn shoe, the brass skillet
> She cooked blueberries for the children in,
> And the wooden board she kneaded on.
>
> All that she handled in good times and bad,
> Hers and yours, it lies here to be seen.

O great treasure despising glitter,
Actress and exile, skivvy and wife! (Reprinted in Pintzka, *Helene Weigel*, 66)

Weigel's work in *Señora Carrar's Rifles* is referenced not just by the net but by the 'old' mirror, stool, and 'tiny pot of greasepaint', which allude to 'The Actress in Exile'. There is, again, no clear boundary between Weigel's 'wretched' circumstances and Teresa's; if anything, the new adjectives for the mirror and the make-up further blur the distinction. The inventory of artefacts from 'the time of flight' includes objects Weigel used as the mother of Brecht's children – the foreign coin, the brass skillet – along with some which could belong either to Weigel's home or to Teresa's. The 'worn shoe' recalls the canvas shoes into which Weigel steps at the end of 'The Actress in Exile', while 'the wooden board she kneaded on' is fully ambiguous. It could be something Weigel used to cook for her children; but it could equally be 'the Basque woman's board on which she bakes her bread', which Brecht references in the later 'Weigel's Props'. Indeed, given the limited resources available to Dudow and Berlau, she may well have used the same board in both roles.

The final stanza piles the tools Weigel uses at all of her jobs – as mother, as 'actress and exile, skivvy and wife' – into the same 'great treasure despising glitter'. The German word rendered as 'skivvy' in this translation is 'Magd', which has some of the same connotations as 'maid' in English; it can refer to a female servant but it can also refer to a virgin or to *the* Virgin (Brecht, 'Die Requisiten Der Weigel', 146). Balanced with 'Frau' (rendered here as 'wife' though it can also mean 'woman') it complicates the final line, poising Weigel between two life stages (maid and wife, young woman and mature woman) while highlighting the hard labour involved in playing all of these feminine roles.

The second version of 'Weigel's Props' strives to restore the separation of performer from role by suppressing this personal dimension, eliminating direct references to the world outside the theatre and restricting itself to the props Weigel used in productions before, during and after the war. Brecht stresses Weigel's intentionality, treating her 'select[ion]' of props as both an art and a science:

Just as the millet farmer picks out for his trial plot
The heaviest seeds and the poet
The exact words for his verse so
She selects the objects to accompany
Her characters across the stage. The pewter spoon
Which Courage sticks
In the lapel of her Mongolian jacket, the party card
For warm-hearted Vlassova and the fishing net

> For the other, Spanish mother or the bronze bowl
> For dust-gathering Antigone. Impossible to confuse
> The split bag which the working woman carries
> For her son's leaflets, with the moneybag
> Of the keen tradeswoman. (Brecht, *Poems*, 427)[24]

By not naming Teresa (identified here only by her nationality and her net) Brecht minimises the personal history to which she is attached; this poem does not mention exile. At the same time, by designating her as 'the other' mother, he implies Teresa's kinship with Vlassova and Courage and suggests that they are versions of the same figure. The particularity so important to Brecht's materialist theatre is nevertheless preserved by Weigel's expert selection of things that instantly convey the circumstances that created each personality. It is thanks to Weigel's props that it is 'impossible to confuse' Vlassova and her choices with Courage and hers. While her performance in these mother roles creates continuity, Weigel also generates a unique reality for each character with densely signifying pieces from the hoard of objects that is her dowry as mother, actress, exile and wife: a pewter spoon, a jar of lard, a net to mend, a chicken to pluck, a board for baking bread.

Brecht ends by celebrating Weigel as a fellow artist and worker whose tools are

> Selected for age, function and beauty
> By the eyes of the knowing
> The hands of the bread-baking, net-weaving
> Soup-cooking connoisseur
> Of reality. (Ibid., 427–8)

Making Weigel a 'connoisseur' (another way to render the German 'Kennerin' would be 'expert') emphasises her critical intelligence, rendering 'reality' a medium over which she exerts artistic control. But the stubborn materiality of the objects themselves, which must be 'hand picked', preserves Weigel's physicality; she remains present not just as a discerning consciousness but as a pair 'bread-baking, net-weaving/ Soup-cooking' hands around which multiple kinds of work, multiple mother figures, and multiple realities now condense. If the emphasis in Brecht's discursive writing has been on Weigel's capacity to 'show' – on the ironic self-consciousness that prevents her from inhabiting a role – the poetry tells a different story. In them, Weigel's unique corporeal body, fully and powerfully present, is the irreplaceable link between art and reality, the gravitational centre holding the system together.

If Brecht's use of *Riders to the Sea* in *Señora Carrar's Rifles* clearly exceeds whatever Synge's intentions might have been, Weigel's creation of Teresa Carrar takes Brecht's play beyond some of the boundaries that restrict Brecht's own theory. As her hands manipulate those household objects, her theatrical character and her role as the mother of Brecht's children interpenetrate, the one becoming as performative or as essential as the other. In the first version of 'Weigel's Props' we see Brecht approaching an insight that might have enabled him to understand maternity itself as a contingent social construct inviting critique – to see in Weigel's conflation of actress, exile, servant and wife the densely layered imperatives that compel the mother's self-sacrifice. As Teresa Carrar, Weigel – herself a militant mother – incarnates her own 'praxis', one which does not so much embody Brecht's theory as push its limits.

Conclusion

The story of Maurya's mobilisation suggests that Brecht's understanding of the emotional exchanges between performer and spectator was more subtle than he was prepared to acknowledge. It suggests, specifically, that by the time Brecht wrote *Mother Courage* – the 'favored text' for those who claim that Brecht's plays succeed in spite of his intentions (Gleitman, 'All in the Family', 148) – he knew how to use the grieving mother to create an intense emotional response which was, nevertheless, not 'empathetic'. *Mother Courage* depends for its impact on the stark divergences that Brecht creates between the mother's expressions and the spectators' feelings. In a scene that Roche identifies as an echo of *Riders*, the body of Courage's son Swiss Cheese is brought to her by the soldiers who killed him (Roche, 'Synge, Brecht, and the Hiberno-German Connection', 29). Courage knows, as the audience knows, that if she betrays her relationship to him, she will be killed. Brecht would also seem to have known, by now, that forcing Courage *not* to express grief was the surest way of inducing spectators to feel it. Brecht enforces another divergence by informing the audience of Eilif's death while Courage is off stage. Since Courage never learns of Eilif's death, she cannot grieve for him; the spectators have to do it for her. Courage is therefore structurally prevented from making the spectators her mirror. To find Courage 'tragic and moving' (ibid.), spectators have to move themselves.

All this might seem, as Jameson would put it, to give 'aid and comfort to Brecht's critics, who always maintained that Brechtian distanciation was impossible' (*Brecht and Method*, 55). But my goal in restoring Teresa Carrar to this sequence of Brechtian mothers is not to argue that identification is unavoidable or that the divergent responses produced by the alienation effect are simply empathy under another name. As Jameson argues, one cannot identify with what is not there. There is a significant difference between 'surrendering' to the mother's grief and *creating* that grief after confronting its terrifying absence. It is the moment of confrontation – the spectator's perception of a mother capable of refusing grief – that suggests alternatives and releases the 'radical' potential of both Maurya and Teresa as models for working-class motherhood. It is only by breaking the mirror of empathy that Brecht can engineer that confrontation.

At the same time, the fact that the spectator is immediately moved to erase that absence by filling the mother with his or her own emotions suggests that the difference between the mirroring and the active generation of emotion is significant in ways that Brecht and his proponents might not wish to acknowledge. Based on this history, in fact, it would appear that the vision of alternative possibilities created by the 'radical absence' of the performer's emotion is fleeting, while the more permanent effect of preventing the spectator from 'surrendering' to empathy is to intensify the spectator's emotional excitement and thereby increase his or her pleasure. In other words, breaking our hearts over Mother Courage is *more* pleasurable to us because we feel *for* her rather than *with* her; we enjoy *Mother Courage*, not 'in spite' of Brecht's intentions, but *because* of them. The catch, from the spectator's point of view, is that this pleasure is inseparable from the play's ideological content. The catch, from Brecht's point of view, is that this pleasure *is* – as both Helen Henry's admirers and bourgeois Brechtians demonstrate – separable from the revolutionary action that 'epic theatre' intends to provoke.

It was perhaps a sense that his technique might not *necessarily* or *inevitably* produce the desired results that kept turning Brecht's attention back to Weigel and her props – that prompted him to challenge what Olga Taxidou calls the 'somatophobia' of modernist performance and foreground instead 'the materiality and the theatricality' of the link between performer and prop (Taxidou, 'Machines and Models', 253). According to Taxidou, the implications of Weigel's props continued to expand the horizons of Brechtian draumaturgy well into the 1940s, as the 'intricate relationship between subject and object on the stage' which is 'a fundamental aspect of the Brechtian *gestus*' (ibid., 251) enables him, Weigel and Berlau to collaborate again in the production of a meaningful artistic response to the 'ruin' of the Second World War (ibid., 253). In Taxidou's reading of the *Antigone-Model 1948* (in which Berlau's photographs document Weigel's performance of Brecht's *Antigone*), the 'image of Helene Weigel attached to the door proposes an interchangeability between subjects and objects on stage' (ibid., 251), and 'confuses the line between actors and objects, granting neither the privilege of agency, ascension, or sublimation' (ibid., 253). Weigel's props take on an inextinguishable yet insufficient 'life', opening a 'rupture' between life and death which is precisely the space of catastrophe that Antigone must inhabit (ibid., 254). If Brecht foresaw that his technique would become 'a type of mediation' (ibid., 257) for someone else's message, that might explain his fascination with a unique and irreplaceable pair of soup-cooking hands capable of transforming the detritus of a ruined world into the 'work of mourning' (ibid., 242) that the postwar world would demand.

Notes

1. The best summary of the genesis of *Señora Carrar's Rifles* is in John Willett and Ralph Manheim's Introduction to Volume 4, part 3 of *Bertolt Brecht: Collected Plays*, xi–xiii.
2. The English title arose in 1938 when Keene Wallis's translation was published in *Theatre Workshop*. Brecht preferred the more literal *Mrs. Carrar's Guns* (Brecht, *Letters*, 288).
3. Critics disagree on the relationship between the two plays. Martin Esslin describes *Señora Carrar's Rifles* as 'vaguely based on' *Riders* (*Brecht*, 69). Keith A. Dickson reads both *Señora Carrar* and *Mutter Courage und Ihre Kinder* as 'counter-projects' (*Towards Utopia*, 107). Johannes Kleinstück claims that the two plays have virtually nothing in common ('Synge in Germany', 275–6). Sidney Poger argues for *Señora Carrar*'s 'significant indebtedness' to *Riders* ('Brecht's *Señora*', 37–8). For the most persuasive discussion of the specific parallels between *Señora Carrar's Rifles* and *Riders to the Sea*, see Roche, 'Synge, Brecht, and the Hiberno-German Connection', 25–7.
4. See Sarah Lennox, 'Women in Brecht's Work', 86; Sue-Ellen Case, 'Brecht and Women', 70–3; and Teresa Ritterhof, 'Ver/Ratlosigkeit'.
5. See Gay Gibson Cima, *Performing Women*, 92–121; Claire Gleitman, 'All in the Family'; and Kim Solga, '*Mother Courage* and its Abject'.
6. These include Elin Diamond's *Unmaking Mimesis*, Gay Gibson Cima's *Performing Women*, Sarah Bryant-Bertail's *Space and Time*, and Sue-Ellen Case and Janelle Reinelt's work in *The Brecht Yearbook*.
7. Brecht acknowledged only Steffin as a collaborator. The question of Brecht's debts to his collaborator-lovers has been a contentious issue since John Fuegi published *Brecht & Co* in 1994. The picture that emerges from Ruth Berlau's memoir and from reputable scholarship (from which category I exclude Fuegi's biography) is that Steffin functioned as editor and amanuensis, Berlau and Brecht brainstormed, and Weigel revised Teresa Carrar's dialogue. See Paula Hanssen, 'Brecht and Weigel', 181–90, and Sabine Gross, 'Margarete Steffin's Children's Plays', 67–88.
8. Maurya starts out convinced that Bartley will not survive his journey; her fears are confirmed by a series of ill omens.
9. The anecdote of the spinning wheel is retailed in Lady Gregory's *Our Irish Theatre*. With regard to the pampooties and flannel, see Saddlemyer's introduction to Synge's *The Aran Islands. Collected Works* (xviii–xix).
10. Roche also follows Dickson in reading *Mother Courage* as a dialectical response to *Riders* (Roche, 'Synge, Brecht, and the Hiberno-German Connection', 28–9).
11. Vlassova's name is transliterated in many different ways. I will retain this spelling throughout.
12. See Willett and Manheim, 'Introduction', vii–xiv.
13. See Brecht's letters to Paul Peters, 215–18.
14. For an analysis of the mismatch between Brecht and the Theatre Union and its audiences, see Bradley, *Brecht and Political Theatre*, 137–54.
15. See notes in the Theatre Union promptbook for performances on 24 November and 3 December.
16. *Variety* (2 November 1935) notes that '[t]he attempts to be different in its staging appear to have resulted in reverse reaction, many first nighters regarding it as distinctly amateurish'. This and all other reviews of the Theatre Union production cited here are taken from clipping files (T-CLP: The Mother and MWEZ+n.c.4648) held in the Billy Rose Theatre Division, The New York Public Library for

the Performing Arts. Many of these clippings do not preserve full publication information.
17. Dash's review appeared in *Women's Wear Daily* (Dash, 'Mother'). John Anderson complains that the show lacked 'the excitement of what a bourgeois critic might consider the theater' (Anderson, 'Drama'); Howard Barnes faults it for having 'little of the bite and excitement of persuasive propaganda' (Barnes, 'The Theaters');' Robert Coleman suggests that the play is so 'boring' that it might have been what drove Brecht and Eisler into exile (Coleman, 'Mother').
18. See John Anderson, 'Drama'.
19. See Burns Mantle, '"Mother"'; Thomas R. Dash, 'Mother' (*Women's Wear Daily*); Robert Garland, '"Mother"'; and John Whitney, 'Broadway Last Night', *Newark Evening News*, n.d., 22.
20. Poger rejects Teresa's political conversion ('Brecht's Señora', 42–3); Roche calls it a 'problem' ('Synge, Brecht, and the Hiberno-German Connection', 28).
21. Wolff's translation of *Riders* was performed in Basel in 1935; but Brecht was in exile in Denmark then, and spent much of 1935 travelling to Paris, London, the Soviet Union and New York (Willett in Brecht, *Letters*, 157).
22. Hanssen quotes this in the original German; I am indebted to Rebecca Haltzel-Haas for the English translation.
23. 'The Actress in Exile', originally published in German in 1937 as 'Die Schauspieleren im Exil', translated by Tom Kuhn. Copyright ©1937 by Bertolt-Brecht-Erben/Suhrkamp Verlag, from *Love Poems* by Bertolt Brecht, translated by David Constantine and Tom Kuhn. Used by permission of Liveright Publishing Corporation.
24. 'Weigel's Props', originally published in German in 1961 as 'Die Requisiten Der Weigel', translated by John Willett. Copyright ©1961, 1976 by Bertolt-Brecht-Erben/Suhrkamp Verlag, from *Bertolt Brecht Poems 1913–1956* by Bertolt Brecht, edited by John Willett and Ralph Manheim. Used by permission of Liveright Publishing Corporation.

5

THE FLAMING SUNFLOWER: THE SOVIET UNION AND SEAN O'CASEY'S POST-REALISM

INTRODUCTION

Sean O'Casey's place in the canon of modern Irish drama is secured by three plays known as the 'Dublin trilogy', all written and produced during the mid-1920s and all dramatising the effects of Ireland's revolutionary conflicts on the inhabitants of Dublin's slums. O'Casey's *Shadow of a Gunman*, *Juno and the Paycock* and *The Plough and the Stars* were phenomenally profitable for the Abbey, partly because O'Casey had created a fusion of realism and melodrama which was eminently accessible to middle-class and working-class spectators. But the plays on which his literary reputation now rests are the only three unambiguously realistic plays O'Casey ever wrote. After Yeats, Gregory and Lennox Robinson rejected O'Casey's experimental 1928 play *The Silver Tassie*, O'Casey settled in England, where he definitively rejected realism with his 1934 play *Within the Gates*. He pursued his quest for a new dramatic form until his death in 1964. We think of O'Casey as a disillusioned realist only because most of the work he produced after his break with the Abbey has dropped out of literary history. The plays O'Casey wrote after *The Silver Tassie* are rarely taught, seldom written about and almost never produced.

O'Casey's experimental phase has gone down the memory hole for two main reasons. The first is that O'Casey's experiments took him in directions directly opposed to some major trends in avant-garde theatre that have shaped our understanding of what constitutes good art. Though O'Casey claimed

Shakespeare and Boucicault as his influences, what we see in his later work is the legacy of the loose and baggy maximalism invented by George Bernard Shaw for his first Irish play – the polar opposite of the stripped-down minimalism so successfully promoted by their compatriot Samuel Beckett. The result is that to contemporary readers, most of O'Casey's later work just seems . . . well . . . bad.

The second reason is that O'Casey's experimental phase is coeval with his left turn from the labour socialism of his Dublin days to a public embrace of the Communist Party and the Soviet Union. What distinguishes O'Casey from many other intellectuals who gravitated towards Communism during the Popular Front era is his deep commitment to the Soviet Union itself, which lasted until O'Casey's death in 1964. In the late 1930s, while British intellectuals scrambled to repudiate the Soviet Union, O'Casey, as they say in baseball, went the other way with it. He joined the editorial board of the *Daily Worker*, defended Stalin's show trials and wrote a four-act glorification of the Soviet Union entitled *The Star Turns Red* which was produced in 1940 by Unity Theatre, a workers' theatre affiliated with and probably bankrolled by the Communist Party of Great Britain. None of the revelations about Stalin's regime altered O'Casey's public stance. O'Casey's unshakeable conviction that Stalin was a 'great man' was and remains a source of distress for his family, friends and supporters.[1] The understandably charged emotions raised by this issue have long distorted treatments of his later work.

In this chapter, I will examine the interpenetration between O'Casey's aesthetic choices and his political allegiances during his red period. By doing so, I argue, we gain greater understanding both of an important period in the life of one of Ireland's most influential modern playwrights, and of the ways in which Soviet literature, culture and gender politics interacted not only with modern Irish drama but with the Cold War-era criticism that played such an important role in defining modernist drama and theatre. The great paradox of O'Casey's reception is that many of those who professed the greatest admiration for both the man himself and his later work – here, I will focus primarily on the influential American drama critics George Jean Nathan and Brooks Atkinson and the indefatigable O'Casey scholars David Krause and Ronald Ayling – were also the most adamant that his politics had nothing to do with his plays. Krause's *Sean O'Casey's World*, for instance, assures us that O'Casey's 'eclectic and unpredictable belief in Communism [was] more emotional than political, more of a personal faith than a party programme' (68). This interpretation was affirmed with enthusiasm and relief by the venerable *New York Times* drama critic Brooks Atkinson, whose review of Krause's 1960 *Sean O'Casey: The Man and His Work* was headlined 'O'Casey's Communism is Really a Dream of A Better Life for Mankind' (Atkinson, *Sean O'Casey*, 151). But as we now know, the 'emotional' and the 'political' have never been separable in left culture – neither in the era of queer socialism, nor in the era of syndicalism, nor in the era of Soviet Communism. And as I will show, the aspects of his later plays that these critics most often cite to prove that O'Casey wasn't 'really' a Communist – the richness of his language, the religious sensibility, the optimistic 'faith in life' (ibid., 9) – are the aspects most obviously *produced* by his exposure both to Larkinite syndicalism and Soviet Communism.

O'Casey's identification with the Soviet Union was founded in part on his belief that it was a society where the kind of writing that *he* had always wanted to do – but which neither the Abbey nor the commercial theatre wanted – had not only *a* place but *the* place of honour. Communism, for O'Casey, was not solely an ideology, but rather a network of organisations, institutions and publications through which he hoped to build an international audience for his work. This network became more important to O'Casey with every bridge he burned; and when it came to bridges, Sean O'Casey was a demolition expert. Like Shaw, O'Casey saw the Soviet Union as the last best hope of the worldwide workers' revolution; but he also saw it as the source of a literary culture with whose aims and forms O'Casey believed he was in sympathy.

Expanding the scope of our enquiry to include the Soviet Union and Soviet literary history changes our perspective on much of O'Casey's later work. Re-reading O'Casey's red period in this context doesn't make it any more flattering; if anything, it demonstrates all the more vividly that O'Casey earned the niche he has long occupied between W. B. Yeats and Ezra Pound in the Hall of Grievously Mistaken Modernists. Restoring this segment of O'Casey's career to the history of twentieth-century Anglophone literature will, however, allow us to examine the impact that the rise of a Communist world power had on Anglophone avant-garde drama and performance – and give us a better understanding of what modern drama lost when Soviet Communism set socialism straight.

Larkin, Labour and Lomonosova

The first step in reassessing O'Casey's red period is arriving at a reasonably accurate understanding of when and how he fell for the Soviet Union. This has been made maddeningly difficult by O'Casey himself, who enjoyed generating revisionist fantasies about his own life. To take just one example of how these fantasies become embodied in criticism: in a special issue on socialism in Ireland published by the *Crane Bag* in 1983, Robert Lowery discusses O'Casey's prescient response to the Russian Revolution of 1917. Citing O'Casey's description of himself eagerly scanning Irish newspapers for news of the Bolsheviks, Lowery praises his foresight: 'It is a tribute to [O'Casey's] socialist consciousness . . . that he was able to read between the lines . . . When the press ceased to mention Lenin's name, the playwright knew that power had been gained in the newly-formed U.S.S.R.' (Lowery, 'Socialist Legacy', 5).

This narrative is based on a piece titled 'Lenin: Logos of Russia' that O'Casey wrote for publication in the Soviet Union after Stalin's death in 1953.[2] O'Casey wrote several similar articles for Soviet media, and there are good reasons not to treat any of them as objective records of actual events. For one thing, O'Casey's identification of the point at which he and the rest of the dejected radical Irish labour movement are electrified by the glorious news from Russia changes with each retelling. In an unpublished piece titled 'The Star Ascending', the big bang is the fall of the Romanovs amidst the general strikes and mutinies of the spring of 1917. But in 'When the News Came to Dublin', published in *Instronnaya Literatura* in 1957, the workers of Ireland are revived by a different revolutionary moment: the seizure of power by the Bolshevik party in October 1917. By the time O'Casey retells this story in 'Lenin', published in 1960 in *Inostrannaya Literatura*, the news from Russia isn't so much a thunderbolt as a constant drizzle:

> Suddenly the news came that the Czar had been dethroned and that the Russian People had declared against monarchy. The workers in Ireland cowed and sullen heard that the Russian workers were in revolt, and joy came into many hearts. Later the news came that the Provisional Government were responsible men ... and the staunch hearts of Irish workers got gloomy again. Then the name of LENIN came suddenly into the papers, saying he was leading a Revolutionary Party which had overhtrown [sic] the Bourgeois Provisional Government, and had declared as Soldiers, Workers, and Peasants Socialist Republic! Minds which had become quiet while the prudent Kerensky was in power now became anxious, and gloomy hearts among the militant workers rejoiced again. (O'Casey, 'Lenin', 2–3)

Sacrificing dramatic impact for the sake of the title character, this version presents the emergence of LENIN into the Irish press as *the* revolutionary moment.

This shifting representation of O'Casey's revolutionary epiphany correlates less closely with O'Casey's life than with market demand. 'The Star Ascending' does not appear to have found a Soviet publisher. The two pieces in which Lenin is identified with and indeed *as* the Revolution, on the other hand, appeared within two days of O'Casey's most outrageously hagiographic tribute to Lenin, 'The Flaming Sunflower':

> I love flowers; love them for their beauty, their economic uses benefiting man, their value in medicine towards stopping pain and helping in illness; I like to know where each came from first, and the family each belongs to; and one of my first favorites is the Sunflower. I love the plant for the beauty of its gold-brown disk and yellow petals raying out like the beams

of a sun; for its sturdiness, its stature, rising higher than its companion plants; its value in producing heat-giving seeds in rich profusion; its majestic look as it stands among the other flowers; and it always faces towards the sun: the plant is a fine symbol of the great Lenin; its characteristics are the same as his – Lenin was, is still, a Flaming Sunflower. (O'Casey, 'The Flaming Sunflower', 5)

This passage showcases three defining characteristics of O'Casey's writing for and about the Soviet Union. First, whereas contemporary readers are more likely to imagine Stalinist Russia as the shade of untreated cement, in O'Casey's imagination the Soviet Union is always saturated with the sensuous beauty so desired by queer socialism. Second, although panegyric was a staple of Soviet propaganda, this Blakean/VanGoghesque/Ginsbergian exaltation of the sunflower marks 'The Flaming Sunflower' as a highly idiosyncratic instance of it, and demonstrates the extent to which Shelley's idealism and Larkin's extravagance continued to find expression in O'Casey's work even after the masculinisation of the revolutionary period. Third, 'The Flaming Sunflower' makes more sense in the context of Soviet history. 'The Flaming Sunflower' was published in *Izvestia* on 21 April 1960. The 22nd of April 1960 was the ninetieth anniversary of Lenin's birthday. The fact that O'Casey composed three tributes to Lenin on this occasion suggests more than a spontaneous overflow of revolutionary ardour. It suggests that O'Casey understood that the ninetieth anniversary would create demand, in the Soviet market, for the kind of overheated eulogy that O'Casey had been producing with ease since *The Story of Thomas Ashe* in 1917.

The archive suggests that O'Casey's interest in the Soviet Union became serious only after Jim Larkin's release from prison and return to Dublin in 1923. In the fall of 1914, Larkin set sail for America with the intention of raising money for the Irish Transport and General Workers' Union (ITGWU) and forging ties with American syndicalism (E. Larkin, *James Larkin*, 177–84). After America entered the First World War in 1917, Larkin was prevented from leaving the USA. During the U. S. government's anti-IWW (Industrial Workers of the World) campaigns of 1919 (Darlington, *Syndicalism*, 162–3), Larkin was arrested, convicted of 'criminal anarchy', and imprisoned. No longer the charismatic leader of 1913, this older, angrier Jim Larkin was recruited to help establish a viable Communist Party in Ireland. Larkin was a very troublesome operative, but he did at least convert O'Casey, who mentions in a January 1925 letter to Lady Gregory that he 'had dinner with [Larkin] and a Communist organiser' (O'Casey, *Letters of Sean O'Casey* 1, 123). In November, O'Casey proudly reports to Lady Gregory that all of a sudden he's huge in Russia:

I happened to mention to a German Labour comrade, whom I met in the Abbey, that I was thinking of writing in the future a Labour play to be called 'The Red Star.' Since then I have received appeals from Leningrad & Moscow to let them know when the play is to be commenced & when finished, & to send on the work to them Scene by scene & act by act so as to avoid all possible delay in production! (Ibid., 155)

O'Casey's reference to 'The Red Star' refers to the years before the Dublin trilogy, when O'Casey still had ambitions to write the next great Irish strike play – and Lady Gregory and Lennox Robinson persuaded him to abandon them.

For labour drama at the Abbey, *The Labour Leader* marked the end of an era. As the War of Independence wore on, it became clearer that Bolshevism would not be reconciled with Gaelic and Catholic nationalism, and that Sinn Féin was not committed to labour's agenda, and that public ownership was not going to become the foundation of the new Irish government. We can see this change of heart in the directors' responses to the scripts that O'Casey started sending them in 1916.[3] Of *Profit and Loss* we know only the title, *The Frost in the Flower* is lost, but *The Harvest Festival* survives, and we have reader's reports on *The Crimson in the Tri-Colour*. *The Harvest Festival*'s central character, Jack Rocliffe, is a lone-wolf labour leader given to long, impassioned speeches with a strong evangelical flavour. Robinson complained, with some justification, that the play was 'seldom dramatic', and encouraged O'Casey to work on character development.

It is not until the discussion around *The Crimson in the Tri-Colour* in 1921 that we clearly see a political agenda at work. O'Casey described *Crimson* to Lennox Robinson as 'a Futurist work, evolved from the passions, ideas & activities of the present' (ibid., 94). Lady Gregory found the play 'puzzling' but 'extremely interesting' and was full of suggestions for revision (ibid., 95–6). Nevertheless, when she met with O'Casey on 21 November 1921, what she told him was that the present moment was not right for his futurist work. The Abbey would not do a play about the conflict between Labour and Sinn Féin while the revolution was in progress. Her reader's report was firm on this point: '[W]e could not put it on while the Revolution is still unaccomplished – it might hasten the Labour attack on Sinn Fein, which ought to be kept back till the fight with England is over' (ibid., 95).

The directors kept the manuscript, however, and in 1922 Robinson and Gregory did reconsider *Crimson*. Explaining their decision not to produce it, Robinson sent O'Casey the least offensive portion of W. B. Yeats's reader report. Yeats disliked the play's hero, who emerges 'suddenly, at the end' as 'some kind of labour leader' (ibid., 102), and objected to its plot: 'It is a story without meaning – a story where nothing happens except that a wife runs away from a husband . . . & the Mansion House lights are turned out because of some wrong to a man that never appears in the play' (ibid.).

In rejecting this ending, Yeats was rejecting the core belief governing syndicalist practice: an injury to one is an injury to all. From a syndicalist point of view, responding to wrongs done to people who have never 'appeared' in the drama of your specific life is not 'without meaning'. It was precisely by persuading people to act on behalf of others whose personalities and histories were unknown to them that syndicalists hoped to accomplish the revolution. Yeats's response points out that syndicalist structures of feeling are incompatible with the Aristotelian framework that undergirds dramatic 'construction'. O'Casey's radically different politics have thus produced the methods against which Yeats reacts so violently; but the objection is articulated purely in aesthetic terms.

O'Casey got the message. 'The reader adversely criticises the fact that an action is performed for a man that never appears on stage', he writes to Robinson. 'I am glad this is mentioned, for I was thinking of writing a play around Jim Larkin – The Red Star – in which he would never appear though [be] responsible for all the action' (ibid., 105). In other words, he is 'glad' to know that he should not bother writing 'The Red Star'. In the rest of the letter, O'Casey shows willingness to adapt to his readers' demands, asking to talk to Robinson in person about his next manuscript before submitting it. This was a tragicomedy originally titled *On the Run*, and eventually called *Shadow of a Gunman*.

Shadow of a Gunman appears to be entirely preoccupied with republican politics. O'Casey's socialism is on view mainly in the representation of tenement poverty and in the pessimistic vision of Ireland's future under republican rule. The only protest O'Casey allows himself against the silencing of *The Crimson in the Tri-Colour* and the preclusion of *The Red Star* is a satire on his protagonist's abuse of Shelley's revolutionary *eros*. Donal Davoren, believed by his fellow-tenement dwellers to be an IRA gunman, is in fact an aspiring poet and Shelley enthusiast. But Davoren, who misunderstands the political games he's playing, also gets Shelley wrong. Davoren's poetry is limited to lyrical descriptions of natural beauty in the context of heterosexual courtship, as in the passage he recites for Minnie:

> One day, when morn's half-opened eyes
> Were bright with Spring's sunshine –
> My hand was clasp'd in yours, dear love,
> And yours were clasp'd in mine –
> We bow'd as worshippers before
> The Golden Celandine. (O'Casey, *Plays 2*, 16)

O'Casey lifted Davoren's lines from his own poem 'A Walk with Eros', an epic hymn to Shelley's revolutionary *eros*. At first, the speaker wanders through a lush spring landscape with his beloved, as descriptions of budding spring flowers and green grass become freighted with the speaker's erotic desires; but when they return to the city, 'Eros's visions lose their beauty' in a place where human desires are thwarted by the evil conditions created by capitalist greed (O'Casey, *Windfalls*, 17). O'Casey doesn't allow Davoren access to the poem's critique of capitalism; that is reserved for *Juno*'s betrayed idealist, Mary Boyle, who quotes the ominous transitional passage of 'A Walk With Eros' immediately after being let down by Jerry Devine.[4] Davoren writes romantic poetry purely to meet girls, without any appreciation of its transformative power. Dejectedly reciting from Shelley's *Epipsychidion* at the beginning of Act II, Davoren approaches epiphany when he notes that the 'cold chaste moon' of Shelley's poem 'couldn't make this thrice accursed room beautiful'; the tenement belongs to 'an ugliness that can only be destroyed' (O'Casey, *Plays 2*, 33). But it never occurs to Davoren that the Shelley of *The Mask of Anarchy*, *The Revolt of Islam* and *Queen Mab* could help destroy it.

In the Dublin trilogy, we are always living in the disillusioned aftermath of idealism; the acrid scent of resentment camouflages whatever else might have wafted up to us from Davoren's golden celandine. At this stage, O'Casey is more concerned with his big break than with his aesthetic and ideological credos. At *Juno*'s premiere, what O'Casey remembers is not Gregory's concern about the revolution but her assertion that his 'gift [was] characterisation' (Gregory, *Journals*, I, 512). Gregory, Yeats and Robinson thus used their gatekeeping function to move O'Casey away from labour as a subject, and helped convince him that realism and Larkinite labour politics were mutually incompatible.[5] They were assisted by history and by Larkin himself. When he finally returned to Ireland, Larkin's attempt to regain power triggered Irish labour's own 'civil war' (E. Larkin, *James Larkin*, 267). After Larkin was expelled from the ITGWU in March 1924, the Larkinite faction established a 'Provisional Committee' which declared itself the legitimate executive of the ITGWU. This faction became the Workers' Union of Ireland (ibid., 282). Each union denounced the other as a 'scab union'. The resulting confusion took its toll, and by 1926 the labour movement was in disarray (ibid., 286).

Committing himself to realism at this time allowed O'Casey to cope with the conflict between his identification with his idealised hero and his disillusionment with a labour movement that was disemboweling itself. To take Larkin's side, O'Casey had to turn his back on the ITGWU and accept Larkin's estimation of the ITGWU's leadership as hypocritical, corrupt and self-serving – as, in fact, much like *Juno*'s Jerry Devine, 'a type, becoming very common now in the Labour Movement, of a mind knowing enough to make the mass of his associates, who know less, a power, and too little to broaden that power for the benefit of all' (O'Casey, *Juno*, 208). O'Casey used realism to indict the movement that had betrayed and expelled his hero, but preserved Larkin's ideal status by keeping him out of the Dublin trilogy.

Looking back at O'Casey's letter about 'The Red Star', then, we might detect just a dash of bitterness in O'Casey's eagerness to let Lady Gregory know that *another* avant-garde national theatre is *very* interested in his labour plays. These 'appeals from Leningrad & Moscow' were relayed to him by Raisa Lomonosova, who was establishing a literary agency in Berlin which she hoped would facilitate exchange between Soviet and Western writers (Davies and McCormack, 'Unpublished Correspondence', 181). Lomonosova, whose husband had been active in the 1917 Revolution and held a diplomatic position, had travelled widely, had been active in the international women's peace movement, and had established herself as a patron of the arts (Cohen, 'Early Endeavors', 191–3). O'Casey's correspondence with Lomonosova suggested that the labour movement that had forged most of O'Casey's lasting personal relationships might also be a network through which his labour plays could find an audience. Lomonosova's interest in O'Casey's work was sparked by the fact that O'Casey happened to mention his idea for 'The Red Star' to a 'German Labour comrade' at a time when the Berlin-based Lomonosova was looking for plays that could be translated for production in the Soviet Union (Davies and McCormack, 'Unpublished Correspondence', 181).

Lomonosova's 'appeals' were O'Casey's first hint that the Soviet Union might be a market for the kind of work that the Abbey gatekeepers had discouraged him from pursuing. Unlike Lady Gregory, Lomonosova wasn't interested in O'Casey's 'gift for characterisation'. Her partner Korney Chukovsky had read *Shadow* and *Juno* and judged them 'not very talented' (quoted in ibid., 182). Though Chukovsky liked some of the Irish peasant plays Lomonosova sent him, he reported in August that they had been 'deemed to be offensive to the dignity of working people' (quoted in ibid.). 'The Red Star' would have suited their needs much better; Jim Larkin was still an international labour hero. Finally, O'Casey had found a buyer for the play he had been trying to write for the past ten years. Alas, he had not yet written it; and at the time, he was too busy with *The Plough and the Stars* to do so. O'Casey had to rebuff numerous requests for 'The Red Star' from a persistent Lomonosova; but her interest ended in 1927, when she and her husband fled Stalin's regime. O'Casey later regretted that 'this faint link with the Soviet Union was severed, and it wasn't till some years later that I got into touch with this energy and enthusiasm again' (O'Casey, 'Rise o' the Red Star', 10).

The Abbey's rejection in 1928 of his experimental anti-war drama *The Silver Tassie*, and the paper war that followed, helped convince O'Casey to sever his ties with both the Abbey and realism, and to pursue his quest for a new anti-realist form on the London stage. Because O'Casey's move to England coincides with the consolidation of Stalin's power in the Soviet Union, however, his exchange with Lomonosova represents O'Casey's only contact with the experimental theatre that flourished during the first decade after the 1917

Revolution. It was not until 1934 that it became apparent to O'Casey that London's commercial theatres would be no more hospitable to his experiments than the Abbey had been, and that the only way he could make his career survive his displacement was to embrace an alternative. By then, the Soviet Union had undergone a stark transformation.

By the time O'Casey began identifying himself as Communist, independent ventures like Lomonosova's were a thing of the past. The Party-controlled Writers' Union had a monopoly, and socialist realism was the official mode of Soviet literature. Through the Comintern, Stalin imposed stricter controls on national Communist parties. The British organisations affiliated with the Communist Party of Great Britain (CPGB) were, by the time O'Casey encountered them, undergoing Stalinisation. O'Casey's ambivalent relationship with the British left derives in part from the marked contrast between O'Casey's idiosyncratic adaptation of queer socialism – inflected by Larkin's romantic idealism, but infused with a resolutely heteronormative Protestant evangelism – and the grimness that Stalinisation had imposed on the British left.

Towards A Rich Theatre

In 'The Green Goddess of Realism', an essay O'Casey published in his collection *The Flying Wasp* (1937), O'Casey argues vehemently against his former style. Calling for 'less of what the critics call "life", and more of symbolism', he argues that illusionistic realism is merely symbolism in another guise: 'A room in a realistic play must always be a symbol for a room. There can never be any important actuality on the stage' (O'Casey, *The Flying Wasp*, 124). Most performance theorists would agree. Because theatre's definitive function is to *show* – to hold out actions, characters and events for the observation of the audience – every element of theatrical performance unavoidably becomes a sign. Even if the playwright, director and performers are committed to replicating actuality, 'the ostending, or presenting' of these objects and actions 'guarantees this result' (Carlson, *Theatre Semiotics*, 7). The sofa on which an actress reclines in a realistic production may be a real sofa, but because it is on stage in front of an audience, it also a sign of the imaginary sofa reclined upon by an imaginary person.

What distinguishes realism is the ease with which it conceals the signifying process. Because it is materialised through iconic props and costumes that could function just as well in an actual room as in the room they represent on stage, realism hides the gap between its signifiers and what they signify. It is through this sleight-of-hand that realism '*produces* "reality" by positioning its spectator to recognise and verify its truths' (Diamond, *Unmaking*, 4). O'Casey denounces realism as more deceptively 'fake' (*The Flying Wasp*, 123) than any other mode because it has convinced spectators to accept the symbolic as the real. The essay never explains why the goddess of realism should be green.

The title is most likely a reference to William Archer's horrible melodrama *The Green Goddess*. But the green also suggests that O'Casey is attacking not just London's drawing-room realism, but the Irish realism to which he had so recently contributed.

O'Casey's frustration with his own tenement realism is evident in *Windfalls*, a collection of short stories and poetry that O'Casey published in 1934 to coincide with the production of *Within the Gates*. In 'The Star-Jazzer', O'Casey uses fiction to expose the elisions of stage realism. The unnamed title character is, like Juno, a Dublin tenement mother. The story begins with her washing her family's laundry in the courtyard of her building on a dark, cold night. Looking up at the sky brings home the contrast between the soul-destroying poverty of her life and the beauty of the stars. Inspired by that beauty, she launches into a dance of defiance – an attempt to prove that 'in spite of seven kids carried in ten years', her body is still capable of sensual enjoyment (O'Casey, *Windfalls*, 94). Ecstatic release soon exhausts a body worn out by hard labour, and the protagonist forces herself to return to her tenement room and her family.

Cloying though his use of the stars may be, O'Casey cannot be accused of sugar-coating his protagonist's return to the 'reality of her one-roomed home' (ibid., 101):

> She groped her way along the darkness, her fingers brushing the wall, her lungs, after the coolness and freshness of the outside air, sensing the hot, human, thicker density of the air in the house that gave breath and took breath from the forty-five breathing bodies that lived there. Her foot slipped on something soft and slimy on the stairs; dirty gang of mellowing apes; some kid misbehaved on the stairs, and nobody bothered to clean it away. (Ibid., 99–100)

Adding injury to insult, O'Casey brings her to the bed she shares with her husband Jack and their four surviving children, where she discovers that her work day is not yet over:

> 'No, no, Jack, not to-night . . . too tired for that sort of business . . . Give it over, give it over, Jack . . .'. She tried to plunge away from him, and one of the kids at the bottom of the bed yelled in fright and pain as her toes ploughed his thigh. 'Shut up, there, you!' she heard her husband say viciously to the kid, 'or I'll leather hell into your hide!' She struggled sleepily and wearily against him so as to hang on to a little rest, for it wasn't fair for him to bully her into his embraces when she was so tired . . . He sank his fingers into the flesh of her shoulders and roughly held her from moving . . . 'Keep quiet for a few moments, can't you?' (Ibid., 104–5)

This is realism with a vengeance, executed in detail that would send any theatrical producer fleeing in terror. The audiences who first flocked to *Juno and the*

Paycock were excited to taste the raw reality of life in Dublin's slums; but had they been forced to breathe tenement air, smell shit on the stairs and witness marital rape carried out in the presence of four children, the result would have been a riot the likes of which the Abbey Theatre has never known. Juno's appeal as a character lies precisely in the strength that saves the audience from having to imagine her submitting to this kind of treatment, just as the appeal of the tenement set is that it constructs a persuasively harsh but considerably sanitised 'realistic' and reassuring poverty.

By revealing what the stage can never represent, 'The Star-Jazzer' exposes the signifying aspect of *Juno*'s realism. The Boyles's tenement is a representation controlled by theatrical conventions which exclude the degradation and humiliation foundational to the 'real life' that *Juno*'s spectators believe they are experiencing. Because – even with a proscenium stage, even with a darkened auditorium – spectators must share the characters' environment, the staging cannot produce conditions that its spectators would consider truly unbearable. Far from putting actuality on stage, the realism of *Juno* substitutes a symbolic representation which is accepted as real because it confirms what its middle-class spectators already suspect: that as bleak as these characters' lives may be, their poverty is not too awful to be borne, not so appalling that it has to be destroyed.

Windfalls models a counter-realism which O'Casey hoped would contribute to the workers' 'moral resurrection' (O'Connor, *Syndicalism in Ireland*, 9) by infusing their world with a beauty that O'Casey saw himself as reclaiming from the elites who had garnished it. 'The Star-Jazzer's' painful portrayal of life inside the tenement is counterbalanced by the romantic idealism that radiates from the stars through the open air into the courtyard:

> She shivered, glanced up at the sky, and wondered what they called the star that glittered right over her head. It seemed to stand out in the black breast of the sky in a fuller and more friendly way than the others . . . Her mother had often told her when she was a kid that God was hiding behind the stars. (O'Casey, *Windfalls*, 92–3)

The star has not yet turned red, but it has become O'Casey's symbol for the resplendent alternative that O'Casey's later plays would seek to offer to the deceptive realism bounded by the tenement set of his greatest success.

The alternative glimpsed in 'The Star-Jazzer' and other stories and poems included in *Windfalls* manifests through a style for which 'highly coloured' would be too pale a descriptor. O'Casey's language is charged with a lust for colour which surpasses even Shelley's. O'Casey's lyric 'The Garland' is a particularly striking example:

> No shining pearls from orient seas,
> No wondrous sapphires brilliant blue,

> Strung on a golden string could make
> A garland rich enough for you.
>
> Nor all the em'rald's glorious green,
> And rubies rich in crimson hue,
> Mix'd with the opal's glow could make
> A garland rich enough for you.
>
> But in the wood's deep shaded bower,
> Where grow rare violets richly blue,
> I'll gather all these gems of bloom,
> And make a garland, love, for you. (Ibid., 27)

The gem metaphor and the persistent return of the word 'rich' suggest that all this brilliant colour represents the sensual and spiritual fulfilment denied by capitalism to those without money. The imagery of 'The Garland' is 'rich' in that it overwhelms the senses; it is also 'rich' in that it is associated with precious materials. The speaker of 'The Garland' tries to glorify 'gems of bloom' – the beauty offered to him by nature free of charge – until they become 'rich enough' to supersede the pearls, sapphires and gold that the speaker cannot give his beloved.

The same attempt structures 'Gold and Silver Will Not Do', in which a penniless 'Dreamer' offers his beloved gifts more valuable than those showered on her by her wealthy suitors. The beloved is presented with a stark choice between love and money:

> They bowed in their pride before her, for they had many possessions, and proud confidence stiffened their bending.
> They drowsily dropped at her feet trinkets of silver and trinkets of gold.
> They touched her white breasts with the tops of their fingers, saying, calm in their pride: these fair things of silver and fair things of gold are for thee in return for the favours thy white body can give. (Ibid., 35)

The wealth concentrated in the hands of the Dreamer's rivals manifests as colour; they offer 'silks of blue and silks of green that gleamed with rich quietness of grace' (ibid., 37). The Dreamer counters by promising 'colours many times more wonderful than these colours that shine in this silken loveliness', which 'are to be found first in the deeper depths of thine own heart and of thine own mind; and, afterwards, in the depths of the hearts and the minds of the poets' (ibid., 38–9).

As we have seen, the idea of socialism as a means of bringing beauty, culture and leisure to the masses has its roots in the idealist tradition that derives from Shelley through Morris, Carpenter and Wilde. As we have also seen, Larkin's incorporation of queer socialism into his self-dramatisation attached it to the family and to the putatively essential masculine capacity for violence. In *Windfalls*, the queer dimension of aesthetic socialism is further obscured by the increasingly stereotyped heterosexual frame within which the battle between riches and richness takes place; 'richness' is deployed in the context of heterosexual romance and its value is confirmed when the desired woman chooses the man who offers it.

In his autobiographies, which he begins publishing in 1939, O'Casey identifies Larkin as the bringer of all this richness. The extravagance that characterised Larkin's speeches becomes part of the prize for which labour was fighting, as Larkin's 'voice of mingled gold and bronze' liberates its hearers simply by giving them the words and images they need to '[picture] themselves – as they were, as they ought to be' (O'Casey, *Autobiographies*, I, 574). The concrete goals of the labour movement are inseparable from the poetry through which Larkin articulates them: 'Gifts of the Almighty, went on the voice, labour – a gift, not a curse – , poetry, dancing, and principles; and Sean could see that here was a man who would put a flower in a vase on a table as well as a loaf on a plate' (ibid.). Through their very superfluity, the excesses of Larkin's style did not just represent but actually *were part of* the existence for which the workers were fighting – an existence in which they, for the first time, would have *more* than they needed.

It is from this conviction that O'Casey's experimental style was born. O'Casey's much-maligned wordiness, his overdone alliterations, the similes that cascade from his characters' lips into confused puddles of sound and image, should be seen as artistic choices motivated – for better or for worse – by a belief in the value of sensory overload. O'Casey's adoption of excess as a style was one way of appropriating Larkin's conception of who the workers were and what they were entitled to. O'Casey insisted to Nathan that 'almost everything I've written (except juvenile stuff) was written as a Communist' (*Letters of Sean O'Casey*, 842) because for him, writing 'as a Communist' meant this prodigality of style, not just ideological content. For that reason, the class politics that informed O'Casey's aesthetics were always at work in the reception of O'Casey's post-Abbey output, even when they were not always visible.

O'Casey explained how in a late essay titled 'Theatre and People':

> Nor ought we dismiss with derisive laughter the heart and vulgar art of an uneducated people. This longing is but a harbinger of finer things. Their tawdry ornaments, the beflowered texts of scriptures, their love of the coloured lights of Broadway and Piccadilly Circus are evidences, dim ones, right enough, but positive evidences of the people's longing for colour and light.
>
> Then there is what is called the Left-Wing manifestation of art and of

the theatre, at which there has been a quick and constant lifting of noses, and loud sniffs of contempt. The little art that may be hiding in it is (it is said) smothered in propaganda ... I submit that because we are often displeased – often rightly so – with 'proletarian' art, we have no authority to declare that it is invariably hollow, tiresome, and worthless. (O'Casey, 'Theatre and People', 10)[6]

O'Casey links the 'lifting of the noses' that greets overtly propagandistic theatre with the 'derisive laughter' evoked by a working-class aesthetic that reads to these critics as mere bad taste. But though he tries to distance himself from this 'vulgar art', that first paragraph is a description of O'Casey's own late style. O'Casey's debt to the 'beflowered texts of scriptures' has been well-established; love of the 'coloured lights of ... Piccadilly Circus' flashes forth from several passages of his story 'I Wanna Woman' (O'Casey, *Windfalls*, 66–8); and nobody could long for 'colour and light' with greater intensity than the speakers of 'The Garland' and 'Gold and Silver Will Not Do'. The socialist basis of O'Casey's pursuit of richness was always visible to him. Most of his critics, however, were unable to recognise the politics of O'Casey's style or of their own reaction to it. That, at least, was the lesson O'Casey took away from the reception of *Within the Gates* in 1934; and it is one reason that O'Casey moved from writing plays 'as a Communist' to 'writing a play on Communism' (O'Casey, *Letters of Sean O'Casey* 1, 842).

Within the Gates is structured by a fundamental conflict between the beauty and richness of visionary language and the impoverished humiliation of working class 'actuality'. The Dreamer and the Young Whore act out the conflict between riches and richness that structures 'Gold and Silver Will Not Do'. Richness is once again presented as both indispensable to the poor *and* the property of heterosexual masculinity. *Within the Gates* begins with a chorus welcoming spring, in which heterosexuality is naturalised in classic *Golden Bough* fashion: 'Our mother, the earth, is a maiden again', alluring 'her Bridegroom, the Sun' with her 'blossom and bud', as she 'feels the warm kiss of his love on her mouth, on her breast, as she dances along' (O'Casey, *Within the Gates*, 3–4). 'Life' in *Within the Gates* always designates, implicitly or explicitly, the reproductive desires which a celibacy-obsessed church attempts to crush: 'They cancel life with their livid love of God!' (ibid., 13). The Dreamer is the play's hero, not just because he is a poet, but because he is free of the sexual hypocrisy and guilt that prevent the Bishop from acknowledging that he is the Young Whore's father.

The Young Whore's fate is decided in a contest between the Bishop, who exhorts her to spend her final moments repenting her sexual sins, and the Dreamer, who urges her to choose life by dedicating her final moments to sensual pleasure:

> Turn your back swift on the poor, purple-button'd deadman, whose name is absent from the book of life. Offer not as incense to God the dust of your sighing, but dance to His Glory, and come into his presence with a song! (Ibid., 164)

Although the Young Whore dies, her determination to dance till she drops prevents her from being absorbed by the 'Down and Outs' – the poor who have been ground into a dehumanised mass by the brutality of their existence (ibid., 163–9).

London critics failed to grasp the connection between the play's politics and its aesthetics. Although O'Casey set *Within the Gates* in London's Hyde Park, and included no identifiably Irish characters, they insisted on reading O'Casey's enriched language as an essential attribute of Irishness. Once it was no longer justified by an Irish setting and Irish characters, O'Casey's poetic language became a 'vulgar' indulgence rather than an aesthetic pleasure. Gordon Beckles complained that 'like every other character (Cockneys included), [the Young Whore] was handicapped by the Hibernian atmosphere and rhetoric' (O'Casey, *Letters of Sean O'Casey* 1, 492). James Agate praised the play's 'beautifully muscled prose – or is it poetry?' but branded such beauty 'essentially' Irish:

> The trouble is that Mr. O'Casey is essentially an Irishman who, while labelling his characters English and dropping the accent, still retains the Irish idiom. Take the Old Woman, for example. Any drunken old lady who is Irish has that poetry in her which befits her for Kathleen-Ni-Houlihan, whereas the capacity to soar is not in the English Mrs. Gamp. (Ibid., 495)

Once 'poetry' is essentialised as Irish, it becomes impossible to lift an Irish character out of realism; any amount of enriched language given to a 'drunken old lady who is Irish' will simply confirm her Irishness. By identifying poetic speech as Irish, Agate denies the poor of his own city the 'capacity to soar' – and therefore their entitlement to the fuller existence that O'Casey's play tries to imagine for them. In 'booing fantasy and poetry out of the Theatre', O'Casey responded, Agate was 'doing his bit to keep [the English Mrs. Gamp] from seeing the shadows of stars shining in the mire' (ibid., 502). If London critics need to keep fantasy and poetry essentially Irish, it is, he implies, because they are afraid of how fantasy and poetry might transform England's working class.

The Star Turns Red was, among other things, O'Casey's response to his critics. It does go home to Mother Ireland, but refuses to be confined there. It uses the heightened language that Agate and Beckles tagged as essentially Irish to translate an Irish story into a parable about the worldwide workers' struggle. It forces O'Casey's reluctant audiences to consider the global implications of both the Irish incident that *The Star Turns Red* re-presents and the medium through which it delivers the message. *Within the Gates*'s allegories allowed O'Casey's critics not to see the connection between O'Casey's politics and his poetics. *The Star Turns Red* spells it out for them. The crudeness of the symbolism is the crudeness of graffiti; it is a response to their refusal to read between the lines. After *The Star Turns Red*, London critics might still greet O'Casey's 'longing for colour and light' with 'derisive laughter' and dismiss the opulence of his language as 'vulgar'; but they could no longer avoid knowing why they were doing so.

Red Jim

The Star Turns Red tells the story of a workers' revolution which takes place on Christmas Eve in an unspecified city and in the near future – 'tomorrow, or the next day'. It begins in a tenement which is home to an Old Man and Old Woman with two sons, Kian and Jack. Kian is a soldier in the Saffron Shirts, a fascist militia under the control of the church hierarchy (represented by the Red Priest).[7] Jack is a Communist and follower of union leader Red Jim. Act I builds to a confrontation in which Kian shoots and kills Jack's comrade Michael (the father of Julia, Jack's love interest). Act II takes place in a union hall, where the Red Priest conspires with the corrupt leadership of the General Workers' Union to remove Red Jim from power. Red Jim wins the battle and goes on to lead the workers' revolution, which culminates in Act IV as his army seizes the Lord Mayor's residence. The silver star shining in the background turns red. The body of Jack, who has fallen in battle, is borne in as the Red Priest, accompanied by Kian, urges Red Jim to surrender his overwhelmed forces. Kian joins Red Jim, and the battle ends in victory when the soldiers refuse to fire on the workers. Soldiers and workers join in singing the 'Internationale' as the red star 'glows, and seems to grow bigger'.

By giving this play to Unity in 1940, O'Casey, as the *New Leader* review put it, 'nailed his colors to the mast' (J. E., 'Sean O'Casey Sees Red', 7). Unity was the flagship of a British left theatre movement that first flourished during the 1920s. Within the context of British left theatre, Communism was a style as well as in ideology, and *The Star Turns Red* is in part a 'tribute to an agitational tradition of left-wing art' to which O'Casey's connection with London's Unity Theatre exposed him (Chambers, *The Story of Unity Theatre*, 205). For the initial audiences of *The Star Turns Red*, the red star and the hammer and sickle were dramatic conventions as well as party symbols, citations not only of the ideology and organisation to which they refer but also of earlier workers' theatre productions. Indeed, by the time *The Star Turns Red* premiered, thanks in part to Unity Theatre's active involvement in the Spanish Civil War propaganda effort, some of these conventions, such as the clenched-fist 'Red Front salute', had already ripened into cliché.[8]

At the same time, within the Stalinised British left, O'Casey's use of these conventions was politically and aesthetically heterodox. As Jack Mitchell suggests, *The Star Turns Red* has been mischaracterised as agitprop only because so many critics know so little about agitprop (Mitchell, *The Essential Sean O'Casey*, 155). A 'flexible, mobile form of theater' (Chambers, *The Story of Unity Theatre*, 27) often performed on short notice in public spaces for found audiences, agitprop was built on a schematic, episodic template that kept the plays cheap and portable. There is nothing cheap or portable about *The Star Turns Red*. Its enormous cast has more than thirty speaking parts. As written, it requires three different interior sets, live and recorded music, and lighting effects. Its running time is comparable to that of grand opera.[9] It could be performed as written only in a conventional theatre, and any company that attempted to tour it would have been committing financial suicide.

What *The Star Turns Red* does is incorporate elements of agitprop's theatrical language into a form of O'Casey's own – a form that almost anyone else would have considered hopelessly incompatible with them. The play's Communist symbols do for O'Casey's stage world what James Connolly believed syndicalism would do for the Irish labour movement: they '[invest] the daily incidents of the class struggle with a new and beautiful meaning and [present] them in their true light as skirmishes between the two opposing armies of light and darkness' (Connolly quoted in O'Connor, *Syndicalism in Ireland*, 8). O'Casey believed that these symbols had the power to universalise the Lockout because the Communist Party linked the local history he had left behind in Ireland and the global community potentially available to him through the British left. By writing a play that would have instant appeal to an audience familiar with workers' theatre, O'Casey was attempting to join that community.

Larkin was, once again, the connection. The Workers' Union of Ireland (WUI) became the organisational home for most of the Larkin loyalists who left the ITGWU with him. Though Larkin eventually cut ties with the Comintern, the WUI remained Communist in spirit if not in name. Identifying as a Communist was one way for the self-exiled O'Casey to maintain his membership in a community that had defined his identity and forged some of his most lasting friendships. For a man who had a phenomenal talent for estranging his friends, O'Casey was extraordinarily loyal to Larkin. In an emotional letter to O'Casey describing Larkin's 1947 Dublin funeral, Jack Carney indicates how bonded – and how isolated – Larkin's Old Guard became: 'Poor Barney [Conway]! The loneliest man in Ireland tonight. As we were leaving he said to me: "I am going to be very lonely now, Jack, will you write to me the letters you used to write to the Big Man." I said I would and I will.'[10] O'Casey wrote to Conway too, for another fifteen years. In 1962, writing for what both men must have assumed could be the last time, O'Casey offers Conway the same gift he offered his characters in *Windfalls*, transfiguring Conway's final days with a glorious description of the Lockout:

> Just think for a minute, Barney, on how we workers were then, living in squalid places, wretchedly paid, hard worked, not daring to say a word of protest against any of these evils. Then Jim Larkin came among us, and all became changed: the workers were on their feet, they had much to say for themselves, and they stood out to do battle. And right well and right long they fought; and you and I were among them, Barney. We, the workers, were on the march! The eloquent roaring voice of the great Jim Larkin became the trumpet of the Irish workers, ay, and of the English workers too, in his glorious Fiery Cross campaign ... We helped to fashion this great power and position in life that the workers now have; we got scarred by how we had to live then, and by what we did, and so did our great and beloved leader, Jim, but he was proud of all he did, and so are we, Barney; so are we.[11]

Thus, 1913 is no longer just part of the international workers' struggle; it becomes the struggle's fulfilment. To Yeats's 'Easter 1916' and its 'all is changed, changed utterly', O'Casey opposes the 1913 Lockout as the crisis through which 'all became changed'. His reimagination of the Lockout ties the personal ('you and I were among them, Barney') to the national ('the trumpet of the Irish workers'), then merges both in the global: 'We helped to fashion this great power and position in life that the workers now have'. Jim Larkin, meanwhile, crosses the line between 'larger-than-life' and 'god among men'.

As O'Casey remembers it from England, then, the Dublin Lockout is both intensely personal and transcendently universal. It sustains his Irishness *because* it incarnates the global battle of capital against labour symbolised for him by the Communist Party – the 'great workers' fight' to which most of his remaining Irish friends are dedicated. *The Star Turns Red* strives to reproduce this fusion of personal, national and global by using the sign language of the Communist Party to translate the personal desires and fantasies bound up with the Dublin Lockout into a story that all the workers of the world can read.

O'Casey's desire to retain the human drama of 'the men and women who fought through the great Dublin lockout in nineteen hundred and thirteen' to whom *The Star Turns Red* is dedicated, while also imbuing the Lockout with eschatological significance, leads him to double the plot. Mitchell reads this doubling in terms of a 'dialectic of the "general-social" and the "private"' (Mitchell, *The Essentialist Sean O'Casey*, 157). But the fundamental conflict structuring *The Star Turns Red* is between realism and idealism; and O'Casey uses this clash between modes to stage the relationship between the local and global aspects of labour politics. The story of Irish labour is retold through two analogous plots which reimagine the traumas of O'Casey's experience with the Irish labour movement. Embedded in the heart of the play is O'Casey's retelling of the 1923–4 ITGWU schism – a revisionist fantasy in which O'Casey engineers a complete 'reversal' (Benstock, *Paycocks and Others*, 138) of history as Larkin, eminently recognisable as the model for Red Jim, saves the union instead of destroying it. O'Casey's investment in this fantasy is demonstrated in earlier drafts, which make it clear that Brannigan, the only union member who comes out of Act II with his integrity intact, is a fictionalised version of O'Casey's fellow-Larkinite Barney Conway.[12] Act II thus embeds O'Casey's personal emotional attachments at the heart of the play. Surrounding and interpenetrating this mini-drama is O'Casey's anti-realist treatment of the 1913 Lockout, in which the personal and local are subsumed in the archetypal and universal. The two plots converge at the end of Act III, when Red Jim rescues Michael's body from the clutches of the Red Priest.

Each plot requires an idealised labour-leader protagonist (Jack for the Lockout plot, Red Jim for the schism plot); each protagonist requires a martyr whose sacrifice he celebrates (Jack's martyr is Michael; Red Jim's is Jack); each protagonist defies and defeats a gang of antagonists (for Jack, the Red Priest and the Saffron Shirts; for Red Jim, the council of the General Workers' Union) with the help of a fallen but redeemed comrade (for Jack, his flighty girlfriend Julia; for Red Jim, the alcoholic Brannigan). For audience members not privy to the history of Irish labour, the main thing distinguishing these two plots is method. The schism plot of Act II is almost but not quite bound by the material and realist present, while the Lockout plot that dominates acts I, III and IV is almost but not quite translated into the symbolic and ideal future. Both plots enact the destruction of the green goddess by the votaries of the red star.

In a reversal of the division of space that Levitas identifies in *The Slough*, the union hall becomes the last bastion of realism and its discontents. O'Casey's choice of 'bright green' for the union hall's walls symbolically conflates bourgeois Irish nationalism with the green goddess of realism. Most of Act II is written in the 'method of *Juno*'. The conflict is driven by a clash of personalities; the cowardice and hypocrisy of the corrupt union officers is played up for comic effect; and (with the occasional exception of Red Jim) all the characters introduced in this act speak in pungent colloquial prose. When Brannigan bursts in on the officers' conspiracy, armed to the teeth and fortified with liquor, he taunts them in language reminiscent of Fluther Good's brawl with the Young Covey in *The Plough and the Stars*:

> EGLISH: We're comrades, after all, don't forget that, Brannigan.
> BRANNIGAN: (furiously) Comrades? I'll leave yous fidgeting about in fragments if you dare to call me comrade! (O'Casey, *The Star Turns Red*, 80–1)

These characters are weak, compromised men of the type the Dublin trilogy made famous. Here, however, they are embedded a symbolic drama which critiques the realistic mode that spawned them, and which is ruled by idealised incarnations of heroic working-class masculinity.

The union officers plotting Red Jim's demise are marked as corrupt by their association with naturalistic props which, once framed by the symbolic mode established in Act I, become visible as signs – of their own corruption, and of the corrupting effect of stage realism. Sheasker's venality is signified by a gilt-framed photographic portrait which has been presented to him along with a 'suite of furniture' by one of the divisions of the General Workers' Union (ibid., 68). Caheer carries a gold cigar case given to him by Sir Jake Jester, 'the bastard who was honoured for his work in keeping the workers down' (ibid., 95). O'Casey represents the union leadership's willingness to be bribed through objects that are, in his mind, already identified with the green goddess. Photography was used by O'Casey's early critics as a metaphor for the method of the Dublin trilogy (Harris, *Gender and Modern Irish Drama*, 168, 225). A suite of furniture is standard equipment for the illusionistic drawing-room against which O'Casey rails in *The Flying Wasp*. Red Jim's first question upon finding the gold cigar case – 'Good God, who owns this property?' (O'Casey, *The Star Turns Red*, 95) – calls attention to its dual status as both a piece of stage property and a symbol of the system of property ownership that has co-opted Caheer. Revealing the signifying function of these bits of actuality, Red Jim's denunciation conflates theatrical realism with the tyranny of private property, implying that the officers have been claimed simultaneously by both.

This realist mini-drama reinforces the dominance of the idealism animating the symbolic plot, as does the play's structure. The realistic men confined to Act II are incapable of standing up to the archetypal heroes who also appear in Acts I, III and IV. At the beginning of the second act, the Red Priest leads the union officers in a sinister liturgy during which they are limited to one-line responses. The officers are momentarily frightened of Brannigan's bayonet, but it is not until Red Jim appears that the power shifts. Red Jim is, like Larkin himself, both real and antirealist. O'Casey allows the spectators to see through the character to the real model: the play references Larkin's 'fiery cross' speech (ibid., 90) and his reputation for playing fast and loose with the union's money (ibid., 98–9). At the same time, Red Jim delivers Shelleyan exhortations to the Brown Priest – 'Stretch not a timid finger towards the holy fire of Revolution;/ But step into the midst of it, man, or flee away' (ibid., 88) – and flattens the corrupt officers with bursts of passionate rhetoric:

> Who found you with hardly a boot on your foot, a ragged shirt flaunting a way out of a breach in your britches? . . . I did! The Union chose you, did it? The men elected you, did they? Who made the Union? Who

made the men men? Who gave you the power you have? I did, you gang
of daws! (Ibid., 100)

Red Jim's claim to have 'made the union' establishes that he – unlike his puny mortal opponents – can command the elemental forces and work on the monumental scale established by the play's symbolism. Red Jim later demonstrates these powers by 'making the men men' – or at least turning Brannigan from a drunken hell-raiser into a sober revolutionary:

> RED JIM: (*putting a hand affectionately on BRANNIGAN's shoulder*) Brannigan, my dear comrade, I want you to do something for me.
> BRANNIGAN: (*eagerly*) Anything, Jim, anything!
> RED JIM: Give up the drink!
> BRANNIGAN: (*frightened*) Oh, for God's sake, Jim, I couldn't! One of the walls at home is covered with printed pledges taken from priests, but I wasn't able to keep one of them.
> RED JIM: You'll keep this one for me, and sign nothing. I want you, Brannigan, I want you. We've enemies everywhere – even here. (*He indicates the Delegates.*) There's a brazen bunch of them! I can't trust you if you drink – sober, I'd trust you with my life eternal!
> BRANNIGAN: (*after a long pause – enthusiastically*) I'll do it, Jim; no drink; not once; no more; never again – so help me God! (Ibid., 102)

Having cured Brannigan of the alcoholism that so undermined working-class masculinity in *The Slough*, Red Jim exits, leaving the union officers imprisoned in the domain of the green goddess 'till their backs bend and their hair grows gray' (ibid., 104). Meanwhile, the symbolic plot that connects Act I to Acts III and IV transmutes the Lockout itself from a gruelling local conflict into a universalised struggle between the forces of good and evil. Instead of concealing the process of signification, O'Casey writes it so large that no one could possibly fail to see it.

The absorption by the symbolic of what O'Casey's audiences have insisted on identifying as reality is dramatised through Jack's parents, the Old Man and Old Woman. Decayed relics of O'Casey's realistic phase, they belong to an obsolete past swiftly being demolished by the approaching future. The Old Woman justifies her passivity and obedience to authority with a tired reprise of Juno's 'poor dead son' pacifism: 'For my sake, Jack; for your mother's sake, let us have a little peace . . . [Kian] is my son; you are my son: therefore you are his brother' (ibid., 16). The Old Man boasts about being a scab while reiterating Juno's rejection of labour politics: 'The workers are getting like the tides now – always either coming in or going out . . . I'm telling you it's dangerous' (ibid., 8). The 'real world' they are trying to preserve, however, is in the process of metamorphosis. O'Casey deploys the politics of colour he developed in *Windfalls* to denaturalise the tenement set in which audiences expect his plays to start: 'The walls are a vivid black, contrasting with the dark blue of the sky outside, seen through windows . . . In the centre of the room, a table, black, covered with a yellow cloth bordered with white – the papal colours' (ibid., 3). Colour, in this dramatic universe, has been captured by the authorities. The 'vivid, dark, rich yellow' (ibid., 50) of the Saffron Shirts' uniform, the 'crimson cassock' of the Red Priest, Joybell's confraternity 'robe of rich blue' (ibid., 28), and the 'thick gold chain of office' worn by the Lord Mayor (ibid., 40) offer the only relief from the black hole of poverty; even the yellow in the table cloth pledges allegiance to the Pope. Colour passes into the ownership of the working classes only through Julia's green and black fancy-dress costume and the red star badge on Jack's coat – symbolic claims to a richer existence which the Red Priest accordingly tries to confiscate.

Red Jim delivers his fellow workers from realism by appropriating the richness that O'Casey models in *Windfalls*. In this universe, that richness has been monopolised by the church. In Act III, when a group of the wretched poor come to Jack's tenement to mourn Michael, their cries of affliction alternate with repetitions of the Red Priest's latest anti-Communist diatribe, which is a parodic version of the atrocity propaganda promoted by the Catholic Church and its allies during the Spanish Civil War:

> MAN WITH CRUTCH: Singing a song, they sawed a priest in two, fair in the open air, and the blessed sun shining.
> BLIND MAN: With a weapon as long as my arm and as thick as my little finger, they knifed a priest, and he murmuring the Mass. (Ibid., 117)

The Red Priest has co-opted queer socialism's discourse on beauty in order to glorify the status quo. Instead of claiming beauty through revolution, these characters have to earn it through their submission to the church, which entitles them to the 'dignity and loveliness that priests say poverty gives the poor' (ibid., 118):

> MAN WITH CRUTCH: What greater can we be than what the holy Red Priest said we were, and he preaching on the twenty-seventh Sunday after Pentecost, during the holy communion of Reparation.
> WOMAN WITH BABY: Kings and priests unto God, Who has called us out of darkness into His marvellous light!
> BLIND MAN: 'In the doze and drab of life', says he, 'we are as pearls quietly aglow with a great beauty'.
> YOUNG MAN WITH COUGH: Could the Communists say more than that – the bowseys! (Ibid.)

The funeral pageant makes explicit the political functions of richness. The church uses its riches to ennoble not the poor but poverty, persuading these characters to embrace their own abjection. The strength of the mourners' desire for 'dignity and loveliness' – to see themselves as something other than the diseases and deprivations to which their programmatic names reduce them – overcomes their self-interest; they follow the Red Priest because they crave the 'great beauty' which he confers on them as long as they accept their poverty. The only way the Communists can break this spell is by proving that they can, literally, 'say more than that'.

Jack can't. He is so consumed by zeal that he cannot rise to poetry. Though he appropriates the church's authority – 'We are the resurrection and the life; whoso worketh and believeth in the people shall never die!' (ibid., 124) – his assertion that 'the clenched fist alone can gather the corn that the earth can give' (ibid., 129) to make the workers' 'daily bread' cannot compete with the sensory power of the Red Priest's anti-Communist invective:

> Communism would banish God from your altars: it would change your holy churches into places where bats hang by day and owls hoot by night; it would soil the sacrament of marriage with lust; it would hack in sunder the holy union of the family; street gutters would run with the blood of your pastors; and all holy thoughts and deeds would sink into a weary heap of blackened ashes! . . . It is the bugle-call of the powers of darkness; it is the fire of hell flaming in its energy! (Ibid., 130)

All the more convinced by the poverty of Jack's language that 'the happiness of the toiling masses is hidden only in the bosom of the holy Church' (ibid., 131), the crowd remains in thrall to the Red Priest until Julia announces the arrival of Red Jim and 'the People's Church' (ibid., 133).

Red Jim then delivers a fiery apostasy punctuated by the anaphora that gives so many of the Red Priest's speeches their incantatory power:

> If your God stands for one child to be born in a hovel and another in a palace, then we declare against him. If your God declares that it takes a sack of sovereigns to keep one child and a handful of pence to keep another, then we declare against him. If your God declares that one child shall dwell in the glory of knowledge and another shall die in the poverty of ignorance, then we declare against him: once and for all and for ever we declare against your God, Who hath filled the wealthy with good things and sent the poor empty away! (Ibid., 135)

Clothing Jack's naked dogma with voluptuous flesh, Red Jim seizes and delivers to the poor the 'good things' that they have until now had to pick up as crumbs fallen from the Red Priest's pulpit. His oratory invests them with 'majesty' more splendid than the church's dream of dignified poverty:

> The life we have lived is coming to an end: life rotten in the eye that it could not see; in the limbs that they could not move; in the mind that it

could not think; and in the heart that it could not love! We have bothered the ear of your God till our tongues were dry; we have crept flat on our bellies to where 'twas said we'd find him, and for our meekness the whip of hunger stung us . . . Now we stand up, we turn, and go our own way, the bent back changing to the massed majesty of the Clenched Fist! (Ibid., 136)

Inventorying the senses that have been starved and withered by poverty, Red Jim reawakens his listeners to their own sensual, emotional and intellectual capacities, instilling in them a hunger for the 'good things' of which this speech is a foretaste. This appeal to the senses is augmented by the pageantry of Michael's funeral procession which is accompanied by drums and a workers' hymn sung in chorus to the tune of 'Shenandoah'.

The end of Act III is what the past ten years of O'Casey's career were building to: a compelling demonstration of the purpose and power of his new style. By defeating the Red Priest, Red Jim activates the transformative richness that O'Casey was working towards in *Windfalls* in a context which spells out the justification for the excesses of O'Casey's post-realism. Ivor Brown's review in the *Observer* picked out 'the mourning over the Red Martyr' as 'one of the play's successes' (Brown, 'At the Play', 11) and even a hostile Stephen Spender singled out the funeral pageant as one of its 'memorable moments' (Spender, 'A Morality Play With No Morals', 363). The Unity Theatre applied for a licence to perform Act III in public as a stand-alone play (Nicholson, *British Theatre*, 111–13).

For all the posturing done by all the stock figures, then, it is Red Jim who lets us know what *The Star Turns Red* – and the ten years of wandering in the wilderness that led up to it – are really about. By leaving behind the poverty of realism for the richness of fantasy, O'Casey tried to pass on the gift he believes Larkin passed on to him from Shelley: the vision of a united working class seizing for itself not only the power but the 'dignity and loveliness' that has been denied to them by the ownership class and by the stage realism that traps them in an impoverished universe, filling the wealthy spectators with good things but sending away the poor characters away empty. By rendering this richness through a vocabulary of signs borrowed from the Communist Party and British left theatre, he forced his audiences to extend this gift to workers all over the world. The power of poetry can no longer be confined to a 'realistic' Ireland defined by its chronic failure to capitalise on that power. *The Star Turns Red* captures for a revolutionary agenda an aesthetic that had become the property of bourgeois high culture, whose icon Shakespeare is ceaselessly invoked on the side of the angels in *The Flying Wasp*.

The Star Turns Red thus straddles the yawning chasm that separates the didactic model of theatre employed by most workers' theatre and the entertainment/enrichment model maintained by London's mainstream houses and critics. In yoking all this grandeur to labour politics, O'Casey was going very much against the grain; and there is a reason the grain runs the way it does. Staging this kind of richness costs a fortune. *The Star Turns Red*'s form demanded a technically complicated and expensive production in a conventional theatre; at the same time, its content ensured that no commercial producer in London would touch it. The fact that O'Casey gave the play's first production to an amateur group has often been cited as an indicator of just how bad *The Star Turns Red* is. It would be more accurate to say that O'Casey gave the play to the sole theatrical company in London capable of interpreting it.

Founded in 1936, Unity Theatre was dedicated to elevating workers' theatre from agitprop to high culture. In hopes of enticing middle-class spectators and established theatre critics, Unity trained actors and crews in techniques that the first wave of British left theatre had rejected as bourgeois. Founding member Herbert Marshall was obsessed with Stanislavski's acting system, and went to great trouble to train Unity's actors in it. Unity's mission was founded on a faith 'in the masses, and in their capability of producing art and culture', and its professed goal was to 'show them how' to fulfil that capacity through 'mastery of the highest [professional] technique'.[13] Unity maintained its 'amateur' status partly as a matter of identity; it was a workers' theatre, and its actors had day jobs. But it was also strategic: as an amateur organisation, Unity evaded state censorship by exploiting the 'private club' dodge invented for *The Cenci*.

The fact that Unity was unique in possessing both the means and the motive to produce *The Star Turns Red* gives us some indication of why O'Casey's experimental work has not survived. On the other hand, the fact that *The Star Turns Red* was produced at all shows that despite his commercial failures O'Casey could still find an audience. The small army of actors, stagehands and spectators who kept the play running for eighty-five performances testifies to the appeal, for this particular community, of O'Casey's new socialist aesthetic. The sight of the soldiers joining the workers in that final chorus of the Internationale would have been especially powerful for them in the spring of 1940. By then, British socialists were repudiating the Soviet Union over the non-aggression pact with Germany, the entry of Britain into the Second World War, and the Soviet invasions of Poland and Finland in the winter of 1939. Unity, however, because of its dependence on the CPGB, could not abandon ship without ceasing to exist. *The Star Turns Red*'s conclusion realised for the Unity audience a vision of universal solidarity and peaceful victory which was, in the real world, utterly lost to them.

The Star Turns Red is thus, fundamentally, a fantasy – one which, for a short time, O'Casey shared with the radical British left. Had O'Casey been as enthusiastic about Unity as Unity was about *The Star Turns Red*, the production could have been the start of a partnership that might have given O'Casey's career a different shape. But O'Casey was always ambivalent about Unity. After a pre-production discussion with Jack Selford, head of Unity's Play Department, O'Casey complained that if Unity was allowed free rein, *The Star Turns Red* would 'hardly look like an O'Casey play'. O'Casey inserted into his contract articles stipulating that Unity could not make changes in the text and that the author and his intermediary Peter Newmark had final authority on creative decisions (O'Casey, *Letters of Sean O'Casey* 1, 825–6). Through Newmark, O'Casey fought the production team over everything from the incidental music to the image on the drop curtain (ibid., 825, 840). In June 1940, when both casts of the Unity production sent a letter to O'Casey thanking him for 'a great opportunity to take part in the production of a poetic masterpiece which represents a new step forward in the development of the drama', they ended with the surprising and plaintive question, 'Will you come and see us before we close?'[14] It is not certain that O'Casey ever did. Ultimately, O'Casey seems to have come to view Unity the way most of his critics would: as a collection of incompetent amateurs whose unflagging enthusiasm for his work only made him feel the rejection of the commercial sector more keenly.

We should not, however, assume that O'Casey's dissatisfaction with British left culture extended to Soviet culture. In fact, O'Casey's postwar writing for and about the Soviet Union shows that it remained the object of all the fantasies with which it is invested in *The Star Turns Red* – and that one of these fantasies was O'Casey's belief in the Soviet Union as the incubator of literary innovation. Time, space and the language barrier all contributed to the formation of this (by then) erroneous impression. But O'Casey did have enough exposure to Soviet culture to prevent us from dismissing his misapprehension as an ignorant mistake, a cognitive failure or an amusing latter-day Irish bull. O'Casey's misunderstanding of Soviet literature transformed his drama just as Brecht's misreading of Synge transformed his own drama – or, to take the analogy farther afield, just as Yeats's misapprehensions about Japanese No drama enabled him to produce new dramatic forms by authorising him to act on desires that were neither imagined nor encouraged by more local models. If O'Casey's new form has not had the future that Yeats's and Brecht's had, that is perhaps partly because it was developed through contact with a literary mode which had been warped by its symbiotic relationship with a ferociously intolerant state.

Mayakovsky and *Cement*

To understand how O'Casey's engagement with Soviet literature transformed his work, it is first necessary to establish that he engaged with it at all. Intuitively, O'Casey's strongly marked personality, his idiosyncratic forms, his uncompromising defence of his own authorial rights, and his demonstrated inability to play well with others suggest that O'Casey would be antagonistic to any attempt on the part of the state to limit the author's autonomy. So does the fact that the Irish left tradition that produced O'Casey is rooted in the individualism shared by Wilde, Carpenter and Morris. The declaration of socialist realism as the officially sanctioned mode of Soviet literature at the Writers' Congress of 1934 has, by contrast, long been treated as the paradigmatic example of state interference with individual creativity. Many of those most involved in editing, publishing and promoting the voluminous output of O'Casey's red period presented him as an 'eccentric' (Atkinson, *Sean O'Casey*, 18) whose love for all things Communist had no real impact on his drama (except for the regrettable *The Star Turns Red*), and who certainly would never have submitted to towing the Communist Party line on literature or on anything else.

In his introduction to his *Sean O'Casey* reader, for instance, Brooks Atkinson gives us O'Casey the irrepressible individualist:

> O'Casey was never a member of the Communist Party. I think his non-membership in a party he actively supported was significant. It indicated not only his fundamental independence, but also his complete distrust of any organization that required so much discipline, whether it was a political party or the Roman Catholic Church. He was incapable of accepting discipline from any external source. There is not much about Lenin or Stalin in his comments on Communism. (Ibid.)

O'Casey was certainly allergic to discipline. But a fanatical commitment to one's *own* autonomy does not necessarily imply an equal commitment to other people's autonomy; and, as we have seen, there is plenty about Lenin and Stalin in the pieces O'Casey published in Soviet journals. After O'Casey's death, Ronald Ayling edited and published the English originals of some of these essays in *Blasts and Benedictions*. Although Ayling noted that two of the 'central tenets of Socialist Realism' – optimism and the positive hero – 'are in fact embodied in much of O'Casey's later work', Ayling also strives to give the impression that this was accidental, asserting that O'Casey's 'consistent repudiation of the theory of Socialist realism' demonstrates his 'fundamental disagreement with "official" communist attitudes toward art' (Ayling, 'Introduction', xvi). As evidence, Ayling cites this passage from 'The Flaming Sunflower':

> Communists everywhere seem to be afraid of any writing or painting that isn't packed with what they consider to be 'socialist realism', which is nonsense. As we have no fear of experiments in science, so we must abandon fear of experiments in art and in literature; and, above all, com-

munists should be more tolerant of the natural gaiety of youth. (Quoted in ibid., xvii)

A slightly longer citation of this passage from the draft preserved in the New York Public Library's Berg Collection shows O'Casey justifying this criticism by appealing to Lenin's authority:

> **Pavlov was a great scientist, and that was enough for Lenin; Mayakovsky was a great poet and that was enough for Lenin, too.** Communists everywhere seem to be afraid of any writing or painting that isnt packed with what they consider to be 'socialist realism', which is nonsense. As we have no fear of experiments in science, so we must abandon fear of experiment in art and literature; and, above all, communists should be more tolerant of the batural [sic] gaiety of youth. [Handwritten] **Remembering Lenin's ... lofty brow and penetrating mind, we must not forget Lenin's kindly eyes and the twinkle that could come into them.** (O'Casey, 'The Flaming Sunflower', 4–5; emphasis added)

This impression of O'Casey's complete artistic and intellectual independence from the Communist Party has been produced in part by a reluctance to historicise. Socialist realism was associated with Stalin's cult of personality, and began to loosen its stranglehold on Soviet literature during the 'thaw' after Stalin's death in 1953. What would have been an oppositional assertion of artistic autonomy in 1935 or 1946 was, by the time 'The Flaming Sunflower' appeared in 1960, no longer remarkable. In addition, we now know that we should be wary of accepting these Lenin birthday tributes as an accurate record of attitudes that O'Casey actually held during the Stalin era. In fact, when we go back to that era, we discover that O'Casey was very much in sympathy with socialist realism – or rather, with what he believed socialist realism to be.

O'Casey's critique of 'proletarian' literature is most often levelled against *Anglophone* literature; and one of O'Casey's chief complaints is that such literature is drab, depressing and gloomy. The romantic belief in the revolutionary value of sensuous beauty survives in O'Casey's review of Unity founder Herbert Marshall's book *Mayakovsky and his Poetry* in the *Anglo-Soviet Journal* in 1946: 'The jacket and the book-cover are far too black and gloomy for such a poet as Mayakovsky. Each should have in them the glow of the songs, the dancing, burning hues that go to the making of a Van Gogh picture' (O'Casey, 'Mayakovsky Immortal', 40). The contrast O'Casey draws between the depressing cover and the radiant content is emblematic of the difference between O'Casey's enthusiasm for Soviet literature and his frustration with the British left through which it reached him. O'Casey devotes his review to singing Mayakovsky's praises, quoting Marshall's text only during a discussion of Mayakovsky's 'battle ... for his own integrity as a poet and a thinker' against the Russian Association of Proletarian Writers (RAPP).

Once again, this review appears to be an example of the iconoclastic O'Casey defending the individual genius against the suffocating dogmatism of Soviet literary culture – until you look at the publication date. Mayakovsky, who was part of the revolutionary avant-garde, was indeed persecuted for his unorthodoxy by RAPP. He finally joined them in 1930, and shot himself shortly thereafter. But in 1932, RAPP was disbanded; and in 1935, Stalin announced in *Pravda* that Mayakovsky was 'the best, most talented poet of our Soviet epoch' and that 'indifference to his memory or his works is a crime' (quoted in Urbaszewski, 'Canonizing', 636). By celebrating Mayakovsky as immeasurably superior to the hacks who plotted his downfall, O'Casey thus follows the party line of 1946.

Some of the more egregious extravagances of O'Casey's postwar writing turn out, upon closer inspection, to express O'Casey's affinity for socialist realism. Let us take, for instance, the piece in which O'Casey reminisces about Raisa Lomonosova. This was a 1946 essay for the *Anglo-Soviet Journal* (*ASJ*), and it is a good example of how O'Casey's propagandistic writing exceeded what most of the British left would consider normal parameters. Apart from book reviews, what British writers generally contributed to the *ASJ* were reports on Soviet life, all calculated to impress the reader with a sense of how remarkably strong and brave the Soviet peoples are and what excellent care Stalin's regime takes of them. For instance, the spring 1946 issue contains an editorial defending Soviet elections, two articles about conditions for workers and professionals in the Soviet Union, write-ups of two events promoting English awareness of Soviet culture – and Sean O'Casey's seven-page fantasia on Soviet themes entitled 'Rise o' the Red Star', which blends in with its surroundings about as well as a rhinoceros at a cocktail party.

Because it is subordinated to a Stalinist world view, none of the *ASJ*'s content is free from absurdity. But however tortured their logic, *ASJ* pieces typically present themselves, *formally* speaking, as rational arguments. This is how Sean O'Casey's contribution to the *ASJ* presents itself:

> It rose, suddenly, through the gloom of a dark horizon, just twenty-eight years ago. It rose while all the sway of earth was shaking like a thing infirm. A portent of good for man; a portent of evil for many. It provoked more agitation, more excitement, more fear, than did the lion that walked around the Capitol, and the sheeted dead gibbering in the streets of Rome; for truly common slaves held up their hands which did flame and burn like twenty torches joined, and yet, not sensible of fire, remained unscorched. And when they saw the star, rulers and fearful leaders of men ran hither and thither with naked swords in their hands. (O'Casey, 'Rise o' the Red Star', 7)

'It' is the Red Star, helpfully identified one paragraph later as 'the symbol of new thought born into the world' (ibid.). This amalgam of biblical imagery, Shakespearean reference and evangelical effusion is not typical for the *ASJ*; but it is eminently typical of the style O'Casey employs in *The Star Turns Red* and in his autobiographies. What this paragraph actually describes is the 1917 Bolshevik Revolution. It begins a review of Soviet history which takes us through the civil war period, the post-civil-war 'rebuilding' of the 1920s, the dark days of the 1930s when the Soviet Union was isolated by her 'enemies' in the hopes that 'she would gradually die of loneliness', and the heroic fight against Hitler (ibid., 12). But this narrative is presented less as history than as the fulfilment of a prophetic vision; and it is self-evidently a literary construct. 'Rise o' the Red Star' turns for evidence not to documents or statistics, but to world literature.

Where most observers can only see 'the fine, gentle, and indomitable face of Lenin ashine in that Red Star', O'Casey perceives 'many faces intermingled there behind the countenance of Lenin' (ibid., 7). The list of spirits promiscuously commingled with Lenin's is dominated by writers, including Ralph Waldo Emerson, Walt Whitman, Carlyle, John Mitchel, Robert Burns, Robert Browning, Elizabeth Barrett Browning and Jonathan Swift (ibid.). For information about the 1920s, O'Casey turns to Feodor Gladkov's novel *Cement*, incorporating a fairly substantial excerpt from Gladkov's text into the essay. The list of writers and thinkers that O'Casey presents as sharing the dream of *Cement*'s protagonist Gleb Chumalov – the 'dream' of 'try[ing] to force from this wide desolation a land of productive bustle and power, a land of pride and beauty, to create a new world out of an old and withering one' – includes Omar Khayyam, Fintan Lalor and Karl Marx (ibid., 8).

Soviet literary history can help explain how O'Casey could celebrate the richly hued Mayakovsky as the Soviet Walt Whitman while also lavishing approval and attention on a socialist realist novel which is, as its name implies, about a cement factory. There are many reasons why an Irish playwright might be attracted to Mayakovsky's poetry. But there's only one reason that O'Casey would have been reading *Cement*; and that's because it was *the* classic Soviet novel. Although *Cement* was written in 1925, it was retroactively designated one of socialist realism's foundational models, and *Cement* was frequently held up as an example for future novelists (Clark, *The Soviet Novel*, 69–70). Part of O'Casey's attraction to that novel can be attributed to the fact that *Cement* was written before socialist realism had been officially formulated and universally prescribed. As Katerina Clark notes, *Cement*'s worker-hero Gleb was atypically 'anarchic and willful' (ibid., 82), which can only have endeared him to O'Casey. But part of it may well derive from the elements that would later be codified as socialist realism, and which would have offered O'Casey another model for the antirealistic form for which he was searching.

To understand why that is not a paradox we have to delve into the vexed question of what 'socialist realism' actually was. According to Clark, the 'proletarian realism' promoted by RAPP 'called for large dollops of verisimilitude and psychological portraiture but cautioned against exaggerating heroism' (ibid., 32). RAPP, in other words, advocated a literary mode closely related to the one against which O'Casey was revolting: the gritty naturalism characterising 'realistic' depictions of working-class life. The 'socialist realism' that replaced 'proletarian realism', on the other hand, was not so much realism as an attempt to yoke the oppositional modes of naturalism and idealism together in a single literary form. Citing Zhdanov's definition of socialist realism in 1934 – 'a combination of the most matter-of-fact, everyday reality with the most heroic prospects' – Clark argues that socialist realism is characterised by the friction between the injunction to represent 'what is' and the equally powerful injunction to represent 'what ought to be' (ibid., 37). While both modes were in theory equally important, '[i]n practice the balance was actually tilted in favor of revolutionary romanticism, with its exaggeration and grand scale' (ibid., 34). Another quality that puts Soviet fiction beyond the pale for most Western critics is 'its . . . proclivity for making sudden, unmotivated transitions from realistic discourse to the mythic or utopian' (ibid., 37).

It does not take long to find these features in abundance in *Cement*. When Gleb returns to the village he left three years ago to fight for the Red Army during the civil war, his perception of it shuttles back and forth between ideal dream and degenerate actuality, sometimes changing from paragraph to paragraph:

> Gleb strode, in the wine-gold lustre, along the path on the mountain slope, through the clumps of still wintry brushwood, along the sparkling yellow flowers. It seemed to him as though the very air sang and chirruped and danced on wings of mother-of-pearl.
>
> In the square, beyond the wall, a mob of dirty children were playing, and paunchy, snake-eyed goats roamed, nibbling at bushes or acacia shoots.
>
> . . .
>
> Splendid! Once again, machines and work. Fresh work. Free work, gained in struggle, won through fire and blood. Splendid!
>
> Like giddy maidens, the goats scream and laugh with the children. The ammoniacal stench of the pig-sty. Grass and weeds besmirched by hens.
> (Gladkov, *Cement*, 2)

The enforced union of two heterogenous literary modes emerges as a feature of O'Casey's experimental drama as early as *The Silver Tassie*. It reaches monumental proportions in *The Star Turns Red*. In *I Knock at the Door*, the first volume of O'Casey's autobiography, 'sudden, unmotivated' transitions between miserable reality and utopian fantasy are effected at the cellular level in the heteroglossic narration and on a larger scale by Johnny's daydreaming.[15] In 'The Dream School', for instance, the hungry and suffering Johnny's imagination lifts him out of his actual school into a heavenly school where well-fed and gorgeously clad children imbibe instruction surrounded by lush pastoral beauty.

My point is not that O'Casey derived all this directly from Gladkov. Clearly, O'Casey's penchant for this kind of juxtaposition predates his exposure to *Cement*. O'Casey's early writing about Larkin and the labour movement is full of overblown idealisation, and 'sudden, unmotivated transitions' between antithetical modes are a hallmark even of his realistic tragicomedies. My point is that when he encountered *Cement*, O'Casey would have recognised in it some of the least respected aspects of his own work. He would have seen Gladkov as a kindred spirit; and the fact that the Soviet Union had so highly prized a novel so close to his own experiments with form would justify the claim he made in an article that he submitted for publication in the Soviet journal *International Literature* in 1938: 'In the USSR alone can mighty experiments be made' (O'Casey, *Letters of Sean O'Casey* 1, 753).

Here again, however, timing matters. O'Casey, who did not speak Russian, read the novel in the English translation published by A. S. Arthur and C. Ashleigh in 1929. He would therefore have been able to savour the 'ornamental' style in which *Cement* was originally written, and about which Katerina Clark complains in terms now achingly familiar to us: '[Gladkov's] prose, highly rhetorical and hyperbolic, often reads like the purple passages of a cheap romance' (Clark, *The Soviet Novel*, 71). To O'Casey, Gladkov's ornamentalism would have been one of *Cement*'s chief pleasures, and another indicator that the Soviet Union nourished a people whose just appreciation of Gladkov's richness of style proclaimed their instinctive love of beauty.

O'Casey would not necessarily have known that by the time he paid his *homage* to *Cement* in 'Rise o' the Red Star', the novel had undergone several revisions which gradually stripped out all that ornamentation (ibid., 78). Precisely because *Cement* was a classic, Gladkov – like many other Soviet authors – was repeatedly pressured to rewrite it to reflect changes in party ideology (Veselá, 'The Hardening of *Cement*', 112–13). In addition to simplifying the style, the revisions toned down Gladkov's critique of the Party, normalised Gleb's wife Dasha's sexuality, and reined in Gleb's willfulness (ibid., 104–5). Most of these revisions took place after 1929 and would not have been reflected the translation O'Casey read (ibid., 113). Like the image of a star that is light-years away, the version of Soviet literature that reached O'Casey through that translation of *Cement* reflected something which, at its point of origin, had long ago ceased to be.

O'Casey's contact with Soviet literature, then – misleading though it was

– encouraged him to continue pursuing something that modernism was supposed to have obliterated: romantic idealism, and the 'optimistic, utopian vision of human perfection' (Moi, *Henrik Ibsen and the Birth of Modernism*, 73) on which it was based. But the support that O'Casey believed that Soviet literature provided to his own literary experiments was always partly imaginary; and this accounts for some of the contradictions of O'Casey's red period. His autobiographies are riddled with *homage* to modernists that were proscribed during Stalin's heyday; they are also bursting with the triumphant optimism that defined the literary mode that Zhdanov promoted as a bulwark *against* modernism. O'Casey's autobiographies fulfilled enough of Zhdanov's requirements to be translated and published in the Soviet Union; they also went far enough beyond those requirements to ensure a significant American following.

Ironically, O'Casey's engagement with Soviet literature helped enable his American champions to position him as a rugged individualist bravely fighting for a richer, fuller life. Atkinson's 1964 elegy for O'Casey celebrates him for maintaining idealism in the face of an increasingly dire reality:

> 'Joyous' may not be too radiant a word to describe [O'Casey's] inner spirit in his last years. He was an optimist about the future of mankind. Despite the many hardships of his life (he once remarked that he regarded himself as a failure) he always enjoyed the experience of being alive: 'Tired, but joyous, praising God for His brightness and the will towards joy in the breasts of men' – to quote a line he once wrote about himself as a tenement boy in Dublin. (Atkinson, *Sean O'Casey*, 163)

Joyousness, optimism, orientation towards the glorious future instead of the past – all of these were things towards which practitioners of socialist realism were exhorted to strive, and all of them infuse the work that Atkinson loyally celebrated throughout the last three decades of O'Casey's life.

Atkinson, following O'Casey's lead, preferred to attribute these qualities to O'Casey's pre-revolutionary models: 'His communism, he says with the pride of an old believer, goes back beyond Lenin to Milton, Keats, Shelley, Byron, Dickens, Emerson and Whitman' (ibid., 151). About that, as we know, Atkinson was absolutely right; and it is partly because the aesthetics of queer socialism survive in O'Casey's writing that it presents to his American critics as an inexhaustible fountain of romantic ecstasy. But one can never step into the same river twice; and by drawing sustenance from socialist realism, O'Casey was not simply returning to bathe in the spring from which Yeats and Shaw once drank. Before it reaches Sean O'Casey, the radical *eros* that inspired Yeats, Shaw and Wilde travels a long way and undergoes, as we have seen, some significant modifications. O'Casey's Communist aesthetic does indeed 'go back beyond Lenin'; but it also moves *forward* towards Stalin.

O'Casey embraces official Soviet culture – as he understands it – because it rhymes with some of his own fantasies in a way that queer socialism never did.

Straight Socialism

The rise of a cult of 'physical and psychological toughness' (Clements, 'Introduction', 11) – designated by the Russian term *zakal*, sometimes translated as 'steeliness' – was one of the hallmarks of early Soviet culture. *Zakal*, which Catriona Kelly glosses as 'the quality known in English as "backbone," "character," "moral fiber," or "strength of will,"' was fundamental to the Soviet 'myth of a society led by supremely fit and committed citizens,' and a major pillar of 'the state-sponsored modernization program' (Kelly, 'The Education of the Will', 133). With the cult of *zakal*, 'the courageous, resolute, and unflinching' hero became the 'ideal of male behavior in the 1920s and 1930s' (ibid.). The Soviet psychiatric community, for a time, considered *zakal* a more important norm than heterosexuality:

> Despite the Party's prevailing suspicion of women who evaded their 'natural' reproductive role, some doctors allowed that masculinization imbued the lesbian with strength, public presence, and skillfulness, all politically admirable attributes. Male femininity, on the other hand, rendered men soft, frivolous, and obsessed with a cozy bourgeois domestic sphere. By the late 1920s a clear public ethic against play and pleasure prevailed, influencing even sympathetic doctors to erase the male homosexual's ironic femininity from their case histories. (Healey, 'The Disappearance of the Russian Queen', 162)

The cult of *zakal* displaces not so much homosexuality itself as femininity, and with it 'play and pleasure'. Female bodies can be made useful, especially in their 'reproductive role'; but *femininity* is now less desirable even for women, and officially 'abhorred' in men (ibid.).

Official Soviet culture thus repudiates the ethos of queer socialism – not only by mandating an 'increasingly negative and confined approach to sexual expression' (ibid.) but by rejecting the value of pleasure. Even before Stalinisation, the pursuit and/or celebration of *zakal* was a prominent feature of Mayakovsky's poetry as well as 'official Soviet novels' (Kelly, 'The Education of the Will', 143). The cult of *zakal* resonated with what Eric Naiman has identified as a deeply misogynistic strain of idealism that the Russian futurists inherited from the pre-Bolshevist avant-garde, which expressed itself in imagery that 'measured the subject's social significance through his violation of a female other' (Naiman, *Sex in Public*, 52). As Naiman puts it, '[i]n the poetry of Vladimir Maiakovsky, the entire cosmos is often in a state of sexual arousal, either lusting after the poet's body or about to be raped by him' (ibid.). O'Casey would therefore have encountered *zakal* and its literary analogues through his perusal of Soviet literature, despite the time warp.

As we have seen, O'Casey's red period writing defies Soviet orthodoxy by remaining faithful to those aspects of queer socialism which were preserved in Larkin's romantic syndicalism, including a belief in the proletariat's right and need for sensory pleasure. But his late writing also participates in the idealisation of strength and toughness, and the intolerance for 'men's refusal of the masculine' (Healey, 'The Disappearance of the Russian Queen', 162), demanded by the cult of *zakal* and supported by the Russian avant-garde's explosive and aggressive idealisation of heterosexual masculinity. *The Star Turns Red*'s Jack, for instance, is made of almost nothing but *zakal*, leavened with a few evangelical allusions; and even the men who are more bearably impure – Michael, Brannigan and Red Jim – are, to use Kelly's terms, infallibly 'courageous, resolute, and unflinching' ('The Education of the Will', 132). The alter egos O'Casey creates in his autobiographies perform amazing feats of 'backbone', among them a lengthy dressing-down of Lady Gregory for the crime of admiring the insufficiently optimistic Upton Sinclair. As Lady Gregory, sitting with him in her library at Coole, reads to O'Casey from Sinclair's *Singing Jailbirds*, O'Casey's fictional self leaps to his feet and silences her with this majestic outburst:

> Oh, stop, woman, for God's sake! ... the Labour Movement isn't a mourning march to a jail-house! We are climbing a high hill, a desperately steep, high hill through fire and venomous opposition. All those who were highest up have dropped to death ... lower still, many will drop to death; but just beneath these is the invincible vast crowd that will climb to the top by the ways made out by their dear dead comrades! (O'Casey, *Inishfallen, Fare Thee Well*, 184–5)

It is scarcely necessary to observe that although Gregory did introduce O'Casey to *The Singing Jailbirds* in 1924 (O'Casey, *Letters of Sean O'Casey* 1, 118), he would never have said any of this to her face while she was alive. More intriguing is the faux-Casey's reiteration of the 'climbing a high hill' metaphor, which could have been drawn either from O'Casey's extensive collection of biblical references or from the 'cult of *turizm* (hiking and mountain-climbing)' that Kelly identifies as part of 'Soviet "revolutionary romanticism"' ('The Education of the Will', 143), or both.

My point, again, is not that O'Casey's gender politics were *formed* by Soviet culture, but that this aspect of Soviet culture authorised O'Casey to indulge in forms of self-expression that had been discouraged by earlier mentors and models. The cult of *zakal* made a virtue of O'Casey's homophobic conflation of desire between men with death and destruction, which manifests subtextually as early as *The Plough and the Stars*.[16] It is only after his left turn that

O'Casey reveals how foundational heterosexism is to his politics, and to the 'abiding faith in life' (Atkinson, *Sean O'Casey*, 60) that steams from every pore of *Within the Gates*.

The foundations of the conception of 'life' that O'Casey celebrates in his later plays are clearly exhibited in O'Casey's vicious attack on the queer English playwright Noël Coward in *The Flying Wasp* (1937). Entitled 'Coward Codology', O'Casey's polemic persistently denies masculinity to Coward, presenting him as an 'infant phenomenon' playing with the 'baby-rattle' of his slender talent (*The Flying Wasp*, 129, 142). The climax of the piece is O'Casey's critique of Coward's 1932 comedy *Design for Living*. *Design for Living* centres on three creative types – Otto the artist, Leo the playwright and Gilda the designer – who are all in love with each other. They spend the first two-and-a-half acts trying to get a decent dyad out of what Gilda's husband calls their 'three-sided erotic hotch-potch' (Coward, *Design for Living*, 138); but none of these permutations are stable, and the play ends with Gilda's husband storming out while Gilda, Leo and Otto collapse onto the couch in uncontrollable laughter.

Wildean echoes abound. Gilda's husband is named Ernest, and Gilda, Leo and Otto breathe an atmosphere of triviality in which Jack and Algernon would feel quite at home. O'Casey's remarks focus on a passage in which Otto justifies his decision to reject the 'ordinary social conventions' that enforce monogamy:

> The Methodists wouldn't approve of us and the Catholics wouldn't either; and the Anglicans and the Episcopalians . . . But the whole point is it's none of their business. We're not doing any harm to anyone. We're not peppering the world with illegitimate children. The only people we could possibly mess up are ourselves, and that's our lookout. (Quoted in O'Casey, *The Flying Wasp*, 144)

O'Casey responds to this mild Wildean individualism by condemning to death all those who murmur against the Child. Coward's queer trio 'would be far closer to life if they were' having illegitimate children (ibid., 146). It is precisely because their desires are infertile that they are debarred from heaven, earth and life itself:

> [I]t isn't this Church or that Church, but life itself that excommunicates these persons. As the wasp tears the sickly grub from its cell and casts it from the nest as a piece of rubbish, so life tears such as these from the bowels of her companionship and drops them down where death is standing. (Ibid., 145)

Since the wasp is O'Casey's favourite metaphor for himself as critic, he has just cast himself as the eugenics-minded mother carrying out selective infanticide, in imitation of a lifeforce whose 'companionship' is refused to creatures who cannot, will not, or should not breed. By uncoupling sex from procreation, Otto has reduced himself and his lovers to parasites – 'poor wincing worms in a winecup' (ibid., 152). The sustained invertebrate metaphor contemptuously excludes the entire trio from *zakal*; they literally have no backbone. Otto and Leo are *so* soft, *so* spineless, *so* helpless, so 'wincing' that they are just begging to be crushed.

Crush them O'Casey does, in an instructive if disturbing outburst of authoritarian spleen. In this passage we can actually watch O'Casey's fear of homosexuality poison the radical *eros* he once borrowed from Shelley, transforming polymorphous and unbounded desire into a single, unidirectional, irresistible compulsion. When 'life' means binding oneself to produce the future, then 'life' excludes personal autonomy: 'not one of us can mess up his life without messing up the life of another'. When 'life' is vouchsafed only to those producing the next generation, individualism is death: 'The man who can do no harm to anyone but himself is dead' (ibid., 145–6). In the womb of 'life' as O'Casey imagines her, there is no room for resistance: 'Everything said or done in this world has to justify itself or be destroyed by either force or neglect. Each has to fit himself in or go' (ibid., 145).

This passage resonates with a strain in George Bernard Shaw's writing which Matthew Yde documents in *Bernard Shaw and Totalitarianism*. Pointing to Shaw's pronouncement in the preface of *Major Barbara* that 'We shall never have real moral responsibility until everyone knows that his deeds are irrevocable, and that his life depends on his usefulness' (Shaw quoted in Yde, *Bernard Shaw and Totalitarianism*, 104), Yde argues that Shaw believed that the path to the utopian future would have to be cleared by the elimination of human beings whose 'usefulness' could not be justified. Shaw 'frequently brought up the idea of liquidating recalcitrant citizens in a lethal chamber' (Yde, *Bernard Shaw and Totalitarianism*, 106), and 'knew of Stalin's efforts to "weed the garden," as he liked to put it, and defended his right to do so' (ibid., 105). Yde reads Shaw's doctrine of Creative Evolution, as dramatised in his five-part post-revolutionary dramatic 'pentateuch' *Back To Methuselah* (1921), as evidence that Shaw 'accepted ... the use of state intervention to assist the supposed fittest members of the race and ensure the speedy elimination of the less fit' (ibid., 129). For Yde, there is no mystery about Shaw's admiration of Stalin; Shaw saw in Stalin's Soviet Union 'a model for the rest of the civilised world', not in spite of but *because* of Stalin's ruthlessness in eliminating human impediments to his vision (ibid., 168). Yde grounds this argument in a reading of Shaw's 1934 play *The Simpleton of the Unexpected Isles*, in which 'an exterminating angel descends from the skies to rid the world of its useless parasites and idlers' (ibid., 170). In all this, Yde argues, Shaw was not *influenced* by Stalin;

he *recognises* Stalin as a proponent of ideas Shaw himself has nurtured for decades (ibid., 172).

O'Casey's rejection of Otto's individualism – 'Everything said or done in this world has to justify itself or be destroyed by either force or neglect. Each has to fit himself in or go' – is a softer and vaguer statement of the same demand for the individual to put himself at the service of society and/or the state. Anything or anyone that cannot 'justify itself' must be 'destroyed', actively or passively. Anyone who cannot 'fit himself in' must 'go' – where? Since we are talking about Life, it would seem that the only place to 'go' is death. And in fact, this section of 'Coward Codology' is subtitled 'Design for Dying'.

But if this comparison sheds some light on why and how Shaw and O'Casey shared an admiration of Stalin for so long, it also highlights a major difference between Shaw and O'Casey's conceptions of the Life Force. Yde insists on constructing Shaw as always-already totalitarian, as far back as *The Quintessence of Ibsenism*; but this is only possible because Yde ignores the anti-authoritarian utopianism established by the queer socialism that was part of Shaw's formation. For Yde, 'utopia' always and only means a totalitarian state-centred society, and 'idealism' always and only means valuing ideology over human life (ibid., 7–15). Knowing what we now know, however, we can see a major shift taking place in the plays that make up *Back to Methuselah*, which were written in the immediate aftermath of the Irish and the Bolshevik revolutions, and in which Shaw decisively repudiates queer socialism and begins 'evolving' in the opposite direction as fast as he can.

We see that shift clearly in the recurrence, in *Back to Methuselah*, of John Todhunter and the long-repressed Avenue Theatre trauma. The last two plays in the series, 'Tragedy of an Elderly Gentleman' and 'As Far as Thought Can Reach', incorporate Todhunter's distinctive neoclassical aesthetic through Hellenistic costumes, Delphic oracles and the Greek dancing that featured in *A Sicilian Idyll* and *Comedy of Sighs*. In both plays, this relic of Shaw's formative years is staged precisely in order to relegate it to a bygone era being superseded by far superior visions. In 'As Far as Thought Can Reach', this neoclassical 'play' is of interest only to children, who soon outgrow it (Shaw, *Back to Methuselah*, 235–8); in 'Tragedy of an Elderly Gentleman', the Oracle explains that she goes through the 'usual mummery' of her Delphic rigmarole only because the benighted short-livers who consult her can't do without it (ibid., 200).

What Yde *has* grasped quite firmly is that Shaw's growing preference for the authoritarian utopia over the anarchist one is driven by overwhelming fear of the human body (Yde, *Bernard Shaw and Totalitarianism*, 3). Unlike *Man and Superman*, *Back to Methuselah* includes heterosexuality in that disgust, just as 'Creative Evolution' takes Samuel Butler's evolutionary theory to a new level by eliminating sex itself. In the future of 'As Far as Thought Can Reach', adults no longer have or want sex, and children are hatched from eggs. *Back to Methuselah* 'is the fantasy of a man in rebellion against Eros, against life itself' (ibid., 140).

O'Casey does not rebel against Eros. On the contrary, after his left turn, O'Casey celebrates *eros* ever more vehemently. What O'Casey rebels against is anything that seeks to prevent a man's *eros* from fulfilling what he holds to be its natural destiny. O'Casey despises Coward and his characters for the same reasons that *Within the Gates*'s Dreamer hates the church; they are enemies of the life-giving *eros* which it is the heterosexual man's pleasure, privilege and duty to disseminate. As time goes on, O'Casey's conception of 'life' becomes more concretely heterosexual. The protagonist of O'Casey's 1949 play *Cock-a-Doodle Dandy* is an actual cock – as in rooster – whose antics are tremendously exciting for the town's women, while most of the action given to Father Domineer and the other men could be fairly described as attempted cock-blocking. In 'The Bald Primaqueera', O'Casey lambasted the entire 'Theatre of the Absurd' – 'the dare-devil Horrorhawks of the theatre of murder, rape, and cruelty' (O'Casey, 'The Bald Primaqueera', 64–5) – as a bunch of 'primaqueeri' warped by their neurotic horror of the female genitals (ibid., 66):

> It was Artaud – the latest trumpeter of the Primaqueeri – or one of his brethren, who gave us a picture of a beautiful girl, naked, with a malignant tarantula spider [sic] between her lovely thighs. An ugly guardian for the seat of life, a vision that could only be seen by a savage Primaqueera – one who is thinking he is looking through a lens which reflects back into the mind of the onlooker, showing that this tarantula spider is squatting, not between the lovely thighs of a woman, but in the searcher's skull, weaving its tendrils in and out of the web of his brain. (Ibid., 66)

O'Casey reminds his readers that in turning away from the vagina these men blot themselves out of the book of life: 'All the greatness of man' begins as 'a little life from between the thighs of a woman', and writers who fail to respect *l'origine du monde* 'blaspheme against humanity' (ibid., 66). O'Casey notes, as one of many reasons to hate David Rudkin's *Afore Night Come*, that it includes 'a psychopath and a homo' (ibid., 68); he complains that the primaqueeri are so anti-life that they wouldn't even tolerate the appearance of a 'flowering plant' (ibid., 72) on their stages; and he concludes by contrasting two real-life women who risked their lives to save children with the perverts of the European avant-garde: 'Ah, to hell with the loutish lust of primaqueera' (ibid., 76).

This is an attitude that O'Casey maintained at some cost to himself. Many directors and producers who might have been interested in his experimental work would have found themselves swept into the pit along with the 'primaqueeri'. About Hilton Edwards and Micheál MacLíammóir, for instance, whose Gate Theatre began producing exactly the kind of expressionist/ experimental drama O'Casey was interested in writing at exactly the time he started writing it, O'Casey wrote to George Jean Nathan in 1948: 'Pity they are Cissies. They've done good work, which makes me feel even worse about them' (quoted in Nathan, *My Very Dear Sean*, 84). This attitude is endorsed by David Krause, whose edition of Sean O'Casey's letters includes a letter that Krause himself wrote to the *Irish Times* after MacLíammóir quipped, in a 1963 lecture, that 'if everybody did what O'Casey did, go off to a foreign country just because a play was turned down, nobody would live anywhere' (quoted in Krause, reprinted in O'Casey, *Letters of Sean O'Casey* 4, 386). Krause defended O'Casey's decision as the laudable action of a husband and father supporting his children: 'At the time when the Abbey rejected his play, he was living in a London flat, struggling to support a wife and small child solely by his writing' (ibid.). Krause received, he notes, 'several letters from Dubliners praising' his correction. The one he chose to reproduce is by a woman signing herself M. O'Donnell: 'I think why so many Irishmen resent O'Casey is firstly because he is 100% male ... I do disagree with you, however, when you refer to MacLíammóir as a MAN – I don't class him as one, and I am sure no other woman could either, and we will never be allowed the opportunity to put him to the test!' (ibid.). Krause included O'Casey's own comment on O'Donnell's letter: 'The women of Dublin have spoken, God bless them' (ibid.).

Apparently, then, O'Casey's '100% male' reputation was well-established in Ireland; and, as is often the way, it is established in Krause's collection through its opposition to a denigrated male homosexuality assumed to be feminine. In the American context, O'Casey's identity as the champion of a specifically *heterosexual* masculinity could be exploited for specific and urgent political purposes. O'Casey's ideologies coincided with rising paranoia about queer influences in the theatre world. Gregory Woods argues that it was 'in the period after the Second World War that claims of homosexual power broker- age in the arts flourished most often on both sides of the Atlantic' (*Homintern*, 14–15). Woods documents the persistence throughout the modern period of 'a widespread, paranoid association of homosexuality with espionage' which he argues derived from 'the suspicion that homosexuals may form stronger allegiances to others of their own kind, across national boundaries, as well as across ... classes, than to their own fellow nationals' (ibid., 7), and which supported the myth of the 'Homintern', an international cabal of queer Communists bent on infiltrating and perverting theatre and culture (ibid., 9).

This paranoia was particularly acute in postwar America, where anti- Communist purges coincided with the purging of known or suspected homo- sexuals from the federal government (Johnson, *The Lavender Scare*, 2–5). The connection between capitalism and the nuclear family, which Edward

Carpenter had articulated so long ago, recurred in nightmare fashion in 'the entanglement of homosexuality in the politics of anticommunism' (D'Emilio quoted in ibid., 11), as a 'nation on "moral alert" because of the Cold War' identified the 'stable, monogamous, heterosexual' marriage as 'a key weapon in the arsenal against degeneracy and internal Communist subversion' (Johnson, *The Lavender Scare*, 11).

No matter how close O'Casey got to the Comintern, he was not a member of the Homintern. Ironically, it was precisely *because* O'Casey embraced the hypermasculinity of Soviet culture that O'Casey just didn't *seem* like a Communist to Atkinson, Krause and Nathan. What could be more moral than a universe dedicated to the triumph of the straight man's libido over the feeble protests of a conspiracy of robe-wearing celibates? What could be less 'subversive' than a universe ringing with evangelical cadences and radiant with divine glory? What could be more American than this worship of Life?

As long as O'Casey's authoritarianism is expressed as a celebration of Life – as a demand for more Life – as a vigorous condemnation of anyone who refuses the service of Life – it remains invisible to those who have never questioned his definition of life. O'Casey's affinity for a totalitarian state baffles the men who celebrate him only because they do not recognise either reproductive futurism or compulsory heterosexuality as coercive – because their own societies are built on the same foundations. Reproductive futurism and compulsory heterosexuality are less visible to heterosexual men because they are aligned with their major desires; it's the women and the queers who feel their disciplinary force. What is obviously an authoritarian demand when made vis-à-vis Coward and his queer characters – that the subject 'fit himself in or go' – is liable to seem like common sense to a subject who is already comfortably ensconced. Similarly, as long as the dominant expression of O'Casey's engagement with Soviet culture is his idealisation of masculine strength and potency, there is no danger that his admirers will perceive the Stalinist provenance of the 'vitality' of O'Casey's late style.

Conclusion

After rebuilding a context that finally makes some sense of O'Casey's late style, it might seem capricious to thus expose it as fed by a tainted source. Can we not simply appreciate O'Casey's restoration of joy, beauty, richness and, yes, life to the theatre during one of the darkest periods of the twentieth century? Does it matter that many of O'Casey's supporters denied the connection between his politics and his plays, re-presenting his later style as if it sprang spontaneously from the pure well of O'Casey's own all-embracing spirit? Does it matter, even, that O'Casey sniped at Coward – whose reputation and career he did not have the power to damage – or that he wrote off an entire generation of avant-garde playwrights as traitors to heterosexuality?

It does; but not in the ways that O'Casey's anti-Communist detractors might expect. My point is not that we should go back to ignoring these plays because they really *are* Communist, or even because they amplify some of the least sympathetic aspects of O'Casey's personality. What matters more is that we can now better appreciate the distorting effect of the quite substantial convergence, on matters of gender and sexuality, between apparently opposed ideologies. Atkinson, Krause, et al., failed to 'make sense' of O'Casey's Communism because the aspects of Soviet culture that appealed most strongly to O'Casey were the ones that most closely resembled the 'common sense' they had absorbed from their own societies.

A utopian vision that fails to perceive that convergence – a vision that is born out of a desire never to acknowledge the implications of that convergence – produces a 'there and then' which is self-defeatingly coincident with the 'here and now'. In addition to opening up the question of what else that convergence might still be preventing us from reading, the story of O'Casey's later style shows us how that convergence increases the difficulties and the dangers of attempting to restore idealism, as a viable dramatic mode, to a world that had witnessed its betrayal on such a vast scale. Atkinson could recognise the surface features of Shelley's idealism in O'Casey's later style; he couldn't see the hole that had opened up behind them. For better or for worse, now we can.

To the extent that O'Casey's late style succeeded, it was not as modernism but as an alternative to modernism and its postwar legacy – maximalism against minimalism, richness against emptiness, idealism against materialism, optimism against despair, hope for the future against a world in which all possibility of regeneration is gone. But transcendence is not the same thing as denial. Idealism is viable, when it is viable, as a living link between what is and what might be, between the present and the future. The more of the present that O'Casey had to ignore, un-see, or misrepresent in order to protect his own fantasies – the more his supporters had to do the same to protect the joy they found in O'Casey's work – the more attenuated that link became. The things that were and are valuable about O'Casey's later work – the insistence on beauty, the richness given to the poor, the sensual pleasures of poetic language – could not be fully activated by a drama that excluded so aggressively the despair, damage and betrayal that the Soviet Union and the 1930s had wrought in the 'here and now' and on the people socialism was invented to serve.

Notes

1. See for instance Eileen O'Casey's draft introduction to *Cheerio, Titan!*, NLI MS 44,703/2.
2. It was published in the Moscow *Literary Gazette* in 1960. The English typescript is preserved in the Henry W. and Albert A. Berg Collection of English and American Literature, New York Public Library, Astor, Lennox and Tilden Foundations. All

citations of Sean O'Casey's writing for Soviet journals are taken from the English-language typescripts in that collection. I thank the curators of the Berg collection and the Estate of Sean O'Casey for their permission to cite these typescripts.
3. The Abbey's 'Plays Received' ledgers for that period record the receipt of a play called *Profit and Loss* by 'Shawn O'Casey' on 2 March 1916. It was returned on 6 March.
4. Mary identifies the stanzas she recites as 'verses [Jerry Devine] read' during a 'lecture in the Socialist Rooms ... on Humanity's Strife with Nature' (O'Casey, *Juno*, 242). They are extremely similar to the stanzas that end the natural idyll in O'Casey's 'A Walk with Eros'.
5. On *The Harvest Festival*'s debt to melodrama, see Stephen Watt's *Joyce, O'Casey, and the Irish Popular Theater*, 148–61.
6. O'Casey, 'Theatre and People', 10. I am citing a typescript prepared by Sean O'Casey and held in the Unity Theatre archive at Southern Illinois University. This typescript is not listed in Ayling and Durkin's *Sean O'Casey: A Bibliography*. Ayling and Durkin do list two other typescript versions of this piece (ibid., 331), both titled 'The People and the Theatre' and held in the Henry W. and Albert A. Berg Collection of English and American Literature, New York Public Library, Astor, Lennox and Tilden Foundations. A significantly revised version of the essay was published under the title 'The People and the Theatre' in *Theatre Today* (March 1946) and reprinted in O'Casey, *Under a Colored Cap*, 213–23. The passage I cite does not appear in the published text.
7. In the version published and performed in 1940, the character representing the church is called the Red Priest. After Agate's review pointed out the irony, O'Casey renamed him the Purple Priest for the *Complete Plays*. I am citing the original edition, so I will use the original name.
8. Chambers, *The Story of Unity Theatre*, 205. Stanley Payne documents the Spanish left's use of these symbols (*The Spanish Civil War*, 96).
9. The rehearsal schedule for the Unity production allots three hours for each dress rehearsal. Unity Theatre Archive, box 6, folder 4.
10. Letter from Jack Carney to Sean O'Casey, 5 February 1947 (Carney, Letter to Sean O'Casey).
11. Letter from Sean O'Casey to Barney Conway, 9 May 1962 (O'Casey, Letter to Barney Conway).
12. An early draft of Act II in O'Casey's holograph notebooks shows a character named Barney Conway bursting in to demand his maternity money; Red Ned (an early name for Red Jim) calms Conway down and convinces him to give up drinking. In the published text, the character's name has been changed to Brannigan. See O'Casey, Holograph Notebooks, vol. 15, pp. 22 and 28–36.
13. Memorandum headed 'PROBLEMS OF THE LABOUR MOVEMENT AND ITS ALLIES', probably written by Unity co-founder Herbert Marshall. Unity Theatre archive, Southern Illinois University, 29/11/7.
14. Letter to Sean O'Casey, 9 June 1940 (Allen, Letter to Sean O'Casey).
15. I borrow the term 'heteroglossia' from Mikhail Bakhtin's narratological theory.
16. See chapter 4 of Harris, *Gender and Modern Irish Drama*.

EPILOGUE:
WHAT THE IRISH LEFT – SEAN O'CASEY, SAMUEL BECKETT AND LORRAINE HANSBERRY'S *THE SIGN IN SIDNEY BRUSTEIN'S WINDOW*

Valediction

In reconstituting the networks, exchanges and interactions through which these Irish playwrights participated in the international socialist and sexual revolutions, my hope is not so much that the individual plays examined here will come back to life but that the work of rediscovering their context will reorient and deepen our understanding of modern theatre. The work of restoring the water in which these strange fish once swam was undertaken in hopes that it would lead us to look for other texts or readings that might be, as it were, moving in the deep. As an example of how understanding the ever-complicating afterlives of idealism, queer socialism, radical *eros*, utopian dreaming, revolutionary mothers and metatheatre might enlarge our understanding of twentieth-century theatre, I want to close with a brief consideration of the impact of the Irish left on American drama during the Cold War. I offer this epilogue, not as a last word, but as a gesture towards a hoped-for future, in which the history of Irish drama and these other revolutions might illuminate other plays, performances and histories.

In the spring of 1956, two Irish playwrights offered the spectators of New York City two dramatically different visions of the human condition. Sean O'Casey's third attempt at a Lockout play, *Red Roses For Me*, opened on Broadway at the Booth Theatre on 8 December 1955. That April, after a disastrous few weeks in Miami, Michael Myerberg's revamped production of

Beckett's *Waiting for Godot* reached Broadway. Having learned the hard way not to market *Godot* as popular entertainment, Myerberg presented Beckett's work as a challenge to New York's 'playgoing intellectuals', daring them to appreciate a play whose dramatisation of the meaninglessness of human existence had been endorsed by the intellectuals of France, England and the USA (Gelb, 'Wanted: Intellects', 177). Brooks Atkinson grasped *Godot*'s 'melancholy truths about the hopeless destiny of the human race' and grudgingly admitted that the play made an impression on him (Atkinson, 'Theatre'). Nevertheless, analogising Beckett's mysteries to those of the inscrutable Soviet Union itself, he subtitled his review of it 'Mystery Wrapped in Enigma at Golden'.[1] *Red Roses For Me*, meanwhile, Atkinson hailed as 'O'Casey's Beautiful Ode to the Glory of Life' (Atkinson, *Sean O'Casey*, 95).

From the point of view of literary history, this meeting of Irish minimalism and Irish maximalism on Broadway in the mid-1950s looks like one of those transitional passages when one movement dies as another is born. Thanks in part to Grove Press's savvy in marketing theatre of the absurd to the American academy, *Waiting for Godot* went on to become the cornerstone of postwar avant-garde drama (Glass, 'Absurd Imprint', 535–40). *Red Roses* went to the remainder bin. But guided by Melas, by Brecht, and by what we have seen about what becomes possible when we take ourselves out of straight time, I want to close by looking at a Cold War text in which *Red Roses* and *Godot* remain suspended forever at their moment of intersection: Lorraine Hansberry's *The Sign in Sidney Brustein's Window*.

When *Red Roses* and *Godot* came to Broadway, Lorraine Hansberry was twenty-six years old and living in Greenwich Village. From 1950 to 1953, she had worked for Paul Robeson's newspaper *Freedom*, which put her 'in the midst of a vibrant Black Left network' (Higashida, *Black Internationalist Feminism*, 57). Kate Baldwin has investigated the complex interactions between African-American modernism and the Soviet Union which helped create that network. Robeson was part of a group of black writers, performers and intellectuals for whom the model of nationalism emerging in the Soviet Union 'seemed to offer . . . a means of contesting the exclusionary practices of citizenship and national belonging on which their understandings of identity were based' (Baldwin, *Beyond the Color Line*, 2). The 'affinity' that Baldwin argues existed between Soviets and African-Americans was based on their 'parallel' positions as 'as marginalized, world historical others' (ibid.) for whom the 'Bolshevik promise of a global internationale offered a means of contesting Western paradigms of identity, subjecthood, and, relatedly, nation' (ibid., 6) as well as a site of opposition to 'the worlding of capitalism' (ibid., 10). The black left's interest in Soviet internationalism survived the disillusionment that sent so many of their white American counterparts fleeing the party in the late 1930s, and lasted well into the postwar period (ibid., 7).

Along with *Godot* and *Red Roses,* however, 1956 brought new disclosures from Khruschev about Stalin's atrocities (ibid., 15); and in November, the Soviet Union's invasion of Hungary destroyed its claim to anti-imperialism. As 'black Bolshevism dropped to an all-time low' in the 1950s, however, Robeson 'strengthened his ties' with the Soviet Union (ibid.). Robeson doesn't seem to have met the similarly contrarian O'Casey, though both men supported Unity Theatre in the late 1930s, and Robeson played the lead in Unity's 1938 production of Ben Bengal's strike play *Plant in the Sun*. Robeson's continued investment in Soviet internationalism helped ensure the continuity of a tradition of black radicalism inspired by the 'Soviet promise', which would stretch to include Angela Davis and Audre Lorde (ibid.).

Cheryl Higashida identifies Hansberry as part of a 'Black internationalist feminism' whose members identified 'the fight against heteropatriarchy' as a crucial aspect of the revolution (Higashida, *Black Internationalist Feminism*, 2–3). Over the past fifty years, Higashida notes, 'racism, patriarchy, and homophobia have combined potently with anticommunism to marginalise and silence radical Black women' (ibid., 5) like Hansberry, consigning them to the oblivion into which so many of the texts and performances we've examined here have subsided. In Hansberry's case, it is not silencing so much as selection. The vast majority of Hansberry scholarship focuses on her 1959 realistic family drama, *A Raisin in the Sun*, which is still widely taught and frequently staged.

Even *Raisin* suffers to some extent from the disappearance of its radical context. As a minor example, we can take up the sickly plant that Lena Younger cherishes, and which she saves at the last minute as the family leaves their apartment forever. The plant is typically read as a symbol of Lena herself, or of Lena's children Walter and Beneatha, or of the family's dream for a better life. True enough; but the line with which Lena introduces the plant – 'Lord, if this little old plant don't get more sun than it's been getting, it ain't never going to see spring again' (Hansberry, *Raisin and Sign*, 40) – is also a reference to *Plant in the Sun*, in which the growing plant is used as a metaphor for the workers' revolution. *Plant in the Sun* puns on the double meaning of 'plant' as vegetation and as factory; it takes place in an American candy factory whose employees are trying to organise. The union is fictional, but clearly syndicalist; workers from different sections gradually put aside their differences and join the sit-down strike started by Robseon's character, Peewee. Homophobia is represented in *Plant in the Sun* as a barrier to solidarity; a file clerk named Henry, who the men tauntingly call 'Susie', nearly scuttles the strike by passing information to the employers.[2] In an unconventional development, Peewee acknowledges that their bullying made Henry a 'stool pigeon', and extracts from the other men the promise that they will treat Henry like one of their own. It's the discovery that the reformed Henry has taken up a collection for the strike fund from the other file clerks that prompts Peewee to exclaim that the strike is 'growin', fellas, growin' fast – like – like a plant in the sun' (Bengal, *Plant in the Sun*, 216).

Lena's wish for a better house for herself and her family thus resonates with the utopian ambitions of American syndicalism, and (more faintly) with the hope that social and sexual liberation might still intertwine with and encourage each other. Lena's fear that the plant will 'never see spring again' unless its environment becomes kinder is also a poignant acknowledgement of the disintegration of all those hopes under Cold War conditions. The disillusioned protagonist of *The Sign in Sidney Brustein's Window* comments ironically on the overuse of 'spring' as a metaphor for the always-deferred revolution: 'I no longer even believe that spring must necessarily come at all. Or, that if it does, that it will bring forth anything more poetic or insurgent than . . . the winter's dormant ulcers' (Hansberry, *Raisin and Sign*, 229).

Precisely because spring has not come, most contemporary American readers won't hear these echoes. The loss of that context harms *Raisin* only slightly; but it has been disastrous for *The Sign in Sidney Brustein's Window*, whose main preoccupation is the crisis of the white American left in the post-McCarthy world. I specify the white left, not only because almost all of the characters are white, but because the African-American civil rights movement – which Hansberry herself was deeply involved in while writing the play – is oddly absent from the world these white progressives inhabit. *Sign* thus allows Hansberry to treat the crisis of faith and confidence in the Soviet Revolution – and the specific damage done by the House Un-American Activities Committee (HUAC) – in comparative isolation (Alton Scales, a 'No-More-Since-Hungary' ex-Communist and the play's only black character, is the only character who makes a connection between Marxist politics and American racial politics). It also allows Hansberry to target, in her critique, a specific problem for the left that emerges at the intersection between whiteness and maleness, and which I will refer to as heroic masculinity.

WAITING FOR LEFTY

The play is set in the bohemian Greenwich Village flat of the eponymous Sidney Brustein, a Jewish intellectual who is approaching the end of his thirties and with it the end of his patience with lost causes and failed revolutions. His bitterness and disillusionment poison his relationship with his younger wife, Iris, and goad him into conflicts with his fellow-Greenwich Village hipsters, including Alton Scales and the gay avant-garde playwright David Ragin. At the same time, Sidney retains his contempt for bourgeois culture, which he vents on Iris's middlebrow sister Mavis. Sidney reluctantly supports the campaign of his friend Wally O'Hara, who is running as a reform candidate against the corrupt New York City machine. (The 'sign' of the title is Wally's campaign sign.) O'Hara's victory renews Sidney's battered idealism – until Iris, just before leaving him, informs Sidney that O'Hara has been co-opted by the very system he has pledged to fight. Sidney is joined in his despondency by Iris's other sister, Gloria, who works as a prostitute. Gloria has returned to New York hoping to build a life with Alton; but Alton has left her a break-up letter. Into this pit of despair wanders David Ragin, whose absurdist play has become a Broadway hit. After Sidney passes out, David asks Gloria to help him consummate his relationship with his lover, who is unable to perform without a woman watching him. Gloria agrees; but she can't bring herself to do it, and instead commits suicide in the Brusteins' bathroom. The next morning, Wally pays Sidney a condolence visit. Sidney declares his renewed commitment to the struggle and vows to fight Wally and what he represents.

Despite the astonishing success of *A Raisin in the Sun*, *The Sign in Sidney Brustein's Window* struggled to reach Broadway. It ran to 101 performances only because Hansberry's ex-husband Robert Nemiroff organised a campaign to support it.[3] Since then, *Sidney Brustein* has suffered from 'utter scholarly neglect' (Hodin, 'Lorraine Hansberry's Absurdity', 745). Mark Hodin blames this in part on the fact that play was perceived as pandering to 'white audiences' (ibid., 745–6). Cheryl Higashida points towards another reason by identifying *Sidney Brustein* as part of Hansberry's critique of the existentialist avant-garde and 'its articulations of sexual and racial others' (*Black Internationalist Feminism*, 72). For Hansberry, as Hodin and Higashida show, the arrival in New York of Beckett and the rest of O'Casey's Horrorhawks provided aid and comfort to a white intelligentsia prone to 'constructing African-Americans as figures of social alienation' and 'existentialist outcasts' with whom they could identify and thus achieve 'their own transcendence from the American mainstream' (Hodin, 'Lorraine Hansberry's Absurdity', 754). *The Sign in Sidney Brustein's Window* engages absurdist drama directly through the callous and self-involved David Ragin, who bears some resemblances to both Samuel Beckett (Carter) and Edward Albee (Higashida), but who could just as easily stand in for Jean Genet, whose *Les Nègres* evoked a strong response from Hansberry when it was staged in New York in 1961 (Hansberry, 'Genet, Mailer, and the New Paternalism'), or Albert Camus, whose critique of the Soviet Union in his 1951 book *The Rebel* fuelled the 'Sartre-Camus debate' that Hansberry describes as part of the play's genesis (quoted in Nemiroff, 'A Portrait', 161). Hansberry's decision to make David the play's most repellent character – even the perfidious Wally O'Hara is more likeable – is typically interpreted as a critique of the 'theater of the absurd' and as a warning about the 'immoral and tragic consequences' of withdrawing from politics into the existential abyss (Higashida, *Black Internationalist Feminism*, 72).

Constant readers will be unsurprised to learn that I intend to complicate this reading. David is indeed judged harshly by *Sidney Brustein*; but once we realise that O'Casey is haunting this play along with Beckett, we can recognise David's dramatic vision as the most potentially generative thing about him. Beckett's dramatic vision is not simply an ordeal that Sidney has to pass through in order to '*realistically* affirm' (Nemiroff, 'A Portrait', 163) the value of humanity and political engagement. It is the necessary partner of the *other* dramatic vision that Sidney has already internalised: the expressionist idealism of O'Casey's later style. Beckettian 'absurdism' in *Sidney Brustein* is offered not as a dead end, but as one term in a synthesis which might produce a way through the impasse in which the white left is trapped.

The 1956 *Waiting for Godot* certainly must have appeared as anathema to the leftmost segments of the largely white New York theatre scene. It would have seemed to them like the final ironic nail in the coffin of the agitational theatre of the 1930s, whose most successful incarnation had always been Clifford Odets's very different execution of a very similar premise in *Waiting for Lefty*. Lefty wasn't any more punctual than Godot; but in Odets's play the non-arrival of the expected saviour is what sparks the revolution. Communism, by returning agency to the rank and file, allows workers to *stop* waiting for someone to lead them out of bondage: 'What are we waiting for ... Don't wait for Lefty! He might never come' (Odets, *Six Plays*, 31). When a messenger arrives with the news that Lefty has been assassinated, Agate – his rank-and-file surrogate – hails the news with ecstatic joy, knowing that the 'WORKERS OF THE WORLD' can now finally give their 'BONES AND BLOOD' to the battle ahead (ibid.). 'And when we die they'll know what we did to make a new world!' Agate shouts. 'We'll die for what is right! Put fruit trees where our ashes are!' (ibid.). When Agate turns to the audience and asks, 'Well, what's the answer?' the cast chants 'Strike!' until the spectators stand up and chant with them. Agency passes from the labour leader into the rank and file while enabling the spectators to feel the thrill of collective action.

Lefty's optimism, however, is founded both on an idealistic view of the Soviet Union as the utopian destination towards which the workers of the world were moving, and on the idealistic community spirit that created and sustained the Group Theatre. By the time *Godot* came to town, both of these things were irretrievably broken. Odets had renounced Communism, gone Hollywood, and betrayed many of his Group comrades by naming them as Communists to HUAC (Smith, *Real Life*, 417). Odets's wounded former comrades would have found in *Godot*'s universe an image of their current nightmare: a world in which, despite the survival of capitalist exploitation, resistance is meaningless and progress impossible. 'Let us do something while we have the chance!' Vladimir cries, with the boss and the worker literally lying helpless at their feet (Beckett, *Waiting for Godot*, 51). But Vladimir and Estragon can neither help nor hurt Pozzo or Lucky; and although class privilege itself seems to be diminishing along with everything else – Pozzo keeps losing the props that confirm his status – *Godot*'s answer to the question 'What is to be done?' is, apparently, 'Nothing.' Even more cruelly, Godot, unlike Lefty, refuses to complete his absence. Like the heaven that Father Keegan could see from Rosscullen, Godot torments Vladimir and Estragon by neither materialising nor disappearing. Queer futurity turns dystopian; deferral, instead of sustaining alterity, traps Vladimir and Estragon in the living death of an eternal present moment.

Hansberry explored the destructive side of deferral in *A Raisin in the Sun*. The play's title is drawn from Langston Hughes' poem *Harlem*, which consists of speculative answers to the question, 'What happens to a dream deferred?' The play's working title was 'The Crystal Stair', drawn from Hughes's poem *Mother to Son*; the change shifts the focus from Lena's endurance to Walter's desperation as he struggles to attain a manhood which he believes is dependent on the economic success denied to him by racism. But *Sidney Brustein*, I will argue, suggests that Hansberry found in Beckett's universe, and in the 'theater of the absurd', not a simple denial of the possibility of change, but ambiguities and possibilties which could – if recuperated – help her paralysed comrades move through the impasse created by Cold War politics. In order to activate it, however, she must first bridge the false opposition between politically committed and absurdist theatre; and that is where O'Casey's late plays come in.

Hansberry finds her grounds for comparison where we found it in Chapter 5: the patriarchal foundation on which both *Godot* and *Red Roses* are built. Through David, Hansberry underlines the exclusion of women, and the feminine itself, from *Waiting for Godot*. *Sidney Brustein*'s engagement with O'Casey's heterosexism is much less clearly marked, but only because O'Casey's world view is so thoroughly integrated into Sidney's consciousness. By using Iris and her sisters to synthesise the antirealist techniques of the two Irish playwrights whose work had been most generative for her, Hansberry reanimates some of the insights of the queer socialism that both Soviet Communism and the American right sought to destroy. She critiques O'Casey and Beckett *by* recuperating them, using their techniques to undo a toxic model of political struggle defined by the cruel optimism that constitutes heroic masculinity.

Loren Berlant defines 'a relation of cruel optimism' as one in which the object you desire is 'an obstacle to your flourishing' (Berlant, *Cruel Optimism*, 1). Unopposed capitalism, Berlant argues, renders 'the good life' increasingly unattainable; yet the dream of 'the good life' cannot be abandoned, because of the unacceptable cost of abandoning optimism. If 'all attachment is optimistic', the only alternative to optimism is solipsism (ibid., 2) – or what Alton dubs 'ostrich-ism' (Hansberry, *Raisin and Sign*, 228). Sidney's situation is especially difficult because he desires a 'good life' that can be lived *in opposition* to capitalism. It is oppositionality itself, I argue, that Hansberry exposes as the object of the white left's cruel optimism. Hansberry's treatment of David suggests that binary oppositions remain stable only for those who can escape or refuse the painful complications of intersectionality. The oscillation between optimism and ostrich-ism that Sidney finds so exhausting is the consequence of his unexamined attachment to an ideal of masculinity founded on an impossible desire for the individual's heroic resistance to overwhelming forces of control. Sidney breaks through when he finally learns – through his mediated encounters with the otherworlds of O'Casey and Beckett – to live without heroic masculinity.

Last Man Left

During the 1930s, like their British and European counterparts, American playwrights, directors, performers and screenwriters rallied to the Popular Front. During and after the Second World War, in the USA, the same people were subjected to two decades of political persecution by the state, the media, their employers and public opinion. In 1938, Congressman Martin Dies founded a House committee with the stated object of ferreting Communists out of the entertainment industry (Kessler-Harris, *A Difficult Woman*, 114). One of their first targets was the Federal Theatre Project, a New Deal relief programme founded in 1935 to provide work for theatre professionals. Hallie Flanagan was called to testify on 8 December 1938, in a public hearing now best remembered for an exchange in which a congressional representative accused Christopher Marlowe and Euripides of being Communists *avant la lettre* (Murphy, *Congressional Theatre*, 14–15). The hearing gave the House Appropriations Committee the ammunition it needed to cut off funding for the Federal Theatre Project, which folded in 1939.

After the war, the Dies Committee was revitalised and renamed the House Un-American Activities Committee. Anyone suspected of a radical past could, from that point on, be subpoenaed by HUAC, dragged down to Washington, and confronted with the question, 'Are you now or have you ever been a member of the Communist Party?' During the 1950s, when Senator Joseph McCarthy embarked upon his own anti-Communist purge in the Senate, that question became far more dangerous. At the same time, in the same national capital, by a different group of government officials, 'another question was posed at least as frequently, if more discreetly: "Information has come to the attention of the Civil Service Commission that you are a homosexual. What comment do you care to make?"' (Johnson, *The Lavender Scare*, 5). To be a healthy, loyal, 'normal' American – as opposed to suspect, subversive and risky – one now had to repudiate the twin perversions of homosexuality and Communism. By the late 1950s, HUAC had interrogated nearly every major radical playwright, director and performer in America.

HUAC was not so much an investigative body as a disciplinary machine designed to destroy anyone fed to it. HUAC staged thousands of iterations of the oppositional confrontation between the individual radical and the state that George Bernard Shaw and William Morris experienced on that day in Trafalgar Square. As on Bloody Sunday, idealism demanded that a *real* man respond with absolute defiance to any threat to his personal autonomy; and as on Bloody Sunday the conditions that created that demand made it almost impossible to meet. Like the Dublin Employers' Federation, HUAC understood the coercive power of long-term denial of employment. Invoking the Fifth Amendment could protect an uncooperative witness from contempt of Congress charges; but it would not protect him from being blacklisted by the film studios, producers, unions, school systems, universities and other institutions who were desperate to avoid being targetted themselves.

But to cooperate – to perform the 'sincere contrition' that confirmed the witness's loyalty and kept him off the blacklist – meant not only confessing, but informing (Kessler-Harris, *A Difficult Woman*, 257). A 1950 Supreme Court decision empowered HUAC to imprison any witness who admitted to Communist Party ties but refused to name people they had worked with (Smith, *Real Life*, 415). Anyone named during a hearing became vulnerable to HUAC and to blacklisting. Over the years, blacklist victims lost their jobs, their health and sometimes their lives (ibid., 414–18).

HUAC enforced its own alternative temporality, conflating past and present in a way that fused change with shame. HUAC was at its most aggressive in the immediate postwar era. By then, many of those who had joined the Communist Party during the Popular Front days, when it seemed to be 'dedicated to the best, most progressive aspects of the American way of life' (ibid., 415), had renounced it. The demand for a yes or no answer left no room for ambivalence about a once-cherished but now-abandoned ideal; nor was the witness permitted to separate what his politics were *now* from what they might *have ever been*. Such a witness could only experience HUAC testimony as self-betrayal. If he said yes, he was declaring loyalty he did not feel to a Communist Party he rejected; if he said no, he was denying convictions he had once deeply held. If he resisted, he was pretending to a resolve falsified by his earlier recantation; if he cooperated, he was exposing his friends to an abusive and tyrannical government. John Proctor's agony over his confession at the end of Arthur Miller's 1953 play *The Crucible* captures the specific dilemma that HUAC created for the apostate witness. Proctor's guilt over his sexual betrayal of Elizabeth makes him unworthy (in his own eyes) of martyrdom, but he can't avoid his own martyrdom without harming other people.

In contrast to *Godot*'s image of defeat, *Red Roses* offered a compensatory fantasy, which included O'Casey himself as a living example of a heroic masculinity which had been violently stripped from so many of his American counterparts. O'Casey's masculinity had never been tested in the HUAC crucible and therefore had never failed there. As a playwright with a working-class background – which he narrated with a wealth of invented detail in his autobiographies – he could purify the now-suspect American theatre by infusing it with a steeliness which, if dangerously *red*-blooded, was nevertheless bracing in its virility. As a playwright *unchangingly* committed both to an anti-commerical artistic vision and to the Communist Party, O'Casey incarnated the purity of commitment – the unflinching, uncomplicated, unbroken resolve – that HUAC was designed to destroy.

O'Casey's Irishness made identification easier for the *white* men of the American left. The role that the Irish played in the formation of a specifically white American, working-class identity has long been a subject of debate among American historians.[4] Diane Negra, writing about the Irish 'boom' in American popular culture in the 1990s, argues that the 'transnationalized Irishness' of the Celtic Tiger era constituted, for white Americans, 'a category of racial fantasy' which compensated for their rising 'terror that whiteness in America [was] losing its social purchase' (Negra, 'The Irish in Us', 2). The embrace of Irishness as 'a form of "enriched whiteness"' – a white identity 'politically insulated' from America's history of racial oppression, and defined by Ireland's cultural and spiritual heritage rather than by racist ideology – is, Negra argues, one of the reasons that '[v]irtually every form of popular culture' in the USA 'has, in one way or another, at one time or another, presented Irishness as a moral antidote to contemporary ills ranging from globalization to postmodern alienation' (ibid., 1–9). We have already seen how, half a century before the era Negra investigates, O'Casey functioned for his American admirers as a 'moral antidote' even to the very Communism that informed his own work. O'Casey's Irishness thus marked him as a fantasy embodiment, not just of left masculinity, but specifically of *white* masculinity.

While Hansberry's identification with O'Casey was necessarily complicated by this, her white male colleagues could simply vicariously enjoy both O'Casey's heroism and the victory represented by this Broadway production of one of his late plays. The director, John O'Shaughnessy, had staged *Red Roses* in Houston in 1951, where it was attacked by anti-Communists and the Catholic Church (Murray, *Sean O'Casey*, 332). In 1953, when a planned New York production of O'Casey's *Cock-a-Doodle Dandy* came under similar attack, Arthur Miller discovered that 'the most powerful names in the theater' were too 'scared or bewildered' to stand up to anti-Communist bullying (Miller quoted in ibid., 305). The backers pulled out; that battle was lost. *Red Roses For Me* on Broadway represented, for Miller and his milieu, a battle won.

Formally and ideologically, *Red Roses* is closer to Broadway norms than most of O'Casey's experimental work. By returning to the Lockout's time and place – Dublin 1913 – and to a mostly-realistic mise-en-scène, *Red Roses* excludes Soviet Communism from its dramatic universe. Borrowing the sacrificial narrative and the sacrificial symbolism of Irish nationalism, *Red Roses* evokes revolution as nostalgia rather than as a contemporary threat. The richness of the play's language is closely identified with its Shakespearean sources by the play's opening scene, in which Ayamonn and his mother are dressed in Elizabethan garb and rehearsing a scene from *Henry VI*. The other characters' collective hostility towards the play's lone atheist confirms its religious sensibility, as does a golden cross of daffodils that conflates Christian symbolism with romanticism. O'Casey's deployment of socialist aesthetics thus provides some protective camouflage for its Communist politics.

So do the play's gender politics, which are fully coincident with the norms demanded by a paranoid culture that had declared war on 'subversion'. The heroic masculinity developed in *The Star Turns Red* also drives *Red Roses*. The worker-hero Ayamonn is compassionate towards his fellow tenement dwellers, but exalted above them; his speech rarely descends from the heroic register. Though his mother, his girlfriend and his rector entreat him to avoid the coming battle between the strikers and the police, Ayamonn never wavers:

> MRS. BREYDON. Stay here, my son, where safety is a green tree with a kindly growth.
> AYAMONN. I go, mother, to fight for the dark places, where there is no green tree and no kindly growth; where we shall yet plant roses of Sharon and lilies of the valley. (*Indicating Men and Women.*) I go with them.
> SHELIA. (*To Ayamonn.*) Stay here when time goes by in sandals soft, where days fall gently as petals from a flower, where dark hair, growing gray, is never noticed. (*Women in crowd murmur against this.*)
> AYAMONN. Sweetheart, I go to fight for them who know no peace from poverty; I am of them, God helping me, with them; and no fear of a threat, no offer of love, can pluck me out of their hands. (O'Casey, *Red Roses For Me*, 66–7)

Ayamonn remains consistent with O'Casey's conception of a socialist realism hero, while an Irish dramatic convention established in Yeats and Gregory's *Cathleen ni Houlihan* – the hero's rejection of his family in order to pursue the immortality of those who die for an ideal – is repurposed to dramatise the hero's acceptance of his destiny as leader of The People.

Ayamonn's real power, however, is revealed not in battle but in the transformation scene of Act III, in which Ayamonn comes upon a crowd of Dublin's wretched poor huddled on a bridge and lifts them out of abjection by inspiring them with his vision of a future in which ownership has returned to the people. O'Casey's stage directions show Ayamonn's speech literally changing the world:

> *The scene has brightened, and bright and lovely colours are being brought to them by the caress of the setting sun. The men that have*

> *been lounging against them now stand stalwart, looking like fine bronze statues, slashed with scarlet.* (Ibid., 58)

As Ayamonn lays on ever richer colour, one of the previously dejected 'men' finds himself suddenly appreciating the sight of 'th' houses . . . gay in purple and silver', jolting one of his fellow-proletariats into an epiphany: 'Our tired heads have always haunted far too low a level' (ibid.). For O'Casey, this transformation scene was about visualising the principle that joins his aesthetics to his politics: before the workers can fight for the loaf of bread, they need the flower in the vase. Like Larkin, Ayamonn struggles to bestow that gift through the superb overabundance of his own imagery. On stage, precisely because all 'actuality' is symbolic, Ayamonn can accomplish the transformation that Larkin could not complete.

Lionel Burch, reviewing the 1946 London production of *Red Roses*, provided a startling revelation of the specifically *masculine* aspect of Ayamonn's creative power. For Burch, the transformation scene produces not catharsis but a kind of metaphysical ejaculation, a 'shattering orgasm' so powerful that we need the first two acts to prepare ourselves to 'receive the impact' (Burch, 'Red Roses for Me', 20) of all this *jouissance*:

> Then, in the stupendous third act, O'Casey consummates the apocalypse, and gives the God-in-everyman a clear fifteen mintues' run. By a lyrical potency of lighting and language, Dublin and the dim, strike-bound Dubliners on the stage are translated from life-as-it-is into a time and place over and beyond the strike . . . in to a golden Dublin, from which the need to strike – like the need to hate, and the need to fear – is seen to have withered away. Sitting, with constricted throats and upheaved stomachs, in the stalls – we go, we come back. We make the golden journey into the Kingdom of Heaven . . . And you, who haven't been there, can't take that away from us. (Ibid., 21)

Ayamonn's 'shattering' power represents a magical efficacy which was being brutally denied to the American cultural left. Because Ayamonn is an aspiring actor and poet as well as an autobiographical figure for O'Casey himself (Atkinson, *Sean O'Casey*, 10, 13, 15), Ayamonn's transformation of his onstage environment thus makes him not just a worker-hero but, specifically, a heroic radical playwright. Journalist Murray Kempton summed up the poignancy of this fantasy for a community that had recently gone through a different kind of shattering: '[A]s long as O'Casey runs this time, there can be nothing like him in this town, for he is life celebrating life', Kempton noted – wistfully adding, 'And how anemic he makes us all seem' (Kempton, 'A Terrible Beauty'). Arthur Miller admitted as much in a conversation with John Calder: 'None of us dares to be direct any more' (Calder quoted in Murray, *Sean O'Casey*, 369).

This impression was no doubt enhanced by the fact that Brooks Atkinson, who during this period was New York's single most influential drama critic, had been cultivating this image of O'Casey's heroic masculinity for the past two decades. In his review of the 1934 Broadway production of *Within the Gates*, Atkinson contrasts the 'gentry idling in the studios', fiddling with their 'nervous realism' while impotently dreaming of the advent of a stronger form, with the muscular strength O'Casey cultivated 'on the streets and docks and in the tenements of Dublin' (Atkinson, *Sean O'Casey*, 64). 'Work does not terrify the laborer', Atkinson declares; O'Casey is so 'confident of his strength' that he has produced in *Within the Gates* 'not merely a technical achievement, but a fantasy impregnated with the joy and terror of life', forged by 'the simplicity of Mr. O'Casey's courage' (ibid.). The artist capable of impregnation on this scale must be a man indeed: 'a man of strength, courage, and honesty' (ibid., 118); 'a man of valor and principle' (ibid., 165); 'a hard man in a fight' (ibid., 120); 'a man of colossal fortitude' (ibid., 146); a 'free man' who scorns to 'bluff, pose, or truckle' (ibid., 120); a 'natural man' (ibid., 64), 'a man who could never surrender to expediency' (ibid., 161). He has 'the hardness of a man who has worked with his hands' (ibid., 117). 'Censors tremble' before O'Casey because they are 'in the presence of a man who is fully alive' (ibid., 68). Atkinson closed a review of *Red Roses* with the line, 'He always was a man' (ibid., 93).

By celebrating O'Casey/Ayamonn's power, Atkinson, Miller and Kempton could identify with and share in O'Casey's heroic masculinity. Hansberry, although among O'Casey's most vocal American admirers, was also very critical of white fantasies of masculinity. Most vividly, Hansberry's attack on Norman Mailer's 1957 essay 'The White Negro' in her 1961 piece 'Genet, Mailer, and the New Paternalism' testifies to her impatience with the white 'hipster's' obsession with attaining oppositionality through identification with an idealised image of someone else's heroic masculinity (Hodin, 'Lorraine Hansberry's Absurdity', 754).

Mailer's construction of 'hipster' masculinity is predicated on a desire for pure oppositionality, which he articulates through his discussion of black masculinity as psychopathic. The central problem that Mailer identifies for white masculinity is that a 'totalitarian society makes enormous demands on the courage of men, and a partially totalitarian society makes even greater demands for the general anxiety is greater' (Mailer, 'The White Negro'). It is in search of the 'disproportionate courage' that masculinity now requires that Mailer turns to 'the Negro' who 'has been living on the margin between totalitarianism and democracy for two centuries' (ibid.). Mailer overtly envies a black masculinity which he imagines has never possessed the 'security' available to 'the average white'; having nothing to lose, 'the Negro' is free from the 'anxiety' that saps the 'courage' of white men. Presented with a choice between 'the simplest of alternatives: live a life of constant humiliation or ever-threatening danger', the 'Negro' has chosen danger, and thus modelled heroic masculinity for the timorous and tempted white hipster (ibid.).

In pursuit of his own masculinity, then, Mailer constructs a romanticised and highly stereotyped black masculinity in which rationality has been completely displaced by pure embodiment. Though he assigns it a positive value, Mailer nevertheless imagines black masculinity as a kind of Molotov cocktail made up of equal parts of violence, sex and jazz. Hansberry was merciless in her dissection of Mailer's 'romantic racism', and especially in his insistence on denying 'the middle-class Negro's search for comfort' (Hansberry, 'Genet, Mailer, and the New Paternalism', 14). 'There is certainly nothing fresh in the spectacle of white people telling all sorts of colored peoples how they should behave to satisfy them', Hansberry observes. 'It is, to say the least, the most characteristic aspect of the nation's foreign policy' (ibid.). Hodin argues that *Sign* continues this critique, 'reveal[ing] white identity as a relatively weak position' (Hodin, 'Lorraine Hansberry's Absurdity', 756). Instead of identifying with O'Casey's heroism, Hansberry turns the fantasy against itself, challenging the white male playwright's sole entitlement to this kind of creative power.

Playing Appalachian

In *To Be Young, Gifted, and Black: Lorraine Hansberry in Her Own Words*, Hansberry tells the story of attending a student production of *Juno and the Paycock* at the University of Wisconsin at Madison which inspired her to become a playwright. Because *Juno and the Paycock* is the only O'Casey play that Hansberry publicly named, most comparative treatments of Hansberry and O'Casey focus on *Juno and the Paycock* and *A Raisin in the Sun*.[5] Indeed, *Raisin*'s 'debt' to *Juno* quickly became a sore spot for Hansberry. In June of 1959, Hansberry published a withering response to one A. Boyle who had written to *The New York Times* accusing her of appropriating *Juno*'s plot, and expressing the hope that 'the O'Casey Club' would mobilise to 'see the Green Crow is treated right' ('Mailbag – "O'Casey – Hansberry"'). Hansberry replied that Boyle's perception of *Raisin* as an adaptation of *Juno* was produced largely by his own ignorance about black life. 'I am the first to say that my play and all the plays I shall ever write "owe" deeply to the great O'Casey', she declared – but only 'in spirit' (ibid.).

This exchange points out some of the pitfalls of comparativism. Our unavoidably limited perspectives can and do lead us to perceive influence where we may be observing coincidence (Lonergan, *Theatre and Globalization*, 108). It is precisely in order *not* to repeat A. Boyle's mistake that I have avoided, to the extent that I can, approaching this book as a study of influence, a term which denies innovation and originality to the more recent text. The implications of 'influence' become exponentially more damaging when the 'original' text belongs to a white man and the more recent one to a black woman. *The*

New York Times reported in 1959, for instance, that Hansberry 'worships Sean O'Casey' (Robertson, 'Dramatist Against Odds', X3) as her 'literary God' ('Her Dream Came True', 37). This was both patronising and inaccurate. Among other things, by situating Walter in the context of institutional racism, *Raisin* administers a powerful rebuke to *Juno*'s indictment of working-class masculinity as inherently irresponsible, thus undermining the counter-revolutionary model of the working-class family that O'Casey inherited from Ervine via Wilson. Just as New York drama critics were so busy finding borrowings from *their* favourite playwrights in *Raisin* that they missed its engagement with Miller's *Death of a Salesman* (Hansberry, 'An Author's Reflections', 8), more contemporary commentators have tended to assume that the only O'Casey play Hansberry knew is the only one that *they* know.

But that is by no means a safe assumption. Elsewhere in *Young, Gifted, and Black*, Hansberry speaks of O'Casey in terms that suggest she was familiar with his later style: 'This, to me, is the playwright of the twentieth century accepting and using the most obvious instruments of Shakespeare' (68–9). In an interview with Studs Terkel, Hansberry admired O'Casey's 'poetic dialogue' (quoted in Carter, *Hansberry's Drama*, 32). Though Nemiroff himself doesn't see the connection, his description of the formal 'problems' that kept *Sidney Brustein* out in the cold points out the play's structural similarities with O'Casey's later plays: a plot which is 'not neat, simple, or well-made', a wide range of 'themes and conflicts' which are not so much interwoven as 'juxtaposed' on a 'sprawling canvas', an attempt to mix realism with other styles, and excessive length (Nemiroff, 'A Portrait', 164–5). This is compelling, if circumstantial, evidence of Hansberry's familiarity with O'Casey's later work, at least on the page. As for the stage, there is no obvious reason to assume that Hansberry – who left *Freedom* in 1953 to devote more time to her own writing – would not have been among the small but dedicated group of fans that Arthur Miller remembered coming to 'cheer on' the 1956 *Red Roses* (Miller, *Arthur Miller*, 48). *Red Roses* was the first chance Hansberry would have had in her lifetime to see a new play by O'Casey; and given the political climate, she might well have assumed that it would be her last.

In *Sidney Brustein*, Hansberry gives Sidney Ayamonn's capacity to alter the staged reality for other characters. In the opening scene of Act II, 'just before daybreak', Sidney uses his banjo to make a new day dawn:

> As he plays the lighting shifts magically, and nonrealistically, to create the mountain of his dreams. Gone is even the distant foghorn; he is no longer in the city. After several phrases of this . . . the IRIS-of-his-Mind appears, barefooted, with flowing hair and mountain dress, and mounts the steps. She embraces him and then, as by the lore of the hill people,

> *is possessed by these rhythms, and dances in the shadows before him.*
> (Hansberry, *Raisin and Sign*, 274)

Superficially, this resembles Walter's transformation scene in *Raisin*, with Iris recovering a deeper, more 'authentic' self rooted in 'the lore of the hill people'. But Iris's Appalachian identity is largely a fabrication – the product of a craving for authenticity and primitivism which, because the men who crave it also have the power to induce women to embody it, ironically converts the 'natural' into the artificial. For the actual Iris, Sidney's refusal to understand this fantasy *as* a fantasy has become intolerable. By Act III, Iris has violently rejected the long hair that is key to the folk aesthetic: '*Her hair has been cut and teased to a stiff sculpture and tinted an entirely unnatural metallic yellow*' (ibid., 311). Shocked as he is, Sidney doesn't get the message until Iris actually screams, 'I DON'T WANT TO PLAY APPALACHIAN ANY MORE!' (ibid., 315).

Iris is from Appalachia; but 'playing Appalachian' doesn't mean being herself. 'Playing Appalachian' means accepting the job that, according to Elin Diamond, realism always assigns the female lead: using her own body to produce the symptoms that allow the protagonist/analyst to produce the 'truth' that realism claims to discover (Diamond, *Unmaking*, 4). Iris is a frustrated actress, who at this moment has just accepted a role in a commercial because she believes she has no real talent. But this belief is the result of years of failed auditions for 'blank director-producer-writer faces' who want something specific but won't tell her what (Hansberry, *Raisin and Sign*, 251). Iris's rebellion against Sidney's fantasy is as tragically ironic as Sidney's support of Wally O'Hara; 'she has broken free from Sidney's objectification only to become the object of another fantasy' (Hodin, 'Lorraine Hansberry's Absurdity', 761).

Appalachian folk music has its roots in the music of Scotch-Irish immigrants, which makes this scene one of several ways in which Hansberry presents Irishness as a false promise of authenticity. A less subtle indicator is Hansberry's decision to bestow the name Wally O'Hara on her apostate politician. David accuses Sidney of 'reading too much Shaw' (Hansberry, *Raisin and Sign*, 264); perhaps he's been borrowing it from Wally, who has fully embraced gradualism. Wally uses alcoholism as a metaphor for utopianism: 'Don't think about all the drinks you've got to give up, just concentrate on the next one . . . Don't think about the ailing world for the time being, just think about your own little ailing neighborhood' (ibid., 229). But as proof of the value of learning to 'negotiate' with power, all Wally can offer at the end of the play is a promise to put up a stop sign at a dangerous intersection (ibid., 336).

On one level, the Act II transformation scene critiques the masculinism of O'Casey's later phase by making visible the gender dynamics of *Red Roses*, in which – with the exception of Ayamonn's mother – all the women are child-like beings dependent on Ayamonn to transform their poverty-stunted souls with the bringing of the Word. *Red Roses* includes a trio of poor Catholic women – Eeada, Dympna and Finoola – who function as an expressionist chorus; each wears make-up representing one of the three stages of a woman's life, and all have 'the same expressionless stare' (O'Casey, *Red Roses For Me*, 13). Catholic opposition to *Red Roses* in Ireland was as much about O'Casey's condescending treatment of this trio as it was about his Communism (Fallon, *Sean O'Casey*, 152–7). Their dependence on the Protestant Ayamonn for salvation is emphasised in the bridge scene, where they become the beneficiaries of Ayamonn's transfiguring vision: '*(To Eeada.)* The apple grows for you to eat. *(To Dympna.)* The violet grows for you to wear. *(To Finoola)* Young maiden, another world is in your womb' (O'Casey, *Red Roses For Me*, 57). At the climax, Ayamonn dances with Finoola; when he first tries to exit, Finoola asks, 'Amn't I good enough for you?' Ayamonn answers by kissing her and running across the bridge towards destiny. The moment he leaves, the vision fades, and the women relapse into their previous torpor.

Sidney Brustein, as Hodin has demonstrated, also treats its female trio – the three sisters Iris, Mavis and Gloria – as a chorus, but looks back to the Ancient Greek model. Mavis points this out to Sidney when she explains the origin of their maiden name, Parodus: 'The parodus is the chorus! And you know – no matter what is happening in the main action of the play – the chorus is always there, commenting, watching . . . Just watching and being' (Hansberry, *Raisin and Sign*, 307). Hodin sees this 'gendered choral structure, in which women are at once marginalised from and yet central to the main action' as an outgrowth of Hansberry's study of Simone de Beauvoir ('Lorraine Hansberry's Absurdity', 757); the Parodus sisters 'materialise' the absurd as meaningless suffering which they are, under patriarchal conditions, compelled to experience and yet powerless to change (ibid., 771). But if they cannot affect the action, the Parodus sisters also cannot be rescued from this absurdity by their would-be male saviours. Hansberry is quite deliberate in making *them* the ones who rescue *him*.

Sidney's transformation scene begins, like *Red Roses*'s bridge scene, with a male creator conjuring up a symbolic woman who responds to the creator's music with an ecstatic dance expressing the faux-liberation of her faux-real self. At the end of the dance, 'the mountain nymph gives [Sidney] a final kiss and flees'. As a 'spent' Sidney 'plucks idly' at the banjo strings, the real Iris enters. The cliché would be for the fantasy to end and for Sidney to make a cutting remark about the pain of his return to reality. What happens instead is that Iris begins collaborating with Sidney.

When Sidney builds the fantasy scene with his words – 'Look at the pines . . . You can taste and feel the scent of them' – Iris replies, 'This is some mountain' (Hansberry, *Raisin and Sign*, 274). She knows it's a fantasy; but she participates in its construction. During the rest of the scene, Iris acts as if they are in fact on the mountain. When she uses 'here', it means the mountain ('You'd like to live right here, in the woods'); when she speaks of her childhood she says she 'was born in country like this' (ibid., 277); when she wants to exit the fantasy she says, 'Take me back to the city, please, Sid', which he does by slinging his banjo and helping her off the porch (ibid., 278–9). Iris makes Sidney's fantasy real – to him, to her, to the spectators – by behaving as if it is. She becomes, in other words, Stanislavsky's ideal performer, who doesn't need a glass of water or a bank draft to make the spectator believe that he is using them. While doing this – *because* she is doing it – Iris can finally tell Sidney that she can't live with this fantasy: 'I'm sorry. The truth is that I am cold and bored' (ibid., 275). She confesses that she hates her long hair, and that he's 'the reason I wear it like this' (ibid., 275–6). For the first time, Iris successfully communicates something important to Sidney, who successfully takes it in: 'I'm not saying anything, Iris. I'm listening' (ibid., 278). She has, by inhabiting and bringing to life a man's lie, told a difficult truth about her authentic self. Which means that as far as the Method is concerned, Iris has just achieved her dream of becoming a great actress.

The transformation scene ultimately produces not Sidney's fantasy but Iris's dream – but only because Sidney is willing to let her direct. Act II scene I thus both exploits and critiques O'Casey's expressionism; this momentary realisation of another possible world *is* transfiguring when and only when it is truly collaborative. Their cooperation enables what is perhaps Sidney's first sincere expression of non-tortured emotion: 'I love you very much' (ibid.). Act II scene 1 is thus a subtle, sophisticated and powerful piece of stagecraft in which Hansberry releases *Red Roses*'s transformative magic from the grip of a man who can only use it to amplify his own power, and enables a woman to turn it into a moment of healing connection from which something real might emerge.

Naturally, in the original production, this scene was cut for time (Nemiroff, 'A Portrait', 166).

Though Iris's monologue was eventually incorporated in to Act I (ibid., 186), the loss of its antirealist context isolates the Act III 'absurdist orgy', which would otherwise be part of a linked pair: O'Casey's vision and Beckett's void. As Sidney has been given O'Casey's powers, David has Beckett's – which are also doing very little to change the world for women. When Mavis asks if there is a part in David's new play for Iris, Sidney snaps, 'There are only two characters in David's play, and they are both male and married to each other and the entire action takes place in a refrigerator' (Hansberry, *Raisin and Sign*, 262). As this joke about Beckettian minimalism highlights the exclusion of women from *Godot*, the refrigerator gimmick establishes frigidity as the defining feature of Beckett's dramatic universe, where the heat of *eros* has been deeply repressed if not entirely extinguished.

Any Two of Anything

Samuel Beckett's admiration for O'Casey was not reciprocated. 'Beckett?' O'Casey demanded in 1956, 'I have nothing to do with Beckett. He isn't in me; nor am I in him' ('Not Waiting For Godot', 51). O'Casey's take on Beckett is, based on what we discovered in the last chapter, predictable: Beckett writes as if everything is already dead and the whole earth is 'a graveyard or a roaring camp', when in fact 'there is life and energy even in decay' (ibid.). Hansberry's own critique of existentialist drama, as Hodin and Higashida argue, revealed a much deeper engagement with postwar catastrophe, which O'Casey wants to bury under an avalanche of 'witnesses' testifying to the glory of human life (ibid., 52). By putting O'Casey and Beckett in dialogue with each other, Hansberry produces her own alternative to the here and now – one that neither Beckett nor O'Casey could have envisioned alone.

In Act III, Sidney, David and Gloria become caught up in the play's second transformation scene, which is described in language that leaves no doubt of its provenance: 'An absurdist orgy is being created in front of us – a disintegration of reality to parallel the disintegration in SIDNEY's world' (Hansberry, *Raisin and Sign*, 328). Carter, Hodin and Higashida are unanimous in treating this scene as a hostile takedown of absurdist drama. But if we see it, not *just* as a dialogue with existentialist/absurdist theatre, but as in dialogue with the Act II transformation scene, the 'absurdist orgy' appears as another moment at which the play enables forward movement by transforming a problematic, but potentially generative, Irish antirealism.

Hansberry's characterisation of David Ragin has 'troubled' critics who read it 'as "tarring" existentialism through its association with homosexual decadence' (Higadisha, *Black Internationalist Feminism*, 73) – a comparison which denigrates both terms. I would argue, however, that in a play where naming is seldom arbitrary, it is significant that David shares a first name with the white narrator of James Baldwin's novel *Giovanni's Room*. Baldwin and Hansberry were close friends and admirers of each others' work, and this nod to one of the most self-absorbed queer characters in the canon of twentieth-century American fiction should cue us to attribute David's most damaging trait – his callous refusal of responsibility to anyone other than himself – less to his homosexuality than to his whiteness.

Hansberry's stage directions specify that David has drained every ounce of camp from his self-presentation: 'his mannerisms intend to suggest the entirely unmannered – but by choice. He is not in the least – "swish"' (Hansberry, *Raisin and Sign*, 259). Her emphasis on David's self-presentation as a 'choice' recalls the self-imposed butchness of Baldwin's David, who is engaged throughout *Giovanni's Room* in a desperate attempt to distance himself from his darker, femmier lovers and the hell he believes they inhabit. Hansberry's

David Ragin is not only white, he is in love with whiteness – specifically, with the memory of a boy named Nelson who David met at the age of seven, whose 'fine golden hair and delicate profile' made him 'a real aristocrat' (ibid., 331).

David, in other words, remains unfree in part because he refuses to understand that his sexuality, instead of isolating him, connects him to a larger community of oppressed people. Sidney's dressing-down of David during the dinner party fiasco of Act II has been interpreted as evidence of Sidney's homophobia; and it is true that, like all of *Sign*'s characters, Sidney is unable to fully achieve the open-mindedness that is the core value of his bohemian milieu. But what Sidney specifically accuses David of is failing to understand his oppression as social rather than existential – to assume that he is experiencing 'the isolation of the soul of man, the alienation of the human spirit, the desolation of all love, all possible communication', instead of the inevitable effects of living in 'a society that will not sanctify your particular sexuality' (ibid., 269). David's conviction that his own suffering is 'something that only the deepest, saddest, the most nobly tortured can know about' (ibid., 269–70), which is what keeps his characters locked in their refrigerator, is a symptom of his whiteness; he has yet to unlearn the sense of superiority inculcated by privilege. But although Sidney says all this, he doesn't understand what it means – because he attributes what he dislikes about David to the sexuality that makes them different, rather than to the privileges that they share.

In her unpublished spoof of *Waiting for Godot*, 'The Arrival of Mr. Todog', Hansberry suggests that Beckett, too, might get over himself by embracing the aspects of queer culture of which David is most afraid. In 'The Arrival of Mr. Todog', Didi and Gogo are renamed Mary and Poopoo – one classic camp name, one reference to anality – and it turns out that what they have really been waiting for is each other. Carter remarks that unlike the 'nearly impotent neuters' Didi and Gogo, Mary and Poopoo are 'active and assertive homosexuals' (Carter, *Hansberry's Drama*, 155) whose only use for a rope is to 'skip with it a bit' (Hansberry, quoted in ibid., 156). When they discover, after the Traveler joins them, that no saviour is coming, they rejoice – 'You mean there isn't anyone to make up the rules?' – and throw a party (quoted in ibid., 157). 'The Arrival of Mr. Todog' suggests that what makes Beckett's universe so empty is not infertility *per se* but the refusal to embrace it: a universe without 'life' as O'Casey has defined it doesn't *have* to be a wasteland, unless you refuse the freedom that comes with loss of the 'rules' that define the 'real' world (quoted in ibid.).

Though it's difficult to assess the tone of 'Arrival of Mr. Todog', its existence suggests that Hansberry shared O'Casey's sense that there was something queer about the theatre of the absurd – but that, unlike him, she was interested enough to explore it. 'Mr. Todog' shows Hansberry playing around with the relationship between 'the absurd' and sexual liberation, and considering the possibility that the Life-less, ruler-less, rule-less landscape of *Godot* might become a kind of queer utopia. *The Sign in Sidney Brustein's Window* complicates this idea by incorporating the entanglement between sexual and socialist politics. Though David, tragically, fails to grasp this, the space he has created in his own plays is a place where those who would be blotted out of O'Casey's Book of Life might find a home – and where Sidney, forced to abandon the oppositional logic that has hitherto structured his identity, might finally stop waiting for Lefty.

When David, who lives in the apartment above Sidney's, enters the apartment at the beginning of Act III, a drunk and despondent Sidney hails him as 'the only man I happen to know personally who is unafraid of the dark' (Hansberry, *Raisin and Sign*, 321). Sidney demonstrates that he now understands and can appreciate David's play:

> All that motion, all that urgency ... for nothing. That's the whole show, isn't it? A great plain where neither the wind blows, nor the rain falls, nor anything else happens. *Really happens*, I mean. Besides our arriving there and one day leaving again ... That's what your plays are about, aren't they? (Ibid.)

Sidney's sudden realisation of what Beckett is 'about' is a direct consequence of his final betrayal by Irish idealism. Celebrating O'Hara's victory in the opening scene of Act III, Sidney indulges in burst after burst of idealist eloquence, spinning an electoral victory in a local race into an omen of the miraculous birth of a new age:

> Alton, *he's a baby!* He's an infant! ... *Man! The human race!* Yesterday he made a wheel, and fire, so today we're all demanding to know why he hasn't made universal beauty and wisdom and truth too! ... A few thousand lousy years he's had to figure out a calendar, and how to make the corn grow; a few lousy years to figure out – *everything*. And we give 'im hell ... All he needs is a little more time ... and he'll be all right, doncha think, Alt? (Ibid., 300)

Sidney is on fire with the 'faith in life' so characteristic of late O'Casey. His own sense of self is enormously bolstered by his Irish hero's victory, which he claims has upended '[t]wenty years of political history' (ibid., 299). But even if O'Hara were honest, none of this would be true. The past does not return, and it is impossible to 'wipe out the Big Boss in one fell stroke' with the election of a single candidate. In the same way, the 'muscular' language to which O'Casey's American adherents respond so strongly comes attached to a conception of the struggle which is unusable – not only is it defined by totalitarian desires, but it hasn't changed in twenty years. As both *The Star Turns Red* and *Red Roses For Me* demonstrate, that conception of the struggle is distinguished by a lust for heroism, battle, glory and victory. That O'Hara's victory is an illusion is one problem; but it is the *desire* for victory – or, to put it another way, for the defeat of one's enemies – that keeps Sidney in the impasse.

Sidney's insistence on the term 'man' in his paean to 'the human race' is not incidental. Wally's victory inspires Sidney to perform his masculinity in newly aggressive ways; he celebrates O'Hara's victory primarily by using it to triumph over male adversaries. His first action in Act III is to tell off his paper's biggest advertiser: 'I'm sure you can understand, we're in no mood to backtrack on anything today' (ibid., 298). Moments after hanging up on him, Sidney decides to find David and 'bait' him (ibid., 299). Sidney's boast that he will 'make that sophomoric little elf eat his nineteenth-century profundities with a spoon' reveals that Sidney's commitment has atrophied into a desire for dominance. When he fantasises about shoving David's own speech down his throat, Sidney is not fundamentally different from any other straight man who has ever shored up his faith in his own masculinity by bashing a queer. Iris has already suggested that Sidney sticks to verbal sparring only because it is more consistent with his progressive self-image than physical abuse: 'Why don't you just hit me with your fists sometimes, Sid?' (ibid., 248).

Sidney's eagerness to get to grips with Beckett's view of the universe in Act III, then, is another sign of the 'capacity for growth' that is his best claim to the title of protagonist (Carter, *Hansberry's Drama*, 86). He has abandoned his attachment to an anachronistic, deceptive, destructive idealism based less on faith in human life than on a desire for conflict and conquest. After learning of O'Hara's betrayal, Sidney renounces this idealism by brandishing a yardstick as 'the sword of his ancestors', then snapping it in half (Hansberry, *Raisin and Sign*, 317). This act is a symbolic self-castration; but it is also a frustrated repudiation of a whole range of phallic political symbolism, including the clenched-fist salute, which promises power and never delivers it. Sidney's trip to Beckett's world doesn't make him, Gloria or David *feel* better; each of them dances 'locked in the vacant isolation of a separate world, from which he speaks' (ibid., 329), and most of what they say is alienating and fragmentary. In the midst of all this, however, Sidney delivers, 'deadpan', the line, 'Any two of anything is totalitarian' (ibid.).

If we take Sidney's line seriously – not everyone does – it appears that Beckettian absurdity has allowed Sidney an insight about the nature of his impasse. The rejection of the social injunction to monogamy – the restriction of relationship to only two people – has been part of queer culture since the days of Oscar Wilde; so has the rejection of the gender binary. Sidney's line could, for instance, stand as a summary of the case against marriage equality so recently made by queer radicals: it's not the insistence on one man and one woman, but the insistence on limiting sexual relationship to *any* two of *anything*, that makes marriage an oppressive institution.

Sidney, David and Gloria are at this moment *almost* forming the kind of queer triangle that O'Casey attacked in 'Coward Codology'. The anti-*eros* aspect of the absurdist idiom, however, mitigates the 'sensual heat' of Sidney's initial dance with Gloria by physically separating the participants, preventing their triple act from becoming a ménage. This chilling of the erotic is what allows 'the absurd' to include Gloria. Gloria, contrary to the expectations that David has derived from avant-garde literature (Hodin, 'Lorraine Hansberry's Absurdity', 763), does not 'like' (Hansberry, *Raisin and Sign*, 323) the sex work she has been doing; she is exhausted and drained and desperate to quit. She has just learned that Alton, the one man she wants, has dumped her after learning her history (ibid., 324–7). Gloria cannot experience sex in the here and now as anything other than battery; and for that reason, it is a relief to enter a dramatic universe in which eroticism is foiled by alienation.

Sidney's insight is thus less about marriage or sexual pleasure than it is about grasping the coercive power of binary opposition. If 'any two of anything is totalitarian', then any system that restricts *any* area of human experience to a binary choice – gender, sexuality, ethics, American presidential politics – is cruel. Just as Iris is not free simply because she has the option of shuttling back and forth between barefoot mountain nymph and Golden Curl Girl, Sidney cannot make himself free simply by selecting, from two available options, the oppositional stance. But since dialectic proceeds via binary oppositions, escape from the totalitarian binary is impossible in a 'rational' universe. The absurd – the place without logic, coherence or debate – is thus the only safe space for either David or Gloria: 'DAVID. Trying to live with your father's values can kill you. Ask me, I know./ GLORIA. No, Sweetie, living *without* your father's values can kill you. Ask *me*, *I* know' (ibid., 330). Neither obedience nor resistance to the 'father's values' is a liveable option for either of them; but only in an absurd universe would it be possible *not* to choose one or the other.

Sidney and David can share some of the blame for Gloria's suicide; but what really kills Gloria is the reassertion of the rule of two. When Sidney loses consciousness, the trio becomes a (superficially) heterosexual dyad – and heteronormativity immediately reasserts itself, pushing Gloria and David into a 'long, wet kiss' (ibid., 331) which neither of them wants. Unlike the Act II scene, in which Sidney and Iris help each other transition to actuality, this unchosen embrace triggers a crash as 'the music comes to an abrupt stop' (ibid.). Gloria asks 'what happened to the music' (ibid.); but there's no diegetic answer. We saw her put the record on; nobody has turned it off. Gloria nevertheless turns the record player on again, prolonging the audience's awareness of the fact that the music is being controlled by an unseen sound operator. Illusionistic realism cannot be fully re-established, but neither can the absurd alternative. The record player opens up a tear in the fabric of the dramatic universe, through which Gloria will fall.

Gloria's annihilation begins at the moment that David tries to turn the 'absurdist orgy' into a realistic one. The lover waiting for David in his apartment upstairs is an adult incarnation of the ethereal and aristocratic Nelson, and is unable to make love without 'the presence of a woman' who can pass for 'somebody of his own class' (ibid., 332). David's callousness in asking Gloria to resume prostitution (without even making it clear whether he intends to compensate her) marks his return to realistic characterisation. It also marks David's failure to activate for other people the potential he creates in his plays. There will be no escape for him or his lover from the binary logic of heterosexism; whatever they do must be interpolated into the idealised heterosexual pairing that Gloria's presence replicates. When Gloria reproaches David, he says, loftily, 'It's not for me. Perhaps you can understand: if he asked for the snows of the Himalayas tonight, I would try to get it for him' (ibid.). If the 'snows' evoke the refrigerator setting of his play, David also uses a vocabulary of exploration and acquisition arising from the imperialist consciousness he shares with the David of *Giovanni's Room* (who identifies himself as white by informing the reader that '[m]y ancestors conquered a continent'). His self-justification merely emphasises her objectification in the scenario he proposes. The fact that he's not asking her to touch either of them seems to David to mitigate the cruelty of his request. But this merely underlines for Gloria that sex work has forever excluded her from 'any two of anything': this job turns her into an object used to generate pleasure for a couple from which she remains excluded. After David leaves, the rule of two reasserts itself more brutally. As Gloria is left alone on stage, '[f]or a long moment her eyes dart frantically and she whimpers, trapped, seeking refuge. There is none. At last she looks at the bottle of pills in her hand' (ibid., 333). Gloria has to choose between two exits, each leading to an unliveable place: the stairs, which mean prostitution, and the bathroom, which – combined with the bottle of pills in her hand – means death.

After Gloria's death, Sidney's confrontation with Wally O'Hara seems anticlimactic. Hodin compares the 'apparent triumph' ('Lorraine Hansberry's Absurdity', 762) of Sidney's renewed commitment unfavourably to similar moments of affirmation for the men of *Raisin* (ibid., 756). Carter tries to salvage it by pointing out that what Sidney vows to fight is not Wally O'Hara himself, but the 'oppressive society' that produced him, and that Sidney wishes redemption on O'Hara rather than destruction (Carter, *Hansberry's Drama*, 99). It is true that Sidney's temporary escape from the totalitarianism of two has enabled him to tell his male adversary something that is definitely not part of O'Casey's script: 'I love you' (Hansberry, *Raisin and Sign*, 339). Using the same words that marked his willingness to release Iris from the Appalachian fantasy, Sidney extends Carpenter's comrade love to include even ex-comrades. He pledges 'to fight' not with the sword of his ancestors, which is broken, but with his heart (ibid.). When he lists what he now 'believes', it doesn't include belief in any one man, or a belief that the fight can be won. Instead of reaffirming his steeliness, he draws strength from his vulnerability: 'I hurt terribly today, and . . . hurt is desperation and desperation is – energy and energy can *move* things' (ibid., 340). If Sidney is going to fight, he's not going to fight like a man.

The play's actual 'victory', in other words, is *not* in Sidney's rededication to the same oppositional battle that has been so corrosive to his body and soul. It is in Sidney's movement away from the agonistic clash with the adversary towards a different understanding of 'struggle' which accepts – even loves – the vulnerability that is an unavoidable consequence of embodiment. Standing up to Wally is something Sidney does out of habit and out of anger, but that's not his future, and Iris knows it: 'For a long time now I've been wanting something. For a long time. I think it was for you to be all of yourself' (ibid.). What she has been wanting is not for him to be stronger or bolder or more fearless, but to activate the parts of his self that have been shut down by years of oppositional conflict. Sidney opens the new struggle at the moment when he *stops* talking and starts to help Iris grieve (ibid.). He promises, not a return to battle, but deferral: 'Let us both weep. That is the first thing: to let ourselves feel again . . . Then, tomorrow, we shall make something strong of this sorrow' (ibid.).

In naming sorrow as the thing from which strength will spring, Sidney enters the future, stepping towards an era of grief-driven activism that includes the ACT UP protests of the 1980s and 1990s as well as the Black Lives Matter activism of the 2010s. *The Sign in Sidney Brustein's Window* looks forward to a there and then which we still have the opportunity to choose as our own, in which 'hurt' – the pain of inhabiting a body targetted (sometimes for multiple reasons) for death and visited by violence – is an engine of the struggle instead of an obstacle to it. It looks forward to a time when taking the time to feel, to stop moving and care for oneself, is a strategy for change instead of a dereliction of duty. It looks forward to the reparation of a breach between class politics and body politics which we are still struggling to heal.

There are no heroes in *The Sign in Sidney Brustein's Window*. There is no true belief and there are no pure victims. Gloria dies a racist, spurred by homophobic disgust to act out one of literature's oldest patriarchal scripts. David betrays his potential as a queer futurist by trying to appropriate Gloria without including her. Sidney's conclusion that Gloria died of 'capitulation' (ibid., 338) is incomplete; she dies of an enforced choice between two lethal capitulations. Sidney and Iris are still limited, they're still guilty, they're still lost. But they go on. They fail better. The affirmative potential of O'Casey's idealism and the terrifying freedom of Beckett's evacuated universe combine in the final image of Sidney and Iris sitting silently, 'physically drained and motionless . . . as the clear light of day fills the room' (ibid., 340). Deferral no longer means defeat, paralysis, the death of meaning or of hope for change. It is instead a pause on the threshold, a hesitation within the archway cleared by a broken impasse, as they let go of the dream of revolution, and wait to see what they can make of their grief.

Conclusion: Attention Must Be Paid

We do not really discover, rescue or re-create the literary works we study. As much time as this book has spent on drama excluded from the canon, it remains true that none of the texts we have encountered is truly lost; they have merely been forgotten. Attention – critical attention, audience attention, political attention – was once paid to them; it left traces; those traces lead us back through the amnesia of the last two or three or five decades to something that was never intended to be a mystery. If anyone is rescued by work like this, it is not the texts themselves, but us – the contemporary readers who have stopped asking the questions that this body of work tried to answer.

In bringing this aspect of modern drama to our attention, I have sought, primarily, to do two things. One is to restore to visibility a tradition of left theatre which originated at the intersection between socialist politics and sexual politics – or, to put it more broadly, between anticapitalist politics and identity politics. The other is to use the history of Irish playwrights and the international left to trace, and thereby render visible to contemporary eyes, an Irish internationalism which is not coincident with either the postcolonial narrative that established the basis of Irish studies as a discipline in the 1970s and 1980s, or the global/world paradigm which informs so much of the new comparative work, and which is predicated on the structures and values of late twentieth-/twenty-first-century global capitalism.

The chapters in this book were written over a period of many years. I began writing the introduction just after the 'Brexit' referendum of 23 June 2016, in which a majority of those who turned out voted for the UK to leave the European Union. I began this conclusion on 10 November 2016, two days after the election to the presidency of the USA of an anti-internationalist, anti-trade candidate whose most consistent campaign promise was to build a wall along the border between the USA and Mexico. Both the Leave campaign and the Trump campaign promoted and were fuelled by anti-immigrant, anti-Muslim and racist sentiment, a phenomenon which testifies to the continued association in the political field between economic protectionism and a paranoid fear of 'outside' influences presumed to threaten an imaginary national 'purity' signified by whiteness. This toxic protectionism has, according to the emerging conventional wisdom, been embraced by large segments of an ageing, white working class whose economic fortunes never recovered from the collapse of the manufacturing sector that coincided with globalisation. Again according to conventional wisdom, this constitutes a new impasse for the left, creating a zero-sum game in which the interests of the white working class are diametrically opposed to those of the left's 'other' constituencies – women, queers, immigrants, the disabled and people of color – who it should be noted make up a significant portion of the working class. The US presidential election, for instance, has produced a rash of opinion pieces counselling the American left to address itself assiduously to the economic concerns of white, male, working-class voters, and abandon its critique of the 'other' oppressions in which those voters might be implicated.[6] But by drawing our attention to the relationship between sexual and social politics as it developed through the involvement of Irish playwrights in the international left – and specifically in demonstrating the pernicious effects of the totalitarian force of reproductive futurism – I hope to have shown that progress is not a zero-sum game. I hope that this book has demonstrated that these revolutions need not and should not be in opposition or in competition, and has strengthened the case for rethinking class politics *through*, rather than *against*, the politics of embodiment.

I have also tried to expand our understanding of the impact of syndicalism on the strain of urban Irish socialist drama hitherto identified almost exclusively with Sean O'Casey, and to recall from oblivion the role that workers' theatre played in mediating the connection between Synge's naturalism and Brecht's epic theatre. In emphasising the role of labour – organised, disorganised, revolutionary – I hope, by returning our attention to the experience of struggle, to have demonstrated the indefensibility of the binary opposition between reason and emotion on which Ervine and Shaw sought to build a firewall between socialist and nationalist politics, and on which Brecht claimed to have founded his conception of epic theatre. Though these chapters were written far in advance of the final months of 2016, they will stand, I hope, as a call to imagine the *integration* of a rational ethics of equality and justice with an affective irrationalism which – like the exiled soul of Oscar Wilde's fisherman – does tremendous damage when it is allowed to roam the world without a heart or a conscience.

Finally, by bringing to light this previously occluded aspect of the Irish dramatic revival's internationalism, I hope to have offered future scholars a new understanding of Irish drama's place in the world of modernist performance, upon which other scholars might build as we enter the increasingly uncertain future. The violent repudiation of globalism that marked the latter half of 2016 will not, of course, end capitalist exploitation. Toxic protectionism is itself a cruel optimism which intensifies the economic sufferings of those who embrace it. But the rise of toxic protectionism only emphasises our need for alternative internationalisms – for ways of thinking about global networks and exchanges which are not indissolubly bound to the foundational structures of a catastrophically exploitative global capitalism.

If nothing else, I hope that *Irish Drama and the Other Revolutions* has demonstrated that there are borders yet to cross and boundaries still to disregard in our pursuit of a truly internationalist understanding of Irish drama, of modernist performance and of the revolutions I have investigated here. The networks I have elaborated in this project expand in all directions, branching off like fractals as they disappear from the circle of our attention. As we emerge from the age of specialisation, there's a lot that we risk: the loss of nuance, the disappearance of the local, the phantom 'influences' and unintentional errors generated by incomplete and uneven knowledge. I have tried to proceed slowly, to read widely, to document carefully, and to renounce the arrogance of discovery; but the risks remain. Nevertheless, they are risks we must take. The 'there and then' we imagine as we enter this present moment must include not only a world without capitalism, but an academy without walls.

NOTES

1. The subtitle references a description of the Soviet Union, attributed to Winston Churchill, as 'a riddle wrapped in a mystery inside an enigma'.
2. Henry is not explicitly identified as homosexual; Bengal's stage directions attribute the shipping clerks' bullying to Henry's middle-class markers (more 'correct' diction and a more white-collar job). However, the shipping clerks read these class markers as feminising and bully Henry on that basis. The file clerks are collectively referred to by the other men as 'lilies of the valley' and 'punks' (Bengal, *Plant in the Sun*, 216).
3. Nemiroff describes the campaign in detail in 'A Portrait: The 101 'Final' Performances of *Sidney Brustein*'.
4. The major interventions here are Noel Ignatiev's *How the Irish Became White* and David Roediger's *The Wages of Whiteness*. Both Ignatiev and Roediger were part of the critical race theory movement of the 1990s, whose objective was to end racism by deconstructing the category of race itself.
5. See, for instance, Frank McGuinness's 'The Mask and the Martyr: Lorraine Hansberry and Sean O'Casey'.
6. Mark Lilla's 'The End of Identity Liberalism' is a prominent example.

WORKS CITED

'Abbey Theatre. A Powerful Strike Play'. *The Irish Times*, 4 November 1914, 6.

Allen, Grace M. '*Señora Carrar's Rifles*: Dramatic Means and Didactic Ends'. *Essays on Brecht: Theater and Politics*. Ed. Siegfried Mews and Herbert Kunst. Chapel Hill: University of North Carolina Press, 1974, 156–73.

Allen, John. Letter to Sean O'Casey. 9 June 1940. National Library of Ireland, MS 38,052.

Anderson, John. 'Drama Tells Old Women's [sic] Struggle Through Dark Bolshevik Period'. 1935. [*New York Journal.*] Clipping file, Billy Rose Theatre Division, New York Public Library for the Performing Arts.

Archer, William. *Royal Court Theatre, Sloane Square, S. W. The Vedrenne-Barker Season, 1904–1905. A Record and Commentary*. Not dated.

——. *The Theatrical 'World' of 1893*. London: W. Scott, Ltd, 1894. Online. Hathi Trust Digital Library, accessed 18 September 2016.

——. *The Theatrical 'World' of 1894*. London: W. Scott, Ltd, 1895. Online. Hathi Trust Digital Library, accessed 18 September 2016.

Atkinson, Brooks. *Sean O'Casey: From Times Past*. Ed. Robert G. Lowery. Totowa: Barnes & Noble Books, 1982.

——. 'Theatre: Beckett's 'Waiting for Godot.' Mystery Wrapped in Enigma at Golden'. *The New York Times*, 20 April 1956, 21.

Ayling, Ronald. 'Introduction'. In Sean O'Casey, *Blasts and Benedictions*. London: Macmillan, 1967, i–xvii.

Ayling, Ronald and Michael J. Durkin. *Sean O'Casey: A Bibliography*. Seattle: University of Washington Press, 1978.

Baldwin, James. *Giovanni's Room*. New York: Delta Trade Paperbacks, 2000.

Baldwin, Kate A. *Beyond the Color Line and the Iron Curtain: Reading Encounters Between Black and Red, 1922–1963*. Durham, NC: Duke University Press, 2002.

Barnes, Howard. 'The Theaters'. *Herald-Tribune*, 20 November 1935. Clipping file, Billy Rose Theatre Division, New York Public Library for the Performing Arts.

Bax, Clifford. *Florence Farr, Bernard Shaw, W. B. Yeats. Letters*. New York: Dodd, Mead & Co., 1942.

Baxandall, Lee. 'Introduction'. *Bertolt Brecht: The Mother. With notes by the author. Translated and with an introduction by Lee Baxandall*. New York: Grove Press, 1965.

Beckett, Samuel. *Waiting for Godot*. New York: Grove Press, 1954.

Beevers, Robert. *The Garden City Utopia: A Critical Biography of Ebenezer Howard*. New York: St. Martin's Press, 1988.

Bellamy, Edward. *Looking Backward*. New York: Houghton Mifflin and Company, 1889.

Bengal, Ben. *Plant in the Sun*. In William Kozlenko (ed.), *The Best Short Plays of the American Social Theatre*. New York: Random House, 1939, 199–228.

Benjamin, Walter. *Understanding Brecht*. Trans. Anna Bostock. London: NLB, 1973.

Benson, Edward Frederic. *Dodo, a Detail of the Day*. Chicago: Charles H. Sergel, 1893.

Benstock, Bernard. *Paycocks and Others: Sean O'Casey's World*. Dublin: Gill & Macmillan, 1976.

Berlant, Loren Gail. *Cruel Optimism*. Durham, NC: Duke University Press, 2011.

Berlau, Ruth. *Living For Brecht: The Memoirs of Ruth Berlau*. Ed. Hans Bunge, trans. Geoffrey Skelton. New York: Fromm International Publishing Corporation, 1987.

Bettany, Frederick George. 'The Playhouses'. *Illustrated London News*, 5 November 1904, Issue 3420, 643.

Bevir, Mark. *The Making of British Socialism*. Princeton: Princeton University Press, 2011.

Boeninger, Stephanie Pocock. *'Submarine Roots': The Drowned Body and Postcolonial Memory in Irish and Caribbean Literature*. Dissertation. University of Notre Dame, 2011.

Bornstein, George. *Yeats and Shelley*. Chicago: University of Chicago Press, 1970.

Bradley, Laura. *Brecht and Political Theatre: The Mother on Stage*. Oxford: Oxford University Press, 2006.

Brecht, Bertolt. *Bertolt Brecht Collected Plays*. Ed. John Willett and Ralph Manheim. London: Methuen, 1983. Volume IV, part iii.

——. *Bertolt Brecht Journals*. Trans. Hugh Rorrison, ed. John Willett. London: Methuen, 1993.

——. *Bertolt Brecht Letters*. Translated by Ralph Manheim and edited with commentary and notes by John Willett. New York: Routledge, 1990.

——. *Brecht on Theatre: The Development of an Aesthetic*. Ed. and trans. by John Willett. New York: Hill and Wang, 1964.
——. *Gedichte*. Volume V. Frankfurt am Main: Suhrkamp Verlag, 1964.
——. *Love Poems*. Trans. David Constantine and Tom Kuhn. New York: Liveright Publishing Corporation, 2015.
——. *Mother*. [Typescript] Promptbook, Acc. No. 927952 A] [N.P.] 1935. Microfilm made by the New York Public Library Photographic Service.
——. *Poems 1913–1956*. Ed. John Willett, Ralph Manheim et al. London: Eyre Methuen Ltd, 1976.
——. *The Good Person of Szechwan*. Ed. and trans. Ralph Manheim and John Willett. Penguin Classics, 2008.
——. *The Messingkauf Dialogues*. Trans. John Willett. London: Eyre Methuen, 1974.
——. *The Mother. With notes by the author. Translated and with an introduction by Lee Baxandall*. New York: Grove Press, 1965.
Brown, Ivor. 'At the Play'. *Observer*, 17 March 1940, 11.
Bruder, Helen P. and Tristanne Connolly (eds). Introduction. *Queer Blake*. New York: Palgrave Macmillan, 2010.
Bryant-Bertail, Sarah. *Space and Time in Epic Theatre: The Brechtian Legacy*. Rochester: Camden House, 2000.
——. 'Women, Space, Ideology: *Mutter Courage und Ihre Kinder*.' *Brecht, Women and Politics: The Brecht Yearbook, Volume 12*. Detroit: Wayne State University Press, 1983, 43–64.
Buder, Stanley. *Visionaries and Planners: The Garden City Movement and the Modern Community*. Oxford: Oxford University Press, 1990.
Bunyan, John. *The Pilgrim's Progress, From That World to That Which is to Come*. Ed. J. M. Hare. London: Simkin, Marshall, & Co., 1856.
Burch, Lionel. 'Red Roses for Me'. *Picture Post*, 1 June 1946, 20–1.
Burch, Stephen Dedalus. *Andrew P. Wilson and the Early Irish and Scottish National Theatres, 1911–1950*. Lewiston: Edwin Mellin Press, 2008.
Burnshaw, Stanley. 'The Theater Union Produces 'Mother'. *New Masses*, 3 December 1935, 27–8.
Butler, Samuel. *Luck, or Cunning as the Main Means of Organic Modification?* London: A. C. Fifield, no date. Accessed 19 February 2014 at http://babel.hathitrust.org/cgi/pt?id=wu.89009354895;view=1up;seq=17
Cardwell, Douglas. 'The Well-Made Play of Eugène Scribe'. *The French Review*, 56 (May, 1983), 876–84.
Carlson, Marvin. *Theatre Semiotics: Signs of Life*. Bloomington: Indiana University Press, 1990.
Carney, Jack. Letter to Sean O'Casey. 5 February 1947. National Library of Ireland, MS 37,989.

Carpenter, Edward. *Homogenic Love, and its Place in a Free Society.* Manchester: Labour Press Society Ltd, 1894.

——. Introduction. In George Barnfield (ed.), *The Psychology of the Poet Shelley.* London: G. Allen & Unwin, 1925.

——. 'Transitions to Freedom'. In *Forecasts of the Coming Century by a Decade of Writers.* Manchester: Labour Press Ltd, 1897, 174–92.

Carter, Huntley. *The New Theatre and Cinema of Soviet Russia.* London: Chapman & Dodd, Ltd, 1924.

Carter, Steven R. *Hansberry's Drama: Commitment and Complexity.* Urbana: University of Illinois Press, 1991.

Casanova, Pascale. *The World Republic of Letters.* Trans. M. DeBevoise. Cambridge, MA: Harvard University Press, 2004.

Case, Sue-Ellen. 'Brecht and Women: Homosexuality and the Mother'. In *Brecht, Women and Politics: The Brecht Yearbook, Volume 12.* Detroit: Wayne State University Press, 1983, 65–78.

Casey, Paul Foley. 'German Productions of the Dramas of J. M. Synge'. *Maske und Kothurn: Internationale Beiträge zur Theaterwissenschaft,* 27 (1981), 163–75.

Cave, Richard Allan. 'On the Siting of Doors and Windows: Aesthetics, Ideology, and Irish Stage Design'. In Shaun Richards (ed.), *The Cambridge Companion to Twentieth-Century Irish Drama.* Cambridge: Cambridge University Press, 2004.

Chambers, Colin. *The Story of Unity Theatre.* New York: St. Martin's Press, 1989.

Chaudhuri, Una. *Staging Place: The Geography of Modern Drama.* Ann Arbor: University of Michigan Press, 1995.

Cima, Gay Gibson. *Performing Women: Female Characters, Male Playwrights, and the Modern Stage.* Ithaca: Cornell University Press, 1993.

Clark, Katerina. *The Soviet Novel: History as Ritual.* Chicago: University of Chicago Press, 1981.

Cleary, Joe. *Outrageous Fortune: Capital and Culture in Modern Ireland.* Dublin: Field Day Publications, 2007.

Clements, Barbara Evans. 'Introduction'. In Barbara Evans Clements et al. (eds), *Russian Masculinities in History and Culture.* New York: Palgrave, 2002, 1–14.

Cohen, Laurie. 'Early Endeavors to Establish a (Soviet) Russian WILPF Section, 1915–1925: A Little Known Episode in Feminist Transnational Peace History'. *Deportate, esuli, profughe: Rivista telematica di studi sulla memoria femminile* (2012), 179–98.

Coleman, Robert. '"Mother." Novel of Gorki Used as Basis of Drama'. *New York Mirror,* no date, 24. Clipping file, Billy Rose Theatre Division, New York Public Library for the Performing Arts.

Connolly, James. *Labour in Irish History*. 1910. In James Connolly, *Labour in Ireland*. Dublin: Colm O Lochlainn, 1950.

———. 'Tram Strike'. *Irish Worker*, 30 August 1913, 2.

Corkery, Daniel. *The Labour Leader: A Play in Three Acts*. Dublin: Talbot Press, 1920.

———. *The Yellow Bittern, and Other Plays*. Dublin: Talbot Press, 1920.

Coward, Noel. *Design for Living: A Comedy in Three Acts*. Garden City: Doubleday, 1933.

'Craobh na nDealg'. '"Independent" and "Herald notes" List of Scabs'. *Irish Worker*, 27 September 1913, 4.

Creese, Walter L. *The Search for Environment: The Garden City, Before and After*. New Haven: Yale University Press, 1966.

Cullingford, Elizabeth Butler. *Gender and History in Yeats's Love Poetry*. Cambridge: Cambridge University Press, 1993.

Darlington, Ralph. *Syndicalism and the Transition to Communism: An International Comparative Analysis*. Aldershot: Ashgate, 2008.

Dash, Thomas R. 'Mother'. *Women's Wear Daily*, 1935. Clipping file, Billy Rose Theatre Division, New York Public Library for the Performing Arts.

'Davena's Diatribes'. Clipping preserved in *The Diaries of Joseph Holloway, 1895–1944 from the National Library of Ireland, Dublin*. Microfilm, 105 reels.

Davies, Richard and W. J. McCormack, 'Sean O'Casey's Unpublished Correspondence with Raisa Lomonosova, 1925–26'. *Irish Slavonic Studies*, 5 (1984), 181–90.

Davis, Tracy C. '"Do you Believe in Fairies?": The Hiss of Dramatic License'. *Theatre Journal*, 57(1) (2005), 57–81.

de Blacam, Aodh. *Towards the Republic: A Study of New Ireland's Social and Political Aims*. Dublin: Thomas Kiersey, 1919.

'Description of a Scab'. *Irish Worker*, 10 June 1911, 1.

Diamond, Elin. *Unmaking Mimesis: Essays on Feminism and Theater*. New York: Routledge, 1997.

Dickson, Keith A. *Towards Utopia: A Study of Brecht*. Oxford: Clarendon Press, 1978.

Edelman, Lee. *No Future: Queer Theory and the Death Drive*. Durham, NC: Duke University Press, 2004.

Ellis, P. Berresford. *A History of the Irish Working Class*. London: Victor Gollancz, Ltd, 197.

Ervine, St. John. *Mixed Marriage: A Play in Four Acts*. Dublin: Maunsel & Co., 1911.

———. *Sir Edward Carson and the Ulster Movement*. Dublin: Maunsel & Co., 1915.

Esslin, Martin. *Brecht: The Man and his Work*. Garden City: Anchor Books, 1971.

Fallon, Gabriel. *Sean O'Casey: The Man I Knew*. Boston, MA: Little, Brown, 1965.

Garland, Robert. '"Mother" produced at Civic Repertory. Tells Story of Transformation of a Woman from a Conservative to a Radical'. [*New York World-Telegram*, date not preserved.] 1935, 28. Clipping file, Billy Rose Theatre Division, New York Public Library for the Performing Arts.

Gelb, Arthur. 'Wanted: Intellects. Myerberg Wants 70,000 of Them to Support Plotless Play'. *The New York Times*, 15 April 1956, 1.

Gladden, Samuel Lyndon. *Shelley's Textual Seduction: Plotting Utopia in the Erotic and Political Works*. New York: Routledge, 2002.

Gladkov, Feodor Vasilievich. *Cement*. Trans. A. S. Arthur and C. Ashleigh. New York: International Publishers, 1929.

Glass, Loren. 'Absurd Imprint: Grove Press and the Canonization of the Theatrical Avant-Garde'. *Modern Drama*, 54 (2011), 534–61.

Gleitman, Claire. 'All in the Family: *Mother Courage* and the Ideology in the Gestus'. *Comparative Drama*, 25(2) (1991), 147–67.

Gray, John. *City in Revolt: James Larkin and the Belfast Dock Strike of 1907*. Belfast: Blackstaff Press, 1985.

Gregory, Lady Augusta. *Lady Gregory's Journals, Vol. 1, Books One to Twenty-Nine, 10 October 1916–February 1925*. Ed. Daniel J. Murphy. Coole Edition of Lady Gregory's Works, Vol. 14. Gerrards Cross: Colin Smythe, 1978.

——. *Our Irish Theatre; A Chapter of Autobiography*. New York: Oxford University Press, 1972.

Grene, Nicholas. *Bernard Shaw: A Critical View*. New York: St. Martin's Press, 1984.

Gross, Sabine. 'Margarete Steffin's Children's Plays: Anti-Illusionism with a Difference'. *Focus: Margarete Steffin, Brecht Yearbook 19* (1994), 67–88.

Halberstam, J. Jack. *In a Queer Time and Place: Transgender Bodies, Subcultural Lives*. New York: New York University Press, 2005.

Halberstam, J. Jack. *The Queer Art of Failure*. Durham, NC: Duke University Press, 2011.

Hall, Peter, Dennis Hardy and Colin Ward. 'Commentators' Introduction'. In Ebenezer Howard, *To-Morrow: A Peaceful Path to Reform*. Ed. Peter Hall, Dennis Hardy and Colin Ward. London: Routledge, 2003, 1–9.

Hansberry, Lorraine. 'An Author's Reflections: Willy Loman, Walter Younger, and He Who Must Live'. *Village Voice*, 12 August 1959, 7–8.

——. *A Raisin in the Sun and The Sign in Sidney Brustein's Window*. New York: Vintage Books, 1995.
——. 'Genet, Mailer, and the New Paternalism'. *Village Voice*, 1 June 1961, 10–15.
——. *To Be Young, Gifted, and Black; Lorraine Hansberry in Her Own Words*. Adapted and edited by Robert Nemiroff. Englewood Cliffs: Prentice-Hall, 1969.
Hanssen, Paula. 'Brecht and Weigel and *Die Gewehre der Frau Carrar*.' *Helene Weigel 100: The Brecht Yearbook 25* (2000), 181–90.
Harris, Susan Cannon. *Gender and Modern Irish Drama*. Bloomington: Indiana University Press, 2002.
——. 'What Still Matters'. Sequels. Annual symposium sponsored by the Ethnic and Third World Literatures graduate specialisation in the Department of English at The University of Texas at Austin. Austin, Texas, 31 March–1 April 2005.
Healey, Dan. 'The Disappearance of the Russian Queen, or How the Soviet Closet was Born'. In Barbara Evans Clements et al. (eds), *Russian Masculinities in History and Culture*. New York: Palgrave, 2002, 152–73.
'Her Dream Came True'. *The New York Times*, 9 April 1959, 37.
Higashida, Cheryl. *Black Internationalist Feminism: Women Writers of the Black Left, 1945–1995*. Urbana: University of Illinois Press, 2011.
Hodin, Mark. 'Lorraine Hansberry's Absurdity: *The Sign in Sidney Brustein's Window*'. *Contemporary Literature*, 50 (2009), 742–74.
Holloway, Joseph. *Joseph Holloway's Abbey Theatre; A Selection from his Unpublished Journal, Impressions of a Dublin Playgoer*. Ed. Robert Hogan and Michael J. O'Neill. Carbondale: South Illinois University Press, 1967.
——. *The Diaries of Joseph Holloway, 1895–1944 from the National Library of Ireland, Dublin*. Microfilm, 105 reels.
Housego, Molly and Neil R. Storey. *The Woman's Suffrage Movement*. London: Bloomsbury Publishing (Shire Library Imprint), 2012. Online.
Howard, Ebenezer. *To-Morrow: A Peaceful Path to Reform*. Ed. Peter Hall, Dennis Hardy and Colin Ward. London: Routledge, 2003.
Ibsen, Henrik. *Four Major Plays*. Oxford: Oxford University Press, 1982.
Irish Independent. 'A Powerful Play: *The Slough* at the Abbey', 2 November 1914, 6.
Jameson, Fredric. *Brecht and Method*. London: Verso, 1998.
'J. E.'. 'Sean O'Casey Sees Red: Flays Fascism, Church'. *New Leader*, 21 March 1940, 7.
Jennings, Rebecca. *A Lesbian History of Britain: Love and Sex between Women since 1500*. Oxford/Westport: Greenwood World Publishing, 2007.
Johnson, David K. *The Lavender Scare: The Cold War Persecution of Gays*

and Lesbians in the Federal Government. Chicago: University of Chicago Press, 2004.

Johnson, Josephine. *Florence Farr: Bernard Shaw's New Woman.* Gerards Cross: Colin Smythe, 1975.

Kearns, Kevin C. *Dublin Tenement Life: An Oral History.* Dublin: Gill & Macmillan, 1994.

Kelly, Catriona. 'The Education of the Will: Advice Literature, *Zakal*, and Manliness in Early Twentieth-Century Russia'. In Barbara Evans Clements et al. (eds), *Russian Masculinities in History and Culture.* New York: Palgrave, 2002, 131–44.

Kempton, Murray. 'A Terrible Beauty'. *New York Post*, 2 January 1956, n.p. available.

Keogh, Dermot. *Ireland and the Vatican: The Politics and Diplomacy of Church-State Relations, 1922–1960.* Cork: Cork University Press, 1995

Kessler-Harris, Alice. *A Difficult Woman: The Challenging Life and Times of Lillian Hellman.* New York: Bloomsbury Press, 2012.

Kiberd, Declan and P. J. Mathews. *Handbook of the Irish Revival: An Anthology of Irish Cultural and Political Writings 1891–1922.* Notre Dame: University of Notre Dame Press, 2016.

Kirchhoff, Frederick. *William Morris: The Construction of a Male Self, 1856–1872.* Columbus: Ohio University Press, 1990.

Kleinstück, Johannes. 'Synge in Germany'. *A Centenary Tribute to John Millington Synge, 1871–1909: Sunshine and the Moon's Delight.* Ed. Suheil B. Bushrui. New York: Barnes and Noble, 1972.

Kostick, Colin. 'Labour Militancy During the Irish War of Independence'. In Fintan Lane and Donal Ó Drisceoil (eds), *Politics and the Irish Working Class, 1830–1945.* New York: Palgrave Macmillan, 2005, 187–204.

Krause, David. *Sean O'Casey's World.* Dublin: Gill & Macmillan, 1976.

Kuch, Peter. 'Wildean Politics – or Whatever One Wants To Call It'. *Irish Studies Review*, 13(3) (2005), 369–77.

Lane, Fintan and Donal Ó Drisceoil (eds). *Politics and the Irish Working Class, 1830–1945.* New York: Palgrave Macmillan, 2005.

Larkin, Emmet. *James Larkin: Irish Labour Leader, 1876–1947.* London: Routledge and Kegan Paul, 1965.

Larkin, James. 'May Day Demonstration'. Editorial. *Irish Worker*, 31 May 1913, 2.

——. 'My Daddy's On Strike'. *Irish Worker*, 15 February 1913, 2.

——. 'Revolution!' *Irish Worker*, 12 August 1911, 2.

——. 'Why This Strike?' Editorial. *Irish Worker*, 1 July 1911, 2.

——. 'Workers' Victory. Sunday's Meeting'. 29 July 1911, 4.

Laurence, Dan H. and Nicholas Grene (eds). *Shaw, Lady Gregory, and the*

Abbey: A Correspondence and a Record. Gerrards Cross: Colin Smythe, 1993.

Lennox, Sara. 'Women in Brecht's Works'. *New German Critique*, 14 (1978), 83–96.

Lesjak, Carolyn. 'Utopia, Use, and the Everyday: Oscar Wilde and a New Economy of Pleasure'. *ELH*, 67 (2000), 179–204.

Levitas, Ben. 'Censorship and Self-Censure in the Plays of J. M. Synge'. *Princeton University Library Quarterly*, 68 (2006/2007), 271–94.

——. 'J. M. Synge: European Contexts'. *The Cambridge Companion to J. M. Synge*. Ed. P. J. Matthews. Cambridge: Cambridge University Press, 2009, 77–91.

——. 'Plumbing the Depths: Irish Realism and the Working Class from Shaw to O'Casey'. *Irish University Review*, 33 (2003), 133–49.

——. *The Theatre of Nation: Irish Drama and Cultural Nationalism, 1890–1916*. Oxford: Oxford University Press, 2002.

——. '"These Islands" Others: *John Bull*, the Abbey and the Royal Court'. In Richard Cave and Ben Levitas (eds), *Irish Theatre in England*. Dublin: Carysfort Press, 2007.

Lilla, Mark. 'The End of Identity Liberalism'. *New York Times*, 18 November 2016. Online.

Livesey, Ruth. 'Morris, Carpenter, Wilde, and the Political Aesthetics of Labor'. *Victorian Literature and Culture*, 32(2) (2004), 601–16.

Lonergan, Patrick. *Theatre and Globalization: Irish Drama in the Celtic Tiger Era*. Basingstoke: Palgrave Macmillan, 2008.

Lowery, Robert G. 'The Development of Sean O'Casey's *Weltanschauung*'. In Robert Lowery (ed.), *Essays on Sean O'Casey's Autobiographies*. Totowa: Barnes & Noble, 1981.

——. 'The Socialist Legacy of Sean O'Casey'. *The Crane Bag*, 7(1) Socialism & Culture (1983), 128–34.

McAteer, Michael. 'A Troubled Union: Representations of Eastern Europe in Nineteenth-Century Irish Protestant Literature'. In Barbara Korte, Eva Ulrike Pirker and Sissy Helff (eds), *Facing the East in the West: Images of Eastern Europe in British Literature, Film and Culture*. Amsterdam: Rodopi, 2010, 205–18.

——. *Yeats and European Drama*. Cambridge: Cambridge University Press, 2010.

McCarthy, Fiona. *William Morris: A Life for Our Time*. New York: Alfred A. Knopf, 1995.

McGarry, Fearghal. *Irish Politics and the Spanish Civil War*. Cork: Cork University Press, 1999.

McGuinness, Frank. 'The Mask and the Martyr: Lorraine Hansberry and Sean O'Casey'. In Maria Stuart, Fionnghuala Sweeney, Fionnuala Dillane and

John Brannigan (eds), *Maintaining a Place: Conditions of Metaphor in Modern American Literature. Essays and Poems in Honor of Ron Callan*. Dublin: UCD Press, 2014, 174–83.

'Mailbag – "O'Casey – Hansberry"'. *The New York Times*, 28 June 1959, 2.1, x3.

Mailer, Norman. 'The White Negro'. *Dissent*, 20 June 2007 (reprinted). Online.

Mantle, Burns. '"Mother" Soviet Primer: Pre-Revolutionary Russia Revealed in Simple Drama Extolling the Workers'. [*New York Daily News*, date not preserved.] Clipping file, Billy Rose Theatre Collection, New York Public Library for the Performing Arts.

Maume, Patrick. *'Life that is Exile': Daniel Corkery and the Search for Irish Ireland*. Belfast: Institute for Irish Studies, Queen's University Belfast, 1993.

Maurer, Sara L. *The Dispossessed State: Narratives of Ownership in Nineteenth-Century Britain and Ireland*. Baltimore: Johns Hopkins University Press, 2012.

Meisel, Martin. *Shaw and the Nineteenth-Century Theatre*. Princeton: Princeton University Press, 1963.

Melas, Natalie. *All the Difference in The World: Postcoloniality and the Ends of Comparison*. Stanford: Stanford University Press, 2006.

Miller, Arthur. *Arthur Miller: Echoes Down the Corridor*. Ed. Steven R. Centola. New York: Penguin Group, 2000.

Miller, C. Brooke. 'Exporting the Garden City: Imperial Development and the English Character in *John Bull's Other Island*'. *Xchanges*. 2.2 (2003). Xchanges.org/xchanges_archive/xchanges/2.2/miller.html

Mitchell, Jack. *The Essential Sean O'Casey: A Study of the Twelve Major Plays of Sean O'Casey*. New York: International Publishers, 1980.

Moi, Toril. *Henrik Ibsen and the Birth of Modernism*. Oxford: Oxford University Press, 2006.

Moody, T. W. *Davitt and Irish Revolution, 1846–1882*. Oxford: Clarendon Press, 1981.

Morris, William. *News From Nowhere: Or, An Epoch of Rest, Being Some Chapters From a Utopian Romance*. London: Reeves & Turner, 1891.

——. 'The Socialist Ideal in Art'. In Edward Carpenter (ed.), *Forecasts of the Coming Century by a Decade of Writers*. Manchester: Labour Press Limited, 1897, 62–72.

'Mr. Shaw's Play. "John Bull's Other Island" at the Court. WIT AND SENTIMENT'. 2 November 1904; no other publication data preserved. In file 'Royal Court, 1904', Victoria and Albert Museum, Theatre and Performance Collection.

Mullen, Patrick. *The Poor Bugger's Tool: Irish Modernism, Queer Labor, and Postcolonial History*. London: Oxford University Press, 2012.
Muñoz, José Esteban. *Cruising Utopia: The Then and There of Queer Futurity*. New York: New York University Press, 2009.
Murphy, Brenda. *Congressional Theatre: Dramatizing McCarthyism on Stage, Film, and Television*. Cambridge: Cambridge University Press, 1999.
Murray, Christopher. *Sean O'Casey: Writer at Work*. Montreal: McGill-Queen's University Press, 2004.
Naiman, Eric. *Sex in Public: The Incarnation of Early Soviet Ideology*. Princeton: Princeton University Press, 1997.
Nathan, George Jean. *My Very Dear Sean: George Jean Nathan to Sean O'Casey, Letters and Articles*. Ed. Robert G. Lowery and Patricia Angelin. London: Associated University Press, 1985.
Negra, Diane. 'The Irish in Us: Irishness, Performativity, and Popular Culture'. In Diane Negra (ed.), *The Irish in Us: Irishness, Performativity, and Popular Culture*. Durham, NC: Duke University Press, 2006, 1–19.
Nemiroff, Robert. 'A Portrait: The 101 "Final" Performances of *Sidney Brustein*'. In Lorraine Hansberry, *A Raisin in the Sun and The Sign in Sidney Brustein's Window*. New York: Vintage Books, 1995, 159–206.
Nichols, Ashton. 'Liberationist Sexuality and Nonviolent Resistance: The Legacy of Blake and Shelley in Morris's *News from Nowhere*'. *The Journal of the William Morris Society*, 10(4) (1994), 20–7.
Nicholson, Steve. *British Theatre and The Red Peril: The Portrayal of Communism 1917–1945*. Exeter: University of Exeter Press, 2000.
O'Casey, Eileen. Typescript. Sean O'Casey Papers. National Library of Ireland, MS 44,703/2.
O'Casey, Sean. *Autobiographies*, Vol. 1. London: Macmillan, 1981.
——. *Blasts and Benedictions: Articles and Stories*. Ed. Ronald Ayling. London: Macmillan, 1967.
——. Holograph Notebooks, Vols 14–15. Henry W. and Albert A. Berg Collection of English and American Literature, New York Public Library, Astor, Lennox and Tilden Foundations.
——. *Inishfallen, Fare Thee Well*. New York: Macmillan & Co., 1949.
——. *Juno and the Paycock*. In John Harrington (ed.), *Modern Irish Drama*. New York: W. W. Norton, 1991.
——. 'Lenin'. Carbon copy of typescript. Articles, Communism, Etc. Sixteen typescripts. 70B6679. #8. Henry W. and Albert A. Berg Collection of English and American Literature, New York Public Library, Astor, Lennox and Tilden Foundations.
——. 'Lenin: Logos of Russia'. Carbon copy of typescript. Typescript. Articles, Communism, Etc. Sixteen typescripts. 70B6679. #9. Henry W. and

Albert A. Berg Collection of English and American Literature, New York Public Library, Astor, Lennox and Tilden Foundations.
——. Letter to Barney Conway. 9 May 1962. National Library of Ireland, MS 37,990.
——. *Letters of Sean O'Casey*. Ed. David Krause. New York: Macmillan, 1975–. Vols 1–4.
——. 'Mayakovsky Immortal'. *The Anglo-Soviet Journal*, 7(1) (1946), 39–40.
——. 'Not Waiting For Godot'. In Sean O'Casey, *Blasts and Benedictions*. London: Macmillan, 1967, 51–2.
——. *Red Roses For Me*. New York: Dramatists Play Service, 1956.
——. 'Rise o' the Red Star'. *The Anglo-Soviet Journal*, 7(1) (1946), 7–14.
——. *Sean O'Casey: Plays 2*. London: Faber and Faber, 1998.
——. 'The Bald Primaqueera'. In Sean O'Casey, *Blasts and Benedictions*. London: Macmillan, 1967, 64–76.
——. 'The Flaming Sunflower'. Typescript. Articles, Communism, Etc. Sixteen typescripts. 70B6679. #5. Henry W. and Albert A. Berg Collection of English and American Literature, New York Public Library, Astor, Lennox and Tilden Foundations.
——. *The Flying Wasp*. London: Macmillan & Co., 1937.
——. 'The Star Ascending'. Typescript. Articles, Communism, Etc. Sixteen typescripts. 70B6679. #15. Henry W. and Albert A. Berg Collection of English and American Literature, New York Public Library, Astor, Lennox and Tilden Foundations.
——. *The Star Turns Red*. London: Macmillan, 1940.
——. 'Theatre and People'. Typescript. Unity Theatre British Manuscript Collection (Collection 29), box 10, folder 3.
——. *Under a Colored Cap: Articles Merry and Mournful with Comments and a Song*. New York: St. Martin's Press, 1963.
——. 'When the News Came to Dublin'. Carbon copy of typescript. Articles, Ireland. Seven typescripts. With O'Casey v. Abbey typescript (xerox). 70B6681. Henry W. and Albert A. Berg Collection of English and American Literature, New York Public Library, Astor, Lennox and Tilden Foundations.
——. *Windfalls: Stories, Poems, and Plays*. London: Macmillan, 1934.
——. *Within the Gates*. London: Macmillan, 1933.
O'Connor, Emmet. 'Labour and Politics, 1830–1945: Colonisation and Mental Colonisation'. In Fintan Lane and Donal Ó Drisceoil (eds), *Politics and the Irish Working Class, 1830–1945*. New York: Palgrave Macmillan, 2005, 27–38.
——. *Reds and the Green: Ireland, Russia and the Communist Internationals, 1919–1943*. Dublin: UCD Press, 2004.
——. *Syndicalism in Ireland, 1917–1923*. Cork: Cork University Press, 1988.

Odets, Clifford. *Six Plays by Clifford Odets*. New York: Random House, 1939.

O'Riordan, Michael. *The Connolly Column: The Story of the Irishmen who Fought for the Spanish Republic 1936–1939*. Dublin: New Books, 1979.

Orme, Michael. [Malcolm Morley.] *J. T. Grein: The Story of a Pioneer 1862–1935*. Foreword written by Conal O'Riordan and censored and revised by George Bernard Shaw. London: John Murray, 1936.

Ormond, Leonee. Preface. In Olga Soboleva and Angus Wrenn (eds), *The Only Hope of the World: George Bernard Shaw and Russia*. Oxford: Peter Lang, 2012.

Payne, Stanley G. *The Spanish Civil War, the Soviet Union, and Communism*. New Haven: Yale University Press, 2004.

Peters, Sally. *Bernard Shaw: The Ascent of the Superman*. New Haven: Yale University Press, 1996.

Pilkington, Lionel. *Theatre and State in Twentieth-Century Ireland*. London: Routledge: 2001.

Pintzka, Wolfgang (ed.). *Helene Weigel: Actress. A Book of Photographs*. Leipzig: VEB Edition, 1961.

Plays Received, 1913–1922. Abbey Theatre Archive.

Poger, Sidney. 'Brecht's *Señora Carrar's Rifles* (*Die Gewehre der Frau Carrar*) and Synge's *Riders to the Sea*'. *The Canadian Journal of Irish Studies*, 10(2) (1984), 37–43.

'PROBLEMS OF THE LABOUR MOVEMENT AND ITS ALLIES'. Unity Theatre Archive. Southern Illinois University, 29/11/7.

Radosh, Ronald, Mary R. Habeck and Grigory Sevostianov. *Spain Betrayed: The Soviet Union in the Spanish Civil War*. Annals of Communism series. Yale University Press, 2001.

Ramert, Lynn. 'Lessons from the Land: Shaw's *John Bull's Other Island*'. *New Hibernia Review/Iris Éireannach Nua: A Quarterly Record of Irish Studies*, 16(3) (2012 Autumn), 43–59.

Review of *The Mother*. *Variety*, 2 November 1935. Clipping file, Billy Rose Theatre Collection, New York Public Library for the Performing Arts.

Ritterhoff, Teresa. 'Ver/Ratlosigkeit: Benjamin, Brecht, and Die Mutter'. *Brecht 100< = >2000: The Brecht Yearbook 24 (1999)*, 246–62.

Robertson, Nan. 'Dramatist Against Odds'. *New York Times*, 8 March 1959, X3.

Roche, Anthony. 'Synge, Brecht, and the Hiberno-German Connection'. *Hungarian Journal of English and American Studies*, 10(1–2) (2004), 9–32.

Saddlemyer, Ann. '*John Bull's Other Island*: "Seething in the Brain"'. *Canadian Journal of Irish Studies*, 25(1–2) (1999), 219–40.

'St. Peter and the Scab'. *Irish Worker*, 27 May 1911.

Scott, Clement. 'The Playhouses'. *Illustrated London News* [London, England], 7 April 1894, 412. *Illustrated London News*. Web. 18 September 2016.

Shaw, George Bernard. *Back to Methuselah*. New York: Brentano's, 1921.

——. *Bernard Shaw: Collected Letters, 1874–1897*. Ed. Dan H. Laurence. New York: Dodd, Mead & Company.

——. *Bernard Shaw: The Diaries, 1885–1897. With early autobiographical notebooks and diaries, and an abortive 1917 diary*. Volume I. Ed. Stanley Weintraub. University Park: Pennsylvania State University Press, 1986.

——. *Bernard Shaw: The Drama Observed*. Volume I: 1880–1895. Ed. Bernard Dukore. University Park: Pennsylvania State University Press, 1993.

——. *Bernard Shaw's Arms and the Man: A Composite Production Book. Compiled and with an Introduction by Bernard F. Dukore*. Carbondale: Southern Illinois University Press, 1982.

——. Draft of letter to Richard Neville. British Library, ADD 50615.

——. 'How William Archer Impressed Bernard Shaw'. Typescript. British Library, ADD 50665. 1926.

——. 'Illusions of Socialism'. In Edward Carpenter (ed.), *Forecasts of the Coming Century by a Decade of Writers*. Manchester: Labour Press Limited, 1897, 141–73.

——. 'Instructions to Producers'. British Library, ADD 50615, 2.

——. *John Bull's Other Island and Major Barbara: Also How He Lied to Her Husband*. London: Archibald Constable & Co., 1907.

——. Lady Gregory's Copy: *John Bull's Other Island*. Typescript. 4 vols. Henry W. and Albert A. Berg Collection of English and American Literature, New York Public Library, Astor, Lennox and Tilden Foundations.

——. *Man and Superman: A Comedy and a Philosophy*. New York: Brentano's, 1903. Accessed 29 April 2014 at http://catalog.hathitrust.org/Record/001909231

——. *Plays Pleasant*. London: Penguin Books, 2003.

——. *Plays Unpleasant*. London: Penguin Books, 1989.

——. 'Preface to the Home Rule Edition, *John Bull's Other Island*'. Typescript draft. British Library, ADD 50615, 16–27.

——. Preface to 'Widowers' Houses'. In *Prefaces by Bernard Shaw*. London: Constable and Company, Ltd, 1934, 667–71.

——. *The Quintessence of Ibsenism*. New York: Brentano's, 1904.

——. 'Shaming the Devil about Shelley'. In *Bernard Shaw's Nondramatic Literary Criticism*. Ed. Stanley Weintraub. Lincoln: University of Nebraska Press, 1972.

——. 'Socialism, Utopian and Scientific'. British Library. ADD 50677A.

——. *Widowers' Houses*. Independent Theatre, 1893. Microfilm.

'Shellback'. [Joseph Foley.] 'The Crime of Blacklegging'. *Irish Worker*, 7 December 1912, 1.

Smith, Wendy. *Real Life: The Group Theatre and America, 1931–1940*. New York: Knopf, 1990.

Solga, Kim. *Mother Courage* and its Abject: Reading the Violence of Identification'. *Modern Drama*, 46 (2003), 339–57.

Solow, Barbara L. 'The Irish Land Question in a Wider Context'. In Fergus Campbell and Tony Varley (eds), *Land Questions in Modern Ireland*. Manchester: Manchester University Press, 2013, 65–80.

Spender, Stephen. 'A Morality Play with No Morals'. *New Statesman and Nation*, 16 March 1940, 363–4.

Stam, Robert. *Film Theory: An Introduction*. Oxford: Blackwell, 2000.

Stepniak, S. Letter to John Todhunter. 12 March 1894, Bedford Park. Todhunter Papers, University of Reading Special Collections. MS 202/1/577-580.

Synge, John Millington. *The Aran Islands. Collected Works of J. M. Synge*. Washington, DC: Catholic University of America Press, 1982, Vol. 2, 47–186.

——. *The Complete Plays of J. M. Synge*. New York: Vintage Books, 1960.

——. *Riders to the Sea. Modern Irish Drama*. Ed. John P. Harrington. New York: W. W. Norton and Company, 1991, 63–72.

Taxidou, Olga. 'Machines and Models for Modern Tragedy: Brecht/Berlau, *Antigone-Model 1948*'. In Rita Felski (ed.), *Rethinking Tragedy*. Baltimore: Johns Hopkins University Press, 241–62.

Tchaprazov, Stoyan. 'The Bulgarians of Bernard Shaw's *Arms and the Man*.' *SHAW: The Annual of Bernard Shaw Studies*, 31 (2011), 71–88.

'The Drama'. *Westminster Review*, 141 (1894), 589.

'The Labour Leader'. Clipping included in *The Diaries of Joseph Holloway, 1895–1944 from the National Library of Ireland, Dublin*. Microfilm, 105 reels.

Todhunter, John. *A Comedy of Sighs*. Typescript. Held in Todhunter Papers at the University of Reading.

——. *A Sicilian Idyll: A Pastoral Play in Two Scenes*. London: Elkin Mathews, 1890.

——. *The Black Cat. A Play in Three Acts*. London: Henry and Co., 1895. Accessed through LION, 18 September 2016.

Ulmer, William A. *Shelleyan Eros: The Rhetoric of Romantic Love*. Princeton: Princeton University Press, 1990.

Unwin, Raymond. 'Edward Carpenter and *Towards Democracy*'. In Gilbert Beith (ed.), *Edward Carpenter: In Appreciation*. London: George Allen & Unwin Ltd, 1931, 234–43.

Urbaszewski, Laura Shear. 'Canonizing the "Best, Most Talented" Soviet Poet: Vladimir Mayakovsky and the Soviet Literary Celebration'. *Modernism/Modernity*, 9 (2002), 635–65.
Valente, Joseph. *The Myth of Manliness in Irish National Culture, 1880–1922*. Urbana: University of Illinois Press, 2011.
Veselá, Pavla. 'The Hardening of *Cement*: Russian Women and Modernization'. *NWSA Journal*, 15 (2003), 104–23.
Walkley, Arthur Bingham. 'The Drama: Irish National Theatre'. *Times Literary Supplement* (69), 146. Friday 8 May, 1903.
Wallace, Alfred Russell. 'Re-Occupation of the Land'. In Edward Carpenter (ed.), *Forecasts of the Coming Century by a Decade of Writers*. Manchester: Labour Press Limited, 1897, 9–26.
Warwick-Haller, Sally. *William O'Brien and the Irish Land War*. Dublin: Irish Academic Press, 1990.
Watt, Stephen. *Joyce, O'Casey, and the Irish Popular Theater*. Syracuse: Syracuse University Press, 1991.
Welch, Robert. *The Abbey Theatre, 1899–1999: Form and Pressure*. Oxford: Oxford University Press, 1999.
Whitney, John. 'Broadway Last Night: "Mother" Paints Pictures of Days in 1912 When Russian Workers Began to Rumble'. [*Newark Evening News*, date not preserved, 22.] Clipping file, Billy Rose Theatre Collection, New York Public Library for the Performing Arts.
Wilde, Oscar. 'The Soul of Man Under Socialism'. In Oscar Wilde et al., *The Soul of Man Under Socialism, The Socialist Ideal-Art, The Coming Solidarity*. New York: Humboldt Publishing Company, 1892.
Willett, John. 'Notes on Individual Poems'. In Bertolt Brecht, *Poems 1913–1956*, 598
Willett, John and Ralph Manheim. 'Introduction'. *Bertolt Brecht's Collected Plays*. Vol. 5, part 2. London: Eyre Methuen, 1980. Vii–xxii.
——. Introduction to *Señora Carrar's Rifles*. *Bertolt Brecht Collected Plays*. Ed. John Willett and Ralph Manheim. London: Methuen, 1983. Volume 4, part 3, vii–xxiii.
Williams, Raymond. *Culture and Materialism*. London: Verso Books, 2005.
Wilson, A. Patrick. 'A Procession and its Banners'. *Irish Worker*, 8 March 1913, 1.
——. '"Larkinism!" The New Word and What it Means'. *Irish Worker*, 5 October 1912.
——. ['Euchan.'] 'Lyres and Liars! Some passing comments on Music Halls and Artistes'. *Irish Worker*, 14 June 1913, 1.
——. ['Euchan.'] 'Some Casual Comments on Rolling Stones and Other Things'. *Irish Worker*, 29 March 1913, 1.
——. 'Strife'. *Irish Worker*, 16 August 1913, 1.

——. 'The Drama – Old and New'. *Irish Worker*, 23 November 1912.
——. 'The Jovial Revolution'. *Irish Worker*, 9 August 1913.
——. *The Slough*. Typescript archived at the British Library, LC 3059.
——. *Victims and Poached*. Dublin: West Trade Union Publishers, no date.
Woggon, Helga. 'Interpreting James Connolly, 1916–23'. In Fintan Lane and Donal Ó Drisceoil (eds), *Politics and the Irish Working Class, 1830–1945*. New York: Palgrave Macmillan, 2005, 172–83.
Woods, Gregory. *Homintern: How Gay Culture Liberated the Modern World*. New Haven: Yale University Press, 2016.
Wright, Arnold. *Disturbed Dublin: The Story of the Great Strike of 1913–14*. London: Longmans, Green and Co., 1914.
Yde, Matthew. *Bernard Shaw and Totalitarianism: Longing for Utopia*. New York: Palgrave Macmillan, 2013.
Yeates, Padraig. *A City in Wartime: Dublin 1914–18*. Dublin: Gill & Macmillan, 2011.
——. *Lockout: Dublin 1913*. Dublin: Gill & Macmillan, 2000.
Yeats, W. B. 'Reasons for Dismissal of Manager, July 17th, 1915'. National Library of Ireland, MS 30,559 TS.
——. *The Autobiography of William Butler Yeats*. New York: The Macmillan Company, 1938.
——. *The Collected Letters of W. B. Yeats*. Ed. John Kelly and Eric Domville. Oxford: Clarendon Press, 1986, Vol. I.
——. *The Land of Heart's Desire Manuscript Materials*. Ed. Jared Curtis. Ithaca: Cornell University Press, 2002.

INDEX

Page numbers in *italics* refer to figures.

Abbey Theatre
  inaugural season, 59
  and O'Casey, 14, 173–8
  and Shaw, 94n3, 122–3
  staging, 73, 127–9
  strike plays, 13, 97; *see also* strike plays
  and Wilson, 112, 122–3
absurdist theatre, 208, 217, 219, 230–6
ACT UP, 237
'The Actress in Exile' (Brecht), 161–3
aesthetic socialism, 19–20, 26, 60, 182, 223
African-Americans, 214–15, 225–6
Agate, James, 184
agitprop, 137, 146, 186, 194
Albee, Edward, 217
alienation, 13, 149, 165, 235
'Alienation Effects in Chinese Acting' (Brecht), 149
Allen, Grace, 160
anarchism, 2, 11, 24, 26, 77, 78
anarcho-syndicalism, 2, 136
Andalusia, 141, 151, 159, 161–2
Anderson, John, 147, 168n17
Andreassen, Dagmar, 159
Anglo-Soviet Journal (ASJ), 198–9
anticapitalist politics, 14, 238
Antigone-Model 1948 (Brecht), 166
antirealism, 14, 134n8, 150, 177, 188–9, 199, 219, 230–1
Antoine, André, 3
Archer, William, 30–1, 44, 45, 56n13
  The Green Goddess, 179
Aristotelian drama, 142–3, 148, 150, 154–5, 175

Arms and the Man (Shaw), 12, 16–19, 45–6, 51–3
'The Arrival of Mr. Todog' (Hansberry), 232
Arts and Crafts movement, 81
'As Far as Thought Can Reach' (Shaw), 207
Atkinson, Brooks, 170, 196, 202, 211, 214, 225
audience *see* spectators
authoritarian socialism, 26, 207
avant-garde theatre, 40, 135, 169–70
  existentialist, 217
  Soviet, 177–8
Avenue Theatre, 12, 17–19, 39, 44–54
Ayling, Ronald, 170, 196

Back to Methuselah (Shaw), 65, 95n16, 206–8
'The Bald Primaqueera' (O'Casey), 208
Baldwin, James, *Giovanni's Room*, 231, 236
Baldwin, Kate, 214
Barnes, Howard, 168n17
Barnfield, George, *The Psychology of the Poet Shelley*, 24
Barrett, William, 106
Basque region, 140, 151
Baxandall, Lee, 144
beauty, 19, 25, 52, 62, 93, 154, 164, 175–6, 201
  and design, 78–9, 81, 93
  of Ireland's landscape, 72–4
  and queer socialism, 100, 173, 191–2

258

INDEX

refusal of, 49
revolutionary value of, 179–84, 197, 210–11
Victorian cult of, 21
Beauvoir, Simone de, 229
Beckett, Samuel, 4, 7, 170, 217, 220, 230–4, 237
  Waiting for Godot, 14, 214–15, 218–19, 221, 230, 232
Beckles, Gordon, 184
Beevers, Walter, 82, 95n13
Belfast, labour movement in, 104
Bellamy, Edward, *Looking Backward*, 61–2, 78, 81, 86
Bengal, Ben, *Plant in the Sun*, 215
Benjamin, Walter, 143–5
Benson, Edward, *Dodo, a Detail of the Day*, 49
Berlant, Loren, 219
Berlau, Ruth, 141, 159, 160, 163, 166, 167n7
Bernliner Ensemble, 158–9
Bersani, Leo, 60
Besant, Annie, 32, 35
Bettany, Frederick George, 91
Bevir, Mark, 77
bisexuality, 36
Bizet, Georges, *Carmen*, 47
The Black Cat (Todhunter), 45, 46, 56n13
Black Lives Matter, 237
black masculinity, 225–6
blacklisting, 221
Blake, William, 9
Bloody Sunday (Dublin, 1913), 103
Bloody Sunday (Trafalgar Square, London, 1887), 18, 28, 29, 31–2, 35, 37, 53, 55n7, 76, 221
Blueshirts, 138
body politics, 237; *see also* embodiment
Bolshevism, Irish interest in, 121, 137–8, 174; *see also* Russian Revolution (1917)
bourgeois domesticity, 39–41
Bradley, Laura, 146
Brecht, Bertolt, 6, 117, 195, 214, 239
  exile, 143, 145–6, 150, 168n21
  gender politics, 139
  WORKS: 'The Actress in Exile', 161–3; 'Alienation Effects in Chinese Acting', 149; *Antigone-Model 1948*, 166; *The Caucasian Chalk Circle*, 145; *Der Messingkauf*, 160; *The Good Person of Szechwan*, 139, 145; *The Mother*, 13, 139, 142–50, 153–6, 159; *Mother Courage*, 165–6; *Señora Carrar's Rifles*, 13, 138–43, 146, 150–2, 155–65; 'Weigel's Props', 162–5
British imperialism, 10, 59, 70, 76
British socialists, 12, 17–21
  and the Soviet Union, 178, 186, 194
  see also Bloody Sunday
Brown, Ivor, 193
Bruder, Helen, 9
Bunyan, John, *The Pilgrim's Progress*, 100
Burch, Lionel, 224
Burch, Stephen, 98
Burns, John, 64
Burnshaw, Stanley, 146–9
Butler, Samuel, 29, 89, 207
  Luck, or Cunning, 65–6

Caballero, Largo, 160
Cadbury, George, 79
Camus, Albert, *The Rebel*, 217
capitalism
  core values of, 66–7
  and cruel optimism, 219–20
  and Garden City movement, 79, 84–7
  growth, 59
  idealised conception of, 9–10
  Ireland's resistance to, 70–1
  and literary value, 6
  and the nuclear family, 209–10
  Shaw's critiques of, 30, 34, 37
  socialism co-opted by, 84–7
  and survival, 144
Carney, Jack, 186
Carpenter, Edward, 11, 18, 19, 23–5, 27–9, 36, 77, 93, 101–3, 110, 181, 196, 210, 236
  Homogenic Love, 27
  Towards Democracy, 81
  'Transitions to Freedom', 25, 63, 74

259

Carter, Steven R., 231, 232, 236
Casanova, Pascale, 11
   The World Republic of Letters, 5–6
Case, Sue-Ellen, 144
catharsis, 148
Cathleen ni Houlihan (Yeats), 71, 223
Catholicism, 105–7, 111, 113, 120, 138, 156–7, 191, 229
The Caucasian Chalk Circle (Brecht), 145
censorship, 22, 194
Charabanc Theatre Company, 100
children
   fairy child, 39–44, 46, 50
   production of, 27
   symbolic politics of, 113–14, 205
   women differentiated from, 39–41
   see also motherhood; reproduction
Chukovsky, Korney, 177
Clark, Katerina, 199–201
Cleary, Joe, 10, 105, 108
   Outrageous Fortune, 5, 9, 20
Cock-a-Doodle Dandy (O'Casey), 208, 222
Cold War politics, 213–16, 219, 220–2
Coleman, Robert, 168n17
collective landownership, 77–8, 82–4, 86–7
Colum, Padraic, *Broken Soil*, 71
A Comedy of Sighs (Todhunter), 12, 16–19, 44–51, 53, 207
Comintern (Communist International), 135–7, 178
commercial theatre, 3, 22, 177–8, 193–4
communes, 77, 82–4, 86, 95n12
Communism, 2
   in Germany, 143
   and HUAC (House Un-American Committee), 220–2
   symbols of, 185–6
   see also Russian Revolution (1917); Soviet Union
Communist Party of Great Britain (CPGB), 170, 178, 194
Communist Party of Ireland, 136, 173
comparativism, 4–7, 226, 238

compulsory heterosexuality, 210;
   see also heteronormativity; heterosexuality
comrade love, 25, 102, 110, 236
Confederacion General del Trabajo (National Confederation of Labor, CNT), 136
Connolly, James, 100, 103, 120, 122, 186
   Labour in Irish History, 101, 121
   'Tram Strike', 101
Connolly, Tristanne, 9
Conway, Barney, 186–8
Cork Dramatic Society, 120
Corkery, Daniel
   The Labour Leader, 13, 98–9, 119–32, 174
   The Yellow Bittern and Other Plays, 122
Countess Cathleen (Yeats), 54–5
Coward, Noël, 208, 210, 235
   Design for Living, 205
Craig, Edward Thomas, 83–4, 86
Crane Bag, 171
Creative Evolution, Shaw's doctrine of, 65, 206–7
Creese, Walter L., 81
Criminal Amendment Act (1885), 27
The Crimson in the Tri-Colour (O'Casey), 174–5

Dáil Éireann, 121
Darwin, Charles, 65, 66
Dash, Thomas R., 146–7, 168n17
Davis, Angela, 215
Davitt, Michael, 17, 87–8
de Blacam, Aodh, *Towards the Republic*, 121
De Valera, Éamon, 138
Deane, Seamus, 10
death drive, 8, 60, 71
deferral, 219, 237–8
demonstrations, 106, 116; *see also* Bloody Sunday; Dublin Lockout (1913); labour agitation
Der Messingkauf (Brecht), 160
design, 12, 60, 65, 79–82, 92–3
desire, 64, 78; *see also eros*; male sexual desire; sexual liberation movements; utopian desire
developmental logic, 12, 59, 89
Diamond, Elin, 158, 228

Dickson, Keith, 143, 167n3
Die Laterne, 146
Dies, Martin, 220
direct action, 97, 102, 113
A Doll's House (Ibsen), 40, 41, 47
domesticity, 144–5
'The Dream School' (O'Casey), 201
Dublin
   Irish dramatic revival, 17; *see also* Abbey Theatre; Irish Literary Theatre
   poverty, 96, 113
   urban housing crisis, 113
Dublin Employers' Federation, 96, 221
'Dublin Kiddies Scheme', 113
Dublin Lockout (1913), 93, 96, 100, 103, 113, 120, 131, 186–8, 190, 213, 222
Dublin United Tramways Company, 96
Dudow, Slatan, 138, 163
Dukore, Bernard F., 52

Easter Rising (1916), 120–1
Eastern Europe, as proxy setting for Ireland, 51
Edelman, Lee, 11, 24, 58, 60, 113
   No Future, 7–8
Edwards, Hilton, 209
Egerton, George, 56n12
Ellis, Havelock, 24
embodiment, 8–10, 20, 31, 126, 226, 239
emotion
   and masculinity, 25
   and politics, 170–1
   of spectators, 139, 142–3, 146–51, 154–7, 165–6
   and syndicalism, 99–106, 119
empathy, 142–3, 148–51, 165–6
England
   dramatic revival, 17
   urban migration in, 76–7
   see also British imperialism; British socialists; London
environmental determinism, 81
epic theatre, 13, 139, 146–51, 159, 166, 239
eros, 102, 110, 230
   and O'Casey, 208
   and political desire, 9

radical, 11, 23–4, 37, 39, 202, 206
   and Shaw, 64–5, 202, 206–7
   and Shelley, 23–4, 63, 175–6, 206
eroticism
   and magic, 51, 71
   male, 41, 236
Ervine, St. John, 3, 123, 239
   Mixed Marriage, 13, 98, 104–12, 114–15, 117–19, 129–32
   Sir Edward Carson, 108–9
Esslin, Martin, 167n3
evolutionary theory, 12, 59, 62, 64–71, 89, 92, 206–7
excess, 182–3
existentialist drama, 231
expressionism, 230
expressionist idealism, 218

Fabianism, 19, 76, 80, 85, 92, 94n1, 105, 108
failure, 7–8
fairy child, 39–44, 46, 50
fairy extravaganzas, 73–4
family
   attacks on, 27, 29
   and capitalism, 209–10
   critiques of bourgeois family, 39–41
   rejection of, 77
   structural unit, 102, 110–11
   see also marriage; motherhood
family plot, 98–9
fantasy, 193–5, 201, 211, 221–30
Farr, Florence, 3, 12, 16–19, 24
   in *Arms and the Man*, 45–6, 51–3
   in *Comedy of Sighs*, 45–51
   in *Countess Cathleen*, 54
   and *Land of Heart's Desire*, 39
   relationships with Yeats, Todhunter, and Shaw, 22, 36, 39, 45, 50, 56n10, 67–8, 74
   in *A Sicilian Idyll*, 36–7, 42, 46
   in *Widowers' Houses*, 35
fascism, 136–8; *see also* Spanish Civil War
Federal Theatre Project, 220
female sexual desire, 12, 18–19, 35–7, 43–50, 203; *see also* reproductive sexuality
femininity, 46, 111, 203
feminisation, 101–2, 240n2

feminism, 1–4, 18, 139, 144
  Black internationalist feminism, 215
Fianna Fáil government, 138
Figgis, Darrell, *The Gaelic State*, 122
'The Flaming Sunflower' (O'Casey), 172–3, 196–7
Flanagan, Hallie, 220
The Flying Wasp (O'Casey), 178, 189, 193
Forecasts of the Coming Century (1897), 63
Foster, Roy, 98
Franco, Francisco, 136, 138, 151–2
Fraser, Winifred, 42
fraternal solidarity, 102; *see also* comrade love
free theatres, 3
Freedom (newspaper), 214, 227
Freie Bühne (Berlin), 3
Fuegi, John, 167n7
future, 59
  predictions of, 89
  see also queer futurity; reproductive futurism; 'there and then'; utopianism

Galsworthy, John, *Strife*, 114, 133n5
Garden City movement, 59–60, 75–88, 135
Garland, Robert, 147
'The Garland' (O'Casey), 180–1
Gate Theatre, 209
Gender and Modern Irish Drama (Harris), 5
gender binary, 110–11, 234–6
gender fluidity, 24–5
gender studies, 5
Genet, Jean, *Les Nègres*, 217
'Genet, Mailer, and the New Paternalism' (Hansberry), 225–6
George, Henry, 76
Gladden, Samuel Lyndon, 23
Gladkov, Feodor, *Cement*, 199–201
Gleitman, Claire, 139
global turn, 4–6, 140
globalisation, 14, 238–9
'Gold and Silver Will Not Do' (O'Casey), 181
Gonne, Maud, 21, 40
The Good Person of Szechwan (Brecht), 139, 145

Gothic, 51
gradualism, 32, 60, 92, 105–6, 228
Graham, R. Cunninghame, 31
Gramsci, Antonio, 10, 23
Grand, Sarah, 56n12
Gray, John, 106
Great Lockout of 1913 *see* Dublin Lockout (1913)
Greece
  neoclassical aesthetic, 36, 207
  as signifier of same-sex love, 36, 46
'The Green Goddess of Realism' (O'Casey), 178–9
Gregory, Lady, 3, 21, 59, 100
  Abbey Theatre productions, 122, 123
  and O'Casey, 169, 173–4, 176, 204
  The Pot of Broth, 71
  Twenty-Five, 72
Grein, J. T., 22
Grene, Nicholas, 34, 69, 94n1
grief
  and activism, 237
  maternal, 13, 147–8, 150, 153, 154–7, 165
Guernica, 151

Halberstam, J. Jack, 11, 61
  The Queer Art of Failure, 7–9
Hansberry, Lorraine
  'The Arrival of Mr. Todog', 232
  'Genet, Mailer, and the New Paternalism', 225–6
  A Raisin in the Sun, 215, 219, 226–8
  The Sign in Sidney Brustein's Window, 14, 214, 216–20, 227–37
  To Be Young, Gifted, and Black, 226–7
Hanssen, Paula, 159
Harvey, David, 9
Hawthorne, Nathaniel, 56n10
hegemonic masculinity, 4, 9, 32
hegemony, 10–11
Henry, Helen, 147–50, 155, 159, 166
'here and now'
  alternatives to, 231
  and capitalism, 86

and the future, 6, 61–2, 69, 71–6, 79, 82–3, 89
and queerness, 27, 61–2
and socialism, 94
heroic masculinity, 14, 31–2, 189, 216, 219–26, 234
heteronormativity, 26, 54, 60–4, 235
heterosexism, 205, 219, 236
heterosexuality, 37, 42, 78, 101, 106, 203–10
  and class ideologies, 51–3
  naturalisation of, 110–11, 183
  as a performance, 49
  see also heteronormativity; reproduction
Higashida, Cheryl, 215, 217, 231
'hipster' masculinity, 225–6
Hodin, Mark, 217, 226, 229, 231, 236
Holloway, Joseph, 134n9, 155
Home Rule, 57–9, 108
Homintern, 209–10
homophobia, 205–6, 215, 232, 237
homosexuality, 24, 209, 231–2
  and anticommunist politics, 209–10, 220
  criminalisation of, 24, 27, 29–30
  see also lesbianism
homosocial relationships, 106–7, 111, 115, 119–20
  and comrade love, 25, 102, 110, 236
Horace, 148, 155
Horniman, Annie, 16, 73
Housego, Molly, 55n7
Howard, Ebenezer, 12, 103
  To-Morrow, 59–60, 75–82, 84, 86, 88, 90
Howson, Gerald, 137
HUAC (House Un-American Activities Committee), 216, 218, 220–2
Hughes, Langston
  Harlem, 219
  Mother to Son, 219
Hugo, Victor, 129
hysterical realism, 158

I Knock at the Door (O'Casey), 200
Ibsen, Henrik, 3, 28, 30, 44–5
  A Doll's House, 40, 41, 47

idealism, 19–23, 28, 37, 52, 181, 211, 233–4
  expressionist, 218
  Irish, 21, 233
  and O'Casey, 176, 187–93
  Victorian, 21
  see also romantic idealism
identification, of audience with protagonist, 148–9, 165
identity politics, 14, 238
Idylls (Theocritus), 36
illusionistic theatre, 142, 146, 151, 155, 178, 189, 235
Independent Theatre, 3, 22
independent theatres, 3
individualism, 27, 30, 196, 205, 207
industrial towns, 79; *see also* Garden City movement
industry, 66–7, 108
infant mortality, 113
Instronnaya Literatura, 172
International Brigade, 136, 140
internationalism, 5–6
  Black internationalist feminism, 215
  Irish, 14–15, 238–40
inversion, rhetoric of, 58
IRA, 137
Ireland
  agrarian violence, 83–4
  colonial past, 10, 59, 70
  dramatic revival, 1–15, 17, 238–40
  Home Rule, 57–9, 108
  internationalism, 14–15, 238–40
  land agitation, 37, 70, 76, 83–4
  land nationalisation, 12, 17, 87
  landscape, 72–5, 88
  militias, 109
  nationalism, 17–18, 70, 72, 76, 94n1, 109, 120–1, 174, 222
  political left, 97
  republicanism, 140–1, 175
  resistance to capitalism, 70–1
  revolution, 12–13, 93–4, 98, 137–8
  unionism, 57–8, 107, 109
Irish Brigade, 138
Irish Christian Front, 138
Irish Citizen Army, 98, 120
Irish Land League, 87
Irish Land War (1879–82), 10
Irish Literary Theatre, 16, 21, 54, 71

263

Irish National League, 18
Irish National Theatre Society, 161
Irish Players, 71–2
Irish studies, 4–6, 238
Irish Times, 97
Irish Volunteers, 109
Irish Women Workers' Union, 133n3
Irish Worker, 98, 100, 101, 112, 115, 118
Irishness, 184, 187, 222, 228
  and anti-productivity, 12
  and re/productivity, 67
irrationalism, 99, 104, 107–11, 115, 120, 126, 130–2, 239
ITGWU (Irish Transport and General Workers' Union), 96, 99, 100, 103, 113, 120, 173, 176, 186, 188
IWW (Industrial Workers of the World), 97, 102
Izvestia, 173

Jameson, Fredric, 9, 149–50, 165
John Bull's Other Island (Shaw), 12, 55, 57–60, 72–6, 82–94
Johnson, Josephine, 56n13
Johnson, Paul, 136
Johnson, Thomas, 121
Juno and the Paycock (O'Casey), 13, 14, 98, 131–2, 144, 169, 176, 177, 180, 226–7

keening, 151, 153, 155–6
Kelly, Catriona, 203, 204
Kempton, Murray, 224, 225
Keough, J. Augustus, 123
Keynotism, 44–5
The King's Threshold (Yeats), 71
Kleinstück, Johannes, 138, 167n3
Krause, David, 170, 209, 211
Kropotkin, Peter, 77
Kuch, Peter, 26
Kuleshov, Lev, 149

labour agitation, 13, 98–103, 119, 123
labour colonies, 77–8
labour councils (soviets), 93
Labour in Irish History (Connolly), 101
The Labour Leader (Corkery), 13, 98–9, 119–32, 174

labour movement, 96–133, 173–6, 239
  local and global aspects, 187–90
  militancy, 12–13, 93, 99–104
  and queer socialism, 93, 181–2
  see also Dublin Lockout (1913); labour agitation; strikes; syndicalism; working-class family; working-class masculinity
Land Act (1903), 76, 87
land agitation, 37, 70, 76, 83–4
land nationalisation, 12, 17, 76–8, 87
Land Nationalisation Society, 78
The Land of Heart's Desire (Yeats), 12, 16–19, 39–44, 46, 50, 54–5
landscape, Irish, 72–5, 88
Larkin, Delia, 100, 133n3
Larkin, Jim, 13, 14, 96–120, 122–4, 126, 131–3, 173, 175–7, 181–2, 186, 189, 193, 204, 224
LeFanu, Sheridan, *Carmilla*, 51
left politics, 2, 3–4, 10, 97
  white left, American, 14, 216–20, 222
  see also aesthetic socialism; anarchism; British socialists; Communism; labour agitation; labour movement; Marxism; queer socialism; socialist movement
Lenin, Vladimir, 143, 144, 172–3, 196–7, 199, 202
'Lenin: Logos of Russia' (O'Casey), 172
Lennox, Sara, 139, 145
lesbianism, 12, 18–19, 29, 35–7, 44–50, 54, 203
Lesjak, Carolyn, 26
Letchworth, 76, 82
Levitas, Ben, 4, 69, 94n1, 98, 105, 116, 117, 120, 131–2, 134n8, 140, 141, 144, 188
  The Theatre of Nation, 20
Liberation War, 120
Licensing Act (1737), 22
Life Force, 64, 69, 71, 90, 207
Linfield, Lily, 37, 43
literary modernism, 3, 5, 69
literary value, 6, 11
Livesey, Ruth, 25
Lloyd, David, 10

Lockout of 1913 *see* Dublin Lockout (1913)
Lomonosova, Raisa, 177–8, 198
London
  commercial theatre, 3, 22, 177–8, 193–4
  independent theatres, 3
  urban housing crisis, 76–7
Lorca, Federico Garcia, *Blood Wedding*, 141, 142
Lorde, Audre, 215
lost or forgotten projects, 7, 131, 238
Lowery, Robert, 98, 171

McAteer, Michael, 40, 51
  Yeats and European Drama, 4
McCarthy, Joseph, 220
MacLíammóir, Micheál, 209
Maeterlinck, Maurice, *The Intruder*, 40
magic, 39–40, 46–7, 51, 71, 227, 230
Mailer, Norman, 'The White Negro', 225–6
Major Barbara (Shaw), 92–3, 95n19, 206
male relationships *see* homosocial relationships
male sexual desire, 41, 47, 236
  and female masculinisation, 46–7
  see also heterosexuality; homosexuality; reproductive sexuality
Malthus, Thomas, 58
Man and Superman (Shaw), 12, 55, 59, 64–71, 88, 207
Mantle, Burns, 147
marriage, 27, 42, 62, 67–9, 90, 234–5
Marshall, Herbert, 194
  Mayakovsky and his Poetry, 197
Martyn, Edward, 3, 21, 71
Marx, Eleanor, 32, 35
Marxism, 2, 3
  abstract universalism, 8–10
  contempt for sexuality, 23
  on motherhood, 144
  postmodern, 9
  romantic idealism and, 21
  utopian desires, 7
masculine dominance, 51–3, 118

masculinisation, 52
  and desire between women, 35–6, 46–50, 54
  and male sexual desire, 46–7
masculinity
  black, 225–6
  and emotion, 25
  hegemonic, 4, 9, 32
  heroic, 14, 31–2, 189, 216, 219–26, 234
  'hipster', 225–6
  idealised in Soviet culture, 203–10
  scabs and, 115–16
  Shaw's, 29
  and syndicalism, 98–104, 119–20, 125–9
  white, 216, 222, 225
  working-class, 12–14, 31–2, 98–104, 119–20, 125–9, 132, 189–90
  see also homosocial relationships
materialism, 11, 21, 80, 164, 211
maternity *see* motherhood
Maume, Patrick, 120
Maurer, Sara, 70
maximalism, 170, 211, 214
Mayakovsky, Vladimir, 197–9, 203
Meisel, Martin, 73
Melas, Natalie, 214
  All the Difference in the World, 6–7
melodrama, 147, 169
Miller, Arthur, 222, 224, 225
  The Crucible, 221
  Death of a Salesman, 227
Miller, C. Brooke, 95n14
minimalism, 161, 170, 211, 214, 230
misogyny, 110, 203
Mitchell, Jack, 186, 187
Mixed Marriage (Ervine), 13, 98, 104–12, 114–15, 117–19, 129–32
modernism, 6, 10–11, 15, 202, 211, 214
  and idealism, 20–1
  literary, 3, 5, 69
Moi, Toril, 23
  Henrik Ibsen and the Birth of Modernism, 20
monogamy, 205, 210, 234
Montefiore, Dora, 113

Moore, George, *The Strike at Arlingford*, 117, 133n5
Morris, William, 11, 12, 18, 19, 23–8, 60, 77, 93, 100–3, 110, 181, 196
  News from Nowhere, 25, 61–3, 72, 81, 93
The Mother (Brecht), 13, 139, 142–50, 153–6, 159
Mother Courage (Brecht), 165–6
motherhood
  maternal grief, 13, 147–8, 150, 153, 154–7, 165
  political consciousness of working-class mothers, 13, 139, 143–5, 150–61, 165–6
  rejection of, 2, 42, 46–9, 154
  see also children; family
Mullen, Patrick, 11
  The Poor Bugger's Tool, 23–4
Muñoz, José, 8, 9, 11, 12, 23, 27, 61
Murphy, William Martin, 96, 100
Murray, Alma, 45, 52
Myerberg, Michael, 213–14
mysticism, 16, 39, 80

Naiman, Eric, 203
Nathan, George Jean, 170, 209
nationalism, 17–18, 70, 72, 76, 94n1, 109, 120–1, 174, 222
naturalism, 20–1, 71–2, 81, 129, 239
Negra, Diane, 222
Negrín, Juan, 160
Nemiroff, Robert, 217, 227
neoclassical aesthetic, 36, 207
Neville, Ralph, 85
New Masses, 146
New Women, 1–3
  rejection of motherhood, 46–9
  social acceptance of, 44–5
  transgressive sexuality, 12, 18–19, 35–7, 43–50
Newmark, Peter, 195
Nichols, Ashton, 25
Nietzsche, Friedrich, 63
normativity, 9, 60–4, 92; *see also* heteronormativity
NUDL (National Union of Dock Labourers), 99, 104, 106

O'Brien, James Bronterre, 17
O'Brien, William, 18

O'Casey, Sean, 2, 4, 100, 239
  on Beckett, 231
  Dublin trilogy, 13–14, 131, 169, 176, 189
  eros, 208
  experimental works, 169–70, 182, 208–11, 219, 222
  gender politics, 204–5, 219, 223, 228–9
  and Hansberry, 217–20, 226–37
  heroic masculinity, 220–6, 234
  richness, 7, 182–3, 191–4, 201, 210–11, 222–3
  and Soviet literature, 195–203
  Soviet Union and Communism, commitment to, 170–8, 184–96
  WORKS: 'The Bald Primaqueera', 208; *Cock-a-Doodle Dandy*, 208, 222; *The Crimson in the Tri-Colour*, 174–5; 'The Dream School', 201; 'The Flaming Sunflower', 172–3, 196–7; *The Flying Wasp*, 178, 189, 193; 'The Garland', 180–1; 'Gold and Silver Will Not Do', 181; 'The Green Goddess of Realism', 178–9; *I Knock at the Door*, 200; *Juno and the Paycock*, 13, 14, 98, 131–2, 144, 169, 176, 177, 180, 226–7; 'Lenin: Logos of Russia', 172; *The Plough and the Stars*, 169, 177, 188, 204; *Red Roses For Me*, 14, 213–15, 221–5, 227–30, 233; 'The Red Star', 174–5, 177; 'Rise o' the Red Star', 198–9, 201; *Shadow of a Gunman*, 169, 175, 177; *The Silver Tassie*, 169, 177, 200; 'The Star Ascending', 172; *The Star Turns Red*, 14, 170, 184–96, 199, 200, 204, 223, 233; 'The Star-Jazzer', 179–80; 'Theatre and People', 182–3; 'A Walk with Eros', 212n4; 'When the News Came to Dublin', 172; *Windfalls*, 179–83, 191, 193; *Within the Gates*, 169, 183–5, 208, 225
occult, 12, 18, 21, 39–40, 48
O'Connor, Emmet, 121
Odets, Clifford, *Waiting for Lefty*, 218

O'Duffy, Eoin, 138
Oneida Community, 95n12
optimism, 219–20
Orme, Michael, 22
O'Shaughnessy, John, 222
ostranenie (making strange), 149
Ouseley, Gideon Jasper, 80
Owen, Robert, 83

paganism, 156
Paget, Dorothy, 39, 41–2
Parker, Barry, 81, 91, 103
Parker, Louis N., *The Man in the Street*, 17
Partido Obrero de Unificación Marxista (POUM), 161
patriarchy, 22, 29, 107–8, 111, 116, 219, 237
Payne, Stanley G., 136–7
Pease, Edward, 80
performativity, 126, 128
perversion, rhetoric of, 57–8
Peters, Paul, 146
Peters, Sally, 24
The Pilgrim's Progress, 100
Pilkington, Lionel, 122
Plato, 20
pleasure, 24–6, 63, 65, 81, 204
The Plough and the Stars (O'Casey), 169, 177, 188, 204
Poger, Sidney, 140, 167n3
political violence, 103, 106–9; *see also* Bloody Sunday
Popular Front, 220, 221
postcolonial studies, 6–7
poverty, 152–3, 161, 179–80, 191–3
praxis, 8, 12, 24, 68, 145, 165
'private club' ruse, 22, 194
production, 62, 112
 anti-productivity, 12
 and pleasure, 24–6, 63
propaganda, 114, 115, 173, 183, 198
 anti-Larkin, 109
 during Spanish Civil War, 7, 136, 138, 185, 191
props, 161–4, 166, 178
Protestantism, 66–7, 105–8, 111, 229

queer futurity, 8, 12, 60–4, 72, 77, 88–9, 219

queer liberation movement, 1–4; *see also* homosexuality; male sexual desire; sexual liberation movements
queer socialism, 8, 11–14, 18, 55, 58, 68–9, 77, 81, 93
 defined, 23–9
 and Larkin, 181–2
 militancy and, 125
 and Soviet Communism, 203–4
 syndicalism and masculinity, 99–104, 110, 112–13, 120, 124–5, 132
queer theory, 7–8, 12, 60–4
queer triangles, 205, 235
queer utopia, 4, 233
The Quintessence of Ibsenism (Shaw), 28–9

racism, 219, 237, 240n4
radical *eros* see *eros*
Radosh, Ronald, 137
A Raisin in the Sun (Hansberry), 215, 219, 226–8
Ralahine commune, 83–4, 86
Ramert, Lauren, 74
realism, 3, 28–30, 117, 120, 128, 131, 134n9, 144, 158
 Brecht's use of, 139, 143, 147, 150, 159, 161
 hysterical realism, 158
 O'Casey's use of, 169, 176, 178–80, 184, 187–93, 222
 and signification, 178–9, 189–90
 socialist realism, 13–14, 178, 196–202, 223
 see also antirealism
'The Red Flag', 130–1
Red Roses For Me (O'Casey), 14, 213–15, 221–5, 227–30, 233
'The Red Star' (O'Casey), 174–5, 177
rent, 18, 76–7, 79, 94n7, 111, 114, 123
reproduction, 68, 112
 as categorical imperative, 64–71
 women's reproductive function, 46–9, 64, 67
reproductive futurism, 8, 12, 58, 60–4, 88, 92, 113, 210
reproductive sexuality, 7–8, 59, 205–8

revolution, 19, 37, 68, 107, 120
  failure of, 130, 132–3
  Irish, 12–13, 93–4, 98, 137–8
  Russian Revolution (1917), 93, 121, 199
  see also sexual liberation movements; socialist movement; workers' revolution
The Revolutionist's Handbook (Shaw), 67–8, 95n12
richness, 7, 116, 171, 182–3, 191–4, 201, 210–11
Riders to the Sea (Synge), 13, 71, 138–43, 150–9, 161, 164–5
'Rise o' the Red Star' (O'Casey), 198–9, 201
Robeson, Paul, 214–15
Robinson, Lennox, 120, 169, 173–6, 211
Roche, Anthony, 4, 140, 143, 152, 156, 158, 165
romance plots, 64, 90, 91, 105
romantic idealism, 2, 21–3, 28–9, 100, 173, 178, 180–1, 202, 211
romanticism, 24, 77, 80, 83, 99, 101, 124, 223
  revolutionary, 200, 204
Rudkin, David, *Afore Night Come*, 208
Ruskin, John, 25
Russell, George, *The National Being*, 122
Russian Association of Proletarian Writers (RAPP), 198, 200
Russian Revolution (1917), 93, 121, 199

Saddlemyer, Ann, 76, 92, 95n15
sado-sexuality, 34–5
Sappho, 36
Sarah-Grandism, 44–5
scabs, 115–16, 118, 119
Scandinavian Experimental Theatre, 3
Scott, Clement, 41, 48, 50, 56n13
sectarianism, 10, 98, 105–10, 115
seduction, 40–1, 46, 48
Selford, Jack, 195
Señora Carrar's Rifles (Brecht), 13, 138–43, 146, 150–2, 155–65
Sexton, James, 106

sexual liberation movements, 1–4, 30, 58, 77, 232–5
  defined, 2
  intersection of socialist and sexual politics, 1–15, 238–40
  see also bisexuality; *eros*; heteronormativity; heterosexuality; homosexuality; lesbianism; male sexual desire; queer socialism; reproduction
Shadow of a Gunman (O'Casey), 169, 175, 177
The Shadowy Waters (Yeats), 16
Shaw, George Bernard, 1–4, 7, 10, 11, 53–4, 59, 239
  and Abbey Theatre, 94n3, 122–3
  and Bloody Sunday, 18, 29, 31–2, 35, 37, 53
  Corkery's critiques of, 122
  on criminalisation of homosexuality, 24, 29–30
  doctrine of Creative Evolution, 65, 206–7
  and *eros*, 64–5, 202, 206–7
  and Florence Farr, 22, 36, 39, 45, 50, 67–8, 74
  and Garden City movement, 82
  and Irishness, 12, 67
  masculinity, 29
  maximalism, 170
  and queer socialism, 207
  and Shelley, 22, 28–9, 52
  socialist politics, 18–20, 27–8, 59, 76, 91–4
  and Stalin, 206–7
  and utopian desire, 12, 20, 55, 59–61, 68, 73, 75–6, 91–2
  WORKS: *Arms and the Man*, 12, 16–19, 45–6, 51–3; 'As Far as Thought Can Reach', 207; *Back to Methuselah*, 65, 95n16, 206–8; *John Bull's Other Island*, 12, 55, 57–60, 72–6, 82–94; *Major Barbara*, 92–3, 95n19, 206; *Man and Superman*, 12, 55, 59, 64–71, 88, 207; *The Quintessence of Ibsenism*, 28–9; *The Revolutionist's Handbook*, 67–8, 95n12; *The Simpleton of the Unexpected Isles*, 206; 'Tragedy of an

Elderly Gentleman', 95n16, 207; *Widowers' Houses*, 30–9, 45, 68, 76
Shelley, Percy Bysshe, 11, 14, 28–9, 55, 93, 101, 193
  radical *eros*, 23–4, 63, 175–6, 206
  romantic idealism, 2, 21–3, 100, 173, 181, 211
  WORKS: *The Cenci*, 22, 52, 194; *Epipsychidion*, 176; *Laon and Cythna*, 63; *The Mask of Anarchy*, 21, 124; *Queen Mab*, 21, 63
Shelley Society, 22
A Sicilian Idyll (Todhunter), 36–7, 207
The Sign in Sidney Brustein's Window (Hansberry), 14, 214, 216–20, 227–37
The Silver Tassie (O'Casey), 169, 177, 200
The Simpleton of the Unexpected Isles (Shaw), 206
Sinclair, Upton, *Singing Jailbirds*, 204
Sinn Féin, 121, 122, 137, 174
skilled labour, 105–6
The Slough (Wilson), 13, 97, 98, 100, 112–19, 131–3, 188, 190
Social Democratic Federation, 17–18
socialist movement, 2
  co-opted by capitalism, 84–7
  intersection of socialist and sexual politics, 1–15, 238–40
  scientific, 19
  see also aesthetic socialism; British socialists; Communism; labour agitation; labour movement; Marxism; queer socialism; workers' revolution; working-class family; working-class masculinity
socialist realism, 13–14, 178, 196–202, 223
Soja, Edward, 9
solidarity, 28, 102, 108–9, 132, 144, 194, 215
Solow, Barbara, 70
'The Soul of Man Under Socialism' (Wilde), 2, 19, 23, 26–7
Soviet Union, 211
  avant-garde theatre, 177–8
  and British socialism, 194
  as destination for utopian desire, 135, 218
  emergence of, 13, 135–7
  idealised masculinity, 203–10
  invasion of Hungary, 215
  literary culture, 171, 195–203
  O'Casey's commitment to, 170–8, 184–96
  and queer socialism, 203–4
  and twentieth-century left, 3
  see also Comintern; Communism; Russian Revolution (1917)
Spanish Civil War, 136–8, 140–1, 151–2, 160–1, 185
spectators
  emotions of, 139, 142–3, 146–51, 154–7, 165–6
  identification with protagonist, 148–9, 165
  and naturalism, 127–9
Spender, Stephen, 193
spiritualism, 21, 28, 71, 77, 80, 82, 83, 92, 181, 222
staging, 73–4, 180, 194
Stalin, Joseph, 160, 170, 177–8, 196–8, 202, 215
Stanislavski, Konstantin, 194, 230
'The Star Ascending' (O'Casey), 172
'The Star-Jazzer' (O'Casey), 179–80
The Star Turns Red (O'Casey), 14, 170, 184–96, 199, 200, 204, 223, 233
steeliness, 93, 203, 222, 237
Steffin, Margarete, 141, 167n7
Stepniak, Baron, 49, 50
Stoker, Bram, *Dracula*, 51
Storey, Neil R., 55n7
straight time, 61–2, 83, 89, 92, 135
strike plays, 13, 96–9, 104–33, 133n5; *see also The Labour Leader* (Corkery); *Mixed Marriage* (Ervine); *The Slough* (Wilson)
strikes, 215–16
  ITGWU, 96
  NUDL, 99, 104
  see also Dublin Lockout (1913)
supernatural elements
  and eroticism, 51, 71
  Todhunter's use of, 39, 44, 46–8
  Yeats' use of, 39–44

symbolism, 178–80, 222
  Christian, 223
  Communist symbols, 185–6
  phallic political, 234
Symons, John Addington, 36
sympathetic action, 102
syndicalism, 2, 10, 12, 96–133, 204, 239
  American, 216
  Comintern and, 135–7
  core beliefs of, 175
  direct action, 97, 102, 113
  emotion and passions, 99–106, 119
  normative irrationalism, 99, 104, 107–11, 115, 120, 126, 130–2
  O'Casey and, 171
  theatricality, 102–4
Synge, J. M., 7, 239
  The Aran Islands, 155
  In the Shadow of the Glen, 71, 154
  Playboy of the Western World, 154
  Riders to the Sea, 13, 71, 138–43, 150–9, 161, 164–5

Taxidou, Olga, 166
Taylor, Helen, 32, 35, 55n7
tenant-right, 70
'Theatre and People' (O'Casey), 182–3
Théâtre Libre (Paris), 3
Theatre Union (New York City), 13, 137, 146–50, 154
theatrical revolution, 3; *see also* free theatres
Theocritus, *Idylls*, 36
'there and then', 89, 211, 237, 240
  and queer socialism, 61, 93
Third International *see* Comintern (Communist International)
thrift, 66–7, 108
Todhunter, John, 3
  and Florence Farr, 22, 36, 56n10
  Shelley as role model for, 22
  supernatural elements, use of, 39, 44, 46–8
  WORKS: *The Black Cat*, 45, 46, 56n13; *A Comedy of Sighs*, 12, 16–19, 44–51, 53, 207; *A Sicilian Idyll*, 36–7, 207

To-Morrow (Howard), 59–60, 75–82, 84, 86, 88, 90
totalitarianism, 60, 225–6
  social engineering, 80
toxic protectionism, 14, 238–9
'Tragedy of an Elderly Gentleman' (Shaw), 95n16, 207
transformation, 73–5, 85–6, 224, 230, 231
transnational projects, 4–6

Ulmer, William, 23
Ulster Volunteer Force, 109
unionists, 57–8, 107, 109
United States
  American drama, influence of Irish left on, 213–16
  anti-IWW campaigns, 173
  Cold War politics, 213–16, 219, 220–2
  presidential election (2016), 238–9
  white left, 14, 216–20, 222
Unity Theatre (London), 137, 140, 170, 185, 193–5, 215
unskilled labour, 105–6, 113, 126–7
Unwin, Raymond, 81, 91, 103
urban migration, 76–7
urban planning, 78–81; *see also* Garden City movement
utopian desire, 7, 12, 61–2, 73, 75
  and the 'here and now', 86
  and pleasure, 24; *see also* pleasure
  Soviet Union as destination for, 135, 218
utopian futurity, 61, 92, 114
utopian socialism, 11, 18, 59–60; *see also* Garden City movement
utopianism, 202, 211, 228
  authoritarian, 207
  left over, forgotten, or unaccomplished projects, 7, 131, 238
  queer, 4, 233
  Victorian, 60–4

Valente, Joseph, 21
vampire tales, 51
Vandeleur, John Scott, 83–4, 86
Variety, 167n16
Victorian idealism, 21

violence
  agrarian, 83–4
  masculine, 53, 100, 119–20, 125–9
  political, 21–2, 103, 106–9; *see also* Bloody Sunday
  women's, 32, 34–6, 53
virility, 114, 118, 222

Waiting for Godot (Beckett), 14, 214–15, 218–19, 221, 230, 232
Waiting for Lefty (Odets), 218
'A Walk with Eros' (O'Casey), 212n4
Walkley, A. B., 71
Wallace, Alfred Russell, 76–8
Wallis, Keene, 167n2
Walshe, Eibhear, 2
War of Independence, 174
Weigel, Helene, 141, 151, 158–66
'Weigel's Props' (Brecht), 162–5
well-made plots, 30, 33–4, 37, 64, 69, 89, 91
Westminster Review, 49, 50
'When the News Came to Dublin' (O'Casey), 172
Where There is Nothing (Yeats), 18
white left, American, 14, 216–20, 222
whiteness, 231–2, 238–9
Whitney, John, 147
Widowers' Houses (Shaw), 30–9, 45, 68, 76
Wilde, Oscar, 1–3, 11, 17, 18, 24, 30, 93, 101, 103, 181, 196, 202, 205, 239
  'The Portrait of W. H.', 23
  'The Soul of Man Under Socialism', 2, 19, 23, 26–7
Williams, Raymond, 9
  'Base and Superstructure', 10–11
Wilson, Andrew Patrick, 13
Wilson, A. Patrick, 100, 101–2, 122–3
  The Slough, 13, 97, 98, 100, 112–19, 131–3, 188, 190
  Victims, 114
Windfalls (O'Casey), 179–83, 191, 193
Within the Gates (O'Casey), 169, 183–5, 208, 225

Woggon, Helga, 121
Wolff, Werner, 141, 168n21
women
  differentiation from children, 39–41
  in labour politics, 99–100; *see also* motherhood; working-class family
  masculinisation, 35–6, 46–50, 54
  militancy and violence, 32, 34–7, 53
  reproductive function, 46–9, 64, 67
  see also bisexuality; gender binary; heterosexuality; lesbianism; New Women
Women's Wear Daily, 168n17
Woods, Gregory, 5, 209
workers' revolution, 93, 171, 185, 215–16, 218; *see also* Communism; labour agitation; labour movement; Russian Revolution (1917)
workers' theatre, 137, 146, 150, 170, 185, 193–4, 239
Workers' Union of Ireland (WUI), 176, 186
working-class family, 112–19, 132; *see also* motherhood
working-class masculinity, 12–14, 31–2, 132, 189–90, 222
  and syndicalism, 98–104, 119–20, 125–9
world literature paradigm, 4–6, 238
World War II, 194
Wright, Arnold, *Disturbed Dublin*, 103
Writers' Union, 178

Yde, Matthew, 19, 61, 76, 94, 95n19
  Bernard Shaw and Totalitarianism, 8, 94n5, 206–7
Yeates, Padraig, 96, 98, 109, 117
Yeats, W. B., 1–4, 7, 11, 29, 100, 195, 202
  Abbey Theatre productions, 122, 123
  on *Comedy of Sighs*, 45, 53
  in Dublin, 54
  fairy plays, 73–4

Yeats, W. B. (*cont.*)
  and Florence Farr, 22, 36, 39
  magical and supernatural elements, use of, 39–44
  and O'Casey, 169, 174–6
  romantic idealism, 21
  Shelley as role model for, 22
  socialist politics, 18
  WORKS: *Cathleen ni Houlihan*, 71, 223; *Countess Cathleen*, 54–5; *The King's Threshold*, 71; *The Land of Heart's Desire*, 12, 16–19, 39–44, 46, 50, 54–5; *The Shadowy Waters*, 16; *Where There is Nothing*, 18

To Be Young, Gifted, and Black (Hansberry), 226–7

zakal, 93, 203–4, 206; *see also* steeliness
Zhdanov, Andrei, 200, 202
Zola, Émile, 3